International Growth of Small and Medium Enterprises

Routledge Studies in International Business and the World Economy

For a full list of list of titles in this series, please visit www.routledge.com

International Growth of Small and Medium Enterprises

Edited by Niina Nummela

Routledge
Taylor & Francis Group
New York London

First published 2011
by Routledge
711 Third Avenue, New York, NY 10017

Simultaneously published in the UK
by Routledge
2 Park Square, Milton Park, Abingdon, Oxon OX14 4RN

Routledge is an imprint of the Taylor & Francis Group, an informa business

First published in paperback 2012

Typeset in Sabon by IBT Global.

Library of Congress Cataloging-in-Publication Data
Nummela, Niina.
    International growth of small and medium enterprises / by Niina Nummela.—1st ed.
      p. cm.—(Routledge studies in international business and the world economy ; 49)
    Includes bibliographical references and index.
    1. Small business. 2. International business enterprises. 3. Business networks. I. Title.
    HD2341.N85 2010
    338.8'81—dc22
    2010012139

ISBN13: 978-0-415-87270-6 (hbk)
ISBN13: 978-0-203-84256-0 (ebk)
ISBN13: 978-0-415-64869-1 (pbk)

Contents

PART III
How Should We Study International Growth?

PART IV
The Role of Networks in the International Growth of SMEs

Tables

Figures

Preface

The majority of SMEs are operating in a networked business environment; these networks extend beyond national and cultural boundaries. In this environment the concept of company growth gets a novel interpretation as the growth processes take various new routes and forms. Instead of linear, positive growth, in the current global business environment international growth is often more cyclical, including periods of stagnation and withdrawal, and even exits. This book focuses on international growth, i.e., how companies expand their operations across national borders through opportunity exploration and exploitation, and identification and development of innovations, i.e., on international entrepreneurship.

The book begins with an introductory chapter which is followed by five parts. Part one focuses on the drivers of international growth of SMEs. Particular interest is paid to the drivers leading to rapid and/or early internationalization and later successful and sustainable growth. However, the "darker side" of growth is also taken into consideration. Part two describes the various routes or paths that SMEs follow when growing internationally. The growth trajectories are evaluated from the viewpoint of process, context, strategy and learning, for example. Part three highlights the need to understand the diversity of internationally growing SMEs and the consequences for research design, particularly from the viewpoint of performance measurement and sample formation. Part four discusses international growth from the viewpoint of networks and social capital. And finally, part five presents three case studies, each with a different story of international growth at a grassroots level, but also with links to the themes presented in the earlier chapters. The book ends with an epilogue—a synthesis of the main themes of the book and suggestions for future research agendas.

It has been a privilege to work with true academic experts from all corners of the world. The thirty-seven researchers of the team represent fourteen countries, and together they have produced an interesting overview of international growth of SMEs. I hope this will be an enjoyable reading experience for both researchers and students interested in the topic.

During the editing process of the book, a surprising and sad message arrived: our friend, colleague and co-author, professor Jim Bell, had passed away. This book is dedicated to Jim, whose memory and work will live among the international business researchers and particularly in the IE-community for years to come.

Niina Nummela

1 International Growth of SMEs
Past, Present and the Future

Niina Nummela and Sami Saarenketo

International growth, or internationalization, is a rather well-studied area. The main body of literature on the subject can be found in the field of international business research, although various streams have their source either in economics or behavioral and social sciences (for more on the development of the international business (IB) research tradition, see, e.g., Weisfelder 2001). In the former field the focus of research has been on international trade and foreign direct investment, in the latter the concept of internationalization has been the central issue. Earlier research on internationalization can be divided chronologically into three eras based on the main focus of interest: (1) the internationalization process, (2) networks in internationalization and (3) new venture internationalization.

A LOOK BACK

In the 1960s Sune Carlson (1966) pointed out that internationalization was an incremental decision-making *process* and later other, both Nordic and North American, researchers (e.g., Johanson and Wiedersheim-Paul 1975, Johanson and Vahlne 1977, Luostarinen 1979, Bilkey and Tesar 1977, Czinkota 1982) developed this idea further. After Carlson's (1966) work, for about a decade researchers concentrated on internationalization as a incremental (learning) process, in which separate phases could be distinguished. The different phases could be identified by following changes in aspects such as operation modes, attitudes toward internationalization, information acquisition and transition, the level of export involvement and successive decisions (for a review of process models, see, e.g., Leonidou and Katsikeas 1996). In spite of numerous attempts, researchers have not been able to agree on one common view of the process. In addition, the stage models have been heavily criticized.

By the 1980s, researchers, including some of the ones mentioned above, understood that internationalization was a much more complex issue than the pioneering models had presented it as. Instead of stages, the focus of research moved to the *network* of an internationalizing firm and, in particular, how it was able to establish and change its network positions during its internationalization (Johanson and Mattsson 1988). In other words, researchers claimed that changes in the internationalization process were mostly due to changes in a company's network position. In addition to studies linking the internationalization process and networks, the importance and utilization of network connections in internationalization has become a central theme in several studies (for a review, see Coviello and McAuley 1999).

Furthermore, and parallel to and overlapping the interest in networks, researchers started to pay attention to *new venture* internationalization. The seminal article on this was written by Patricia McDougall (1989), in which she compared domestic and international new ventures and pointed out that there was an emerging phenomenon of new, resource-constrained firms entering international markets. Other researchers—among the pioneering ones Christensen (1991)—were also able to verify that the time lag in SME internationalization had begun to shorten in many countries. The introduction of the entrepreneurial viewpoint and the notion of the increasing speed of internationalization resulted in a whole new research field called international entrepreneurship—at the intersection of international business and entrepreneurship.

THE CURRENT DRIVERS OF CHANGE

From the viewpoint of the international growth of SMEs, the three main drivers of change are: (1) the transition to a service-based economy, (2) the change in the role of location, and (3) the development and convergence of technology. However, all these three themes are partly interrelated and overlapping, as can be seen from the following discussion.

First, the importance of the "non-manufacturing sector" has been growing steadily, and it can be argued that at the moment we are experiencing a *service*-driven business revolution (Möller et al. 2008). Also in international business the trend toward the increasing importance of services has been noticeable, as, for example, the composition of foreign direct investment has been shifting toward services worldwide (World Investment Report 2004). This development is in line with the current service dominant logic in business: i.e., customers play a crucial role in creating end value together with a service provider (cf. Vargo and Lusch 2004) and in order to be able to do that service providers need to be close to the customer. However, it needs to be highlighted that this emerging trend is not restricted to the service sector. On the contrary, the service logic can be transferred to goods, because in manufacturing customer value is often now created in interaction with the customer (Grönroos 2006). Additionally, the boundary between a physical product and services is nowadays blurred, as most tradable products also include a service or a knowledge-related element.

However, from the viewpoint of the international growth of SMEs, the escalation of services is important because it is clearly underdeveloped in international business research. In addition, services offer a very fertile research context because of their multi-faceted properties. Services are not a homogeneous group, but can be divided into hard or soft services (Erramilli 1990), or location-intensive and information-intensive services (Ball et al. 2008). Both classifications are significant as they have implications for how a firm will internationalize. It has been argued that hard service providers resemble manufacturers in their internationalization (Ball et al. 2008). However, there is a lack of empirical research that would compare the internationalization of different types of service providers. Furthermore, the internationalization of location-intensive service providers—such as tourism companies—highlights the often neglected aspect of internationalization, i.e., inward internationalization (cf. Korhonen et al. 1996), which takes place in a domestic market. Altogether it seems that both the service-based economy and the fact that value is created differently in the service sector indicates that the international growth of these companies would deserve more investigation.

Second, the concept of *location* has always been central in international business research, not least because of the eclectic paradigm applied in research on foreign direct investment and multinational enterprises (cf., e.g., Dunning 2000). However, recently the importance of location has been challenged, particularly due to the "global shift" (Dicken 1998) in the economy. Multinational enterprises are moving their mobile assets (including technology, skills, brands and production) around the globe in order to create a perfect fit with their immobile assets, which are situated in different locations (UNCTAD 2003), and as a result the value chain of the company (cf. Porter 1985) or value network is disintegrated and scattered worldwide. The outcome is a "global factory," i.e., a structure that reflects the combination of the innovation, distribution and production of both goods and services (Buckley 2009, Buckley and Ghauri 2004).

This development is reflected on various levels, e.g., on the industry or the regional level one can argue that regional clusters may be de-clustered to other nations (Gupta and Subramanian 2008) but this also raises the question of balance between local and global operations (Buckley and Ghauri 2004), as both of them are required for value creation. For example, in the biotech industry business is based both on global markets and scientific advances, as well as on the accumulation and dissemination of local knowledge and capital (Brännback et al. 2007). Thus, it seems that the mainstream understanding of international growth provides only a poor fit for internationalizing SMEs. Despite the fact there have been arguments for the "death of distance" and the "end of geography" in international business, location still matters (Buckley and Ghauri 2004) but the question of in what way remains unanswered.

Third, one key argument behind the claims for "death of distance" and the decreasing role of location is the development of *technology*. In addition to the service-driven revolution, one might argue that a parallel technological revolution has been in progress for some time, due to the advances in information and communications technology (UNCTAD 2003). It is a commonly shared opinion that the development of technology will profoundly reconstitute the nature of international business, resulting in changes in all elements of a company's value chain (for a more detailed discussion of the impact on international business research, see De la Torre and Moxon 2001).

In the literature we have already seen evidence of the impact of this development. The shortening of product life cycles, the drive for innovation, the need for technology transfer, the rapid development of information technology and global telecommunications are all factors that have particularly encouraged knowledge-intensive firms to enter international markets more rapidly than they previously had done (Jones 1999, Madsen and Servais 1997). Empirical studies also verify that companies do benefit from technological advances in the form of opportunity identification, the execution of strategy, and as knowledge and resource-building tools (Loane 2005, Aspelund and Moen 2004). On the other hand, the same technology also creates additional challenges in the form of an excess of information and markets. When combined with limited resources and an overload of information the result is that strategic decision-making becomes more complex and crucial to a company's success (see also Jones 1999). Consequently, advances in technology have opened new avenues for international growth but also introduced novel challenges, both of which are factors that do not match well with our dominant understanding of the phenomenon.

WHERE WILL THE FUTURE LEAD US?

There are several potential future avenues for research on the international growth of SMEs. However, it is fairly clear that the landscape in business is about to change as the focus is shifting (again) from the west and northern hemisphere to the east and south. New global players are entering the international business arena, and we are witnessing an increase in the number of emerging economies, i.e., *"regions of the world that are experiencing rapid informationalization under conditions of limited or partial industrialization,"*[1] which will have implications for research as well.

With the developed markets becoming ever more saturated, the importance of the so-called BRIC countries (Brazil, Russia, India, and China) to the world economy is growing substantially. Most projections suggest that China will overtake the US as the world's largest economy by around

2035. India's GDP is also projected to pass that of the US by around 2045 (Wilson and Purushothaman 2003). According to the much cited report for Goldman Sachs (2003) it is expected that by 2050, the world's three largest economies will be China, India, and the US, in that order (Wilson and Purushothaman 2003). Indeed, the rise of China and India is impressive and it is evident that to grow and prosper in the new world order firms will have to connect with China and India, not China *or* India.

So far, it has been noted that most entry efforts by Western firms into these markets have only touched the tip of the proverbial iceberg, as they have focused exclusively on the wealthy elite that possess offerings and business models similar to those applied in the developed world (Prahalad and Lieberthal 1998). Nevertheless, it will be the lower-income markets in emerging economies that present the true opportunities for and challenges to the international growth of SMEs. However, questions such as how operating in these markets will influence firm performance and how these new contexts will challenge the existing knowledge base of firms still remain. Furthermore, there is still limited evidence whether smaller, growth oriented firms fit into the so-called "flying-geese paradigm" of structural upgrading (cf. Akamatsu 1962), in which operations shift from simpler activities toward higher skills (e.g., from low-cost production to the outsourcing of core R&D) as their economies go through their industrial progression and begin to learn in a more open economy context.

Another important area worthy of further study will be the global configuration of the value-adding activities of firms. It will definitely be of importance to study how even new, small ventures leverage their value chains in terms of the resources and the market opportunities that global markets offer. With the emergence of various "hybrid organizational forms" we should attempt to discover what the future architecture of globally operating smaller business will be (Griffith et al. 2008). We should come up with new ways of measuring the globalization of company value chains and dig deeper into what the future level of efficiencies achieved by firms through the global configuration of value activities will be. We also need to ascertain if the worldwide orchestration of value-added activities will lead to better performance in growth seeking SMEs, and if it does then we need to find out how that better performance has been achieved. To this end, this book can be seen as a call for new models, paradigms and strategies that advance our collective understanding of the antecedents, processes and consequences of the international growth of SMEs.

NOTES

1. This definition of emerging economies is by the Center for Knowledge Societies in the 2008 Emerging Economy Report.

BIBLIOGRAPHY

Akamatsu, K. (1962) 'A historical pattern of economic growth in developing countries,' *Journal of Developing Economies*, 1 (1): 3–25.
Aspelund, A. and Moen, O. (2004) 'Internationalization of small high-tech firms: the role of information technology,' *Journal of Euromarketing*, 13 (2/3): 85–105.
Ball, D.A., Lindsay, V.J. and Rose, E.L. (2008) 'Rethinking the paradigm of service internationalisation: less resource-intensive market entry modes for information-intensive soft services,' *Management International Review*, 48 (4): 413–431.
Bilkey, W.J. and Tesar, G. (1977) 'The export behavior of smaller-sized Wisconsin manufacturing firms,' *Journal of International Business Studies*, 8 (1): 93–98
Brännback, M., Carsrud, A. and Renko, M. (2007) 'Exploring the born global concept in the biotechnology context,' *Journal of Enterprising Culture*, 15 (1): 79–100.
Buckley, P.J. (2009) 'The impact of the global factory on economic development,' *Journal of World Business*, 44 (2): 131–143.
Buckley, P.J. and Ghauri, P.N. (2004) 'Globalisation, economic geography and the strategy of multinational enterprises,' *Journal of International Business Studies*, 35 (3): 81–98.
Carlson, S. (1966) 'International business research,' Doctoral dissertation. Acta Universitatis Upsaliensis: Uppsala.
Center for Knowledge Societies (2008) 'Emerging Economy Report', available at http://www.emergingconomy-report.com (accessed May 29, 2010).
Christensen, P.R. (1991) 'The small and medium-sized exporter's squeeze: empirical evidence and model reflections,' *Entrepreneurship & Regional Development*, 3 (1): 49–65.
Coviello, N. and McAuley, A. (1999) 'Internationalisation and the smaller firm: a review of contemporary empirical research,' *Management International Review*, 39 (3): 223–256.
Czinkota, M.R. (1982) *Export Development Strategies. U.S. Promotion Policy*, Praeger Publishers: New York
De la Torre, J. and Moxon, R. (2001) 'E-commerce and global business: the impact of the information and communication technology revolution on the conduct of international business,' *Journal of International Business Studies*, 32 (4): 617–639.
Dicken, P. (1998) *Global shift: transforming the world economy*, London: Paul Chapman.
Dunning, J.H. (2000) 'The eclectic paradigm as an envelope for economic and business theories of MNE activity,' *International Business Review*, 9 (2): 163–190.
Erramilli, M. (1990) 'Entry mode choice in service industries,' *International Marketing Review*, 7 (7): 50–62.
Griffith, D.A., Cavusgil, T.S. and Xu, S. (2008) 'Emerging themes in international business research,' *Journal of International Business Studies*, 39 (7): 1220–1235.
Grönroos, C. (2006) 'Adopting a service logic for marketing,' *Marketing Theory*, 6 (3): 317–333.
Goldman Sachs (2003) 'Dreaming with BRICs: The path to 2050' avilable at: http://www2.goldmansachs.com/ideas/brics/brics-dream.html (accessed May 29, 2010).
Gupta, V. and Subramanian, R. (2008) 'Seven perspectives on regional clusters and the case of Grand Rapids office furniture city,' *International Business Review*, 17 (4): 371–384.

Johanson, J. and Wiedersheim-Paul, F. (1975) 'The internationalization of the firm—four cases,' *Journal of Management Studies*, 12 (3): 305–322.

Johanson, J. and Mattsson, L.-G. (1988) 'Internationalisation in industrial systems—a network approach,' in N. Hood and J.-E. Vahlne (eds) *Strategies in global competition*, 287–314, London: Routledge.

Johanson, J. and Vahlne, J.-E. (1977) 'The internationalization process of the firm—a model of knowledge development and increasing foreign market commitments,' *Journal of International Business Studies*, 8 (1): 23–32.

Jones, M.V. (1999) 'The internationalization of small high technology firms,' *Journal of International Marketing*, 7 (4): 15–41.

Korhonen, H., Luostarinen, R. and Welch, L.S. (1996) 'Internationalization of SMEs: inward-outward patterns and government policy,' *Management International Review*, 36 (4): 315–329.

Leonidou, L.C. and Katsikeas, C.S. (1996) 'The export development process: an integrative review of empirical models,' *Journal of International Business Studies*, 27 (3): 517–551.

Loane, S. (2005) 'The role of the internet in the internationalisation of small and medium sized companies,' *Journal of International Entrepreneurship*, 3 (4): 263–277.

Luostarinen, R. (1979) 'Internationalization of the firm,' Doctoral dissertation. Helsinki School of Economics and Business Administration: Helsinki.

Madsen, T.K. and Servais, P. (1997) 'The internationalization of born globals: an evolutionary process?' *International Business Review*, 6 (6): 561–583.

McDougall, P.P. (1989) 'International vs domestic entrepreneurship: new venture strategic behavior and industry structure,' *Journal of Business Venturing*, 4 (6): 387–400.

Möller, K., Rajala, R. and Westerlund, M. (2008) 'Service innovation myopia? A new recipe for client-provider value creation,' *California Management Review*, 50 (3): 31–48.

Porter, M.E. (1985) *Competitive advantage: creating and sustaining superior performance*, New York: The Free Press.

Prahalad, D.K. and Lieberthal, K. (1998) 'The end of corporate imperialism,' *Harvard Business Review*, 76 (4): 68–79.

The Center for Knowledge Societies (2008) *Emerging economy report*, http://www.emergingeconomyreport.com/ (accessed 14 May 2009).

UNCTAD (2003) *Investment and technology policies for competitiveness: review of successful country experiences*, Publications of the United Nations Conference on Trade and Development, New York and Geneva, http://www.unctad.org/en/docs//iteipc20032_en.pdf (accessed 28 October 2008).

Vargo, S.L. and Lusch, R.F. (2004) 'Evolving to a new dominant logic for marketing,' *Journal of Marketing*, 68 (1): 1–17.

Weisfelder, C.J. (2001) 'Internationalisation and the multinational enterprise: development of a research tradition,' *Advances in International Marketing*, (11): 13–46.

Wilson, D. and Purushothaman, R. (2003) *Dreaming with BRICs: the path to 2050*, Global Economics Paper 99, Goldman Sachs Workbench, Available at http://www.gs.com (accessed 5 May 2009).

World Investment Report (2004) http://www.worldinvestmentreport.org/ (accessed 28 October 2008).

Part I
Drivers of International Growth of SMEs

2 Entrepreneurs' Human and Relational Capital as Predictors of Early Internationalization

Evidence from Latin America and Southeast Asia

*Juan Federico, Hugo Kantis,
Alex Rialp and Josep Rialp*

INTRODUCTION

It is generally acknowledged that new globalized business conditions, the recent ICT revolutions and the progressive reduction of barriers to international trade are creating new opportunities in international markets. Small businesses and new ventures are uniquely positioned to take advantage of these changes, and, indeed, a marked increase in the number of new international firms has been noted (McDougall and Oviatt 2000). From a theoretical point of view, the emergence of these new players challenges the traditional postulates regarding firm internationalization process (Johanson and Vahlne 1977). Instead of a sequential path of firm internationalization, new contributions have been developed to understand not only the emergence but also the behavior and effects of these international new ventures (e.g., Andersson and Wictor 2003, Autio et al. 2000, Bloodgood et al. 1996, McDougall and Oviatt 1996, McDougall et al. 1994).

Despite the great efforts that has been made, some critical reviews of the state of the art in this field of research have pointed out the need to deepen our understanding of this early internationalization process and its determinants (Coviello and McAuley 1999, Jones and Coviello 2005, Rialp et al. 2005, Zahra and George 2002). Moreover, some recent contributions state that despite the research attention devoted to this phenomenon, some of its characteristics are still not well understood (Fan and Phan 2007, Westhead et al. 2001).

In particular, some limitations of past empirical research in this area have been highlighted. Past research on this topic has generally been characterized by (i) the use of case studies or small samples, (ii) a tendency to focus on US or European countries and/or high-tech firms, and (iii) descriptive and comparative statistical approaches. As a consequence, there is a need for a more systematic research approach that incorporates larger samples, cross-national comparisons and multivariate statistical methods (Coviello and Jones 2004, Rialp et al. 2005, Zahra and George 2002).

Following these suggestions, we conducted this study, whose primary objective was to analyze the effects of entrepreneurs' human and relational capital on the likelihood of creating an early internationalizing firm (hereafter, EIF). In particular, we focus on less studied regions, by comparing nearly 1,400 young SMEs in eleven countries and two different regions (Latin America and Southeast Asia). The contribution of this article is threefold. First, it extends the country coverage of empirical EIF studies to include understudied, less developed nations. Second, this paper tests the cross-regional validity of a resource-based approach to explain the emergence of EIFs as well as a stricter operational definition of what indeed constitutes an EIF. Finally, our work presents an empirical model using the Rare Events Logistic Regression technique (King and Zeng 2001a, 2001b) a useful statistical tool for conducting further research in this area.

The remainder of this paper is organized as follows: in the next section, we describe the theoretical framework as well as our conceptual model. We subsequently explain the empirical model to be tested, providing details of the data, the estimation method and the variables included in our analysis. Thereafter, we present and discuss the main empirical results of the study, focusing on observed cross-regional differences. Finally, we conclude with some implications of this study.

THEORETICAL FRAMEWORK AND CONCEPTUAL MODEL

The Influence of Human and Relational Capital

Since the emergence of the international entrepreneurship as a scientific research field (cf. McDougall and Oviatt 2000, Jones and Nummela 2008) several scholars have demonstrated that EIFs are generally led by entrepreneurs with higher levels of human and relational capital (e.g., Bloodgood et al. 1996, Madsen and Servais 1997, McDougall et al. 1994, Zou and Stan 1998). Adopting a perspective focused on the human and relational capital has been considered by many authors as an adequate framework for analyzing the influences of entrepreneurs' abilities, knowledge, experiences and networks on firm strategic behavior, including early internationalization (Bloodgood et al. 1996, Westhead et al. 2001).

Likewise, adopting a resource-based view of the firm, Alvarez and Busenitz (2001) stated that, especially in the case of start-ups or young companies, entrepreneurs constitute the firm's unique resources. This uniqueness is mostly derived from the human and relational capital of these individuals. Entrepreneurs may help create a critical level of firm-specific capabilities that allow their companies to be involved in international markets right from their inception.

Entrepreneurs' human capital has been the subject of many empirical studies. It includes founders' educational background, career history, occupational choices, and so on (Brüderl et al. 1992). Two of the most studied sources of human capital are entrepreneurs' level of education and previous work experience. Regarding entrepreneurs' educational background, it is expected that formal education plays a key role in business performance. In the context of early export behavior, a growing number of scholars have identified a positive correlation between entrepreneurs' educational level and firm export behavior (Andersson and Wictor 2003, Westhead et al. 2001). Managing the complexity associated with an emerging international firm requires a critical set of competencies, some of which are acquired through education (McDougall et al. 1994, Manolova et al. 2002). In addition, postgraduate studies often offer the opportunity for international travel and/or contact with other cultures. Both of these elements can improve entrepreneurs' global mindset, knowledge of and familiarity with foreign markets (Nummela et al. 2004).

Similarly, prior work experience among founders has been usually studied as a means of explaining firm behavior (Stuart and Abetti 1990). In particular, work experience has been shown to be a crucial "entrepreneurial training," through which entrepreneurs learn not only codified knowledge but also implicit know-how regarding markets and the world of business—key information that could not be fully acquired in another way.

In terms of the influence of entrepreneurs' previous work experience on their early export behavior, the empirical evidence is not conclusive (Westhead et al. 2001, Zou and Stan 1998). Regardless of the type of work experience, industry-specific knowledge is what really impacts firms' export behavior (Westhead et al. 2001). As these authors point out, entrepreneurs who found a new company in the same industry as the one in which they had previous experience have a more in-depth knowledge about the sector and the technology. They also are better acquainted with suppliers and customer needs, both in domestic and international markets, and so are better prepared to identify market opportunities.

A singular case of previous work experience refers to those individuals with previous entrepreneurial experience. Some scholars have demonstrated that new businesses created by habitual entrepreneurs have distinct advantages compared with ventures founded by novice entrepreneurs (Colombo and Grilli 2005, Sapienza et al. 2006, Westhead and Wright 1998). In particular, previous entrepreneurial experience may enable entrepreneurs not only to accumulate more specific and tacit knowledge about the market, but also to develop more specific business networks, local as well as international. The positive influence of previous entrepreneurial experience on export behavior has also been recently demonstrated by Jantunen et al. (2008) and Nummela et al. (2005), among others.

Human capital is accumulated in the course of people's lives, so we also consider entrepreneurs' age as another important variable of human capital. At the simplest level, older entrepreneurs have generally had more time to accumulate valuable human capital. In this vein, Westhead et al. (2001) concluded that entrepreneurs' age exerts a positive influence on export propensity. Aside from the supposedly positive effect of age on human capital accumulation, older entrepreneurs are expected to have more extensive social and business networks. In sum, this enriched resource platform as well as the considerable experience of older entrepreneurs may be of great importance when it comes to international sales and marketing.

Finally, one's human capital could be combined with others' human capital in building an entrepreneurial team, extending the concept of entrepreneurs' human capital at the firm level. Businesses owned by teams have a more diversified base of skills and other intangible resources, which allow them to identify and exploit new opportunities in foreign markets (Westhead et al. 2001). The number of partners contributes to the whole firm resource platform, adding not only knowledge and experiences but also networks and personal contacts. In addition, Cooper et al. (1994) pointed out that entrepreneurial teams increase venture legitimacy, reducing some of the liabilities associated with young ventures. Finally, entrepreneurial teams are also more likely to have accumulated a broader base of financial resources.

Relational capital, on the other hand, could be defined as the number, characteristics and content of all the external relationships established at the firm level with other firms and institutions, or at the personal level, with people outside the firm. Empirical evidence derived from case studies has highlighted the importance of networks on export behavior. Sharma and Blomstermo (2003) proposed three main reasons for the importance of networks to the internationalization process. First, networks may provide access to information about foreign markets and may help identify the needs of potential international customers. Second, networks may be a useful way to find potential partners abroad. Finally, networks may help identify new international business opportunities. In a subsequent publication, the same authors extended the aforementioned arguments, making explicit other positive benefits from a knowledge-based view. Later on, they also highlighted the importance of networks as a pervasive vehicle for knowledge transfer (Sharma and Blomstermo 2003). Previous research also demonstrates that new firms with extensive networks are able to internationalize earlier and more successfully than their competitors (e.g., Andersson and Evangelista 2006, Coviello 2006, Knight and Cavusgil 1996, Oviatt and McDougall 1995).

However, the positive effects of networks may be mediated by the nature of such networks. Szarka (1990) divided networks into social and professional ones. Social networks include not only family members but also all relatives, friends and acquaintances with whom the entrepreneur relates primarily on a social basis. In contrast, professional networks include all those individuals (institutions, suppliers, customers, etc.) with whom the relationship is primarily established at the business level. Empirical evidence showed that a higher usage of professional networks is associated with better performance (Ostgaard and Birley 1996). From a resource-based perspective, information, knowledge and experience drawn from professional networks may generate more firm-specific relational capital than social networks.

Conceptual Model

Based on the reviewed literature, we develop a conceptual model where the influence of human and relational capital on the likelihood of being an EIF is mediated by environmental- and firm-specific attributes, as Figure 2.1 illustrates.

Based on a resource-based view of internationalization, it could be argued that larger and older firms tend to have a more developed resource base and hence a richer set of capabilities to deal with complex business conditions, such as exports to a foreign market. Consequently, a positive relationship is expected, although the empirical evidence is somewhat mixed (Bloodgood et al. 1996, Zahra and George 2002, Zou and Stan 1998).

Regarding firm's activity, past research on EIFs has traditionally focused on high-tech or knowledge-based firms (Rialp et al. 2005, Zahra and George 2002). High-technology activities, either manufacturing or services, have been "hot areas" not only for the emergence of new, dynamic ventures but also for the creation of EIFs in particular. The shortening of product life cycles in technology-based businesses usually requires a much faster rate of expansion. Therefore, a quicker process of internationalization is also needed. We would accordingly expect a higher proportion of EIFs in these particular sectors.

Regarding environmental conditions, previous research shows that the attractiveness of the domestic markets—measured in terms of their relative size—may play a negative role in the emergence of EIFs (Fan and Phan 2007, Madsen and Servais 1997). Accordingly, new firms in smaller countries face more competitive pressure to enter international markets earlier in

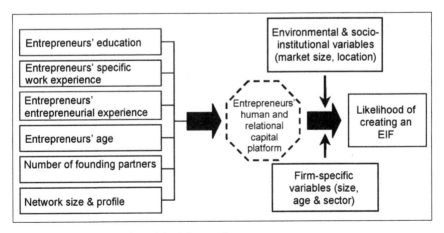

Figure 2.1   Conceptual model of this study.

order to gain scale and specialization (Madsen and Servais 1997). In addition, firm location may also influence export orientation. Urban areas are expected to have much more suitable, up-to-date infrastructure compared to small provincial cities or rural areas. From a cultural perspective, large urban areas are also expected to be more cosmopolitan than small towns. People living in large cities may have more contact with individuals of different backgrounds, reducing the "cultural distance" between markets. All these arguments would indicate that new firms located in large cities would have a greater tendency to engage in export activities than their counterparts located in small provincial towns (Westhead et al. 2001).

RESEARCH DESIGN AND THE EMPIRICAL MODEL

Data Collection

Data for this study was obtained from the combination of two different databases. The first derived from the research project *Entrepreneurship in Emerging Economies*, developed by the Universidad Nacional de General Sarmiento (Argentina), the Development Bank of Japan and the Inter-American Development Bank (Kantis et al. 2002). The second database was generated by the research project *Developing Entrepreneurship*, an initative of the Universidad Nacional de General Sarmiento, the Inter-American Development Bank and FUNDES International (Kantis et al. 2004). Both databases include data on entrepreneurs' backgrounds, firm characteristics and the venture creation process in eleven countries, seven in Latin America (Argentina, Brazil, Peru, Mexico, Costa Rica, El Salvador and Chile) and four in Southeast Asia (Japan, Korea, Singapore and Taiwan). In total, more than 1,700 founders of young businesses were personally interviewed between 2001 and 2003 using a structured and standardized questionnaire.[1] After controlling for missing cases and incomplete information, we ended up with a sample of 1,411 valid observations, of which 65 percent (919) were in Latin America and 35 percent (492) were based in Southeast Asia.[2]

Description of the Variables and the Empirical Model

The dependent variable in this model is the likelihood of creating an EIF. Researchers have usually defined this type of firms using two variables: (i) the extent of the international activities, and (ii) the speed of internationalization. Actually, one of the most referred operational definitions of an EIF is a firm that exports more than 25 percent of its total sales within three years of its inception (Knight and Cavusgil 1996).

Based on this empirical definition, we have developed a stricter definition of an EIF that also takes into account two additional factors: (i) the regularity of the export activity, and (ii) the growth in its importance over time. From questionnaire response data we have information about each firm's export behavior at three different time points: at the first year, at the third year of operations, and at the time of the survey (which, on average, corresponded to the firm's eighth year). In light of the aforementioned comments about the empirical definition of an EIF, and in trying to fully exploit our dataset, we operationally define an EIF as a firm that has experienced some export activity in the first year, has exported at least 25 percent of its sales by the third year and has exported at least 50 percent of its sales by the year of the survey (on average the eighth year). The 25 percent third-year cut-off value could be interpreted as restrictive, but it has been widely adopted by several studies. In contrast, the 50 percent cut-off value has less empirical support in the literature. It was established in order to focus our study on those firms that experience not only a sustainable export performance during their early years, but also a relevant growth in its importance during this period.

As other studies have shown, EIFs—regardless of the specific operational definition being used—only constitute a small percentage of all new firms (Westhead et al. 2001). In this study, the proportion of EIFs, as identified by our definition, is even lower; barely 4 percent of the total sample, with some regional variability, as shown in Table 2.1.

Regarding the independent variables, we first consider the educational level of the principal founder of the firm. This variable is evaluated using a set of dummy variables, one for those who graduated with a university degree, and the other for those who completed some level of postgraduate study. The reference (omitted) category includes those entrepreneurs who did not complete university-level study. Similarly, we include entrepreneurs' industry-specific and entrepreneurial experience, both measured through dichotomous variables. Finally, entrepreneurs' age was considered, including not only the age but also the square of this value to capture potential non-linear relationships. Some recent qualitative research has suggested the presence of such non-linear effects (Andersson and Evangelista 2006).

Concerning variables associated with relational capital, the size of the entrepreneurial team was measured by the number of partners who were involved in founding the business. To capture network size and profile, we decided to build a dichotomous variable that equals 1 for firms with networks of more than eight people (and zero otherwise) provided that those networks were predominantly of a commercial and institutional nature, rather than purely social networks.[3]

Table 2.1   Regional Distribution of Early Internationalizing Firms in the Sample

Region	EIFs		Non-EIFs		Total
		%		%	
Latin America	20	2.18	899	97.82	919
Southeast Asia	34	6.91	458	93.19	492
Total	54	3.83	1,357	96.17	1,411

Regarding firm-specific variables, we decided to consider firm initial size as a proxy of firm size due to the relative youth of the surveyed companies.[4] Initial size was measured as the number of employees by the end of the first year of operations. Firm age was measured as the difference between the year of the survey and the year of founding. We also included a binary variable that equaled 1 if the firm performed a knowledge-intensive activity (software, internet-based businesses and applied electronics) and 0 if the firm performed conventional manufacturing activities. Likewise, binary variables were included to evaluate firm location (large metropolitan cities = 1) and domestic market's size (large countries = 1).[5]

A general description of the dependent, independent and control variables being used in this research can be found in Table 2.2.

Table 2.2 Descriptive Statistics of Dependent, Independent and Control Variables by Region

	Latin America				Southeast Asia			
Variables	*Mean*	*Std. Dev.*	*Min.*	*Max.*	*Mean*	*Std. Dev.*	*Min.*	*Max.*
Likelihood of being an EIF	0.02	0.15	0	1	0.07	0.25	0	1
Independent variables								
University studies	0.42	0.49	0	1	0.47	0.50	0	1
Postgraduate studies	0.16	0.37	0	1	0.13	0.34	0	1
Industry experience	0.60	0.49	0	1	0.69	0.46	0	1
Entrepreneurial experience	0.40	0.49	0	1	0.18	0.39	0	1
Entrepreneur's age	43.33	9.53	23	80	46.64	8.67	26	75
Entrepreneur's age squared	1,967.84	863.78	529	6,400	2,250.54	855.07	676	5,625
Team size	3.38	2.56	2	64	3.60	3.37	2	51
Network size & profile	0.08	0.27	0	1	0.05	0.22	0	1
Control variables								
Initial size	11.00	17.50	1	204	11.67	17.14	1	161
Firm age	7.85	2.68	2	15	7.93	2.46	4	11
Sector	0.30	0.46	0	1	0.55	0.50	0	1
Location	0.70	0.46	0	1	0.75	0.43	0	1
Domestic market's size	0.49	0.50	0	1	0.71	0.45	0	1

The empirical model to be tested was as follows:

Likelihood of creating an EIF $= \hat{\beta}_0 + \hat{\beta}_1$University studies $+ \hat{\beta}_2$Postgraduate studies $+ \hat{\beta}_3$Age $+ \hat{\beta}_4$Age$^2 + \hat{\beta}_5$Industry experience $+ \hat{\beta}_6$Entrepreneurial experience $+ \hat{\beta}_7$Team $+ \hat{\beta}_8$Network size and profile $+ \Sigma$ ($\hat{\beta}_i$ Control variable$_i$) $+ \varepsilon$

The relevance of sociocultural factors in shaping entrepreneurial decisions is widely accepted. It has been largely demonstrated that sociocultural as well as institutional variables may affect not only the decision to become entrepreneur but also a new venture's future success. Thus, in order to consider the differentiating role of socio-cultural and institutional frameworks in human and relational capital variables as well as in the likelihood of EIF creation, we estimate two different models, one for each region (Latin America and Southeast Asia).

The Estimation Method

The decision to create an EIF could be interpreted as the result of a binary choice model. Accordingly, to identify the main factors affecting EIF creation, we can apply a logit regression model. However, using a standard logit regression model in the presence of a dependent variable whose distribution tends to $\hat{p}_i \cong 0$ may lead to biased results due to an underestimation of the parameters. In an attempt to resolve this difficulty, King and Zeng (2001a, 2001b) developed a new method that corrects standard logit model estimates for the presence of few positive responses (defined as "rare events") or small samples. The main difference between this method and the standard logit is that it adjusts the regression at the observed mean value, $\hat{p}_i = \bar{y}$.

Due to the fact that the proportion of EIFs in the sample data was nearly 4 percent on average, with a minimum in Latin America (2.18 percent) and a maximum in Southeast Asia (6.91 percent), it seems appropriate to adopt this Rare Events Logit Model. Despite this technical advantage, this kind of model is rarely seen in the empirical literature—for some recent examples, see Lafuente et al. (2007) or Wagner (2005).

Empirical Results

Table 3 shows the results of the models for each region. Overall, our results show that entrepreneurs' human and relational variables both affect the likelihood of EIF creation. The corresponding Wald tests for both models are statistically significant, whereas the pseudo-R^2 values are on average around 23 percent. Regarding the goodness-of-fit of the models, the overall percentage of correctly classified observations is 78.78 percent for Latin America and 74.39 percent for Southeast Asia. In particular, correctly classified percentages among EIFs are 85 percent and 76.47 percent, respectively.

We will comment first on the results concerning the influence of entrepreneurs' human capital variables (see Table 2.3). Regarding the educational

Table 2.3 Rare Events Logit Results for the Different Regions

	Latin America	Southeast Asia
Independent variables		
University studies	-0.01 (0.54)	0.81 (0.47)†
Postgraduate studies	1.26 (0.61)*	1.21 (0.59)*
Industry experience	-0.89 (0.47)†	0.48 (0.46)
Entrepreneurial experience	0.45 (0.47)	0.85 (0.43)*
Entrepreneur's age	-0.37 (0.16)*	0.41 (0.20)*
Entrepreneur's age squared	0.004 (0.002)*	-0.005 (0.002)*
Team size	0.12 (0.03)***	-0.03 (0.04)
Network size & profile	1.35 (0. 60)*	0.21 (0.72)
Control variables		
Firm size	0.01 (0.01)	0.01 (0.01)
Firm age	0.27 (0.09)**	-0.10(0.08)
Sector	-1.48 (0.74)*	-0.96 (0.43)*
Localization	1.07 (1.02)	0.98 (0.56)†
Domestic market's size	-1.23 (0.67)†	-2.08 (0.45)***
Intercept	2.01 (3.22)	-12.61 (5.05)*
Log likelihood	-71.49	-99.04
Wald (χ^2)	51.01***	51.93***
Pseudo-R^2	0.26	0.20
Correctly predicted (EIF)	85.00%	76.47%
Correctly predicted (non-EIF)	78.64%	74.24%
Correctly predicted (full sample)	78.78%	74.39%
N observations	919	492

Notes: Robust standard errors are in parentheses. † if $p < 0.10$; * if $p < 0.05$; ** if $p < 0.01$; *** if $p < 0.001$.

level of the principal founder, our analysis reveals that in Latin America, as well as in Southeast Asia, those firms whose entrepreneurs have more formal education are more likely to become EIFs. This confirms the results of previous research in more developed areas (Andersson and Wictor 2003, Andersson and Evangelista 2006). In particular, both regions exhibit positive and statistically significant coefficients with respect to postgraduate studies. Postgraduate studies may be considered as more than just additional specific knowledge to help business people to manage more complex situations. In many cases, taking postgraduate courses would also involve international travel and a closer exposure to other cultures and languages.

This may lead entrepreneurs to increase their knowledge of foreign markets. Postgraduate studies may also contribute to enhance entrepreneurs' international networks.

Regarding the influence of entrepreneurs' industry knowledge on the likelihood of creating an EIF, it appears to be negative in Latin America, whereas in Southeast Asia there is no statistically significant relationship, contradicting to some extent empirical evidence from other regions (McDougall et al. 2003, Westhead et al. 2001). In Southeast Asia, a possible explanation for this result could be that almost 70 percent of the surveyed entrepreneurs started their businesses in the same industry as that in which they were previously employed. Thus, having this industry-specific experience does not contribute to explaining the probability of creating an EIF. In contrast, the less favorable entrepreneurship conditions in Latin American companies lead to a very different scenario. It could be argued in this case that the creation of a new business, especially one in a different sector, is a manifestation of a higher level of skills and capabilities, an expected characteristic of entrepreneurs that found EIFs. Alternatively, the fact that EIF's founders do not have industry-specific experience could indicate that these EIF will not reproduce the same existing industrial structure. Thus, these firms will contribute to diversification by incorporating new activities.

A different picture appears when considering the effect of past entrepreneurial experience. In this case, the Southeast Asian sample shows a positive and significant relationship between a founder's prior entrepreneurial experience and the probability of creating an EIF. In contrast, no significant relationship was found in Latin America. This is consistent with the evidence presented by Westhead et al. (2001). Again, some caution should be used in interpreting this result due to the fact that the proportion of habitual entrepreneurs in Southeast Asia (18 percent) is significantly lower than in Latin America (40 percent).

In terms of entrepreneurs' age, we found some interesting results. In both regions, age plays a very significant role in determining the likelihood of creating an EIF. However, the meaning of this effect largely varies by region. In Latin America, we found evidence that suggested a non-linear U-shaped relationship between the age of the principal founder and the likelihood of creating an EIF. This confirmed the results of previous qualitative studies in other contexts (Andersson and Evangelista 2006). According to our results, it seems that younger Latin American entrepreneurs (who may have a global business vision, based upon more connections abroad and thus a more internationally oriented profile) seem to be significantly more likely to create an EIF (cf. Nummela et al. 2004). However, at the same time, the accumulation of experiences, networks and resources that takes place as an entrepreneur gets older also increases the probability of EIF creation.

In contrast, we found evidence in Southeast Asia of an inverted U-shaped relationship, suggesting that entrepreneurs' age, as a proxy of the human capital accumulation process, exerts a positive influence on the probability of creating an EIF. However, this effect occurs only up to a certain age limit, after which the probability starts to diminish. To some extent, this result confirms empirical evidence regarding the importance that age and experience might have in Asian cultures in general, and in the entrepreneurial process in particular (Kantis et al. 2002, 2004).

Concerning the effect of entrepreneurs' relational capital, we noted statistically significant correlations only in Latin America. As we expected, the larger the founding team, the higher the probability of EIF creation. Indeed, complementing the principal founder's human capital with a number of partners with different skills, knowledge and experiences, contributes significantly to a firm's resource endowments. According to our conceptual model, this should increase the likelihood of EIF creation. Similarly, those firms with larger networks that are primarily professional in nature exhibited a higher probability of being an EIF in this particular region. This confirms that relational capital would actually complement human capital in order to achieve earlier internationalization (Andersson and Evangelista 2006, Coviello 2006). Both results may reveal the existence of higher barriers to international business growth in Latin America as compared with other parts of the world. Therefore, the need to strengthen a firm's resource platform by incorporating additional partners and/or qualified networks would be more pressing in these less favorable contexts than in other more developed regions (Kantis et al. 2004).

Regarding control variables, a few points are worth mentioning. First, in terms of firm-specific variables, only in the Latin American sample did we find that firm age positively influences the likelihood of a company being an EIF. Although firms in our sample are generally young, this result may indicate a more gradual internationalization process in this region. On the other hand, the absence of a significant relationship between a firm's initial size and the dependent variable is consistent with other empirical evidence (Zahra and George 2002, Zou and Stan 1998).

Against our expectations, knowledge-based firms showed a lower probability of being EIFs in both regions. This result may to some extent contradict previous empirical data. One possible explanation in the case of Latin America would be related to some of the characteristics of knowledge-based firms, namely software development companies (Kantis et al. 2004). In most cases, these firms were mostly founded to provide local solutions to domestic problems or to produce products that are highly customized to the local customer, and which are therefore difficult to sell abroad. Alternatively, there might be an interaction between the size of the domestic market and the specialization of EIFs as Madsen and Servais (1997) proposed. Thus, in smaller countries, EIFs may produce many different goods, whereas in larger countries EIFs may be more focused on high-technology sectors.

Finally, we found evidence that suggested a negative influence of domestic market size on the likelihood of creating an EIF in both regions. This confirmed our expectations and was consistent with the reviewed literature (Fan and Phan 2007, Madsen and Servais 1997, Oviatt and McDougall 1999). In addition, the positive effect of large metropolitan cities was significant only in the Southeast Asian sample.

However, the coefficients of a rare events logistic regression only indicate the direction of the effect of each independent variable on the likelihood of EIF creation. To measure the effects of certain variables on the overall probability, we also estimated first differences (or attributable risks). First differences are defined as the change in the probability as a function of a specific change in a variable while all other variables are held constant at their means (Lafuente et al., 2007). The results of the first differences for those independent variables that were statistically significant at a 95 percent confidence level are presented in Table 2.4.

From Table 2.4 it is clear that entrepreneurs' age has the most significant influence on the probability of creating an EIF in both regions, assuming all other variables are held constant. In Latin America, as the age increases from 25 to 35 years, the likelihood of founding an EIF decreases by almost

Table 2.4　First Differences of the Significant Independent Variables for the Different Regions

	Latin America %	*Southeast Asia %*
Entrepreneur's age (25–35 years old)	-57.01	0.00
Entrepreneur's age (35–45 years old)	-17.15	2.11
Entrepreneur's age (45–55 years old)	-0.01	54.50
Entrepreneur's age (55–65 years old)	-0.00	32.39
Postgraduate studies	1.94	7.54
Entrepreneurial experience		4.41
Team size (2–4 members)	0.24	
Team size (4–8 members)	0.69	
Team size (8–16 members)	2.79	
Network size & profile	2.48	

Notes: First differences estimate the change in the probability due to a discrete change in the variable. Therefore, to illustrate the effects of entrepreneur's age and team size we chose different intervals. In the case of binary variables, the first difference is the effect of a discrete change from 0 to 1 in the variable. The standard error of the first differences is obtained by bootstrapping. Thus, it may lead to different results for the same variable. Taking this into account, we estimate the first differences several times for the same variable in order to test whether the effect is statistically significant. All the coefficients included in the table are statistically significant at the 95% confidence level. The rest are omitted.

60 percent. When we look at the data for older entrepreneurs, the likelihood of creating an EIF also diminishes, but at a decreasing rate. In contrast, in Southeast Asia the most significant effect of entrepreneurs' age on the probability of EIF creation is found between the ages of 45 and 55, when the likelihood of creating an EIF increases by 54 percent.

In the case of Latin America, the probability of creating an EIF increased by 2 percent if the founder had completed some postgraduate education, as well as if he/she had a larger and more professionally oriented network. Interestingly, team size shows a positive influence on the probability of EIF creation, but this influence only starts becoming relevant when we consider larger teams. For instance, in our Latin American sample, doubling the number of partners from 8 to 16 increased the likelihood of creating an EIF by 3 percent. Additionally, in the case of Southeast Asia, having completed some postgraduate studies increased the likelihood of creating an EIF by 7 percent, whereas having previous entrepreneurial experience improved the chances by 4 percent.

Concluding Remarks and Implications

This study aimed to analyze the influence of entrepreneurs' human and relational variables on the likelihood of creating an EIF, comparing two different regions (Latin America and Southeast Asia). One of the key findings of this work is that EIFs still represent only a limited proportion of all firms, especially in Latin America. The lower level of internationalization of firms—especially SMEs—along with higher barriers to growth and export may explain the still limited proportion of EIFs in this region.

In terms of human capital variables, this study has found evidence for their importance in EIF creation in both regions, confirming and extending empirical studies in this research field. However, significant contrasts between the two investigated regions were identified. In the case of Latin America, this study confirms the relevance of entrepreneurs' education level on the likelihood of EIF creation. In particular, having a postgraduate degree appears to be positively associated with the probability of creating an EIF. Interestingly, the most important factor is the age of the entrepreneur. Specifically, younger as well as more senior entrepreneurs may have a higher likelihood of creating an EIF.

Entrepreneurs' education level is also relevant in determining the probability of EIF creation in Southeast Asia. Equally important is previous entrepreneurial experience. Unlike in Latin America, entrepreneurs' age exhibits a positive but non-linear correlation with EIF creation. In summary, in the case of Southeast Asia, the results of this study confirm the importance of both generic human capital (education) and specific human capital (experience) in EIF creation.

This study also reveals that particularly in Latin America, entrepreneurs should complement and extend their human capital platform by incorporating additional partners into the entrepreneurial team. At the same time, they should work to develop larger and more professionally focused external networks in order to better cope with an unsupportive environment and gain a competitive advantage over other firms. We found evidence supporting the idea that in less developed contexts human capital endowments are necessary but not sufficient conditions to successfully create an EIF. Less developed regions characterized by more adverse entrepreneurial business conditions and, in particular, higher barriers to internationalization, emphasize the importance of both human and relational capital in the early internationalization process.

Some limitations of our study should be highlighted. Given the nature of our database—originally designed to analyze factors that determine the emergence of new ventures—some relevant variables were lacking. These include the names of the foreign countries to which the firms had exported their products and information about entrepreneurs' previous international experience. Similarly, strategic as well as marketing issues could not be evaluated.

As a corollary, this study has some additional implications. First, in terms of policy implications, this study reveals the importance of considering both human and relational capital within the context of activities that foster the emergence of EIFs. Training courses and networking activities that connect entrepreneurs to international markets, potential partners and customer needs are particularly relevant. In particular, in the case of Latin America, this study identifies some important "seedbeds" of potential EIF founders, such as young entrepreneurs and those who have some postgraduate education. Finally, regarding implications for further research, it is important to state that this research constitutes an initial effort to incorporate new evidence about EIFs in under-explored regions, extending the coverage of less developed countries in this field. Nevertheless, more research is needed. In particular we propose that future work should incorporate evidence from more countries not only in these investigated regions but also in other ones. In addition, we would recommend exploration of other variables not covered by this study, such as firm's strategic orientation (cf. Jantunen et al. 2008), or managers' cognitive attributes, such as the attitude toward international competition and risk (cf. Acedo and Jones 2007).

ACKNOWLEDGMENTS

We appreciate the contributions and helpful comments of Niina Nummela and Esteban Lafuente on earlier versions of this chapter. Financial support from the MAEC-AECID scholarship program is also acknowledged.

NOTES

1. Young firms were defined as those between 3 and 10 years of age. However, in some countries we were forced to extend this general criterion and include certain younger or older firms (but no older than 15 years of age). Nevertheless, 94 percent of the sample was between 3 and 10 years old.

2. Unfortunately we do not have information about the foreign markets to which firms were exporting, and are consequently not able to include this dimension in our operational definition.
3. Pearson chi-square statistic between the size of the network and the simultaneous presence of both commercial and institutional ties is 0.682 (Latin America) and 0.135 (Southeast Asia). Both values are statistically significant at the 99 percent confidence level. The cut-off value of eight contacts was confirmed by papers that report on empirical studies of firm growth (Greve and Salaff, 2003).
4. In fact, there is a significant correlation between initial size and current size (the size of the firm at the moment of the survey). The Pearson chi-square statistic is 0.602 and is significant at the 99 percent confidence level.
5. A detail of all the areas that were defined as large metropolitan areas and as small towns can be found in Kantis et al. (2002). For the calculation of country size, we computed the total population and the GDP for each nation and compared them with the regional average.

BIBLIOGRAPHY

Acedo, F. and Jones, M. (2007) 'Speed of internationalization and entrepreneurial cognition: insights and a comparison between international new ventures, exporters and domestic firms,' *Journal of World Business*, 42 (3): 236–252.

Alvarez, S. and Busenitz, L. (2001) 'The entrepreneurship of resource-based theory,' *Journal of Management*, 27 (6): 755–775.

Andersson, S. and Evangelista, F. (2006) 'The entrepreneur in the born global firm in Australia and Sweden,' *Journal of Small Business and Enterprise Development*, 13 (4): 642–659.

Andersson, S. and Wictor, I. (2003) 'Innovative internationalisation in new firms: Born-globals—the Swedish case,' *Journal of International Entrepreneurship*, 1 (3): 249–275.

Autio, E., Sapienza, H.J. and Almeida, J.G. (2000) 'Effects of age at entry, knowledge intensity, and imitability on international growth,' *Academy of Management Journal*, 43 (5): 909–924.

Bloodgood, J., Sapienza, H.J. and Almeida, J. (1996) 'The internationalization of new high-potential US ventures: antecedents and outcomes,' *Entrepreneurship Theory and Practice*, 20 (4): 61–76.

Brüderl, J., Preisendörfer, P. and Ziegler, R. (1992) 'Survival chances of newly founded business organizations,' *American Sociological Review*, 57 (2): 227–242.

Colombo, M. and Grilli, L. (2005) 'Founders' human capital and the growth of new technology-based firms: a competence-based view,' *Research Policy*, 34 (6): 795–816.

Cooper, A., Gimeno-Gascon, F. and Woo, C. (1994) 'Initial human and financial capital as predictors of new venture performance,' *Journal of Business Venturing*, 9 (5): 371–396.

Coviello, N. (2006) 'The network dynamics of international new ventures,' *Journal of International Business Studies*, 37 (5): 713–731.

Coviello, N. and Jones, M. (2004) 'Methodological issues in international entrepreneurship research,' *Journal of Business Venturing*, 19 (4): 485–508.

Coviello, N. and McAuley, A. (1999) 'Internationalisation and the smaller firm: a review of contemporary empirical research,' *Management International Review*, 39 (3): 223–256.

Fan, T. and Phan, P. (2007) 'International new ventures: revisiting the influences behind the 'born-global' firm,' *Journal of International Business Studies*, 38 (7): 1113–1131.

Greve, A. and Salaff, J. (2003) 'Social networks and entrepreneurship,' *Entrepreneurship Theory and Practice*, 28 (1): 1–22.

Jantunen, A., Nummela, N., Puumalainen, K. and Saarenketo, S. (2008) 'Strategic orientations of born globals—do they really matter?' *Journal of World Business*, 43 (2): 158–170.

Johanson, J. and Vahlne, J. (1977) 'The internationalization process of the firm: a model of knowledge development and increasing foreign market commitments,' *Journal of International Business Studies*, 8 (1): 23–32.

Jones, M. and Coviello, N. (2005) 'Internationalisation: conceptualising an entrepreneurial process of behaviour in time,' *Journal of International Business Studies*, 36 (3): 284–303.

Jones, M. and Nummela, N. (2008) 'International entrepreneurship: expanding the domain and extending our research questions,' *European Management Journal*, 26 (6): 349–353.

Kantis, H., Ishida, M. and Komori, M. (2002) Entrepreneurship in emerging economies: the creation and development of new firms in Latin America and East Asia, Washington: Inter-American Development Bank.

Kantis, H., Moori-Koening, V. and Angelelli, P. (2004) *Developing entrepreneurship. Experience in Latin America and worldwide*, Washington: Inter-American Development Bank.

King, G. and Zeng, L. (2001a) 'Logistic regression in rare events data,' *Political Analysis* 9 (2): 137–163.

King, G. and Zeng, L. (2001b) 'Explaining rare events in international relations,' *International Organization*, 55 (3): 693–715.

Knight, G. and Cavusgil, S. (1996) 'The born global firm: a challenge to traditional internationalization theory,' in S. Cavusgil and T. Madsen (eds) '*Export internationalizing research—enrichment and challenges*,' *Advances in International Marketing*, 8: 11–26. New York, NY: JAI Press.

Lafuente, E., Vaillant, Y. and Rialp, J. (2007) 'Regional differences in the influence of role models: comparing the entrepreneurial process of rural Catalonia,' *Regional Studies*, 41 (6): 779–796.

Madsen, T. and Servais, P. (1997) 'The internationalization of born globals: an evolutionary process?' *International Business Review*, 6 (6): 561–583.

Manolova, T., Brush, C., Edelman, L. and Greene, P. (2002) 'Internationalization of small firms: personal factors revisited,' *International Small Business Journal*, 20 (1): 9–31.

McDougall, P. and Oviatt, B. (1996) 'New venture internationalization, strategic change, and performance: a follow-up study,' *Journal of Business Venturing*, 11 (1): 23–40.

McDougall, P. and Oviatt, B. (2000) 'International entrepreneurship: the intersection of two research paths,' *Academy of Management Journal*, 43 (5): 902–906.

McDougall, P. Oviatt, B. and Shrader, R. (2003) 'A comparison of international and domestic new ventures,' *Journal of International Entrepreneurship*, 1 (1): 59–82.

McDougall, P., Shane, S. and Oviatt, B. (1994) 'Explaining the formation of international new ventures: the limits of theories from international business research,' *Journal of Business Venturing*, 9 (6): 469–487.

Nummela, N., Puumalainen, K., and Saarenketo, S. (2004) 'A global mindset—a prerequisite for successful internationalization?' *Canadian Journal of Administrative Science*, 21 (1): 51–64.

Nummela, N., Saarenketo, S. and Puumalainen, K., (2005) 'International growth orientation of knowledge-intensive small firms,' *Journal of International Entrepreneurship*, 3 (1): 5–18.

Ostgaard, T. and Birley, S. (1996) 'New venture growth and personal networks,' *Journal of Business Research*, 36 (1): 37–50.

Oviatt, B. and McDougall, P. (1995) 'Global start-ups: entrepreneurs on a worldwide stage'. *Academy of Management Executive*, 9 (2): 30–43.

Oviatt, B. and McDougall, P. (1999) A framework for understanding accelerated international entrepreneurship, in RugmanA. M. and Wright, R. W. (eds.) *International Entrepreneurship: Globalization of Emerging Businesses, Research in Global Strategic Management*, Vol. 7, 23–40. JAI Press: Stamford, CT.

Rialp, A., Rialp, J. and Knight, G. (2005) 'The phenomenon of early internationalizing firms: what do we know after a decade (1993–2003) of scientific inquiry?' *International Business Review*, 14 (2): 147–166.

Sapienza, H., Autio, E., George, G. and Zahra, S. (2006) 'A capabilities perspective on the effects of early internationalization on firm survival and growth,' *Academy of Management Review*, 31 (4): 914–933.

Sharma, D. and Blomstermo, A. (2003) 'The internationalization process of born globals: a network view,' *International Business Review*, 12 (6): 739–753.

Stuart, R. and Abetti, P. (1990) 'Impact of entrepreneurial and management experience on early performance,' *Journal of Business Venturing*, 5 (3): 151–162.

Szarka, J. (1990) 'Networking and small firms,' *International Small Business Journal*, 8 (2): 10–22.

Wagner, J. (2005) 'Nascent and infant entrepreneurs in Germany: evidence from the regional entrepreneurship monitor (REM),' *IZA Discussion Paper No. 1522*. Available at SSRN: http://ssrn.com/abstract=684007 (accessed 24 June 2009).

Westhead, P. and Wright, M. (1998) 'Novice, portfolio and serial founders: are they different?' *Journal of Business Venturing*, 13 (3): 173–204.

Westhead, P., Wright, M. and Ucbasaran, D. (2001) 'The internationalization of new and small firms: a resource-based view,' *Journal of Business Venturing*, 16 (4): 333–358.

Zahra, S. and George, G. (2002) 'International entrepreneurship: the current status of the field and future research agenda,' in M. Hitt, D. Ireland, M. Camp and D. Sexton (eds) *Strategic leadership: creating a new mindset*, 255–288, London: Blackwell.

Zou, S. and Stan, S. (1998) 'The determinants of export performance: a review of the empirical literature between 1987 and 1997,' *International Marketing Review*, 15 (5): 333–356.

3 The Board's Influence on the Internationalization Process in SMEs

Johanna Nisuls, Anette Söderqvist and Sören Kock

INTRODUCTION

The internationalization process involves both risks and challenges for the company (Buckley 1997, 72). Some authors even consider internationalization to be one of the most difficult strategies for a company to implement (Fernández and Nieto 2005, 77). Bearing in mind that at the end of the day the board of directors is responsible for the development and success of the company (Lainema 2006, 21), the internationalization process is, or should be, an important matter on the board's agenda.

Overall, research on boards of directors has shown that boards can be active or passive. Moreover, a well-functioning active board has been seen as a resource for the company, as it becomes a forum for sharing knowledge and experiences (Castaldi and Wortman 1984, 9, Stiles 2001, 647) as well as an additional source of network contacts (Borch and Huse 1993, 23). However, even though research on boards has increasingly focused on the role of the board for the strategic development of companies (Carpenter and Westphal 2001, 639), there is still a limited amount of research and empirical evidence concerning the relationship between the board and the internationalization process (Sanders and Carpenter 1998, 159, Sherman et al. 1998, 32). Research on the relationship between boards and the internationalization process specifically in a SME context is even more scarce (Zahra et al. 2007, 310).

The purpose of the study presented in this chapter is to analyze the influence of the board on the internationalization process in SMEs. Moreover, the study seeks to explore through which board role or roles this potential influence is expressed, that is, how the board takes part in the internationalization process. The study focuses on internationalization as a process according to the definition by Johanson and Vahlne (2003, 98), that is, internationalization is a continuous process where a company gradually internationalizes by developing knowledge and by increasing the commitment to both international markets and to new and existing members of the company's business network.

The remainder of the chapter is structured as follows: the next two sections present a theoretical discussion, first on board roles in general, then more specifically on boards in relation to internationalization. Then the methodology is described and the empirical findings presented and discussed. Finally, conclusions of the study are drawn.

THE ROLES OF THE BOARD

Previous research on the roles of the board has identified three specific board roles, namely a control role, a service role and a strategic role (Zahra and Pearce 1989, 303). The *control role* is based upon the board's responsibilities to guard the interests of the shareholders by controlling and supervising the management. The control role originates from the agency theory; its purpose is to minimize the risk of agency costs appearing when the management governs the company according to their own interests and not according to the interests of the shareholders (Fama and Jensen 1983, 311). Board tasks related to this role are, for example, to appoint and dismiss the CEO and to supervise and control as well as to evaluate and reward the management (Pearce and Zahra 1992, 413). The *service role* implies that the board's task is to give advice and guidance to the management (Forbes and Milliken 1999, 492, Johnson et al. 1996, 411). According to Pearce and Zahra (1992, 412), this role also includes the board's tasks, for example, to take part in various activities within the company, to represent the company and to establish contacts with the external environment. These service tasks represent various advantages to the company. The *strategic role* focuses on the board's participation in the strategic process of the company, for example, defining and developing the business plans and mission of the company (Pearce and Zahra 1992, 412). However, Ingley and Van der Walt (2001, 176) stress the fact that different points of view can be found regarding which tasks ought to be linked to this board role. On one hand, there are those who consider the board's strategic role to merely be about approving, supervising and inspecting different strategies and, on the other, there are those who consider it to be also the board's responsibility to take part in developing and defining goals, values and principles for these strategies.

Arguments exist against the categorization of the board's roles made by Zahra and Pearce (1989). Hillman and Dalziel (2003, 386) consider it relevant to focus on only two board roles, that is, the control role and the resource-based role, since the latter includes both the service role and the strategic role. Forbes and Milliken (1999, 492) also emphasize two main board roles; the control role and the service role. These have also been applied by Gabrielsson and Winlund (2000, 314–315). According to this division, the tasks associated with the strategic role of the board are divided into the control role and the service role depending on the characteristics of each task. Van den Heuvel et al. (2006, 479) also apply these two board roles. However, in their case the service role is composed of the resource dependence role, the strategic role and the service role. Considering this discussion, it is more or less a question of interpretation as to what the roles of the board are. This chapter will, however, follow Zahra's and Pearce's (1989) categorization of three board roles. These board roles were identified by collecting research material from a period of 25 years, giving Zahra's and Pearce's (1989) research a strong scientific base.

THE BOARD AND THE
INTERNATIONALIZATION PROCESS

The importance of the board in the internationalization process in SMEs can be argued to depend to a large extent on the companies' need for both tangible and intangible resources. Westhead et al. (2001, 341) state, for example, that if the company does not have enough international knowledge this can prevent the internationalization process, however, valuable information, knowledge and resources for this process can instead be acquired through external advisors. Reuber and Fischer (1997, 807) also argue that the lack of resources and knowledge is not necessarily a disadvantage for the company as long as the company develops different methods in order to obtain these resources. The authors focus on the international experience of the management as a possible resource for international knowledge. However, the board could also, either instead of or in addition to the management, be a source of international resources and experience for the company. Moreover Zahra et al. (2007, 324) conclude that in addition to the control role of the board, which is important in order for the management to develop various knowledge-based resources required for the company to be able to survive and succeed on the international market, the board also needs to support the management in this task by sharing expertise, experiences and relations.

According to Zahra et al. (2007, 324), the board can be a valuable resource for SMEs in the internationalization process through their external board members. These external board members might have different international experiences, and thus, they can give advice and inform the company about both risks and opportunities associated with the internationalization process. Sanders and Carpenter (1998, 171) also found a positive correlation between the number of external board members and the company's internationalization. Pearce and Zahra (1992, 412) state that external board members are in fact selected based upon their expertise, name and experience. External members are generally considered to have an important impact on the company's ability to create and implement new strategies (Sherman et al. 1998, 45). Furthermore, the empirical results of Brunninge et al. (2007, 304) reveal that external board members bring a variety of knowledge, relationships and legitimacy to the company. These factors are considered important in order for SMEs with a concentrated ownership structure to achieve strategic change in the company. However, in contradiction to the results above, there is also empirical evidence indicating a positive relation between the number of internal board members and the company's internationalization. Sherman et al. (1998, 44–46) found that internal board members are to a greater extent actively taking part in strategic decision making when the company is experiencing uncertainty, due to the fact that the internal board members tend to be more familiar with the company and can therefore more rapidly reach a decision regarding strategy.

Another aspect to take into consideration is the fact that the purpose of internationalization within the company is often growth (Czinkota and Ronkainen 2007, 238, Hollensen 2004, 32, Leonidou et al. 2007, 740). There are researchers who argue that companies in the growth phase tend to choose their board members based upon the resources they need to acquire (Lynall et al. 2003, 423). Huse (2007, 111) also emphasizes that in the growth phase the main task of the board is to give advice and to support the company. In SMEs the board's service role and strategic role are in general argued to be of greater importance (Brunninge et al. 2007, 299, Daily and Dalton 1993, 75, Huse 2005, 46, Van den Heuvel et al. 2006, 479). However, there is no previous empirical evidence of differences in importance regarding the control role, the service role and the strategic role in the internationalization process in SMEs.

Figure 3.1 illustrates the central aspects regarding the board's influence on internationalization based on the theoretical discussion.

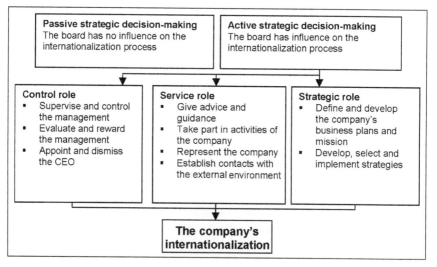

Figure 3.1   Overview of the board's influence on the internationalization process.

The board's activity in the internationalization process can vary from passive to active regarding its participation in strategic decision making. Active strategic decision making implies that the board is involved on a deeper level. Even though the level of activity can vary, this perspective indicates that if the board takes an active role in strategic decision making, the board has an influence on the internationalization process. Consequently, the board's influence on the internationalization process results in three board roles, namely the control role, the service role and the strategic role.

METHODOLOGY

A qualitative research method has been applied to study the influence of the board on the internationalization process in SMEs. The advantage of using a qualitative method is that a comprehensive picture of the phenomenon can be achieved; at the same time the opinions, attitudes and thoughts of each and every informant can be analyzed. In addition this research method is characterized by a large flexibility as well as an interactive process with the informants (Holme and Solvang 1997, 79–80, Jacobsen 2002, 142–143). Also due to the fact that the present study concentrates on the board members' experiences and opinions, which cannot easily be quantified, a qualitative method is more favorable. Furthermore, multiple case studies were conducted in four SMEs altogether, which is in line with the recommendations of Eisenhardt (1989, 545). Various aspects speak in favor of using case studies. For example, according to Dubois and Gadde (2002, 554) "The interaction between a phenomenon and its context is best understood through in-depth case studies." Moreover, case studies are characterized by in-depth analysis of a specific research object (Ghauri 2004, 109), and this approach is favorable to apply when there is a limited amount of previous empirical evidence to build one's theories on (Eisenhardt 1989, 548–549). The empirical material has been mainly collected through individual semi-structured interviews with the majority of the board members in the four case companies. However, here it is important to bear mind that in SMEs the roles of the owners, the managers and the board members tend to correlate with each other (Lainema 2006, 143). Due to the scope of the chapter, the analysis will focus only on the influence of the board and the board members on the internationalization process; in cases where the informants had multiple roles they were asked to focus on the role of board member during the interviews.

The case selection procedure is based on theoretical sampling (Eisenhardt 1989, 537), given that the purpose of the study is not to attain statistically representative material, but to increase and deepen our knowledge on a relatively unexplored topic. Consequently, the cases have been carefully chosen based on the questions that we aimed to answer (cf. Eisenhardt

1989, 537). Potential case companies were selected from a data set previously collected from boards of small Finnish companies. The selection was made in accordance with the following criteria. First, the study focuses on companies with active boards alone, as passive boards tend not to have any board tasks and consequently no influence on the internationalization process. Active refers to the fact that all boards in the study take part in the strategic processes of the firm. Some differences in activity can be found between the companies, but based on the high level of commitment and ability to influence expressed by all board members interviewed, the boards are considered as active and thus having the possibility to influence the internationalization process. Second, the companies taking part in the study were required to have international activities and third, fit within the definition of SMEs by the European Commission (2005, 14).

Company A was founded in 1983. The company has 34 employees and a turnover in 2007 of €14.7 million. This is a web-based company specialized in developing and marketing skincare products. The company has subsidiaries in Sweden, Estonia and Russia, and since 2006 the company's products have been available to all countries within the European Union. Additional international activities consist of international suppliers and production in different countries in Europe as well as sales through agents. The board in company A consists of two full members, joint owners of the company, who were both interviewed. Two deputy members are also part of the board; one of these, who is both owner and employee of the company, was also interviewed.

Company B has 16 employees and a turnover in 2007 of €2.5 million. The company was established in 2003 when the CEO bought a company which was manufacturing components for bicycles. Today the company manufactures bicycle components as well as sliding door profiles and profiles for industry. To this point it is only the bicycle component business that has been internationalized, components being exported to Denmark, Sweden and Hungary. However, within the near future the plans are to internationalize the profiling business as well, and the company's strategic goal is to become one of the leading manufacturers in Europe within this business area. The board was founded in 2003 and has all in all four members, of whom three are external members, who have neither ownership nor employment in the company. The fourth member is the owner of the company. All four board members took part in the study.

Company C produces bakery products. The company was founded in 1939. Nowadays the company has 29 employees and a turnover in 2007 of €4 million. This company started its international activities in the 1960s through the import of machinery, raw materials and pastry products. However, it was not until 2000 that the company actively started internationalizing by exporting its products. At the moment the company's products are exported to Sweden, Denmark and England. The company has also recently started to develop new products and niches for international business. The board in company C was founded in 2005 after a company succession. The board has four internal members, three of whom participated in this study.

Company D was founded in 1956 and specializes in logistic services. The company has 45 employees and a turnover in 2007 of €10.2 million. The first international transport service took place in 1989, and today the company transports goods between Finland and the following countries: Germany, the Benelux countries, Austria, Italy, France, Poland, the Czech Republic, Slovakia, Hungary as well as the Baltic countries. International transports represent 97 percent of the business. In 2007 the company also established a subsidiary in Poland. An active board with external board members had been a vision of the owners for many years, and in 2000 when the company became a joint-stock company, this vision was realized. There have been several different compositions of the board over the years, with the external board chairpersons and members mainly being chosen from larger family companies. Two of the three board members who were part of the board during the internationalization process have been interviewed for this study. One of these two board members is internal and the other is external.

FINDINGS

The key findings of the case studies are illustrated in Table 3.1. The table consists of an overview of the composition of the four boards, the main board tasks in the internationalization process, a simplified decision-making process related to the internationalization process, and the overall influence of the board on the internationalization process found in the companies.

The companies in this study are managed by the CEO alone or together with a small management group. Consequently, there is a limited amount of human capital when considering the number of people managing the company and making the strategic decisions. Previous research also shows that SMEs generally have a limited amount of resources especially intangible ones (Buckley 1997, 72, George et al. 2005, 211, Huse 2007, 109, Reuber and Fisher 1997, 808). Furthermore, in SMEs the internationalization process tends to depend on the experience and knowledge of one person (Holmlund and Kock 1998, 51), and due to the fact that internationalization is a demanding process when analyzed from a knowledge perspective this process can be of great risk for the company without such knowledge (Buckley 1997, 72).

Various risks and challenges related to the internationalization process were brought up during the interviews. Some informants said that there may be decisions related to internationalization that can even overturn the business if they turn out unsuccessful. Further analysis shows that the international experience of the management at the beginning of

Table 3.1 Summary of Findings

Company and board members	Board tasks in the internationalization process	Decision-making process	The influence of the board
A 1) Owner, chairperson 2) Owner, CEO 3) Deputy member, Owner, employee 4) Deputy member	- Develop, decide on and evaluate the overall international strategies - Decide on the allocation of resources - Gather information and external opinions - Critically evaluate aspects from different points of view - Bring insights from various perspectives - Evaluate and shape comprehensive pictures of the external environment - Share contacts and experience - Find contacts, references, partners and entrances in new potential markets - Visit new potential markets and partners - Follow up, compare and evaluate international decisions and make assessments for future development	Initiatives: CEO → Advice and decision: board → Execution: CEO	- The board takes an active part in the internationalization process from the very beginning and during the whole process - There is an interactive decision-making process between the board and the operative management - The board influences through advisory and decision-making functions
B 1) Owner, CEO, chairperson 2) External member 3) External member 4) External member	- Give ideas, advice and contacts - Critically evaluate situations and possibilities from different points of view - Bring insights from various perspectives - Reduce the risks of the internationalization	Initiatives: CEO → Advice: board → Decision and execution: CEO	- The board takes an active part in the internationalization process from the very beginning - The board influences through various advisory functions

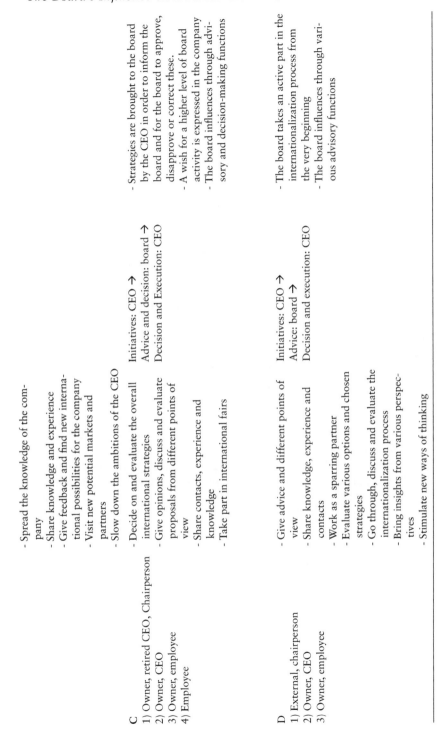

	CEO	Board		
C 1) Owner, retired CEO, Chairperson 2) Owner, CEO 3) Owner, employee 4) Employee	- Spread the knowledge of the company - Share knowledge and experience - Give feedback and find new international possibilities for the company - Visit new potential markets and partners - Slow down the ambitions of the CEO	- Decide on and evaluate the overall international strategies - Give opinions, discuss and evaluate proposals from different points of view - Share contacts, experience and knowledge - Take part in international fairs	Initiatives: CEO → Advice and decision: board → Decision and Execution: CEO	- Strategies are brought to the board by the CEO in order to inform the board and for the board to approve, disapprove or correct these. - A wish for a higher level of board activity is expressed in the company - The board influences through advisory and decision-making functions
D 1) External, chairperson 2) Owner, CEO 3) Owner, employee	- Give advice and different points of view - Share knowledge, experience and contacts - Work as a sparring partner - Evaluate various options and chosen strategies - Go through, discuss and evaluate the internationalization process - Bring insights from various perspectives - Stimulate new ways of thinking		Initiatives: CEO → Advice: board → Decision and execution: CEO	- The board takes an active part in the internationalization process from the very beginning - The board influences through various advisory functions

the internationalization process has been limited in all four companies. Instead, this experience has developed during the internationalization process. However, in spite of limited experience, the management teams have always been very optimistic and positive towards internationalization of the companies. One of the informants said, for example, that internationalization has never felt unfamiliar, even though the management lacked previous experience and knowledge when making international decisions.

Within the companies the CEO, in some cases together with the management, mainly takes the initiatives related to the internationalization process. Thus, the results are in line with Czinkota and Ronkainen (2007, 286) and Hollensen (2004, 38) who state that the CEO tends to be the initiator of internationalization in SMEs. However, even though the board members are not the main initiators, they feel, on the whole, that they influence the internationalization process.

The Roles of the Four Boards in the Internationalization Process

The board's influence on the internationalization process in terms of board roles is in general quite similar within the four companies. An important board task related to the internationalization process mentioned by informants in all four companies is to *evaluate various international ideas and proposals brought up by the management.* This implies that different internationally related opportunities, alternatives, potential consequences and scenarios are discussed and evaluated by the board members. It was pointed out by several informants that when the management alone develops strategies, certain aspects that need to be taken into consideration might be forgotten. Two other tasks partly related to the one mentioned above are to *evaluate aspects from different points of view*, which was emphasized by all companies in the study, and to *bring insights from various perspectives*, which was particularly relevant in companies with external members who are not involved in the everyday activities. Through these board tasks the companies want to evaluate the internationalization ideas and strategies in order to see if they can survive on an international market and what the possible outcomes might be. In companies A, B and D, where external board members are found, the board is considered a valuable resource in the evaluation of strategies from an external perspective, as they possess experiences and knowledge from other companies and situations. For example, in company B, where all board members apart from the CEO are external, a crucial task of the external board members is to critically evaluate international opportunities and strategies. One of the board members stressed that the external members' participation in the development of international strategies reduces the risks;

> It feels safer to develop these strategies together; the risks of hitting a mine somewhere along the way are reduced, though some mines will always be hit, but the effects on the company will be smaller, so to say.

The informants in company B also experienced that by engaging the board in the internationalization process and by avoiding knowledge about the company being tied to only one person, a certain level of safety can be obtained. The board members in company D also stressed the fact that management tends to look at the international aspects from a too positive point of view and consequently forget the negative aspects and risks, and therefore the external board members' knowledge and experience can be very valuable when included in the internationalization process.

The companies analyzed consult their boards in the decisions and strategies related to the internationalization process. When the board is consulted the task of its members is to *give advice* and to *share their experiences and knowledge* and to *be a sparring partner* for the management. In addition, in all four companies it is considered important for the board to *share both national and international contacts* that can be of help in the internationalization process, which corresponds to the results of Holmlund and Kock (1998, 59) regarding the importance of social networks in the internationalization process in SMEs. For example, in company A the chairman emphasized the importance of contacts and references by describing the internationalization process in the board as follows:

> Usually this kind of establishment begins by going through the contacts of the board members, that is, what kind of people the members know, as well as the impressions and impulses of the board members, and the board also goes through various scenarios in order to get a grip on the process.

In three of the companies (A, B and C) *operative tasks* performed by the board members related to internationalization could be observed. The whole board or some specific members had, for example, visited potential markets, customers or trade fairs together with the management.

In addition to these, some more company-specific board tasks were also identified. In company B it was pointed out that *the feedback of the board members* can be of value for the internationalization of the company. The external members can, for example, find international opportunities for the company when they, as CEOs in their own companies, are doing business internationally. An interesting point that came up in company B was that the CEO at an early stage had the ambition to internationalize the profiling business of the company. However, the board advised the CEO against this, in order for the company to first develop its activities on the national market as well as establish a portfolio of products. The task of the board in this situation was in fact to hold back the international ambitions of the CEO. This example supports Lainema's (2006, 66) theories that the entrepreneur's board members sometimes need to tone down the ambitions and goals of the CEO. This can also be seen as a strategic role of the board related to the internationalization process. In company A, the tasks of the board in the internationalization process were also to *gather information and external opinions* as well as to *follow the development of international markets* and to *decide on the amount of resources* to put into the internationalization strategy. Furthermore, the CEO of company D mentioned that the board has *stimulated new ways of thinking* regarding future international strategies. Last but not least, two of the companies (A and D) also identified the board's task as being to *follow up* on the international strategies chosen.

The board tasks above can either be related to the service role or the strategic role defined by Pearce and Zahra (1992, 412). Thus, the boards in our study have tasks that are to varying extents related to the service role, such as giving advice and guidance, taking part in the company's functions, establishing contacts and links to the external environment and representing the company in the internationalization process. Moreover, three of the boards (A, B and D) are involved in the internationalization strategies at an early stage. The board's strategic tasks are then first and foremost to evaluate the presented ideas. The board also takes part in developing these strategies by giving advice, sharing knowledge and experiences. All in all the board's involvement in the strategic role is based upon an interaction where the board is consulted during the development and implementation of the international strategies. However, in company C the board mainly approves the international strategies developed by the management.

Keeping in mind the arguments of Huse (2007, 242), which are based on the theories of McNulty and Pettigrew (1999, 55), the board should participate during the strategic development process in order to be able to actually influence the strategies. The question is therefore if this behavior in company C can be classified as a strategic role of the board. On the other hand, the results show that this board is responsible for drawing up the general outlines for the company, according to which the management develops internationalization strategies, which still indicates a strategic involvement by the board. Furthermore, according to the results, none of the boards take part to any larger extent in the actual implementation of the strategies, since this is considered to be the role of management. Lastly, in two companies (A and D) the informants emphasized the boards' task to follow up on the internationalization strategies after their implementation which can also be considered as a strategic role of the board.

An interesting aspect, which also confirms the importance of and the expectations on the service role and the strategic role of the board in the internationalization process are some of the motives behind the selection of the external board members. As mentioned previously, external members tend to be elected to the board based on their expertise, name and experience (Pearce and Zahra 1992, 412). This is also the case in companies A, B and D when analyzing their selection of external members, implying the expectations on the board as a source of tangible and intangible resources in the internationalization process. Company A had, for example, at one stage of the internationalization, an international board, consisting of two Danish board members along with the two owners. Through these members the company gained international knowledge and valuable international networks and contacts as well as "a general fearlessness towards new international markets."

These results can be related to the arguments of George et al. (2005, 228) that the CEO's propensity to take risks tends to decrease when there are external owners taking part in board activities and strategic decision making in SMEs. Also, in company B, the owner has taken international experience into consideration when selecting the external board members in order to compensate for his own lack of experience. In company D, the owners have selected the external board members mainly based upon their experience of financial questions, leadership and growth in companies.

The Varying Influence of the Four Boards on the Internationalization Process

Further analysis of the results shows that the motives for including the board in the internationalization process and the expectations on the board in the decision-making process differ to some extent between the companies. In companies B and D where external members are found, the board's supporting functions as a sparring partner, as a discussion forum and as an external observer are stressed. However, the board as a decision-making institution is of less importance. One of the board members in company B said, for example, that the role of the board is more about "discussions than concrete decisions." In company D, the informants described the decision-making process in the following way: the management first presents international strategies to the board, then the board discusses and evaluates the strategies and thereby approves them, and thereafter leaves the final decision making to the management.

In company C, the chairman of the board expressed his thoughts on the board's influence on internationalization strategies in this way:

> Of course the board has an influence; I do not believe that the management would go through with something without discussing it here first, considering that there are always two alternatives – one that is better and one that is worse.

In this company, internationalization strategies are presented to the board in order to keep them informed and assure that all the board members are on the same page. The board members have the opportunity to object to the strategies and consequently take part in the decision-making process. What needs to be taken into consideration, though, is that the board in this case very seldom objects to the decisions presented by management. The board works as a forum of discussion and then the sales department decides on which international customers to concentrate on, etc. During the interviews, two of the board members expressed a wish for a higher level of overall activity, as well as the ability for the board to take initiatives regarding internationalization. The informants would also like the board to have a stronger involvement in decision making regarding the amount of resources and time to invest in internationalization. Thus, board tasks based on both an advisory role and a decision-making role linked to internationalization could be identified in company C, although not as clearly as in the other companies in the study.

Company A can be found somewhere in between companies B and D, on one hand, and company C on the other hand, when analyzing the motives behind the board's participation in the internationalization process. Internationalization strategies are discussed among the board members in order to act as a sparring partner, but also because strategies are the responsibility of the board and the members ought to be on the same page regarding these strategies and decisions. One informant said, for example, that "once a decision is made by the board, this is the way it is and the decision is to be implemented." In company A the board as a group acts on the decisions related to internationalization. In one interview it was said that "we trust the experience and knowledge of the chairman very much, and if the chairman is doubtful and reluctant about the strategies then we all, including the CEO, listen to him." These two statements emphasize the board's role in taking strategic decisions, and also the board's advisory role.

Based on the results of this study, the board's influence on the internationalization process is captured in a strategic role and a service role (see Figure 3.2). Overall the service role includes the way in which the board functions as a sparring partner by giving advice and guidance based on the

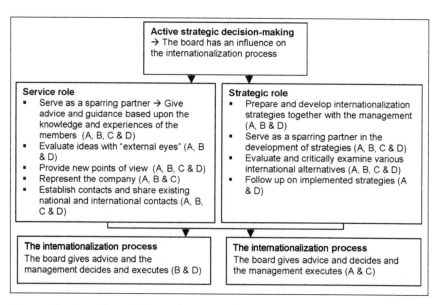

Figure 3.2 Overview of the results on board roles in the internationalization process in SMEs.

knowledge and experiences of the members, as well as the board's function to evaluate the questions, ideas and proposals brought to the board by the CEO or the management team with external eyes. The board should provide the management with new points of view and look at matters from various perspectives. In addition, the national and international contacts of the board members were highlighted in all four companies. The strategic role of the board is formed by the board's task to prepare and develop internationalization strategies together with the management. These occur to a large extent through the board's function as a sparring partner. Another important strategic task is to evaluate and critically examine the strategic initiatives and alternatives brought up on the agenda by the management. In two of the companies the board members also stress the board's task to follow up on implemented strategies.

According to the results of this study, the board actively takes part in the internationalization process of the company and decides on the outlines of the internationalization. However, whether actual decisions regarding international activities are taken by the board or the management team differs from one company to another.

CONCLUSIONS

The analysis of the four case companies shows that the board influences the internationalization process in various ways as well as to varying extents in SMEs. Overall the roles of the board in the internationalization process identified in this study are to a large extent related to supporting functions. This implies that in SMEs the initiative to internationalize and the plans regarding how to develop international activities do not tend to come from the board, but from the CEO, either alone or with the management team. However, the board seems to play an important supporting role in evaluating the plans, contributing with their insights, and sometimes even slowing down the ambitions of the CEO. Moreover, the results show that the management actively strives to reduce the risks associated with the internationalization process by consulting and using the board as a sparring partner in strategic decision making. As one of the chairmen said "the more experience there is in the board, the fewer mines will be hit." By including the board in the internationalization process, the knowledge, experience, contacts and perspectives available will increase significantly and, thus, the board plays a significant role in increasing the intangible capital available to the company.

The influence of the board in terms of the board's involvement in the strategic decision-making process related to internationalization differs somewhat between the cases. In one group of companies the board performed both an advisory and a decision-making role, while in the other group of companies the board's advisory role was emphasized, leaving the management with both the final decision making and the execution of the strategies. Another interesting aspect found in the analysis is that even though the external board members do not have any ownership, the opinions of these board members are taken into consideration and these members have a real ability to influence the strategic development of the company through their advisory role. As such, the results reveal that the influence of the board on the internationalization process can be equally significant when based on an advisory role as when based on direct participation in strategic decision making.

All in all, the findings of this study show that the board in SMEs mainly has two roles related to the internationalization process: a service role and a strategic role. Furthermore, the results show that the control role is more or less insignificant in the internationalization process in SMEs, which partly can be explained by the fact that the control role generally tends to be of less significance in SMEs due to concentrated ownership. Last but not least, this study highlights first of all the value of having an active board taking part in the internationalization process, and second the importance of analyzing the board of directors in order to be able to fully understand the strategic decisions and choices made in the internationalization process of SMEs.

ACKNOWLEDGMENTS

The authors wish to thank the Academy of Finland, which in part has funded this research through the Liike2 program.

BIBLIOGRAPHY

Borch, O.J. and Huse, M. (1993) 'Informal strategic networks and the board of directors,' *Entrepreneurship Theory and Practice*, 18 (1): 23–36.

Brunninge, O., Nordqvist, M. and Wiklund, J. (2007) 'Corporate governance and strategic change in SMEs: the effects of ownership, board composition and top management teams,' *Small Business Economics*, 29 (3): 295–308.

Buckley, P.J. (1997) 'International technology transfer by small and medium-sized enterprises,' *Small Business Economics*, 9 (1): 67–78.

Carpenter, M.A. and Westphal, J.D. (2001) 'The strategic context of external network ties: examining the impact of director appointments on board involvement in strategic decision making,' *Academy of Management Journal*, 4 (4): 639–660.

Castaldi, R. and Wortman, M.S. (1984) 'Boards of directors in small corporations: an untapped resource,' *American Journal of Small Business*, 9 (2): 1–10.

Czinkota, M.R. and Ronkainen, I.A. (2007) *International Marketing*, 8th ed., Mason, OH: Thomson South-Western.

Daily, C.M. and Dalton, D.R. (1993) 'Board of directors leadership and structure: control and performance implications,' *Entrepreneurship Theory and Practice*, 17 (3): 65–81.

Dubois, A. and Gadde L.-E. (2002) 'Systematic combining: an abductive approach to case research,' *Journal of Business Research*, 55 (7): 553–560.

Eisenhardt, K.M. (1989), 'Building theories from case study research,' *Academy of Management Review*, 14 (4): 532–550.

European Commission (2005) *The new SME definition*, Available at: http://ec.europa.eu/enterprise/enterprise_policy/sme_definition/sme_user_guide.pdf (accessed 24 March 2009).

Fama, E.F. and Jensen, M.C. (1983) 'Separation of ownership and control,' *Journal of LAw and Economic*, 26(2): 301–325.

Fernández, Z. and Nieto, M.J. (2005) 'Internationalization strategy of small and medium-sized family business: some influential factors,' *Family Business Review*, 18 (1): 77–89.

Forbes, D.P. and Milliken, F.J. (1999) 'Cognition and corporate governance: understanding board of directors as strategic decision-making groups,' *Academy of Management Review*, 24 (3): 489–505.

Gabrielsson, J. and Winlund, H. (2000) 'Boards of directors in small and medium-sized industrial firms: examining the effects of the board's working style on board task performance,' *Entrepreneurship and Regional Development*, 12 (4): 311–330.

George, G., Wiklund, J. and Zahra, S.A. (2005) 'Ownership and internationalization of small firms,' *Journal of Management*, 31 (2): 210–233.

Ghauri, P. (2004) 'Designing and conducting case studies in international business research,' in R. Marschan-Piekkari and C. Welch (eds.) *Handbook of qualitative research methods for international business*, 109–124, Cheltenham, UK: Edward Elgar.

Hillman, A.J. and Dalziel, T. (2003) 'Board of directors and firm performance: integrating agency and resource dependence perspectives,' *Academy of Management Review*, 28 (3): 383–396.

Hollensen, S. (2004) *Global marketing a decision-oriented approach*, 3rd., Harlow, UK: FT Prentice Hall.

Holme, I.D. and Solvang, B.K. (1997) *Forskningsmetodik*, 2nd ed., Lund: Studentlitteratur.

Holmlund, M. and Kock. S. (1998) 'Relationships and the internationalisation of Finnish small and medium-sized companies,' *International Small Business Journal*, 16 (4): 46–63.

Huse, M. (2005) 'Corporate governance: understanding important contingencies,' *Corporate Ownership and Control*, 2 (4): 41–50.

Huse, M. (2007) *Boards, governance and value creation*, Cambridge: Cambridge University Press.

Ingley, C.B. and Van der Walt, N.T. (2001) 'The strategic board: the changing role of directors in developing and maintaining corporate capability,' *Corporate Governance*, 9 (3): 174–185.

Jacobsen, D.I. (2002) Vad hur och varför? Om metodval i företagsekonomi och andra samhällsvetenskapliga ämnen. Lund: Studentlitteratur.

Johanson, J. and Vahlne, J.-E. (2003) 'Business relationship learning and commitment in the internationalization process,' *Journal of International Entrepreneurship*, 1 (1): 83–101.

Johnson, J.L., Daily, C.M. and Ellstrand, A.E. (1996) 'Boards of directors: a review and research agenda,' *Journal of Management*, 22 (3): 409–438.

Lainema, M. (2006) *Strateginen hallitus*. Espoo: Boardman.

Leonidou, L.C., Katsikeas, C.S., Palihawadana, D. and Spyropoulou, S. (2007) 'An analytic review of the factors stimulating smaller firms to export,' *International Marketing Review*, 24 (6): 735–770.

Lynall, M.D., Golden, B.R. and Hillman A.J. (2003) 'Board composition from adolescence to maturity: a multitheoretic view,' *Academy of Management Review*, 28 (3): 416–431.

McNulty, T. and Pettigrew, A. (1999) 'Strategists on the board,' *Organization Studies*, 20 (1): 47–74.

Pearce, J.A. and Zahra, S.A. (1992) 'Board composition from a strategic contingency perspective,' *Journal of Management Studies*, 29 (4): 411–438.

Reuber, A.R. and Fischer, E. (1997) 'The influence of management team's international experience on the internationalization behaviors of SMEs,' *Journal of International Business Studies*, 28 (4): 807–825.

Sanders, W.G. and Carpenter, M.A. (1998) 'Internationalization and firm governance: the roles of CEO compensation. Top team composition, and board structure,' *Academy of Management Journal*, 42 (2): 158–178.

Sherman, H., Kashlak, R. and Joshi, M.P. (1998) 'Inside board members, regulatory change and internationalization: the case of the U.S. telecommunication industry,' *The International Journal of Organizational Analysis*, 6 (1): 32–49.

Stiles, P. (2001) 'The impact of the board on strategy: an empirical examination,' *Journal of Management Studies* 38 (5): 627–650.

Van den Heuvel, J., Van Gils, A. and Voordeckers, W. (2006) 'Board roles in small and medium-sized family businesses: performance and importance,' *Corporate Governance*, 14 (5): 467–485.

Westhead, P., Wright, M. and Ucbasaran, D. (2001) 'The internationalization of new and small firms: a resource-based view,' *Journal of Business Venturing*, 16 (4): 333–358.

Zahra, S.A., Neubaum, D.O. and Naldi, L. (2007) 'The effects of ownership and governance on SMEs' international knowledge-based resources,' *Small Business Economics*, 29 (3): 309–327.

Zahra, S.A. and Pearce, J.A. (1989) 'Boards of directors and corporate financial performance: a review and integrative model,' *Journal of Management*, 15 (2): 291–334.

4 International Growth Orientation of SME Managers and Entrepreneurs

A Three-Year Follow-up Study

Arto Kuuluvainen and
Eriikka Paavilainen-Mäntymäki

INTRODUCTION

According to numerous authors, the success of a venture in international markets is often related to the entrepreneur's or manager's orientations and intentions towards risk-taking and internationalization (Zahra and Covin 1995, Cliff 1998, Leonidou et al. 1998, Zahra and Garvis 2000, Harveston et al. 2002, Wiklund and Shepherd 2005, Hutchinson et al. 2006). Their innovative and proactive risk-taking behavior (Lumpkin and Dess 1996) is often influenced by prior experience, such as travel, having been born abroad, an international education or work background, access to global networks, or foreign language skills (Aaby and Slater 1989, Coviello and Munro 1997, Madsen and Servais 1997, Welch and Welch 1996).

In SMEs, many company issues are connected to the personality of the owner or founder. This is due to the fact that SMEs are often quite unhierarchical organizations and the entrepreneur can choose not to delegate power (see, e.g., Steinmetz 1969, Hanks et al. 1993) and can structure and organize the firm on the basis of personal preferences. The individual's or the entrepreneur/manager team's ambitions, beliefs, attitudes, capabilities and agenda have a major influence on the direction in which a small firm will develop (Miles and Snow 1978, Stuart and Abetti 1990, rDyke et al. 1992, Cliff 1998, Glancey 1998, McGaughey et al. 1997, Valliere 2006). Therefore, the management skills, education and experience of the entrepreneur are considered to be among the key determinants of internationalization and growth (Collinson and Houlden 2005, Packham et al. 2005, Loane et al. 2007). These findings are supported by Sadler-Smith et al. (2003), who found a statistical link between entrepreneurial style (Covin and Slevin 1988) and fast growth, and by Zahra and Garvis (2000), who found that entrepreneurial activities and orientation are important prerequisites for successful foreign market expansion. Earlier research has also indicated a relationship between strategic orientations and the markers of a company's international performance, such as international growth (Jantunen et al. 2008).

In strategic decision making, the personality of the entrepreneur or manager, together with the external business environment and the enterprise characteristics, influences the attitudes and goals of the leader and the enterprise (Knight 2001, Jantunen et al. 2008). These factors together shape the orientations and intentions of the enterprise, e.g. the ability to take risks, innovate (Wiklund 1998, Valliere 2006) and be proactive (Knight 2001, Lee et al. 2001).[1] The nature and execution of the strategies, which include international growth, derive from these orientations and intentions (Nummela et al. 2004). In this study, success in international markets is defined in terms of international growth, and hence the purpose of this article is to study the possible changes in the international growth orientation (IGO) of Finnish SMEs that have or have not grown during 2004–2007.

INTERNATIONAL GROWTH ORIENTATION AND INTENTION

Existing literature dealing with SME behavior has studied many different kinds of orientations and intentions when trying to explain the decisions and moves enterprises make. Studies have focused on *strategic orientation* (Miles and Snow 1978, Stevenson and Jarillo 1990), *market orientation* (Kohli and Jaworski 1990, Narver and Slater 1990), *foreign market orientation* (Dichtl et al. 1984), *entrepreneurial orientation* (Lumpkin and Dess 1996, Wiklund 1998, Lee and Peterson 2000), *entrepreneurial intentions* (Orser et al. 1998, Hmieleski and Corbett 2006), *achievement orientation* (Crockett and Lowenthal 2007), *international entrepreneurial orientation* (Knight 2001), *international growth orientation (IGO)* (Nummela et al 2005), *international orientation* (Dichtl et al. 1984), *growth orientation (GO)* (Stevenson and Jarillo 1990, Packham et al. 2005), *growth intentions* (Orser et al. 1998), on *innovative strategic orientation* (Wiklund 1998), *entrepreneurial mindset* (McGrath and MacMillan 2000) and the *global mindset* (Nummela et al., 2004).

It is generally understood that the *attitudes* and *beliefs* of entrepreneurs and managers toward SME development help to shape their orientations and intentions (Fishbein and Ajzen 1975, Roux 1987, Cliff 1998, Valliere 2006). Some authors have also discussed the *motives* behind the orientations and intentions (Dichtl et al. 1984, Orser et al. 1998, Matlay and Mitra 2004). According to several authors (Bartlett and Ghoshal 1989, Barkema and Vermeulen 1998, Barney 2002, Jantunen et al. 2008), long-term international success is dependent on firms having an international orientation. In this study, *the focus is on the international growth orientations and intentions of SMEs.*

Theoretically speaking, general growth orientation (GO) and IGO are separate concepts (Nummela et al. 2005). For example, McDougall and Oviatt (1996) state that international growth and enterprise growth do not necessarily correlate positively. In addition, it is important to bear in mind that while some of the driving forces behind growth may be the same, international growth presents exceptional challenges to an enterprise, which differ from the challenges of growth in the home market (see, e.g., Reuber and Fischer 2002, Heinonen et al. 2006). In relation to this, McGaughey et al. (1997) found that the majority of traditional manufacturing SMEs had been operating and growing in the domestic market for over 25 years before internationalizing. This suggests that the foreign expansion of some SMEs is different from the foreign expansion that takes place in born globals (see, e.g., Madsen and Servais 1997, Jantunen et al. 2008).

Despite the fact that GO and IGO are separate, though overlapping, concepts, their differences have not been fully outlined (Heinonen et al. 2004, Jantunen et al. 2008). This may partly explain why earlier results have been contradictory and difficult to understand. For example, when Davidsson et al. (2002) studied Swedish SMEs, they found that enterprises with foreign subsidiaries grew more slowly than others. In fact, researchers themselves noted that the results were difficult to explain. One explanation might be that the phenomenon was observed on too general a level, so the joint effect of the different types of growth gave a partially distorted picture. (Heinonen et al. 2006)

However, there is a clear lack of fundamental IGO and GO research. Consequently, measuring IGO is in itself challenging (see, e.g., Hmieleski and Corbett 2006, Jantunen et al. 2008). For the purposes of this study, a preliminary framework is provided (Figure 4.1). The formation of IGO is depicted below; in it, internal and external factors affecting the enterprise play a central role in providing the decision maker with indicators of the feasibility of the international growth aim. The current state of the firm, its size, age, resource base and the conception of the fruitfulness of international growth, i.e., its belief in success, all affect the nature of the

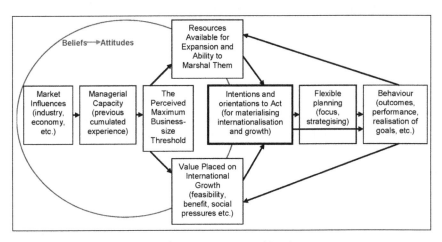

Figure 4.1   The formulation of IGOs on a general level.

intentions and orientations (Wiklund 1998, Matlay and Mitra 2004, Packham et al. 2005, Valliere 2006). According to Fishbein and Ajzen (1975), beliefs precede attitudes, which precede intentions and orientations, which, in turn, precede behavior. Behavior and the materialization of aims, again, affect the resources allocated for reaching the goals and the impression of the benefit received from reaching the goal (see, e.g., Stevenson and Jarillo 1990, Brown et al. 2001).

Particularly in growth literature, the earlier materialized growth, as well as the positive orientation and intention toward growth and the beliefs regarding the fruitfulness and benefits of growth are seen as strongly affecting subsequent growth behavior (Orser et al. 1998, Wiklund 1998, Valliere 2006). Jantunen et al. (2008), however, note that overly high levels of entrepreneurial and international growth orientations do not necessarily improve a company's international performance.

The purpose of this article is to study the possible changes in the IGO of Finnish SMEs during the years 2004–2007. The IGO is surveyed with a measure developed by Nummela et al. (2005). Finland's small and open economic context was selected as it is considered to prompt SMEs to seek growth from abroad (Gabrielsson and Kirpalani 2004, Luostarinen and Gabrielsson 2004, McGaughey 2007), and therefore the data was collected with a survey conducted at the TSE Entre, including Finnish SMEs in different industries (for details, see Heinonen et al. 2006).

SAMPLE FORMATION AND DATA COLLECTION

This study is based on three-year follow-up panel data collected from Finnish SMEs in the years 2004 and 2007. The sample frame consists of data from Statistics Finland (2005), which has the contact information of all Finnish businesses registered in Finland. The data was based on a stratified random sample of Finnish SMEs across all industries. The definition of an SME is based on a recommendation by the European Commission (2003) and the sample included only enterprises with fewer than 250 employees. The final representative sample included 1,300 SMEs, of which 498 participated in the survey in 2004.

Follow-up data from these respondents was collected during spring 2007. In both rounds the same questionnaire template was used. However, in the second round, some modifications were made to include questions that the earlier questionnaire did not address. This structure for studying the development of attitudes, orientations and intentions of SMEs is in line with that suggested by Wiklund (1998) and Wiklund et al. (2003), who similarly used a longitudinal panel data set to explore the relationship between entrepreneurial orientation and SME performance on the one hand, and entrepreneurial behavior, as well as SME managers' motivation to expand their firms, on the other.

The data was collected through telephone interviews in both cases. The aim was ideally to reach the owner-manager or entrepreneur working in the enterprise, and if this person was unavailable, then a co-owner (e.g., a member of the board). If neither of them could be reached, the interview was conducted with a management representative. The follow-up survey consisted of 276 observations. Of the 498 enterprises that entered the survey in 2004, 102 enterprises declined to participate in the follow-up, making the response rate of the follow-up 55.4 percent. The rest of the non-participating enterprises in the follow-up, 120 in total, had either closed down or could not be reached despite multiple attempts. The sample formation is illustrated in Figure 4.2.

The chi-square test and students' *t*-tests were conducted to check for non-response bias. Analyses were done regarding the demographics of respondents and how they compared with those of non-respondents. No statistically significant differences were found.

The results of the questionnaires were compared, providing an opportunity to study the possible short-term changes that had occurred within the enterprises during the last couple of years. At the beginning of the analysis, the decision was made to compare the differences in general GO between grown and non-grown companies. At this point there were 241 respondents (35 enterprises were excluded due to missing data for the question on general GO).

After this analysis, the enterprises that had not answered all of the questions regarding IGO were omitted from the study. Additionally, some SMEs had not answered the questions measuring the proportion of their international operations in relation to their total annual revenue; these enterprises were excluded due to missing data. After these omissions there were altogether 165 SMEs left in the sample for analysis. These SMEs were divided into three categories based on their actions relating to international growth. International growth development was measured by calculating the percentage of the enterprise's total annual turnover coming from exports during the research period (2003 to 2006).

The first group was comprised of those enterprises that had grown internationally during the research period, meaning that in 2006 they received

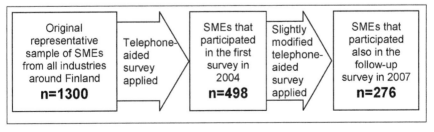

Figure 4.2 Formation of the research sample.

a larger share of their total turnover from international markets than they had in 2003. This group was named the *internationally grown enterprises*. The second group was made up of enterprises that had either declined or remained stable in terms of international growth during the research period; these enterprises were called the *international enterprises*. The third group consisted of those enterprises that had no international business operations in 2006. These SMEs formed the group of *home-market enterprises*, which also included 13 SMEs that had cancelled their international business operations during the research period. In order to compare internationally growing enterprises with enterprises that were growing in the domestic market, two additional groups of enterprises were formulated. Thus, a fourth group was comprised of enterprises that had grown in their domestic market but not in foreign markets during the research period. These firms were called the *grown enterprises*. The fifth group of SMEs, *the not-grown enterprises,* consisted of enterprises that had not grown between years 2003 and 2006.

RESULTS OF THE STUDY

The study began with measurements of the general GO of studied grown and not-grown enterprises in 2004. This conveyed the situation of growth-oriented grown and not-grown enterprises in the early phases of the study. This was done for the sake of comparison between IGO and general GO.[2]

There were no significant differences between the GO of grown and not-grown enterprises when measured in the early phases of this study. There were some differences within the group that had aimed to grow quite a lot. On the other hand, in both groups a similar proportion of enterprises had aimed to grow very much (around 11 percent of the respondents). For some reason, some succeeded and others did not. In all, the differences between the grown and not-grown SMEs were minor and the majority of the SMEs in both groups had a positive GO. However, this study concentrates particularly on the IGO of the participant SMEs, so the IGO of the SMEs was measured next. The analysis, which included 165 firms, is presented in Table 4.1.

The SMEs in the study disagreed somewhat with the statements presented in Table 2. There were no statistically significant attitudinal differences between the internationally grown, international and home-market enterprises in 2004 and 2007. However, it was observed that the orientation towards internationalization had grown more positive, although the rate of change had been very slow. This observation is in line with the fact that changes in attitudes, and thus also in orientations and intentions, evolve slowly (see, e.g., Fishbein and Ajzen 1975). It is also notable that the SMEs did not identify great risks in the internationalization of their operations (in 2007, mean 3.33 and standard deviation 1.548).

Table 4.1   Attitudes Toward International Growth among Finnish SMEs

Item	SMEs 2004 (n=165)	Standard deviation	SMEs 2007 (n=165)	Standard deviation	Change	Significance 2-tailed
We aim at growth mainly through internationalization	3.80	1.523	3.76	1.547	-0.04	0.691
We have to internationalize to succeed in the future	3.67	1,605	3.64	1.616	-0.03	0.771
Internationalization is the only way to achieve the growth targets we have set	4.10	1.376	4.12	1.419	+0.02	0.769
It is important for our enterprise to internationalize rapidly	4.19	1.285	4.18	1.302	-0.01	0.952
There is enough growth potential in our home markets	1.88	1.246	1.82	1.260	-0.06	0.489
The risks brought by internationalization are too great	3.01	1.553	3.33	1.548	+0.32	0.058

Paired samples t-test
(Scale 1=Agree completely, 2=Agree somewhat, 3=Neither agree nor disagree, 4=Disagree somewhat, 5=Disagree completely*)*

After a general overview of SME attitudes towards internationalization, we applied the classification developed for this study and divided the 165 SMEs into the aforementioned three categories based on international growth behavior. The following distribution was found:

1) *Internationally grown enterprises* (enterprises whose share of international operations grew during the research period in proportion to total turnover) *n=31*
2) *International enterprises* (enterprises that operated internationally during the research period but whose share of international operations remained the same or decreased in proportion to total turnover) *n=32*
3) *Home-market enterprises* (enterprises that had no international operations in 2006; this category also included 13 SMEs that had cancelled their international operations during the period) *n=102*.

Next, we examined the IGO of these categories one by one. First we focused on the enterprises that had grown internationally between 2003 and 2006, the group termed internationally grown enterprises. In order to analyze the IGO of this group, the IGO of the managers of these enterprises were reviewed for 2004 and 2007.

Table 4.2 shows that internationally grown enterprises had increased their internationalization efforts since 2004. In addition, at the later date, more SMEs believed that they had to internationalize in order to achieve future success. This is in line with the literature stating that earlier internationalization and growth experience has a positive effect on later behavior. Conversely, fewer SMEs felt that internationalization was the only way to grow or that it was now more important to internationalize rapidly than in 2004. Indeed, SMEs saw internationalization as involving less risk than they had before. Most of these changes, however, were relatively minor. There were no statistically significant differences regarding the IGO of the internationally grown enterprises between 2004 and 2007.

In the next phase, the IGO of the second category, the international enterprises, was analyzed. The second group included enterprises that ran international operations during the research period, but experienced either no change or a decrease in the extent of their international operations.

When the changes in the IGO of these international enterprises were considered, it was observed that the orientation and intention of these SMEs towards internationalization as a main road to growth had taken a slight negative turn (Table 4.3). On the other hand, a larger proportion of these SMEs had begun to feel that they had to internationalize to succeed in the future. It is noteworthy that the international enterprises now considered the risks brought by internationalization to be less significant than in 2004.

Table 4.3 also shows some differences between the international orientations and intentions of internationally grown enterprises and international enterprises. SMEs that had recently grown in international markets naturally had more positive feelings regarding internationalization than SMEs whose international operations were stable or had decreased. This is closely related to the concept of organizational life cycles, where the attitudes of an enterprise at the different stages of the life cycle reflect the state of the enterprise (see, e.g., Valliere 2006).

Third, the IGO of home-market SMEs was examined. Unsurprisingly, these enterprises clearly had more negative orientations and intentions towards internationalization than the other two categories studied above. This could be linked to the findings of Orser et al. (1998) and Valliere (2006) that the desirability of an aim, such as growth, is closely linked to the earlier experiences of the enterprise. In light of this observation, it could be suggested that for SMEs with no experience in international growth, such growth is not as interesting a goal as for SMEs possessing earlier experience of this sort.

Table 4.4 shows home-market enterprises feeling that there was still enough growth potential in the domestic markets. As a result, internationalization was not seen as a crucial strategic move as far as the future success of these enterprises was concerned. Changes in the IGO of these home-market enterprises were even less substantial than those of the two previous SME categories. The changes were not statistically significant.

Table 4.2 Orientation and Intention Changes among Internationally Grown SMEs

Item	Internationally grown enterprises 2004 (n=31)	Standard deviation	Internationally grown enterprises 2007 (n=31)	Standard deviation	Significance (2-tailed)	Change between 2004 and 2007
We aim at growth mainly through internationalization	2.42	1.628	2.19	1.352	0.462	-0.23
We have to internationalize to succeed in the future	2.35	1.644	2.10	1.248	0.428	-0.25
Internationalization is the only way to achieve the growth targets we have set	2.84	1.753	2.90	1.720	0.870	+0.06
It is important for our enterprise to internationalize rapidly	2.84	1.635	3.06	1.526	0.543	+0.22
There is enough growth potential in our home markets	2.87	1.607	2.87	1.648	1.000	0
The risks brought by internationalization are too great	3.84	1.344	4.13	1.176	0.319	+0.29

Paired samples t-test
(*Scale* 1=Agree completely, 2=Agree somewhat, 3=Neither agree nor disagree, 4=Disagree somewhat, 5=Disagree completely)

Table 4.3   Orientation and Intention Changes among International SMEs

Item	International enterprises 2004 (=no international growth during research period, n=32)	Standard deviation	International enterprises 2007 (=no international growth during research period, n=32)	Standard deviation	Significance (2-tailed)	Change between 2004 and 2007
We aim at growth mainly through internationalization	2.72	1.529	2.78	1.518	0.820	+0.08
We have to internationalize to succeed in the future	2.69	1.615	2.47	1.586	0.555	-0.22
Internationalization is the only way to achieve the growth targets we have set	3.38	1.497	3.38	1.641	1.000	0
It is important for our enterprise to internationalize rapidly	3.66	1.335	3.53	1.414	0.601	-0.13
There is enough growth potential in our home markets	2.31	1.306	2.31	1.469	1.000	0
The risks brought by internationalization are too great	3.29	1.419	3.71	1.395	0.152	+0.42

Paired samples t-test
(Scale: 1=Agree completely, 2=Agree somewhat, 3=Neither agree nor disagree, 4=Disagree somewhat, 5=Disagree completely.)

Table 4.4   Orientation Changes among Home-market SMEs

Item	Home-market enterprises 2004 (n=102)	Standard deviation	Home-market enterprises 2007 (n=102)	Standard deviation	Significance (2-tailed)	Change between 2004 and 2007
We aim at growth mainly through internationalization	4.56	0.851	4.54	0.982	0.869	-0.02
We have to internationalize to succeed in the future	4.38	1.108	4.47	1.069	0.515	+0.09
Internationalization is the only way to achieve the growth targets we have set	4.71	0.653	4.74	0.730	0.765	+0.03
It is important for our enterprise to internationalize rapidly	4.77	0.581	4.73	0.786	0.685	-0.04
There is enough growth potential in our home markets	1.45	0.828	1.34	0.682	0.316	-0.11
The risks brought by internationalization are too great	2.65	1.550	2.91	1.577	0.244	+0.26

Paired samples t-test
(Scale 1=Agree completely, 2=Agree somewhat, 3=Neither agree nor disagree, 4=Disagree somewhat, 5=Disagree completely.)

Again, it was observed that even home-market enterprises did not perceive internationalization as very risky. Therefore, even though these enterprises neither seemed to be planning on internationalizing their activities nor considered it to be beneficial for them, the reason behind this attitude was not fear of the risks of internationalization.

DISCUSSION

The demographic characteristics of the entrepreneurs and managers in SMEs are considered to have a significant influence on their orientations and intentions, and consequently on the growth of their enterprises (Zahra and Covin 1995, Cliff 1998, Leonidou et al. 1998, Zahra and Garvis 2000, Harveston et al. 2002, Wiklund and Shepherd 2005, Hutchinson et al. 2006). The willingness to take risks and the interest in international markets and growth were among the most central factors affecting an SME's internationalization and growth development. In general, the results of the analysis showed that the majority of SMEs were positive towards growth, the perceived risks related to internationalization had generally decreased, and SMEs that had earlier international experience were particularly likely to regard internationalization as a promising growth strategy. Although the majority of the SMEs in the study were home-market SMEs, these findings are in line with earlier research, which stresses the impact of earlier growth and internationalization (Orser et al. 1998, Wiklund 1998, Matlay and Mitra 2004, Packham et al. 2005, Valliere 2006), as well as an earlier entrepreneurial background, on subsequent internationalization and growth (Collinson and Houlden 2005, Packham et al. 2005, Loane et al. 2007).

Some of the low interest towards internationalization recorded among domestic SMEs can be explained in terms of industrial factors. Almost one-third (32.4 percent) of these home-market enterprises operated in the service sector, which has not traditionally been very international in Finland when compared to, for example, heavy manufacturing industry. The rapid development of the Information and Communication Technology (ICT) field has created new internationalization opportunities for service enterprises and has evened out competition between different industries. On the other hand, construction (16.7 percent), trade (20.6 percent), and manufacturing (13.7 percent) had a remarkable representation among the home-market enterprises. During the last couple of years there has been a construction boom in Finland, and therefore it is not very surprising that these enterprises currently consider their home market to have enough potential for their purposes. Also statistics (Statistics Finland 2005) support the observation that the construction industry is mainly very domestic.

To some extent, the lack of interest in international growth can be attributed to the age and size of the enterprises and the evidenced high failure rates of SMEs in foreign markets. According to McGaughey et al. (1997) and Matlay and Mitra (2004), among others, many SMEs operate in the domestic market for a long time before internationalizing. From this fact, three conclusions can be drawn. First, the home-market SMEs in our sample had not yet reached the critical age when they might start to consider internationalization as a viable option. Second, the sample enterprises may be firmly entrenched in the home market and embedded in local networks and long-term partnerships. Third, the small size of the SMEs in the sample—closely linked to resources—may have represented a barrier to international growth (Wiklund 1998, Matlay and Mitra 2004, Packham et al. 2005, Valliere 2006).

Earlier experience in growth and internationalization appears to strongly influence the further development of an SME (Aaby and Slater 1989, Coviello and Munro 1997, Madsen and Servais 1997, Welch and Welch 1996). Regarding GO, 74.2 percent of the grown SMEs had a positive stance towards further growth. Again, internationally grown SMEs and international SMEs alike were of the opinion that to reach their goals they would need to continue growing internationally. Interest in growth among not-grown SMEs was also relatively high, accounting for 64.8 percent, whereas international growth was not generally seen as a lucrative choice for future development among home-market SMEs.

An interesting finding in terms of orientations and intentions was the fact that risks are more often associated with IGO than GO. However, it is highly unlikely that growth would be free of risks. Another observation is that many SMEs experience GO and IGO simultaneously, and often enterprises that have GO are more apt also to have IGO. In the sample, however, having GO was more popular than having IGO, but the conclusion cannot be drawn that GO is a prerequisite for IGO.

CONCLUSIONS

Key decision makers are widely regarded as the drivers behind a company's development and as the single most important factor when a firm's international orientation is studied (Aaby and Slater 1989, Cavusgil 1984, Chetty and Hamilton 1993, Leonidou et al. 1998). The decision makers are also responsible for influencing both the firm's strategic orientation (Miles and Snow 1978, Stevenson and Jarillo, 1990) and the patterns and pace of internationalization. Consequently, our research studied SME managers' and entrepreneurs' IGO. Results indicated that between the years 2004 and 2007, the IGO of Finnish SMEs had become more positive; however, the changes were relatively subtle. Our results also show that there were no significant differences at the beginning of the study between the general GO of the enterprises that grew and that of the enterprises that didn't grow during the research period.

Prior literature states that orientations and intentions are influenced by the decision makers' conception of the external business environment (Knight 2001, Jantunen et al. 2008). As the Finnish market is becoming increasingly competitive, it is surprising that this competition did not have more of an effect on orientations and intentions towards international growth, and that these were not consequently more positive. Despite the fact that attitudes and thus also behavior evolve slowly, a faster change could perhaps now be in order from the viewpoint of Finnish SME survival.

Earlier studies have also suggested that the success of an enterprise is often determined by entrepreneur/managers' willingness to take risks by entering new export markets (Harveston et al. 2002, Hutchinson et al. 2006). The SMEs included in this study did not seem to consider internationalization to be too risky. However, home-market enterprises in particular did not seem to be interested in the opportunities that international markets might offer. Managers and entrepreneurs of domestic enterprises clearly stated that enough potential for growth remains in the Finnish home markets. Additionally, they did not seem to think that future success, including growth, would require internationalization.

It is possible to challenge this kind of thinking. Many large foreign corporations are already operating in several industries in Finland. Moreover, it is easy to predict an increasing invasion of Finnish markets by foreign enterprises, in line with globalization. On the other hand, if the majority of home-market enterprises claim that the Finnish market offers enough potential for future growth on its own, we may conclude that the competition between Finnish enterprises is fierce and will become even tougher in the future. Whereas some firms acknowledge that they have to grow and internationalize to survive, some lucky others may survive without these measures, and some unlucky others will wither away. On the other hand, wouldn't this type of scenario, when applied to internationalization, just follow the rules of Schumpeter's (1954) creative destruction? Suggestive events in the markets, particularly among SMEs, may result in a shake-up of the structure of the Finnish business environment.

ACKNOWLEDGMENTS

The authors wish to thank the Academy of Finland which in part has funded this research through the Liike2 program.

NOTES

1. Some authors, such as Lumpkin and Dess (1996) and Stevenson and Jarillo (1990) have also identified competitive aggressiveness and autonomy as elements of entrepreneurial orientation. However, in this study the focus is on risk-taking, innovativeness and proactivity.

2. During this phase there were 241 respondents; however, at later phases of the research, the number decreased dramatically to 165, several enterprises being excluded due to missing data regarding international business.

BIBLIOGRAPHY

Aaby, N.E. and Slater, S.F. (1989) 'Management influences on export performance: a review of the empirical literature 1978–88,' *International Marketing Review*, 6 (4): 7–26.

Barkema, H.G. and Vermeulen, G.A.M. (1998) 'International expansion through start-up or through acquisition; an organizational learning perspective,' *Academy of Management Journal*, 41 (1): 7–27.

Barney, J. (2002) *Gaining and sustaining competitive advantage* (2nd ed.), Upper Saddle River, NJ: Prentice Hall.Bartlett, C. and Ghoshal, S. (1989) *Managing across borders: the transnational solution*, Boston: Harvard Business School Press.

Brown, Terrence E., Davidsson, P. and Wiklund, J. (2001) 'An operationalization of Stevenson's conceptualization of entrepreneurship as opportunity-based behavior,' *Strategic Management Journal*, 22 (10): 953–968.

Cavusgil, Tamer S. (1984) 'Differences among exporting firms based on their degree of internationalization,' *Journal of Business Research*, 12 (2): 195–208.

Chetty, S. and Hamilton, R.T. (1993) 'Firm-level determinants of export performance: a meta-analysis,' *International Marketing Review*, 10 (3): 26–34.

Cliff, J.E. (1998) 'Does one size fit all? Exploring the relationship between attitudes towards growth, gender, and business size,' *Journal of Business Venturing*, 13 (6): 523–542.

Collinson, S. and Houlden, J. (2005) 'Decision-making and market orientation in the internationalization process of small and medium-sized enterprises,' *Management International Review*, 45 (4): 413–436.

European Commission (2003) *SME Definition*, Commission Recommendation 2003/361/EC, Available at http://europa.eu.int/comm/enterprise03_fi.htm (accessed 2 January 2007).

Coviello, N.E. and Munro, H. (1997) 'Network relationships and the internationalization process of small software firms,' *International Business Review*, 6 (4): 361–386.

Covin, J.G. and Slevin, D.P. (1988) 'The influence of organisational structure on the utility of an entrepreneurial top management style,' *Journal of Management Studies*, 25 (3): 217–37.

Crockett, D. and Lowenthal, J. (2007) 'Discriminating between international corporate innovators and international corporate entrepreneurs: the role of achievement orientation,' Paper presented at the 10th Anniversary McGill International Entrepreneurship Conference at UCLA, 27–29.9.2007, Los Angeles, USA.

Davidsson, P., Kirchhoff, B., Hatemi-J., Abdulnasser and Gustavsson, H. (2002) 'Empirical analysis of business growth factors using Swedish data,' *Journal of Small Business Management*, 40 (4): 332–349.

Dichtl, E., Leibold, M., Köglmayr, H.G. and Müller, S. (1984) 'The export-decision of small and medium-sized firms: a review,' *Management International Review*, 24 (2): 49–60.

Dyke, L.S., Fischer, E.M. and Reuber, R. (1992) 'An inter-industry examination of the impact of owner experience on firm performance,' *Journal of Small Business Management*, 30 (4): 72–87.

Fishbein, M. and Ajzen, I. (1975) *Beliefs, attitude, intention, and behaviour*, Reading, Massachusetts: Addison, Wesley.

Gabrielsson, M. and Kirpalani, V.H.M. (2004) 'Born-globals: how to reach new business space rapidly,' *International Business Review*, 13 (5): 555–571.

Glancey, K. (1998) 'Determinants of growth and profitability in small entrepreneurial firms,' *International Journal of Entrepreneurial Behaviour and Research*, 4 (1): 18–27.

Hanks, S.H., Watson, C.J., Jansen, E. and Chandler, G. N. (1993) 'Tightening the life-cycle construct: a taxonomic study of growth stage configurations in high-technology organizations,' *Entrepreneurship Theory and Practice*, 18 (2): 5–30.

Harveston, P.D., Osborne, D. and Kedia, B. (2002) 'Examining the mental models of entrepreneurs from born global and gradual globalizing firms,' Paper presented at the High Technology Small Firms Conference, University of Twente, Enschede, The Netherlands.

Heinonen, J., Nummela, N. and Pukkinen, T. (2004) 'To grow or not to grow? An analysis of internationally growth-oriented Finnish SMEs,' in the *Proceedings of the 30th EIBA Conference*, Ljubljana, 5–8 December, 2004.

Heinonen, J., Nummela, N. and Pukkinen, T. (2006) 'The international growth orientation of Finnish SMEs,' in J. Heinonen (ed.) *The nature and elements of growth—Finnish SMEs in focus*, 107–120, Turku: Small Business Institute, Turku School of Economics.

Hmieleski, K.M. and Corbett, A.C. (2006) 'Proclivity for improvisation as a predictor of entrepreneurial intentions,' *Journal of Small Business Management*, 44 (1): 45–63.

Hutchinson, K., Quinn, B. and Alexander, N. (2006) 'The role of management characteristics in the internationalization of SMEs: evidence from the UK retail sector,' *Journal of Small Business and Enterprise Development*, 13 (4): 513–534.

Jantunen, A., Nummela, N., Puumalainen, K. and Saarenketo, S. (2008) 'Strategic orientations of born globals—do they really matter?' *Journal of World Business*, 43 (2): 158–170.

Knight, G.A. (2001) 'Entrepreneurship and strategy in the international SME,' *Journal of International Management*, 7 (3): 155–171.

Kohli, A.K. and Jaworski, B.J. (1990) 'Market orientation: the construct, research propositions, and managerial implications,' *Journal of Marketing*, 54 (2): 1–18.

Lee, C., Lee, K. and Pennings, J.M. (2001) 'Internal capabilities, external networks, and performance: a study of technology-based ventures,' *Strategic Management Journal*, 22 (6/7): 615–640.

Lee, S.M. and Peterson, S.J. (2000) 'Culture, entrepreneurial orientation, and global competitiveness,' *Journal of World Business*, 35 (4): 401–416.

Leonidou, L.C., Katsikeas, C.S. and Piercy, N.F. (1998) 'Identifying managerial influences on exporting: past, present and future directions,' *Journal of International Marketing*, 6 (2): 74–102.

Loane, S., Bell, J.D. and McNaughton, R. (2007) 'A cross-national study on the impact of management teams on the rapid internationalization of small firms,' *Journal of World Business*, 42 (4): 489–504.

Lumpkin, G.T. and Dess, G.G. (1996) 'Clarifying the entrepreneurial orientation construct and linking it to performance,' *Academy of Management Review*, 21 (1): 135–172.

Luostarinen, R. and Gabrielsson, M. (2004) 'Finnish perspectives of international entrepreneurship,' in L.-P. Dana (ed.) *Handbook of research on international entrepreneurship*, 383–403, Cheltenham, UK: Edward Elgar Publishing.

Madsen, T.K. and Servais, P. (1997) 'The internationalization of born globals: an evolutionary process?' *International Business Review*, 6 (6): 561–583.

Matlay, H. and Mitra, J. (2004) 'The internationalization efforts of growth-oriented entrepreneurs: lessons from Britain,' in H. Etemad (ed.) *International entrepreneurship in small and medium size enterprises. Orientation, environment and strategy*, 221–240, Cheltenham, UK: Edward Elgar Publishing.

McDougall, P.P. and Oviatt, B.M. (1996) 'New venture internationalization, strategic change and performance: a follow-up study,' *Journal of Business Venturing*, 11 (1): 23–40.

McGaughey, S.L. (2007) Narratives of internationalisation. Legitimacy, standards and portfolio entrepreneurs, Cheltenham, UK: Edward Elgar.

McGaughey, S., Welch, D. and Welch, L. (1997) 'Managerial influences and SME internationalization,' in I. Björkman and M. Forsgren (eds.) *The nature of the international firm. Nordic contribution to international business*, 165–188, Copenhagen: Handelshøjskolens Forlag, Copenhagen Business School Press.

McGrath, R. and MacMillan, I. (2000) *The entrepreneurial mindset*, Boston: HBS Press.

Miles, R.E. and Snow, C.C. (1978) *Organizational strategy, structure, and process*, New York: McGraw-Hill.

Narver, J.C. and Slater, S.F. (1990) 'The effect of a market orientation on business profitability,' *Journal of Marketing*, 54 (4): 20–35.

Nummela, N., Puumalainen, K. and Saarenketo, S. (2005) 'International growth orientation of knowledge-intensive small firms,' *Journal of International Entrepreneurship*, 3 (1): 5–18.

Nummela, N., Puumalainen, K. and Saarenketo, S. (2004) 'A global mindset—a prerequisite for successful internationalization?' *Canadian Journal of Administrative Sciences*, 21 (1): 51–64.

Orser, B.J., Hogarth-Scott, S. and Wright, P. (1998) 'On the growth of small enterprises: the role of intentions, gender and experience,' in P. D. Reynolds, W. O. Bygrave, N.M. Carter, S. Manigart, C.M. Mason, G.D. Meyer and K.G. Sharer (eds.) *Frontiers in entrepreneurship research*, 366–380, Massachusetts: Arthur M. Blanc Center for Entrepreneurship, Babson College.

Packham, G., Brooksbank, D., Miller, C. and Thomas, B. (2005) 'Climbing the mountain: management practice adoption in growth oriented firms in Wales,' *Journal of Small Business and Enterprise Development*, 12 (4): 482–497.

Reuber, A.R. and Fischer, E. (2002) 'Foreign sales and small firm growth: the moderating role of the management team,' *Entrepreneurship: Theory and Practice*, 27 (1): 29–45.

Roux, E. (1987) 'Managers' attitudes toward risk among determinants of export entry of small- and medium-sized firms,' in P.J. Rosson and S.D. Reid (eds.) *Managing export entry and expansion. Concepts and practice*, 95–110, New York: Praeger Publishers.

Sadler-Smith, E., Hampson, Y., Chaston, I. and Badger, B. (2003) 'Managerial behavior, entrepreneurial style and small firm performance,' *Journal of Small Business Management*, 41 (1): 47–67.

Schumpeter, J.A. (1954) *Capitalism, socialism and democracy*, London: Allen & Unwin.

Statistics Finland (2005) *Structure Statistics*.

Steinmetz, L.L. (1969) 'Critical stages of small business growth. When they occur and how to survive them,' *Business Horizons*, 12 (1): 29–36.

Stevenson, H.H. and Jarillo, J.C. (1990) 'A paradigm of entrepreneurship: entrepreneurial management,' *Strategic Management Journal*, 11 (Special Issue, Summer): 17–27.

Stuart, R.W. and Abetti, P.A. (1990) 'Impact of entrepreneurial and management experience on early performance,' *Journal of Business Venturing*, 5 (3) 151–162.

Valliere, D. (2006) 'Consequences of growth. Shaping entrepreneurial attitudes,' *Entrepreneurship and Innovations*, 7 (3): 141–148.

Welch, D.E. and Welch, L.S. (1996) 'The internationalization process and networks: a strategic management perspective,' *Journal of International Marketing*, 4 (3): 11–28.

Wiklund, J. (1998) 'Entrepreneurial orientation as predictor of performance and entrepreneurial behaviour in small firms—longitudinal evidence,' in P.D. Reynolds, W.D. Bygrave, N.M. Carter, S. Manigart, C.M. Mason, G.D. Meyer and K.G. Shaver (eds.) *Frontiers in entrepreneurship research*, 283–296, Massachusetts: Arthur M. Blank Center for Entrepreneurship, Babson College.

Wiklund, J., Davidsson, P. and D. Frédérik (2003) 'What do they think and feel about growth? An expectancy-value approach to small business managers' attitudes toward growth,' *Entrepreneurship Theory and Practice*, 27 (3): 247–270.

Wiklund, J. and Shepherd, D. (2005) 'Entrepreneurial orientation and small business performance: a configurational approach,' *Journal of Business Venturing*, 20 (1): 71–91.

Zahra, S.A. and Covin, J.G. (1995) 'Contextual influences on the corporate entrepreneurship—performance relationship: a longitudinal analysis,' *Journal of Business Venturing*, 10 (1): 43–58.

Zahra, S.A. and Garvis, D.M. (2000) 'International corporate entrepreneurship and firm performance: the moderating effect of international environmental hostility,' *Journal of Business Venturing*, 15 (5/6): 469–492.

5 The Dark Side of International Growth

Jarna Heinonen and Ulla Hytti

INTRODUCTION

It is often taken for granted that most small firms aim to grow (e.g., Autio et al. 2000, Yli-Renko et al. 2002, Heinonen and Pukkinen 2006). Given the limitation of growth opportunities within national boundaries in small economies and among firms operating in niche markets in particular, the logical continuation of this aim would be to grow internationally. However, research has demonstrated that not all small firms seek growth, and that the ones that do may also focus on regional and domestic markets (Heinonen et al. 2004, Nummela et al. 2005). Indeed, empirical evidence of a relationship between firm growth and internationalization is scarce (Antoncic and Hisrich 2000), and there is a misconception that internationalization automatically leads to growth (Paavilainen and Kuuluvainen 2008).

There is a substantial amount of literature on the organizational and environmental antecedents of growth and internationalization, their processes and modes, as well as on subsequent company performance (see, e.g., Antoncic and Hisrich 2000). Most studies on internationalization and growth focus on firm-level concerns and neglect or underemphasize the role of the entrepreneur or company managers, not to mention their mindsets (Cort et al. 2007). Furthermore, research exploring the consequences of entrepreneurship on the lives of entrepreneurs remains limited. For example, analyses of firm success seldom refer to its effects on the entrepreneur, or connect it with the hard work and the sacrifices, and the potential consequences such as stress, burn-out, depression, intensified work-family conflicts and increasing work-life imbalance. Further research in this area is needed given the evidence that company success and the well-being of the entrepreneur do not always go hand in hand (e.g., Hmieleski and Corbett 2008). This would complement existing research on the individual level, which has focused largely on characteristics of the decision maker such as experience (Zucchella et al. 2007), attitude and mindset (Zhou 2007, Acedo and Jones 2007) and age (Westhead et al. 2001) that have an impact on the internationalization of the firm.

Moreover, the consequences and outcomes of growth and internationalization, be they economic or non-economic (Wiklund et al. 2003), have not been widely studied either. The idea that they coexist promotes a normative attitude to internationalization—it is considered attractive in that it implies firm growth through wider markets. However, the possible undesired consequences of growth in general and of international growth in particular should be explored and discussed given the multitude of beliefs about the future consequences and outcomes.

As Jones and Nummela (2008) suggest, there seems to be an urgent need to "launch a call for fresh ideas and questions that might extend understanding of IE [international entrepreneurship] as a phenomenon, and incorporate perspectives from other disciplines with the potential to add depth to understanding within the field." We therefore assume a critical approach in this paper, and investigate the potential negative consequences of international growth from two complementary perspectives—those of the firm and of the individual. According to Carr (2006), the critical perspective implies framing the activity, in this case international growth, within a broader context, going beyond being negative and faultfinding in attempts to reject the self-evident nature of reality, and drawing attention to social totality in relation to international growth.

The aim of this conceptual study is to contribute to filling the above-mentioned research gaps by exploring the consequences of international growth in firms. We take a critical stand in assuming that international growth may imply undesired firm- and individual-level consequences, which may also influence future decisions and behavior. The discussion in the following sections is based on the previous literature on such consequences, and we consider their role in the future behavior and endeavors of firms. We conclude by offering some theoretical and managerial implications.

FIRM-LEVEL CONSEQUENCES

Internationalization is not necessarily an intended strategic choice, but it may represent an option if the firm is not able to meet the goals it has set in the domestic market, for example (Wennberg and Holmquist 2008). According to a recent Finnish study, internationalization among SMEs was relatively seldom proactive, highly ambitious or opportunity-driven action, but was rather reactive behavior to unsatisfactory firm performance in limited or even shrinking local markets (Heinonen and Kovalainen, 2009). This idea is further emphasized, but from another angle, in a recent Australian case study: the management team was skilled at taking advantage of slack resources in one part of its portfolio of firms in order to facilitate the internationalization of another part (McGaughey 2007). Although firm growth and internationalization are typically considered highly intentional and of strategic importance, they may thus also be a result of unfavorable internal or external conditions that the firm faces. Similarly, not all firm-level consequences are necessarily desirable by any means. Such consequences are discussed in the following section.

Uncertainty

Internationalization implies increased uncertainty and dynamics in a firm (Anderson et al. 2001), as well as radical changes in business characteristics (Wiklund and Shepherd 2003, Wiklund et al. 2009). It is impossible to plan everything in advance and only then to exhibit planned internationalization and growth strategies, because unplanned, serendipitous encounters take place and influence the process unexpectedly (Crick and Spence 2005). Due to increased uncertainty growing firms are, indeed, believed to face the risk of ending up in a serious crisis (Heinonen and Pukkinen 2006). Furthermore, if increased size brings a reduction in flexibility the firm may lose some of its crisis-survival ability (Wiklund et al. 2003). Perks and Hughes (2008) suggest that internal resources and management's tolerance of risk both influence attitudes toward uncertain and risky international endeavors.

Working Modes and Personnel

In order to manage the increased uncertainty and risk involved in growth and internationalization, firms need to be innovative in terms of coordination, delegation and flexibility. There is usually an implied need for new and more formal working modes and practices as they attempt to prepare for international development. A stronger resource base is required in order successfully to manage more complex strategies, more customer and partner relationships and a wider business environment. Broadening the resource base implies new recruitment on both the managerial and employee levels, which again calls for more formalized resource planning and coordination. In addition, it needs research and development activities in order to meet the changing requirements of the new clientele. (Crick and Spence 2005) All in all, as the firm grows and internationalizes it starts to apply more formal and planned managerial practices in order to be able to coordinate its expanding activities in the new business environment. Although this development may be rational and intended, the fundamental cultural change within the firm may be challenging and time-consuming, and may expose it to crisis.

Changes in working modes and practices also influence employee well-being. Moving from a flat and family-like structure towards a more hierarchical and formal organization with several layers may restrict the room for maneuver among employees and cause dissatisfaction. On the other hand, a larger organization may offer better career opportunities. Interestingly, Wiklund et al. (2003) found that managers in Sweden expected company growth to have an unfavorable impact on employee well-being.

Clientele

A growing and internationalizing firm needs to reposition itself among its customers. Internationalization usually implies expanding the client base from local and national markets to other countries, but at the same time the firm may face some alarming changes due to the increasing power of a few dominating customers (Wiklund et al. 2003). Internationalization may consume much managerial and operational attention, possibly leading to some neglect of domestic customers and a decrease in domestic turnover, although in some cases the decrease in domestic sales may have been the main reason for going international in the first place. In this sense it could be interpreted as an investment in a more profitable future, but on the other hand the shift in attention may be unintentional and lead to negative long-term consequences.

Changes in the Product/Service and Implications for Quality

Growth and internationalization often require changes in current products and services. Sometimes the need for such modifications comes unexpectedly or has been underestimated. Modifications combined with increased detachment from direct control on account of the organizational changes may raise quality concerns, which again may increase the need to introduce formal and usually expensive quality-control systems (Wiklund et al. 2003).

Moreover, the decision to go international is not only a matter of entering new markets and developing services. There are national and cultural factors such as the differing technical standards involved, which create difficulties and incur costs for firms aspiring to enter international markets (Zhang and Dodgson 2007). Product specification and marketing and sales procedures and policies were the main operational changes reported as a consequence of international activities. These changes were more evident and concrete than changes in management style or organizational structure, for example (Anderson et al. 2001). Changes in products and services thus not only require more managerial attention, they may also influence the quality of the offering. Most important, modification and specification may impose a financial burden on a growing and internationalizing company.

Financial Issues

Internationally growing companies usually require an increasing amount of working capital in order to finance their growth (Gabrielsson et al. 2004). Growth usually implies new investments, organizational changes and product modifications, all of which are usually quite costly (Anderson et al. 2001) and thus place a financial burden on the company. In order to cope with the tight financial situation it may need to take additional loans or to share equity with venture capitalists, for example (Wiklund et al. 2003). Small firms tend to have limited access to financial capital, which limits their growth (Hartarska and Gonzalez-Vega 2006).

Financial challenges are further emphasized in international growth due to the physical and mental distance from the markets, as well as to national conventions for paying invoices, which may dramatically differ from country to country. Late payment, for example, may be the normal way of doing business in some, whereas in others, such as the Nordic countries, payment delays are highly disapproved of. The profits gained from international markets may thus be eaten up by increased financial costs and even credit losses. Currency deviations and exchange-rate fluctuations also influence a firm's profitability. (Crick and Spence 2005, Anderson et al. 2001) In the worst case it is not able to finance the business and cash flow becomes the issue to which management needs to devote an increasing amount of its time and effort (Crick and Jones 2000).

Independence and Networks

Increased size due to international growth is likely to increase the firm's independence in relation to its customers, suppliers and financiers (Wiklund et al. 2003, Wiklund et al. 2009). Gaining access to new resources and the skills needed in internationalization and growth requires new internal working modes and a changing relationship with networks, for example: there is a need for increased openness to cooperation. It has been suggested that in the early phases of internationalization firms exploit personal and existing, mostly dyadic entrepreneurial networks. These are characterized by high levels of both trust and commitment (Sasi and Arenius 2008), which have been found to be highly important in international cooperation (Fink et al. 2008). International growth requires the extension of existing networks and the establishment of multilateral networks (Sasi and Arenius 2008). As Prashantham (2008) emphasizes, internationalization necessitates the acquisition of new knowledge and an innovative approach to the development of internationally appropriate offerings. He suggests that new and small firms might best meet this expectation by forming partnerships with those that are more internationally experienced and connected. This type of networking activity, or international cooperation, has been proposed elsewhere as an attractive option for overcoming the disadvantages of smallness and newness in international cooperation (Nummela and Pukkinen 2006, Fink et al. 2008, Sasi and Arenius 2008). In particular, when the internationalization process is sudden and a considerable increase in the company's resource base is needed (Chetty and Campbell-Hunt 2003) it is necessary to develop new networks in order to enter new markets successfully (Crick and Spence 2005).

Prashantham (2008) argues that the issue of power difference should be considered when small firms form and manage relationships with multinational subsidiaries. Given the differences in structure, size, mindset and power, for example, they may find it difficult to negotiate terms with the multinationals. Indeed, opportunistic behavior and the question of interdependence between partners have been experienced as negative sides of collaboration (Spence et al. 2008). On the more concrete level, e.g., in joint ventures, firms encounter a range of operational and managerial problems due to dissimilarities in resources, operating methods and strategy, as well as in national and corporate cultures (Owens and Quinn 2007). Therefore collaboration, although perceived as an important and complementary asset for a company, could also be understood as a loss of independence, and thus as something to be avoided.

Sales and Profitability

Increased sales and higher profits are usually referred to when the consequences of international growth are discussed. Common indicators of internationalization performance include international sales, export intensity, export-sales growth and their profitability in comparison with domestic sales, and the geographic scope of foreign sales. Internationalization is considered to be worth the effort when organizational performance in terms of growth and profit improves (Antoncic and Hisrich 2000). Empirical evidence of such development is scarce, inconclusive and inconsistent, however (Riahi-Belkaoui 1998, Bloodgood et al. 1997, Antoncic and Hisrich 2000). Indeed, in their conceptual paper Antoncic and Hisrich propose a non-linear (reversed U-shape) association between internationalization performance and profitability, indicating a negative relationship as the level of internationalization begins to increase, then positive and finally negative again.

The outcomes of internationalization and growth discussed above could imply that international growth does not necessarily equal better profits after all. The cost of doing business internationally could easily be underestimated, whereas sales and turnover predictions tend to be over-optimistic.

INDIVIDUAL-LEVEL CONSEQUENCES

Previous studies on SMEs stress the need to analyze the consequences of growth not only from the firm's perspective but also from the point of view of the decision maker or owner-manager, who is the one who largely determines the behavior of the firm (Lloyd-Reason and Mughan 2002, Fillis 2002). Hence, decisions are taken in order to achieve the goals not only of the firm but also of the owner-manager. It has been suggested that the entrepreneur aiming at (international) growth will have to change as the structure of the organization changes (Ennis 1999). These changes may not be altogether positive for the individual, especially from the job and life satisfaction perspectives (Dolan et al. 2008). This is discussed below.

Work Tasks and the Workload

Andersson and Florén (2008) explicitly call for individual-level analyses within internationalization research, and suggest combining two streams, managerial behavior in SMEs and internationalization, in order to enhance understanding of SMEs' international behavior. They hypothesize that although entrepreneurial work in small international firms and small domestic firms may be similar in many respects, there may also be major differences. In particular they suggest that having to change their working modes and to delegate jobs in order to be able to direct their own efforts towards the international market makes the working days of internationalized entrepreneurs less fragmented than those of other non-international SME owners. It thus follows that the type of work in which they engage changes: they are involved less in the day-to-day running of the firm and more in planning activities. They also spend less time in their own firm and travel more than their peers in other small firms (Andersson and Florén 2008). Hence, it is to be assumed that the delegation of work is a crucial task for managers wishing to pursue internationalization and international growth. It enables them to focus on strategic rather than operational matters, and to off-load some of the decisions and activities. In order to do this they have to rely on and trust others within the firm to carry out these tasks. This may be a challenge and a possible source of discomfort to owner-managers and entrepreneurs, especially if they define themselves as craftsmen and resist the transition into full-time management that internationalization may necessitate (Wiklund et al. 2003). In addition, for fear of lowering the quality, they may resist the change to mass production or the mass customization of their services that international growth might require (Fillis 2002).

It is open to question whether entrepreneurs can handle the sharing of information and decision-making with the new professionals hired in the firm (Ennis 1999). The delegation of work may also reduce the variety in their working life: it has been demonstrated that variety in terms of activities and necessary skills, along with the autonomy and feedback, constitute a source of entrepreneurial satisfaction (Schjoedt 2009).

On the other hand, if entrepreneurs are not willing to delegate but assume full responsibility for their current tasks and for the new ones associated with the international business, their workload increases. Previous studies have demonstrated that they expect firm growth to result in an increased workload (Heinonen and Pukkinen 2005), and the same may apply to international growth. In general, entrepreneurs report working more hours than employees (e.g., Benz and Frey 2008b), and internationalization may increase the gap even more. These direct work-related factors such as an increase in workload and in time spent away from home may also be linked to indirect factors such as higher levels of work-family conflict and lower levels of family satisfaction (Parasuraman and Simmers 2001). This, in turn, may be negatively associated with overall life satisfaction even if entrepreneurs generally enjoy the new work challenges internationalization involves. In particular, work-family interference seems to be particularly prevalent in the case of (married) female entrepreneurs (Stoner et al. 1990), due to excessive expectations among family members (Ufuk and Ozgen 2001) or to having the major responsibility for household chores and childcare (Kim and Ling 2001). Hence the negative consequences of international growth may be gendered.

Although managers of small firms generally prefer to use informal means of communication (O'Gorman et al. 2005), it is hypothesized that due to the geographical and cultural distances involved managers of international ventures need to rely more on formal sources such as reports and management-information systems, and to make more use of management tools and techniques (Andersson and Florén 2008). This may mean a loss of direct contact with customers, for example, which may have a negative effect on job and life satisfaction: entrepreneurs are known to enjoy the feedback they receive from their work contacts (Schjoedt 2009).

Autonomy and Independence

There are several large-scale panel studies suggesting that entrepreneurs are more satisfied with their work and life than wage earners, even though their work is characterized by factors generally associated with job dissatisfaction (Danna and Griffin 1999, Schjoedt 2009). Autonomy is one of the most significant explanatory factors in this case (Schjoedt 2009). Entrepreneurs are satisfied with unfavorable outcomes such as long hours and lower pay because they find the process of entrepreneurship to be "good" and inspiring. This is mainly attributable to the more interesting jobs and to the greater autonomy they enjoy: "doing what you like to do" is assumed to provide procedural utility, which is valued beyond material outcomes (Benz and Frey 2008a). They also report that they have free choice and control over their lives (Blanchflower 2004).

However, as stated previously in connection with firm-level consequences, internationalization, especially for small firms, often necessitates networking and cooperation with other firms. This need for cooperation and mutual trust may be difficult for entrepreneurs to manage and understand. For many of them the independence and autonomous decision-making and the freedom involved in entrepreneurship compared to a hierarchical workplace constituted the main motivation for becoming an entrepreneur in the first place and the main source of satisfaction in their current lives. They may wish to remain independent and to retain ownership of their enterprise, and to simplify life by keeping it small and more easily manageable

(Ennis 1999, Carson et al. 1995). International growth may thus reduce their autonomy and independence.

Control and Personal Income

Internationalization requires both financial and other resources. However, various studies on venture capital and external finance suggest that in fact many entrepreneurs are not ready to accept venture financing due to the fear of losing control (Berggren et al. 2000). The dilution of ownership is also connected to personal income: how willing are they to give away ownership and consequently future profits? This may be a trivial question. Although entrepreneurship is often implicitly associated with wealth, i.e., it is assumed that money is important for individuals becoming entrepreneurs and aspiring towards growth and/or internationalization, several studies suggest the opposite: other motives such as innovation, vision, independence and challenge are more important than wealth generation (Amit et al. 2001, Wiklund et al. 2003).

In fact, most research on entrepreneurs suggests that their income is lower than that of waged workers in similar professions, although the differentials are much higher (Cooper and Artz 1995). They accept lower initial earnings and growth than waged workers in comparable positions (Hamilton 2000), but most seem to be satisfied with their pay (Taylor 2004), or with their job irrespective of the pay (Benz and Frey 2008b). The goal of starting the firm may be related to achieving a good quality of life, and the economic objectives limited to making a living (Reijonen 2008). The acknowledged wide variation in expectations of financial success and actual success may give some insight into why international growth may prove to be a personally negative experience for some, whereas others may enjoy it.

BELIEFS ABOUT CONSEQUENCES AND FUTURE BEHAVIOR

Beliefs play a crucial role in explaining why people behave the way they do (Wiklund et al. 2003). The consequences of international growth discussed in previous sections represent beliefs about the outcomes—either potential or real—that are likely to influence entrepreneurs' and managers' attitudes towards international growth. Recent research findings have challenged the causal structure of motivation and future behavior. Delmar and Wiklund (2008), for example, suggest that the reverse relationship exists in company growth, i.e., previous outcomes affect future motivations, which change over time depending on whether the intended outcomes materialize or not.

Be they beliefs or actual outcomes, the future behavior of a firm is likely to be influenced by the feedback, which in turn influences the desire for future growth (see Cort et al. 2007, Delmar and Wiklund 2008). The feedback loop may be positive or negative (or neutral), either encouraging or discouraging international growth in the future. Even negative consequences, through learning by doing or learning by failing, may encourage a firm to grow or prevent it from growing. Wiklund et al. (2003) found that non-economic consequences, such as employee well-being, were more important for future growth motivation than the possibility of personal economic gain or loss, for example. On the individual level, what is most important is the manager's ability to keep full control over the operations of the firm.

In a similar vein, Heinonen and Pukkinen (2005, 2006) found that growth was more likely to take place if it was believed to improve the manager's prospects of following and directing the activities of his enterprise, increasing his independence or improving his ability to cope with a crisis situation. Hence, firm-level consequences, especially product quality and control, were considered of importance in relation to future growth aspirations. This suggests that individuals are likely to value the consequences of international growth in different ways in different contexts, and that there is not a one-size-fits-all outcome or belief that universally explains future behavior in relation to international growth. This idea is supported in Wiklund et al. (2003). They suggest that this type of expected outcome may have a substantial effect on some managers, but not all, as the result was not statistically significant although it was consistent in three separate analyses.

Although the vast majority of literature on company growth and internationalization considers sufficient resources, skills and knowledge prerequisites or antecedents of international growth, many of these can be gained during the process, through trial and error. For example, failure as a negative consequence does not need to discourage international growth, but could rather be seen as a means of acquiring experiential knowledge to be exploited in the future. Zidonis (2007) demonstrated that, regardless of its lack of knowledge and experience a company may, through trial and error, be successful in the internationalization process. International growth, especially in new emerging markets, is very often driven by idealist motivations or unrealistic ambitions, and is not supported by sufficient resources, competences or networks. In fact, knowing too much may sometimes block innovative and courageous thinking and behavior. The interpretation of fragmented knowledge creates beliefs and assumptions about growth and foreign market attractiveness, which in turn serve as a basis for international opportunity recognition. International opportunity is perceived as the picture of reality according to which entrepreneurs organize their future activities (Zidonis 2007). It is worth pointing out, however, that international growth should be viewed in the context of a particular firm at a given point in time. Unplanned, serendipitous encounters that challenge management behavior further strengthen this contingency view. (Crick and Spence 2005, Spence et al. 2008) Therefore, lessons learned from one venture cannot necessarily be transferred to the next one.

CONCLUSIONS AND SUGGESTIONS FOR FURTHER RESEARCH

Previous research has demonstrated that researchers focusing on small businesses should analyze the consequences of international growth for the firm and the individual, or entrepreneur, since the entrepreneur largely determines the firm's behavior (Lloyd-Reason and Mughan 2002). Entrepreneurs therefore assess the consequences of international growth for the firm and also for themselves personally (Heinonen and Pukkinen 2005). Firm success and the personal well-being of the entrepreneur do not always go hand in hand (Hmieleski and Corbett 2008), and therefore even if the firm is highly successful in its international growth the entrepreneur may experience a decrease in job or life satisfaction or well-being. Previous research explicitly demonstrates or implicitly suggests that international growth means changes in the entrepreneur's role and work within the firm. There may be a need to delegate and to be less involved in the day-to-day running, to focus more on planned than ad hoc activities, to rely on informal information, and to spend less time in the home base and travel relentlessly. On the other hand, there may be a major increase in workload. In either case the outcome may be the exact opposite of the owner's life and work goals, even if the firm is successful in its international growth. Entrepreneurs have been reported to be more satisfied with their jobs than non-entrepreneurs, which stems in particular from the autonomy, variety and feedback in their work (Schjoedt 2009). According to previous research it is these particular aspects that are at risk from internationalization and the related changes in work practices (Andersson and Florén 2008).

However, we should not expect opinions on international growth to be unanimous (Wiklund et al. 2003). Depending on the motivations, expectations and primary goals for being an entrepreneur and running the firm, the consequences may prove to be either positive or negative. For individuals motivated by independence, autonomy, having full control over the firm, and perceiving themselves as craftsmen actively involved in the day-to-day and operational activities, the decision to pursue international growth, as suggested by policymakers, may have detrimental consequences for their personal lives. However, those who seek liberation from the day-to-day and operational aspects of the business, who can delegate decision-making and enjoy developing more formalized routines and practices, and who adopt a learning-by-doing approach to the international activity, may find internationalization a major source of job and life satisfaction.

Research on the consequences of international growth is scarce and there may be a number of misconceptions about its outcomes. It is hard to differentiate between beliefs and reality. Therefore, it is suggested that future empirical research on international growth should focus on its consequences on the individual and firm levels. In addition, both non-economic and economic consequences deserve attention, given the suggestion in this study that the role of non-economic individual consequences in particular may have been underestimated. Finally, exploring the dark side of growth will deepen understanding of the phenomenon and balance normative assumptions.

ACKNOWLEDGMENTS

The authors wish to thank the Academy of Finland (WORK programme) for financial support.

BIBLIOGRAPHY

Acedo F.J. and Jones, M. (2007) 'Speed of internationalization and entrepreneurial cognition: insights and a comparison between international new ventures, exporters and domestic firms,' *Journal of World Business*, 42 (3): 236–252.

Amit, R., MacCrimmon, K., Zietsma, C. and Oesch, J.M. (2001) 'Does money matter? Wealth attainment as the motive for initiating growth-oriented technology ventures,' *Journal of Business Venturing*, 16 (2): 119–143.

Anderson, V., Boocock, G. and Graham, S. (2001) 'An investigation into learning needs of managers in internationalising small and medium-sized enterprises,' *Journal of Small Business and Enterprise Development*, 8 (3): 215–232.

Andersson, S. and Florén, H. (2008) 'Exploring managerial behavior in small international firms,' *Journal of Small Business and Enterprise Development*, 15 (1): 31–50.

Antoncic, B. and Hisrich, R.F. (2000) 'An integrative conceptual model', *Journal of Euromarketing*, 9 (2): 17–35.

Autio, E., Sapienza, H.J. and Almeida, J.G. (2000) 'Effects of age at entry, knowledge intensity, and imitability on international growth,' *Academy of Management Journal*, 43 (5): 909–924.

Benz, M. and Frey, B.S. (2008a) 'The value of doing what you like: evidence from the self-employed in 23 countries,' *Journal of Economic Behavior & Organization*, 68 (3–4): 445–455.

Benz, M. and Frey, B.S. (2008b) 'Being independent is a great thing: subjective evaluations of self-employment and hierarchy,' *Economica*, 75 (2): 362–383.

Berggren, B., Olofsson, C. and Silver, L. (2000) 'Control aversion and the search for external financing in Swedish SMEs,' *Journal Small Business Economics*, 15 (3): 233–242.

Blanchflower, D.G. (2004) 'Self-employment: more may not be better,' *Swedish Economic Policy Review*, 11 (2): 15–73.

Bloodgood, J.M., Sapienza, H.J. and Almeida, J.G. (1997) 'The internationalisation of new high-potential U.S. ventures: antecedents and outcomes,' *Entrepreneurship, Theory and Practice*, 20 (4): 61–76.

Carr, A. (2006) 'What it means to be 'critical' in relation to international business. A case of the appropriate conceptual lenses,' *Critical perspectives on international business*, 2 (2): 79–90.

Carson, D., Cromie, S., McGowan, P., Hill, J. (1995) *Marketing and entrepreneurship in SMEs: an innovative approach*, Hemel Hempstead: Prentice Hall.

Chetty, S. and Campbell-Hunt, C. (2003) 'Explosive international growth and problems of success amongst small to medium-sized firms,' *International Small Business Journal*, 21 (5): 5–27.

Cooper, A.C. and Artz, K.W. (1995) 'Determinants of satisfaction for entrepreneurs', *Journal of Business Venturing*, 10 (6): 439–457.

Cort, K.T., Griffith, D.A. and White, D.S. (2007) 'An attribution theory approach for understanding the internationalization of professional service firms,' *International Marketing Review*, 24 (1): 9–25.

Crick, D. and Jones, M. (2000) 'Small high-technology firms and international high-technology markets,' *Journal of International Marketing*, 8 (2): 63–85.

Crick, D. and Spence, M. (2005) 'The internationalisation of 'high performing' UK high-tech SMEs: a study of planned and unplanned strategies,' *International Business Review*, 14 (3): 167–185.

Danna, K. and Griffin, R.W. (1999) 'Health and well-being in the workplace: a review and synthesis of the literature', *Journal of Management*, 25 (3): 357–384.

Delmar, F. and Wiklund, J. (2008) 'The effect of small business managers´ growth motivation on firm growth: a longitudinal study', *Entrepreneurship, Theory and Practice*, 32 (3): 437–457.

Dolan, P., Peasgood, T. and White, M. (2008) 'Do we really know what makes us happy? A review of the economic literature on the factors associated with subjective well-being', *Journal of Economic Psychology*, 29 (1): 94–122.

Ennis, S. (1999) 'Growth and the small firm: using causal mapping to assess the decision-making process—a case study', *Qualitative Market Research: An International Journal*, 2 (2): 147–160.

Fillis, I. (2002) 'Barriers to internationalisation. An investigation of the craft microenterprise', *European Journal of Marketing*, 36 (7–8): 912–927.

Fink, M., Harms, R. and Kraus, S. (2008) 'Cooperative internationalization of SMEs: self-commitment as a success factor for international entrepreneurship', *European Management Journal*, 26 (6): 429–440.

Gabrielsson, M., Sasi, V. and Darling, J. (2004) 'Finance strategies of rapidly-growing Finnish SMEs: born internationals and born globals', *European Business Review*, 16 (6): 590–604.

Hamilton, B.H. (2000) 'Does entrepreneurship pay? An empirical analysis of the returns of self-employment', *Journal of Political Economy*, 108 (3): 604–631.

Hartarska, V. and Gonzalez-Vega, C. (2006) 'What affects new and established firms' expansion? Evidence from small firms in Russia', *Small Business Economics*, 27 (2–3): 195–206.

Heinonen, J. and Kovalainen, A. (eds.) (2009) *Yrityskasvun mekanismit* [Mechanism of company growth], Turku School of Economics, CRE/TSE Entre, Series A Research Reports A2/2009.

Heinonen, J. and Pukkinen, T. (2005) 'How about expanding the business? Analyzing entrepreneurs' attitudes toward growth', *The ICFAI Journal of Entrepreneurship Development*, II (3): 64–77.

Heinonen, J. and Pukkinen, T. (2006) 'Entrepreneurs´ perceptions of growth', in J. Heinonen (ed) *The nature and elements of growth—Finnish SMEs in focus*, 80–106, Small Business Institute, Turku School of Economics, Tampere: Kirjapaino Esa Print.

Heinonen, J., Nummela, N. and Pukkinen, T. (2004) 'To grow or not to grow? An analysis of internationally growth-oriented Finnish SMEs', *Proceedings of the 30th EIBA Annual Conference*, Ljubljana, December 2004.

Hmieleski, K.M. and Corbett, A.C. (2008) 'The contrasting interaction effects of improvisational behavior with entrepreneurial self-efficacy on new venture performance and entrepreneur work satisfaction', *Journal of Business Venturing*, 23 (4): 482–496.

Jones, M. and Nummela, N. (2008) 'International entrepreneurship: expanding the domain and extending our research questions', *European Management Journal*, 26 (6): 349–353.

Kim, J.L.S. and Ling, C.S. (2001) 'Work-family conflict of women entrepreneurs in Singapore', *Women in Management Review*, 16 (5): 204–221.

Lloyd-Reason, L. and Mughan, T. (2002) 'Strategies for internationalisation within SMEs: the key role of the owner-manager', *Journal of Small Business and Enterprise Development*, 9 (2): 120–129.

McGaughey, S.L. (2007) 'Hidden ties in international new venturing: the case of portfolio entrepreneurship', *Journal of World Business*, 42 (3): 307–321.

Nummela, N. and Pukkinen, T. (2006) 'What makes export co-operation tick? Analysing commitment in Finnish export circles', *Journal of Euromarketing*, 16 (1&2): 23–35.

Nummela, N., Puumalainen, K. and Saarenketo, S. (2005) 'International growth orientation of knowledge-intensive SMEs', *Journal of International Entrepreneurship*, 3 (1): 5–18.

O'Gorman, C., Bourke, S. and Murray, J.A. (2005) 'The nature of managerial work in small growth-orientated small businesses', *Small Business Economics*, 25 (1): 1–16.

Owens, M. and Quinn, B. (2007) 'Problems encountered within international retail joint ventures: UK retailer case study evidence', *International Journal of Retail & Distribution Management*, 35 (10): 758–780.

Paavilainen, E. and Kuuluvainen, A. (2008) 'International growth of Finnish small and medium-sized enterprises', *Proceedings of the ICSB 2008 World Conference in Halifax, Canada*.

Parasuraman, S. and Simmers, C.A. (2001) 'Type of employment, work-family conflict and well-being: a comparative study', *Journal of Organizational Behaviour*, 22 (5): 551–568.

Perks, K.J. and Hughes, M. (2008) 'Entrepreneurial decision-making in internationalization: propositions from mid-size firms', *International Business Review*, 17 (3): 310–330.

Prashantham, S. (2008) 'New venture internationalization as strategic renewal', *European Management Journal*, 26 (6): 378–387.

Reijonen, H. (2008) 'Understanding the small business owner: what they really aim at and how this relates to firm performance: a case study in North Karelia, Eastern Finland', *Management Research News*, 31 (8): 616–629.

Riahi-Belkaoui, A. (1998) 'The effects of the degree of internationalization on firm performance', *International Business Review*, 7 (3): 315–321.

Sasi, V. and Arenius, P. (2008) 'International new ventures and social networks: advantage or liability?' *European Management Journal*, 26 (6): 400–411.

Schjoedt, L. (2009) 'Entrepreneurial job characteristics: an examination of their effect on entrepreneurial satisfaction', *Entrepreneurship Theory and Practice*, 33 (3): 619–644.

Spence, M., Manning, L. and Crick, D. (2008) 'An investigation into the use of collaborative ventures in the internationalization of high performing Canadian SMEs', *European Management Journal*, 26 (6): 412–428.

Stoner, C.R., Hartman, R.I. and Arora, R. (1990) 'Work-home role conflict in female owners of small business: an exploratory study', *Journal of Small Business Management*, 28 (1): 30–38.

Taylor, M. (2004) 'Self-employment in Britain: When, who and why?' *Swedish Economic Policy Review*, 11 (2): 139–173.

Ufuk, H. and Ozgen, O. (2001) 'Interaction between the business and family lives of women entrepreneurs in Turkey', *Journal of Business Ethics*, 31 (2): 95–106.

Wennberg, K. and Holmquist, C. (2008) 'Problemistic search and international entrepreneurship', *European Management Journal*, 26 (6): 441–454.

Westhead, P., Wright, M. and Ucbasaran, D. (2001) 'The internationalisation of new and small firms: a resource-based view', *Journal of Business Venturing*, 16 (4): 333–358.

Wiklund, J. and Shepherd, D. (2003) 'Aspiring for, and achieving growth: the moderating role of resources and opportunities', *Journal of Management Studies*, 40 (8): 1919–1941.

Wiklund, J., Davidsson, P. and Delmar, F. (2003) 'What do they think and feel about growth? An expectancy-value approach to small business managers' attitudes towards growth', *Entrepreneurship, Theory and Practice*, 27 (3): 247–270.

Wiklund, J., Patzelt, H. and Shepherd, D.A. (2009) 'Building an integrative model of small business growth', *Small Business Economics*, 32 (4): 351–374.

Yli-Renko, H., Autio, E. and Tontti, V. (2002) 'Social capital, knowledge, and the international growth of technology-based new firms', *International Business Review*, 11 (3): 279–304.

Zhang, M.Y. and Dodgson, M. (2007) "A roasted duck can still fly away': a case study of technology, nationality, culture and the rapid and early internationalization of the firm', *Journal of World Business*, 42 (3): 336–349.

Zhou, L. (2007) 'The effects of entrepreneurial proclivity and foreign market knowledge on early internationalization', *Journal of World Business*, 42 (3): 281–293.

Zidonis, Z. (2007) 'Entrepreneurial internationalisation: a case study of Libra company', *Baltic Journal of Management*, 2 (3): 273–287.

Zucchella, A., Palamara, G. and Denicolai, S. (2007) 'The drivers of the early internationalization of the firm', *Journal of World Business*, 42 (3): 268–280.

Part II

International Growth Trajectories of SMEs

6 Growth and Internationalization of French and Danish SMEs

Mathieu Cabrol, Frederic Nlemvo, Erik Rasmussen, Per Servais and Arild Aspelund

BACKGROUND

What happens to a highly international firm after it has been founded and how and why the firm grows—or does not grow—is the focus of this book, as introduced in the previous chapters. It is the intention of this chapter to elaborate on this theme by comparing SMEs from France and Denmark. The focus is on two types of firms that are international right from the outset: the born internationals and the born globals. A third group—the export SMEs—are used as a reference group. In accordance with previous research (McDougall et al. 1994, Oviatt and McDougall 1994), the first two groups can be labeled international new ventures (INVs), while the third group is the more traditional exporters.

During the past few decades the scholarly and popular international business literature has given considerable attention to international new ventures (Rialp et al. 2005, Zahra 2005, Aspelund et al. 2007). Though multiple names for and definitions of this phenomenon exist, they are frequently defined in line with the terminology from the seminal work of Oviatt and McDougall, as *"a business organization that, from inception, seeks to derive significant advantages from the use of resources and the sale of output in multiple countries"* (Oviatt and McDougall 1994, 49).

INVs have deserved this attention because they are clearly distinct from other types of international firms (Madsen et al. 2000, Moen and Servais 2002, Aspelund and Moen 2005), they challenge the traditional views of how firms should internationalize (McDougall et al. 1994, Bell 1995, Knight and Cavusgil 1996, Moen and Servais 2002), they perform an important role in disseminating technologies worldwide (Keeble et al. 1998, Autio et al. 2000, Zahra et al. 2000) and because recent studies suggest that they are growing in numbers in most open economies (Rialp et al. 2005; Zahra 2005, Aspelund et al. 2007). The significance of the INV phenomenon might be most apparent in small and open economies such as in Scandinavia, but there is also evidence of widespread occurrence in larger economies such as that of the US (Bloodgood et al. 1996, Shrader et al. 2000), Japan (Lu and Beamish 2001), UK (Coviello and McAuley 1999;

Burgel and Murray 2000, Crick and Jones 2000) and France (Moen and Servais 2002, Cabrol and Nlemvo 2008).

Even though the emergence and growth of INVs is consistent in a broad range of countries, there seems to be a great deal of heterogeneity in terms of characteristics and strategy among INVs (Jones 1999, Aspelund et al. 2007). This heterogeneity might stem from the industry in which they occur (Boter and Holmquist 1996; McAuley 1999) or from the characteristics of the entrepreneurs (Crick and Jones 2000), but these factors would only account for some of the variation. Since strategic decisions made in the very early stages of the founding process have been found to have long-term effects on the international development of the venture (Moen and Servais 2002), it is tempting to look at other factors related to the founding environment to explain more of the heterogeneity of INVs. One prime candidate would arguably be the national business environment from which they are born.

This chapter thus seeks to investigate whether some of the INV heterogeneity can be explained from the INV's country of origin. More specifically, the purpose is to examine the strategy of INVs from two different countries, namely Denmark and France, to see whether there are any systematic differences that can be attributed to differences in the business environment of these two countries. The study is based on survey data from Denmark and from an area of France that is comparable to Denmark—the Rhone-Alps region—that will make it possible to analyze the differences and similarities.

METHODOLOGY

In this section the research design of two separate studies—one conducted in France, one in Denmark—are presented. As they were not coordinated before the actual collection of data, adjusting them into one comparable data set was a challenge. The original data sets were aligned in terms of founding year of the company and the type of company—they were mainly SMEs in a number of manufacturing industries.

The French Study

The objective of this study was to examine the internationalization French SMEs, all registered in the Rhone-Alps region. Due to the diversity of its economic activities and lack of dominating metropol, the region is considered to be the most representative of the economic landscape of France. With six million inhabitants and an area of 43,698 sq. km., it is the second largest and wealthiest region of France, and one of the ten wealthiest regions within the European Union.

The sample for the study was derived from Telexport, which is a database that gathers data on French exporting companies. First, exporters from the selected region were separated. They represented all main industrial sectors (all in all, 25 categories of NACE codes), but only companies meeting the definition of SME in the European Union (less than 250 employees) were included. This resulted in 2,774 companies, but only 550 of them met the criteria of being founded between 1993 and 2000, and having international sales activity between 1193 and 2002. Subsidiaries, spin-offs or companies which had been created as a result of a merger were excluded from the study (cf. Zahra 2005).

In 2003, mail questionnaires were sent to these 550 firms, and after discarding some for database errors or unfilled questionnaires, 111 valid questionnaires were obtained, i.e., a response rate of approximately 25 percent. In order to assess the extent of internationalization, several relevant criteria derived from the literature were used (Reuber and Fischer 1997, Zahra et al. 2000). The criteria included: (i) the international sales as a percentage of the total sales; (ii) the entry mode adopted to approach foreign markets; and (iii) the geographical areas targeted. The authors then compared the evolution of the above-mentioned indicators over time, which was from the first year of internationalization to the last year considered in this study (2002). The data were also checked using the Telexport database—including the percentage of exports and imports over time, turnover, number of employees, existence of a subsidiary, countries targeted, presence of an export manager, name of the manager, and NACE codes. Of the 111 respondents, 80 met the chosen criteria and were considered eligible for the study.

The Danish Study

Due to the lack of natural resources and the small size of the country—approximately five million inhabitants—small and medium-sized enterprises dominate, and the Danish economy has produced only a very limited number of multinational companies. Danish companies increasingly operate abroad, just as many foreign companies establish themselves in Denmark. Due to the decline in trade barriers and the advances in technology and logistics, Danish SMEs are internationalizing at an accelerating rate. For many of them, the internationalization process does not, however, follow traditional patterns of building upon a stable domestic position before gradually and sequentially engaging in international activities (cf. Johanson and Vahlne 1977, Johanson and Vahlne 1990, Cavusgil 1980). On the contrary, prior research suggests that a new pattern of international entrepreneurship—based on rapid, if not instant, internationalization—is emerging.

Data in this study was collected for a research project "Market Strategy of Firms in Global Environments," which primarily focused on industrial international new ventures. Firms established in 2002 or later were disregarded, as no economic performance data were available, and only firms with a minimum of ten employees were included. Firms established before 1982 were included only if they had more than 50 employees. The population of business firms studied was identified by means of a public database, which lists all private Danish business firms; 3,048 firms met the criteria.

Initially, a letter was sent directly to the CEO of each of the firms. Attached to the letter were seven questions of central importance for the total project. These seven questions were the basis for classifying firms as different types of ventures. As a next step, as mentioned in the initial letter, all CEOs were approached by telephone in order to ask them to participate in the survey and to answer the seven questions. In 2004, a marketing research company carried out this part of the data collection, supported by the team of researchers. After the elimination of incorrect registrations and unreachable firms (the firm was closed, further duplicates, firms with wrong NACE codes, etc.) the population was reduced to 2,527 firms.

About 57 percent of the firms in the effective population of 2,527 firms, altogether 1,456 firms, refused to participate in the survey. A non-response bias test showed no significant differences between the two groups in terms of size, year of establishment, and turnover. The test led to the conclusion that no significant differences were present and that the sample was representative.

The Population of the Study

In order to make the two data sets comparable, only exporting SMEs (meeting the EU definition) that were founded after 1990 or later were included in this study. Next, the companies were classified into three groups. Several alternative classifications exist for this purpose. The seminal articles by Oviatt and McDougall (McDougall et al. 2003, 1994, Oviatt and McDougall 1994, 1995, 1997, 2005a, 2005b), divide firms into four groups in accordance with the type of international activities and number of countries served. These include the multinational trader, the geographically focused start-up, the global start-up, and the export/import SMEs. However, this typology is difficult to use in an empirical setting; for example, it is not clear exactly how one defines a "few" or a "large" number of countries.

Another possibility is to use the classical born global definition of 25 percent or more export during the founding period of the firm—which is typically seen as three years, but may be from one to six years (see Knight and Cavusgil 1996, Knight 1997, Knight and Aulakh 1998, Knight et al. 2000). Yet another alternative is to define the born global firm or INV as a firm with export and sourcing outside its own continent within the first three years, as in Knight et al. 1999, Rasmussen and Madsen 2002, Servais et al. 2006, Moen and Servais 2002, Kuivalainen et al. 2007.

As the focus of this book and this chapter is on how internationalization and growth are interlinked, the authors have chosen to set up a relatively simple typology. The born global group consists of the firms with a rapid internationalization, i.e., their share of exports exceed 25 percent of turnover during the first three years after inception. The born internationals are also international during the first three years, but at a much slower rate—their share of exports is less than 25 percent of turnover during the first three years after inception. The export SMEs have internationalized after the first three years. The first two groups can be labeled INVs in accordance with the literature mentioned earlier; the born global group also meets the criteria used earlier (cf. Madsen and Servais 1997, Madsen et al. 2000, Knight et al. 2000, Rasmussen and Servais 2002, Gabrielsson and Kirpalani 2004, Rialp et al. 2005). The last group—which is used for comparison—is made up of the more traditional exporters that develop the home market first and then go international.

The proportion of born globals in the two data sets is quite close (34 percent in the French set, 39 percent in the Danish one), while the proportion of born internationals and export SMEs differs considerably. The number of born internationals is much higher in France than in Denmark (47 percent vs. 27 percent), thus meaning that the majority of French firms start their internationalization within the first three years after foundation, whereas in Denmark a large group of firms (approximately one-third) do not go international within the first three years.

A more detailed overview shows that while only a third of French firms can be considered as born global firms (BG), almost half of the sample is made up of born internationals (BI) (see Table 6.1). It seems also that the French firms belonging to both aforementioned categories recorded their

Table 6.1 Overview of the Two Data Sets

| | FRANCE | | | | DENMARK | | | |
	BI	BG	Export SME	Total	BI	BG	Export SME	Total
Sample	38	27	15	80	91	130	116	337
% of the sample	48	34	19	100%	27	39	34	100%
Age of the firms in 2002	7,1	5,6	8,3	N=80	7,0	6,4	8,4	N=337
Time lag between the founding year and the first year of internationalization	0,75	0,3	5,3	N=80	2,18	0,70	7,92	N=333
Percentage of firms which had the idea of internationalization before the inception of the company or during the venture creation process (1) (2)	53	96	13	N=80	35	76	44	N=337

1) The internationalization speed was given by the respondent. For Denmark, in a few cases the number of years was extremely high (more than 100 years) indicating that it must be an error. These few outliers have been deleted before calculating the mean.

2) For Denmark, "Did the founder focus on international sales from the establishment of the company?" Answer from 1=not at all to 7=to a great extent. The percentage here includes the answers in category 5, 6, and 7.

first international sales during the year of their inception. On average, it was during the first quarter for born global firms, but at the beginning of the fourth quarter for born international firms. Export SMEs, however, went international much later—on average five years after their inception.

As far as French born global firms are concerned, almost all of them (96 percent) had the idea of going international before the inception of the company or during venture creation, while seven out of ten went international on their own initiative. This picture contrasts with French born international firms, as only half of them had the idea of internationalization before their inception as well as themselves initiating international sales proactively. It is also worth mentioning that only 13 percent of French exporting SMEs thought of internationalization before or during the creation of the venture. This is consistent with their later arrival in international markets. But more than 50 percent of such firms initiated international sales on their own initiative.

Taking a closer look at the Danish firms in Table 6.1, the percentage of born global firms is almost the same as in France, but in France the percentage of born internationals is much higher than in Denmark. Instead, there was a high percentage of exporting SMEs in Denmark. As can be seen in the table, the French and the Danish firms are in many ways similar to each other. The youngest firms in both countries are the born global type of firms. The time between the founding and the first year of internationalization is very short in both countries for the born global firms. And in both countries the founders of the born globals focused on the international markets right from the beginning.

Table 6.2 shows that the industrial distribution in all three groups of French firms—born internationals, born globals or export SMEs—is

Table 6.2   Industrial Distribution in the French Data Set

Industry (EU NACE code)	BI N=38 obs.		BG N=27 obs.		Export SMEs N=15 obs.		Total
Code 1: food industry, tobacco, textiles	4	10%	5	19%	2	13%	11/14%
Code 2: chemistry, plastic, mineral products, metal equipment, machinery	20	53%	9	33%	4	27%	33/41%
Code 3: furniture, computer, electrical equipment, radio, television, communication, electrical products; medical, optical products, car industry	8	21%	7	26%	3	20%	18/23%
Code 7: computer activities (software)	6	16%	6	22%	6	40%	18/23%
TOTAL		100%		100%		100%	101%

Table 6.3 Industrial Distribution in the Danish Data Set

Industry (EU NACE code)	BI N=91 obs.		BG N=130 obs.		Export SMEs N=116 obs.		TOTAL
Code 1: food industry, tobacco, textiles	9	10%	15	12%	9	8%	33/10%
Code 2: chemistry, plastic, mineral products, metal equipment, machinery	58	64%	54	42%	79	68%	191/57%
Code 3: furniture, computer, electrical equipment, radio, television, communication, electrical products, medical, optical products, car industry	21	23%	48	37%	23	20%	92/27%
Code 7: computer activities (software)	3	3%	13	10%	5	4%	21/6%
TOTAL	91	100%	130	101%	116	100%	100%

rather diverse. Moreover, no particular industry seems to be characteristic to born globals. In fact, while born internationals are most often active in the Code 2 industries (53 percent of such firms belong to that category) and export SMEs in computer-related activities (Code 7 industries), born globals have no particular typical industry background. Although the small sample size does not allow strong conclusions, the data indicates that other factors than the type of industry better explain the choice of this international growth strategy.

Tables 6.2 and 6.3 both show differences between the two countries studied, independent of the group of firms studied. However, the data sets also share some similarities, particularly in terms of the profile of born global firms: The majority of these firms are active in the Code 2 or Code 3 industries.

ANALYZING THE DATA—PATHS OF GROWTH

In this section, the patterns of growth in both countries are presented. However, as the data was not collected using identical questionnaires, not all information was available in both countries.

Regarding the French data, the extent of internationalization was measured through three variables: the foreign sales percentage, the entry modes adopted and the geographical areas entered. In so doing, the evolution of these indicators was compared over time—that is, the time between the first year of internationalization and the last year observed (2002). In order to identify the path of growth, two indicators of growth were introduced: the turnover and the number of employees. In fact, whatever the indicator considered, growth is measured as the variation (increase/decrease) in the value of that indicator between the first year of internationalization (year 0) and the last year observed (2002) divided by the value of the indicator considered during the first year. For instance, in terms of turnover, growth is measured as: turnover in year 2002 – turnover in year 0/turnover in year 0. Table 6.2 provides an overview of their growth patterns.

For all indicators examined, Table 6.4 shows shifts in values between the two dates considered, with some differences in amplitude depending on the variable considered. In fact, the average number of employees is three times higher in 2002 as compared to the first year of internationalization, whatever the group considered (born international or born global firms). An exception of this is for export SMEs with a lesser—but still important—increase of 80 percent. This may suggest that ceteris paribus born global firms, as well as born international firms, have a much higher potential for growth than export SMEs. During the same period, the average turnover increased significantly as it is multiplied by numbers ranging from three, in the case of exporting SMEs, to more than four (4.28) for born global firms and even close to six (5.7) for born international firms.

At the same time, there is also an increase in the average percent of international sales for each of the three types of firms studied: very low in the case of born globals (only 5 percent) but particularly high for exporting SMEs (63 percent) and born international firms. For born global firms, the quasi-stability can be explained by the fact that their market is international

Table 6.4   Comparison of International Sales, Turnover, Number of Employees and Geographic Areas Entered between the Three Types of French Firms

	BI firms			*BG firms*			*Export SMEs*		
	Year 0	*2002*	*Growth*	*Year 0*	*2002*	*Growth*	*Year 0*	*2002*	*Growth*
Turnover (KEuros)	497	2849	473%	1038	4453	329%	921	2961	221%
% of international sales	11%	25%	127%	63%	66%	5%	8%	13%	63%
Number of employees	6	17	183%	9	25	178%	15	27	80%
Average number of geographic areas targeted	1.4	2.2	57%	1.7	3	76%	1.3	1.6	23%
Western Europe only	-	21%			19%			36%	
Europe only	54%	38%	-30%	44%	22%	-50%	54%	50%	

N.B.: Year 0 signifies the first year of internationalization.

by essence, insofar as their presence in international markets is optimized or maximized soon after their date of origin. As a result, few improvements are expected over time in this area.

Despite the lack of a control sample, shifts observed in the values of variables studied over time seem to be indicative of an accelerated internationalization. Regarding the geographical areas reached by the firms in the sample, Table 6.4 indicates a tendency of stability for exporting SMEs, but a possible acceleration insofar as the increase goes beyond 50 percent for born international firms and born global firms. It appears also that, on average, over the period examined, both born international and born global firms entered an additional geographical area. Moreover, whereas the same half of exporting SMEs have their international activities focused solely in Europe, the percentage of born international and born global firms with sales activities restricted to Europe ("Western Europe" and "All Europe") decreases strongly, from 44 to 22 percent for born global firms and from 54 to 38 percent for born international firms.

These results partially contradict the PTI perspective—particularly for born global companies but also to a small degree for born international firms as well—because during the first year of international activities, the majority of them do not develop their international activities merely in countries geographically close to France. It seems that during the last year studied, geographical diversity was more important for born global firms, as sales activities of such companies covered, on average, included three different geographical areas a couple of years after their creation. This is consistent with Jones and Crick (2004) who found that INVs—particularly high-tech ones—do not necessarily have the opportunity to gradually develop on the domestic market before going international. Market demand for high-technology products may also limit the window of opportunity for exploitation of new products, thus moving firms quickly to the most attractive rather than the most culturally similar markets.

Table 6.5 Comparison of International Sales, Turnover, Number of Employees and Geographic Areas Entered between the Three Types of Danish Firms

	BI firms			*BG firms*			*Export SMEs*		
	-5 years	2001/ 2002	*Growth*	-5 years	2001/ 2002	*Growth*	-5 years	2001/ 2002	*Growth*
Balance (1000 D.kr.)	24.486	50.618	N=62 106%	28.717	38.595	N=76 34%	26.041	34.196	N=85 31%
Number of employees	25	33	N=56 32%	33	45	N=68 36%	39	46	N=82 20%

Due to legal constraints we have data only from the year of survey (2001/2002) and five years before. Only firms with information from both years have been used.

On the other hand, the data from our Danish study indicates to a large extent the same patterns of growth as the French data, even if not all the same data is available (Table 6.5). Initially, the largest firms are the export SMEs, followed by the born globals and the born internationals. However, the international new ventures are growing at a faster pace than the export SMEs. Furthermore, the data show that the born globals are, nearly all of them, survivors, while one finds a large number of failures among the export SMEs.

HOW AND WHY SMES GROW—OR DO NOT GROW?

Next, the possible linkages between internationalization and growth are discussed from two points of view. First, how do firms—especially international firms—grow? The starting point here is data driven: which types of firms grow, when do they grow and what are the differences between regions or countries? Secondly, why do firms grow, or what are the drivers behind the growth? The theoretical background for this discussion can be found in prior research related to networks and growth (see e.g., Zahra and Garvis 2000, Zahra et al. 2000, Zahra 2005, Zahra et al. 2005, Nummela et al. 2005, 2004, Freeman et al. 2006, Gabrielsson and Kirpalani 2004, Autio and Yli-Renko 1998, Brüderl and Preisendörfer 1998). The following themes are of interest here:

- Differences in the macroeconomic environment and their influence on internationalization and growth
- Drivers of growth, including the role of networks
- Consequences for growth in the case of rapid internationalization

In this study we classified the companies studied into three groups: born globals, born internationals and export SMEs. Contrary to what one might expect, the authors found that the share of born globals in Denmark and France is almost the same. If the general impression of the differences between France and Denmark is correct, the share of born globals should have been much lower in France than in Denmark. On the other hand, the French data set included a relatively large number of born international firms compared to Denmark, while Denmark had considerably more export SMEs. This indicates that the small firms in France tend to be more internationally active after the foundation of the firm than in Denmark.

From the viewpoint of industry, we can conclude that both studies confirmed a rather diverse industrial distribution. The notion that born global firms ought primarily to be found in high-tech industries is thus not confirmed, either in France or in Denmark.

In both countries, the born international firm is the most growth oriented, followed by the born globals. But the "largest" firms are found among the export SMEs, which are not internationally oriented from the onset. In addition, the export SMEs are not growing as fast as the two other groups. We can thus conclude that internationalization and growth are not necessarily linked. Seen from a resource perspective, the born global firm is restrained in its resources because of its focus on international activities, typically in several countries at the same time. Its resources are used to develop contacts and relations in these countries and to build a sales organization capable of handling the large complexity of a highly international firm. In contrast, an export SME will typically be a sub-supplier to a large number of domestic customers, which enables it to start on a much larger scale than the two INV types of firms.

Looking at the growth of the three types, it is interesting to see that the highly international firms—while starting out at a small scale—are growing much faster than the domestically oriented type of firms. It can thus be expected that the INVs will outgrow the domestic firms if they do not extend their internationalization.

Regarding differences in the number of INVs, their internationalization, growth and development, no major differences between France and Denmark were found. The percentage of born global firms was almost the same in the two countries, but there were more born international firms in France than in Denmark. In contrast, there were more export SMEs in Denmark. These firms can be seen as typically Danish sub-suppliers with a focus on specialized production processes. Compared to the INVs they will have a larger number of employees from the foundation of the firm, but will tend not to grow further—and internationalization, if there is any, happens slowly. Whether this type of firm will survive in the long run is an open question, but it is clear that there are fewer and fewer of them either in Denmark or in France.

It could have been argued that the export SMEs would have a large potential for growth in France as this country has a huge home market, but this is clearly not the case. They grow faster than the same type of firms in Denmark, but not as fast as the two INV types of firms. We can thus—with some caution—conclude that a prerequisite for growth among SMEs is an international strategy, both in France and Denmark.

When we first started the discussion of how to compare French and Danish SMEs and their internationalization and growth, we expected to find huge differences between the two countries. Instead, we have found very small differences in, for example, the number of born global firms in the two countries. It can be argued that this is due to the specific area of France that we have used in our research—the Rhone-Alps region—but as this part of France is often used as an "average" part of France we do not believe that this is the case.

Instead, we see this research as documentation of the similarities among the smaller firms in the EU. When one looks at the facts and ignores the few large world-renowned companies, the reality for the small firm is, to a large extent, the same in a number of European countries as we have seen in France and

Denmark. The manager of a small firm in both countries—and in a number of other European countries—has to think and act on an international scale, and the growth of the firm comes to a large extent from its international activities.

BIBLIOGRAPHY

Aspelund, A. and Moen, Ø. (2005) 'Small international firms: typology, performance and implications,' *MIR: Aspects of the Internationalization Process in Smaller Firms*, 45 (3): 37–57.

Aspelund, A., Madsen, T.K. and Moen Ø. (2007) 'A review of the foundation, international marketing strategies, and performance of international new ventures,' *European Journal of Marketing*, 41 (11): 1423–1448.

Autio, E., Sapienza, H. and Almeida, J.G. (2000) 'Effects of age at entry, knowledge intensity, and imitability on international growth,' *Academy of Management Journal*, 43 (5): 909–924.

Bell, J. (1995) 'The internationalization of small computer software firms: a further challenge to 'stage' theories,' *European Journal of Marketing*, 29 (8): 60–75.

Bloodgood, J.M., Sapienza, H.J. and Almeida, J.G. (1996) 'The internationalisation of new high-potential US ventures: antecedents and outcomes,' *Entrepreneurship Theory and Practice*, 20 (4): 61–76.

Boter, H. and Holmquist, C. (1996) 'Industry characteristics and internationalization processes in small firms,' *Journal of Business Venturing*, 11(6): 471–487.

Bruderl, J. and Preisendorfer, P. (1998) 'Network support and the success of newly founded businesses,' *Small Business Economics*, 10 (3): 213–25

Burgel, O. and Murray, G.C. (2000) 'The international market entry choices of start-up companies in high-technology industries,' *Journal of International Marketing*, 8 (2): 33–62.

Cabrol, M. and Nlemvo, F. (2009) 'The internationalisation of French new ventures: the case of the Rhone-Alps region,' *European Management Journal*, 27(4): 255–267.

Cavusgil, S.T. (1980) 'On the internationalization process of firms,' *European Research*, 8 (6): 273–281.

Coviello, N.E. and McAuley, A. (1999) 'Internationalisation and the smaller firm: a review of contemporary empirical research,' *Management International Review*, 39 (3): 223–256.

Crick, D. and Jones M.V. (2000) 'Small high-technology firms and international high-technology markets,' *Journal of International Marketing*, 8(2): 63–85.

Freeman, S., Edwards, R. and Schroder, B. (2006) 'How smaller born-global firms use networks and alliances to overcome constraints to rapid internationalization,' *Journal of International Marketing*, 14 (3): 33–63.

Gabrielsson, M. and Manek Kirpalani, V.H. (2004) 'Born globals: how to reach new business space rapidly,' *International Business Review*, 13 (5): 555–571.

Johanson, J. and Vahlne, J.-E. (1977) 'The internationalization process of the firm: a model of knowledge development and increasing foreign market commitments,' *Journal of International Business Studies*, 8 (000001): 23–32.

Johanson, J. and Vahlne, J.-E. (1990) 'The mechanism of internationalization,' *International Marketing Review*, 7 (4): 11–24.

Jones, M.V. (1999) 'The internationalization of small high-technology firms,' *Journal of International Marketing*, 7(4): 15–41.

Jones, M.V. and Crick, D. (2004) 'Internationalising high-technology-based UK firms' information-gathering activities,' *Journal of Small Business and Enterprise Development*, 11 (1): 84–94.

Keeble, D., Lawson, C., Smith, H.L., Moore, B. and Wilkinson, F. (1998) 'Internationalisation processes, networking and local embeddedness in technology-intensive small firms,' *Small Business Economics*, 11 (4): 327–342.

Knight, G., Madsen, T.K., Servais, P. and Rasmussen, E.S. (2000) 'The born global firm: description and empirical investigation in Europe and the United States,' *American Marketing Association Conference*, Winter 2000.

Knight, G.A. (1997) 'Emerging paradigm for international marketing: the born global firm,' Ph.D. Thesis. Michigan State University, Department of Marketing and Supply Chain Management.

Knight, G.A. and Aulakh, P. (1998) 'A taxonomy of born-global firms,' unpublished paper.

Knight, G.A. and Cavusgil, S.T. (1996) 'The born global firm: a challenge to traditional internationalization theory,' *Advances in International Marketing*, 8: 11–26.

Kuivalainen, O., Sundqvist, S. and Servais, P. (2007) 'Firms' degree of born-globalness, international entrepreneurial orientation and export performance,' *Journal of World Business*, 42 (3): 253–267.

Lu, J.W. and Beamish, P.W. (2001) 'The internationalization and performance of SMEs,' *Strategic Management Journal*, 22 (6–7): 565–586.

Madsen, T.K., Rasmussen, E.S. and Servais, P. (2000) 'Differences and similarities between born globals and other types of exporters,' *Advances in International Marketing*, (10): 247–265.

Madsen, T.K. and Servais, P. (1997) 'The Internationalization of born globals: an evolutionary process?' *International Business Review*, 6 (6): 561–583.

McDougall, P.P., Oviatt, B.M. and Shrader, R.C. (2003) 'A comparison of international and domestic new ventures,' *Journal of International Entrepreneurship*, 1 (1): 59–82.

McDougall, P.P., Shane, S. and Oviatt, B.M. (1994) 'Explaining the formation of international new ventures: the limits of theories from international business research,' *Journal of Business Venturing*, 9 (6): 469–487.

Moen, O. and Servais, P. (2002) 'Born global or gradual global? Examining the export behavior of small and medium-sized enterprises,' *Journal of International Marketing*, 10 (3): 49–72.

Nummela, N., Puumalainen, K. and Saarenketo, S. (2005) 'International growth orientation of knowledge-intensive small firms,' *Journal of International Entrepreneurship*, 3 (1): 5–18.

Nummela, N., Puumalainen, K. and Saarenketo, S. (2004) 'A global mindset–a prerequisite for successful internationalization?' *Canadian Journal of Administrative Sciences*, 21 (1): 51–64.

Oviatt, B.M. and McDougall, P.P. (1994) 'Toward a theory of international new ventures,' *Journal of International Business Studies*, 25 (1): 45–64.

Oviatt, B.M. and McDougall, P.P. (1995) 'Global start-ups: entrepreneurs on a worldwide stage,' *The Academy of Management Executive*, 9 (2): 30–43.

Oviatt, B.M. and McDougall, P.P. (1997) 'Challenges for internationalization process theory: the case of international new ventures,' *Management International Review*, 37 (2): 85–99.

Oviatt, B.M. and McDougall, P.P. (2005a) 'Defining international entrepreneurship and modeling the speed of internationalization,' *Entrepreneurship Theory and Practice*, 29 (5): 537–554.

Oviatt, B.M. and McDougall, P.P. (2005b) 'The internationalization of entrepreneurship,' *Journal of International Business Studies*, 36 (1): 2–8.

Rasmussen, E.S. and T.K. Madsen (2002) 'The born global concept,' The 28th EIBA conference 2002, Athens.

Rasmussen, E.S. and Servais, P. (2002) 'Industrial districts, networks and born global firms,' in T. Knudsen, S. Askegaard and N. Jørgensen (eds) *Perspectives on marketing relationships*, 125–148, Copenhagen: Thomson.

Reuber, A.R. and Fischer, E. (1997) 'The influence of the management team's international experience on the internationalization behaviors of SMEs,' *Journal of International Business Studies*, 28 (4): 807–825.

Rialp, A., Rialp, J. and Knight, G.A. (2005) 'The phenomenon of early internationalizing firms: what do we know after a decade (1993–2003) of scientific inquiry?' *International Business Review*, 14 (2): 147–166.

Servais, P., Madsen, T.K. and Rasmussen, E.S. (2006) 'Small manufacturing firms' involvement in international e-business activities,' in *Advances in International Marketing, International Marketing Research—Opportunities and Challenges in the 21st Century*, JAI, 297–317.

Shrader, R.C., Oviatt, B.M. and McDougall, P.P. (2000) 'How new ventures exploit trade-offs among international risk factors: lessons for the accelerated internationalization of the 21st century,' *Academy of Management Journal*, 43 (6): 1227–1247.

Yli-Renko, H., and Autio, E. (1998) 'The network embeddedness of new, technology-based firms: developing a systemic evolution model,' *Small Business Economics*, 11(3): 253–267

Zahra, S.A. (2005) 'A theory of international new ventures: a decade of research,' *Journal of International Business Studies*, 1 (36): 20–28.

Zahra, S.A. and Garvis, D.M. (2000) 'International corporate entrepreneurship and fi rm performance: the moderating effect of international environmental hostility,' *Journal of Business Venturing*, 15 (5/6): 469–492.

Zahra, S.A., Ireland, R.D. and Hitt, M.A. (2000), 'International expansion by new venture firms: international diversity, mode of market entry, technological learning, and performance,' *Academy of Management Journal*, 43 (5): 925–950.

Zahra, S.A., Korri, J.S. and Yu, J. (2005) 'Cognition and international entrepreneurship: implications for research on international opportunity recognition and exploitation,' *International Business Review*, 14 (2): 129–146.

7 International Growth Strategies in Different Marketing Contexts

Svante Andersson

INTRODUCTION

Internationalization is an important strategy for firms that want to grow, especially in countries with a small home market. Even if the phenomenon has been studied for some time, there still is need for more research dealing with the different contexts within which different firms operate. In this study international growth strategy is regarded as a process (cf. Melin 1992), and important parts in that process include what is produced (goods, services), where the products are sold (markets) and how the firms enter foreign markets (entry modes) (on dimensions of internationalization, see Welch and Luostarinen 1988).

Many different models have been developed to increase the understanding of international growth strategies (e.g., Andersson 2000, Autio 2005, Doole and Lowe 2008, Johanson and Vahlne 1977, 1990, Oviatt and McDougall 1994). Common to these models is that they do not focus on the different marketing contexts that are valid for different firms (e.g., differences between consumer, service and industrial marketing). The theories and models developed discuss internationalization of firms on a general level or use other determinants to discuss different international growth strategies.

In marketing literature, however, separate research streams exist for consumer marketing, industrial (business-to-business) marketing and service marketing (Gummesson 1999). There it is also suggested that firms should adapt different strategies in the different marketing contexts. And yet, although international growth is an important part of many firms' marketing strategies, there have been few attempts to discuss international growth and marketing strategy together and to explore the relationships between different marketing contexts and firms' international growth strategies (Andersson 2002, Coviello and Martin 1999).

To fulfill this gap, this study aims to explore international growth strategies in different marketing contexts, from the viewpoint of marketing theories. Different international growth strategies will be identified and explanations why those patterns have emerged will be discussed. In other words, this study attempts to explore if firms in different marketing context develop different international growth strategies and whether different streams of internationalization literature are more applicable in different marketing contexts.

First, a literature review is carried out. Next, the methodology adopted in this study is presented. Thereafter follows a discussion based on case studies that focuses on firms' international growth strategies in different marketing contexts. The different theoretical approaches are compared with the cases and conclusions are drawn. Finally, some practical implications, limitations and propositions for future research are brought forward.

INTERNATIONALIZATION LITERATURE

Internationalization Process of the Firm

Different models have been developed to increase the understanding of the firm's internationalization process (e.g., Johanson and Vahlne 1977, Bilkey and Tesar 1977, Cavusgil 1980, Reid 1981). One of the most frequently applied models in this field of research is the 'Uppsala model'" (Johanson and Vahlne 1977, 1990), in which the internationalization process is considered to be cyclical, and market knowledge to be the explanatory variable (Johanson and Vahlne 1990, Andersen 1993). Theoretically it is based on the behavioral theory of the firm (Cyert and March 1963) and on the theory of the growth of the firm (Penrose 1959).

In line with Penrose (1959), two types of knowledge are distinguished, objective and experiential. Experiential knowledge, which can only be acquired by personal experience, is viewed as the main way to reduce market uncertainty. The learning-by-doing aspect is central in explaining a firm's international behavior. The internationalization process is seen as a learning process, in which resource commitment and market knowledge are the basis for proceeding (Johanson and Vahlne 1977).

The Uppsala model has been operationalized in two ways: in terms of the sequence of foreign market entry, and the pattern describing the increasing commitment to a single market. The concept of psychic distance has been developed to understand firms' choice of geographical markets and is defined as *"factors preventing or disturbing the flow of information between firm and market. Examples of such factors are differences in language, culture, political systems, level of education, level of industrial development, etc."* (Johanson and Wiedersheim-Paul 1975, 308). The firm's international behavior in a single market is a consequence of a successively greater commitment; i.e., at the beginning there are no regular export activities, then export takes place via independent representatives, later through sales subsidiaries and eventually a manufacturing subsidiary is established (Johanson and Wiedersheim-Paul 1975). In this tradition firms relate to their market via relationships with other organizations. The model has mainly applied to firms operating in business-to-business markets.

International Marketing: The Textbook View

An alternative approach to internationalization has its roots in strategic management and economics. According to this tradition, international marketing decisions are made after a rational analysis of, for example, transportation costs, tariffs and non-tariff barriers, transaction costs, relative wages and market size. Additionally, it is argued that a firm has to analyze firms' internal and external factors to come up with the best alternative. Based on these analyses, an international marketing plan can be developed and be implemented using various marketing mix tools. This view is frequently presented in numerous textbooks in international marketing and strategy (see, e.g., Hollensen 2007, Doole and Lowe 2008).

International Entrepreneurship

An increasing number of researchers argue that the dominant views on internationalization, such as the ones reviewed earlier, are not enough to understand the marketing strategies of small, young and resource-constrained firms, the "Born Globals"(Andersson and Wictor 2003, Autio 2005, Knight and Cavusgil 1996). These firms are international from their inception, and enter markets rapidly without time for learning from earlier market entries (Oviatt and McDougall 1994). In contrast to other internationally operating firms, they rely more often on complementary competencies of other firms. For example, their distribution channels are often based on hybrid structures with a network of partners (Andersson, Gabrielsson and Wictor 2006, Crick and Jones 2000, Gabrielsson et al. 2002, Madsen and Servais 1997, Petersen and Welch 2002). From the viewpoint of marketing strategy, the entrepreneurs' attitude toward marketing (Andersson 2000) and the entrepreneurs experience and networks (Andersson and Wictor 2003) are decisive.

MARKETING LITERATURE

Marketing Management for Consumer Goods

The management of marketing consumer goods is the marketing school that is dominant in marketing literature (Vargo and Lusch 2004). Most textbooks in the area (e.g., Kotler 2003) and most theories and models in marketing are developed mainly for marketing of consumer goods. The underlying assumption in this research tradition is that there is one large seller who needs to reach many individual customers (for a more detailed review of the approach, see Grönroos 1994, Brown 1995 or Vargo and Lusch 2004).

To be able to obtain information from customers, and to communicate with them, they are commonly classified into a number of segments, and the seller may focus their marketing activities on one or several segments. Several ways to segment a market exist: for example, geographic, demographic, psychographic and behavioral criteria may be used (Kotler 2003). After selecting the optimal number of segments, the marketing offer is targeted to them with an attempt to differentiate compared to competitors. In this context, brand building and advertising are the most important promotion tools (Kotler 2003).

Industrial Marketing

In industrial (business-to-business) marketing, both parties—the buyer and the seller—are organizations. In many cases the buyer may be bigger and more powerful than the seller, thus having an influence on the exchange process. The offering is often more complex, and therefore the information flow between seller and buyer is more multifaceted. Altogether, business-to-business relationships are typically more complex than relationships in consumer markets (Håkansson 1982). Therefore these markets are not based on single transactions but on long-term interactions between sellers, buyers, and other parties across multiple firms for mutual benefit (Håkansson 1992, Coviello et al. 1997). This is facilitated by the fact that the number of customers is smaller, so the needs of these significant stakeholders can be handled individually.

In industrial markets, the buyers are professionals who spend all their time buying more efficient and higher quality products. However, the formal buyers are not the only ones who influence the buying process; other actors, such as technical experts, CEOs and other decision makers, and users are important actors in the buying process (Webster and Wind 1972) and each seller-customer relationship is of importance. Existing research on industrial marketing has mainly focused either on organizational buying behavior (Webster and Wind, 1972) or relationships and networks (Anderson et al. 1994, Håkansson 1982), both being central themes in these markets.

The relationship among the different actors in the network is important in order to understand the network (Håkansson and Johanson 1992). Over time, mutual knowledge and the trust that has been developed in relationships form the basis for future business in the network. The actors can be linked to each other through technical, social, cognitive, legal, economic or other ties (Hammarkvist et al. 1982).

The network is difficult for outsiders to grasp (Forsgren and Johanson 1992), as it is not controlled by one actor but changes continuously, which has consequences for the internationalization of the firm. For example,

Axelsson and Johanson (1992) found in their study that the traditional textbook view of foreign market entries was not applicable, as it was not possible to gather important information from a market (network) without being a part of it. This finding is in line with Penrose's (1959) concept of experiential learning. The entry process gradually evolved through interactions among the actors in the network and involved trial and error learning processes. In other words, the network view shares the same theoretical base with the Uppsala model, which was described earlier. In both of these research streams, knowledge seems to be the main explanatory factor behind international growth (Johanson and Vahlne 1990, 2003).

Services Marketing

Services differ from goods in a couple of crucial aspects: they are intangible, that is, they cannot be seen, felt, heard or tasted before they are consumed, and cannot be protected with patents. They are also produced and consumed simultaneously. Therefore, it is not possible to manufacture a service in one place, distribute it to another place, and consume it later. The consumer is also involved in the production, sometimes together with other consumers. Services are also perishable and cannot be stored. They do not provide economies of scale from centralized mass production, standardization is challenging, and quality is difficult to control (Zeithaml et al. 1990). Recently, a new dominant logic has emerged to understand them better, focusing on their intangible characteristics such as skills, information and knowledge and ongoing relationships (Vargo and Lusch 2004).

Services are consumed in direct interaction between the consumer and producer, and therefore the behavior and appearance of front-line staff is of great importance. To complement the intangible side of services, physical evidence can be used to communicate high quality to the consumers (cf. Shostack 1984). For example, hotels and restaurants may pay a great deal of attention to interior décor. Consumers are a part of the production process, and firms can try to educate consumers to take even more responsibility for the process. For example, banks try to share some of the routine work with their consumers via information technology (IT) services and cash machines.

Because of their unique features, internationalization of services requires more resources and is therefore more risky (Carmen and Langeard 1980, Cowell 1991, Grönroos 1990). Tariff barriers have also decreased in the service sector, but non-tariff barriers have continued to increase, which complicates the international growth of the service sector (Javalgi and White 2002). Also the marketing context is of importance: Coviello and Martin found (1999) that internationalization of services was quite similar to internationalization in business-to-business markets, as the importance of networks was stressed in both sectors.

INTERNATIONAL GROWTH STRATEGIES IN DIFFERENT MARKETING CONTEXTS

Previous research on internationalization has developed theories and models applicable to all types of firms. The advantage of such an approach is that the models are simple and may be generalized to a larger population. But they are probably not detailed enough to catch the complex phenomena of individual firms' international growth strategies. Arguably, it is not possible to catch the variety of firms' internationalization with a single approach; several approaches focusing on different perspectives would be preferred.

Our literature review concluded that internationalization literature is based on different theoretical origins. Internationalization process literature has its base in organizational literature (Cyert and March 1963) and focus on organizational learning. The textbook view in international marketing literature has its base in economics and strategic management and has a marketing view similar to mainstream consumer marketing (Coviello et al. 2002). International entrepreneurship literature focuses on the entrepreneurs' experience and personal networks (Rialp et al. 2005). However, in all these research streams there is no deep discussion on how the firms' relations to their marketing contexts influence the international development in the firms.

In marketing the research streams also have their roots in a variety of theories and dominant logics (Vargo and Lusch 2004). Marketing management for consumer goods has its base in economics, and as already mentioned is close to the textbook view in international marketing. Industrial marketing has connections to the internationalization process literature, and literature on service marketing is also linked with the internationalization process literature, both highlighting the role of relationships. In other words, overlap and linkages are prevalent, and therefore by using input from both the internationalization literature and the marketing literature, a matrix can be developed that can be used to analyze how firms implement international growth strategies in different marketing contexts.

Based on the literature review, four aspects of international growth have been identified to be relevant in analyzing the different contexts. They are (1) speed, (2) barriers, (3) markets, (4) entry modes. All these will be used in further analysis of the international growth of selected case companies.

CONDUCTING THE STUDY

Case Selection

Ahrens Rapid Growth (a Swedish consultancy firm focusing on growing firms) publishes regularly a list of high-growth firms in Sweden. They are

Table 7.1   Case Companies in Terms of Type of Buyer and Offer

	Type of buyer	
Type of offer	*Organization*	*Consumer*
Goods	Roxtec	Hästens
	Jomed	H&M
		Electrolux
Services	IBS	Hemfrid
	Intentia	
	IFS	

firms with an average growth of turnover of more than 25 percent over the last six years. This list was the main source of information for selecting the illustrative cases for this study, although some complementary information from business press and Stockholm Stock Exchange was used to identify business-to-business service firms. In order to demonstrate the variety of different marketing contexts, altogether nine cases were selected (Table 7.1). Please note that the size of the companies varies considerably, and some of them (such as Electrolux and H&M) do not fit the criteria for SME.

Data Collection and Analysis

As this study is exploratory in nature, a case study approach was considered to be the most appropriate (cf. Yin 1994). Eisenhardt (1989) also recommends case studies as a fruitful way to give a deeper insight when viewpoints in earlier literature are conflicting, which is also a central feature of this study. The case descriptions are mainly based on data from face-to-face interviews, but complemented with secondary data, such as articles from business magazines, annual reports and internal documents.

The interviews were conducted among key decision makers and people implementing companies' international growth strategies. The interviewees included both CEOs and middle management (export directors, export salesmen and subsidiary managers). However, access to corporate elite was not straightforward (cf. Welch et al 2002), and there was clearly a difference across sectors. In Nordic countries, there has been a tradition of corporate elites being willing to cooperate with academic researchers (Welch et al. 2002). However, in this study a distinctive difference could be noticed between firms marketing to organizations and those marketing to consumers. It was much easier to get access to firms marketing to organizations. An explanation could be that business-to-consumers firms are much better known to the public, and therefore overloaded by numerous requests for collaboration from academics and students. Nevertheless, although access was also granted to the two largest case companies—Electrolux and H&M—the top management could not be interviewed.

A semi-structured interview guide was used, including questions on where, when, how and why the firm had grown, with a focus on foreign markets. A snowball technique was used; i.e., former interviews led to the identification of individuals who were central in the decision making and implementation concerning international growth strategies (cf. Mason 1996, Welch et al. 2002).

The data collection resulted in an extensive amount of data, which was analyzed in several phases. First, the information from interviews and other sources was written down in descriptive narratives, including graphs on, for example, the development of international sales. This helped to cope with the large volume of data (cf. Pettigrew 1988, Mintzberg and McHugh 1985), and allowed the researcher to become intimately familiar with each case and also the unique patterns from each case to emerge before cross-case comparison (cf. Eisenhardt 1989). Following Eisenhardt's (1989) recommendations, the analysis included several iterations between theory and data.

In order to improve the reliability and validity of findings, the interviewees were given the opportunity to read and comment on the drafts of narratives (cf. Yin 1994). Usually it was the most knowledgeable informant from each case company who was asked to do that. However, this revision round did not bring much new information, the requested changes in the narratives were minor in nature. Altogether, no significant sources of error or serious concerns of the validity of the findings were identified. The power gap between interviewer and interviewee was not considered to be a problem (cf. Welch et al. 2002), perhaps because the interviews were carried out in Sweden, which is regarded as a country with a low power distance (Hofstede 2001). The interviewees were also very open (cf. Welch et al. 2002), although the top management seemed to be a bit more open than the middle management. This can be explained by the possibility that the middle management might fear their comments could be scrutinized and used against them by top management.

INTERNATIONALIZATION IN DIFFERENT MARKETING CONTEXTS

International Growth of Business-to-business Firms with a Product Offering

The first case company to be introduced is Roxtec, which was founded by four colleagues in 1990. Their main product is a standardized system of rubber cable entries and seals, although it also sells tailor-made systems. Since its inception, the management of Roxtec has considered their markets to be global, and by 1999 85 percent of the company's turnover already came from sales outside Sweden. The company entered into approximately ten new markets per year, and by 2001 they had a presence in 80 countries. In the early phase of its international expansion, global presence was achieved with the help of independent distributors. This was a deliberate strategy in order to be able to enter many markets simultaneously with small resources. The fact that their product was easy to transport and required little service or education naturally facilitated this process. By 2005, the company had also established seven sales subsidiaries, two of them having also regional responsibilities (Madrid serving both Spain and Latin America, and Dubai serving the Middle East region).

Another example of a rapid international expansion is Jomed, which is in the medical high-tech sector. In 1991, a Swedish entrepreneur bought a German production company and founded Jomed as a medical R&D company, and three years later the company started the sales of a monoleaflet heart valve. In 1995, the company began the R&D for stents and other products for interventional cardiology, and a year later the first generation of their coronary stent was launched. An extremely rapid international expansion followed: their products were distributed and sold in 46 countries around the world within six months. In 1997, the group was brought together under the umbrella of the Dutch holding company; in the same year the company launched a second generation of coronary stents, and a year after a third generation. A new manufacturing and development facility in Rangendingen, in southern Germany, was established, as well as the new distribution and logistics center in Maastricht, in the Netherlands. Direct sales activities started in Europe, where the main markets were located. R&D continued and they next developed a self-expanding nitinol stent. The market expansion was rapid, and further direct sales activities in Europe, Japan and Brazil were commenced. In 2000, the company was represented in approximately 70 countries globally.

These two cases are good examples of an extremely rapid international expansion. This was facilitated by the fact that both companies were started and managed by entrepreneurs with international experience and international networks. It was also possible to manufacture a product in one place and ship it easily and efficiently to another country. Technology development and lower costs in the transport and communication sector have made it easier for entrepreneurs to carry out their international business ideas. Therefore, no significant external barriers prevented them from internationalization.

International growth of business-to-business firms with a product offering has dominated the internationalization of Swedish economy for a long time, and therefore it is quite natural that most of earlier Swedish research has focused on them (starting from the seminal work of Johanson and Vahlne 1977). However, the emerging research on international entrepreneurship has also concentrated on these type of firms, though the interest has been particularly in high-tech firms (Bell 1995, Crick and Jones 2000). Also the case studies presented here show that rapid international growth is possible for both those in the high-tech sector (Jomed) and those in a traditional manufacturing industry (Roxtec), in the latter case particularly if they use a resource-lean market-entry strategy.

International Growth of Business-to-consumer Firms with a Product Offering

Earlier research has shown that it is easier to internationalize products than services (Javalgi and White 2002). However, there are differences in the marketing context that make the barriers for international growth higher for firms offering products directed toward consumers than for those directed toward organizations. The following case descriptions illustrate this well.

Hästens is a company producing high-quality beds for the premium class segment of customers. The company has grown rapidly in Sweden using an aggressive and expensive advertising campaign. The brand name Hästens is now well established in Sweden, and since the end of the 1990s the company has expanded abroad, In 2004, it had activities in Norway, Denmark, Finland, Holland, Spain, France, Italy, the United Arab Emirates, the UK and the US. However, despite its advertising, international expansion would not have been possible without a distribution network. Both supporting the brand and creating a network require significant financial resources, but they can be considered as prerequisites to enter new international markets.

H&M is a fashion company that first focused on the home market before entering the international arena. H&M was founded in 1947 and their first international venture was in Norway in 1964, followed by another in Denmark in 1967: nine years later H&M opened a store in the UK. Also, for H&M, entering new markets is a strategic decision, as successful entry requires a lot of resources for marketing. Instead of a distributor network H&M has chosen another entry mode: it operates internationally through wholly-owned subsidiaries.

Our third example is Electrolux, which manufactures stoves, among other things. Although a stove is a common appliance in most countries,' the requirements for the size of the oven, for example, differ from one country to another. In Sweden a medium-sized oven is required—in order to bake and cook with the oven regularly—whereas in the UK and the US a larger oven is required, and again, in France they traditionally have a smaller oven, as they seldom make their bread at home. This case illustrates how consumer goods are influenced by national culture and habits.

As the number of potential customers on the home market is considerable, a company offering goods to consumers can grow on the home market for a longer time before looking for opportunities abroad. Because of the number of potential customers, personal selling is not the dominant promotion activity; on the contrary, advertising has been the decisive part of the promotion mix of our case companies. This naturally has its challenges, because of the media structure and language differences in diverse countries. Additionally, in the highly competitive environment that consumer products compete in, branding is an important part of their marketing strategy. However, branding requires heavy investments in order to be effective. Because of these marketing-related aspects, the strategic decision to enter foreign markets is considered to be an investment decision with risks. Therefore, potential markets and entry modes are carefully scanned and compared based on collected market information.

International Growth of Business-to-business Firms with a Service Offering

As mentioned earlier, for business-to-business firms with a service offering international growth poses many barriers, because services are consumed and produced simultaneously and therefore internationalization of services requires strong presence on the chosen markets. Compared with consumer goods markets, relatively few—but extremely important—customer relationships exist.

In this study the case companies—IBS, IFS and Intentia—were selected from the Swedish Enterprice Resource Planning (ERP) industry. The ERP industry consists of companies producing business systems software. The software is used to increase the efficiency of business processes in, for example, manufacturing and distribution. Besides the systems, as an elementary part of their whole offering—these firms also offer services (implementation, education, upgrading, etc.) and about 50 percent of the firms' turnover normally comes from services.

The case companies had an incremental international growth strategy: first they aimed at establishing partnerships, which would then be developed into joint ventures and gradually into wholly-owned subsidiaries. This development is in line with the development described in the Uppsala internationalization model (cf. Johanson and Vahlne 1977, 1990). However, the main reason behind incremental internationalization was not lack of market knowledge—as suggested in the Uppsala model—but lack of financial resources.

However, this barrier was significantly lowered as two of the case companies listed themselves on the Swedish Stock Exchange (Intentia in 1996, IFS in 1997). This decision offered them additional resources, which allowed them to grow faster through acquisitions, instead of gradual organic growth. As a result, for example, the annual foreign turnover of IFS grew from 32 percent to 52 percent in 1997. Nevertheless, compared to the manufacturing case companies in business-to-business markets (e.g., Roxtec), these companies were not as international.

Business-to-business markets are based on close customer interface, and therefore internationalization is also more dependent on the relationship with the customer than cultural differences. Also, for the case companies, the concept of psychic distance could not explain the market chosen; rather they entered in accordance with customers' demand. Usually, if the customer was present in numerous countries, the company was asked to serve them in every location. Additionally, network relationships with third parties are important for the firms' international development. For example, in this industry the firms are dependent on the operating platform. Both Intentia and IBS use IBM's platform and have been able to cooperate with IBM in their international expansion.

International Growth of Business-to-consumer Firms with a Service Offering

One could argue that firms offering services to consumers have the highest barriers and they need most resources to implement an international growth strategy. In order to illustrate this, a company called Hemfrid— supplying home services—was chosen for the study. For this company it is not possible to transfer the service overseas easily, as local presence on the market served is always required. Consumer services are also more culturally sensitive than industrial products, which complicates their internationalization. Marketing is expensive, as a lot of potential customers have to be reached, and as personal relationships are important in service marketing, more resources are required compared to marketing of consumer goods, thus making international growth very expensive.

The case company started in Stockholm, Sweden and their growth strategy was to enter other large Swedish cities. Its first product was a cleaning service, and they then added other home services (such as laundry and childcare) to their selection. Gradually it expanded to other large cities within Sweden, but it has not entered international markets yet.

CONCLUSIONS AND IMPLICATIONS

International growth is a strategy dependent on many external and internal factors (Andersson 2003). However, our illustrative cases show that depending on the firms' marketing context, there are different barriers for international growth and different international growth strategies are more likely to be chosen (Table 7.2).

It can also be added that international growth for firms that offer tangible goods to other organizations is less complicated than in other marketing contexts, as there are fewer barriers, and therefore rapid internationalization is possible without large resources. Firms do not have to grow large or have extensive external capital to be able to expand abroad, and born globals are more often found in this context (cf. e.g., Andersson and Wictor 2003). Therefore previous research which has been conducted under the title "international entrepreneurship" (cf., e.g., Autio 2005; Rialp et al. 2005) is often applicable in this marketing context (Table 7.3).

Table 7.2 Comparison of the International Growth of Strategies in Different Marketing Contexts

Type of offer	Type of buyer	
	Organization	Consumer
Goods	1. Rapid internationalization 2. Low barriers for international growth 3. Many markets are entered simultaneously 4. Many different entry modes simultaneously	1. Moderate internationalization 2. Some barriers for international growth: - There are more potential customers in consumer markets; consequently the home market is larger and the firm can grow within a country before expanding abroad. - High marketing costs due to brand building and advertising, which are important but costly marketing tools. - Consumer goods are more affected by cultural differences, which often implies costly product adaptation. 3. Markets are entered after strategic analysis, including sales potential. 4. Entry mode is an important strategic decision following the firms' business idea.
Services	1. Moderate internationalization 2. Some barriers for international growth: - Services cannot be stored or transported. - Local production is required, which requires large resources. 3. Markets are entered incrementally, client-following is a usual way to choose a market 4. Incremental growth via export, middle-men and subsidiaries	1. Slow internationalization 2. High barriers for international growth: - There are more potential customers in consumer markets; consequently the home market is larger and the firm can grow within a country before expanding abroad. - High marketing costs due to brand building and advertising, which are important but costly marketing tools. - Consumer goods are more affected by cultural differences, which often implies costly product adaptation. - Services cannot be stored or transported. Local production is required, which requires large resources. 3 and 4. Focus on the home market

Among our case firms, the ones offering goods to consumers internationalize later than firms offering goods to organizations. This is due to the fact that it takes longer for them to saturate the demand on the home market, but also because entering foreign markets would require more resources.

Table 7.3   Relevance of Internationalization Literature in Understanding the International Growth in Different Marketing Contexts

	Type of buyer	
Type of offer	*Organization*	*Consumer*
Goods	International entrepreneurship	International marketing text-book view
Services	Internationalization process literature	n.a.

For these firms it is not possible to grow incrementally as with industrial products (cf. the Uppsala model, Johanson and Vahlne 1977, 1990). On the contrary, to be successful you need resources to be able to compete with local competitors. Consumer goods are also more influenced by local culture, which makes entry into new countries more expensive, as products need to be adapted to fit different markets.

A firm producing consumer goods should therefore start to penetrate the home market before it enters new international markets. It should also concentrate its resources on fewer markets than firms in business-to-business markets. The traditional textbook view of international marketing fits this context. Entering a new market is a large investment, and as both market and entry mode choices are important strategic decisions, market research and careful planning are needed to cope with the risk involved.

For firms offering services to organizations the individual relations with customers are more important than national cultures. As their relationships are relatively few, it is possible to handle them individually. However, as services are labor- and resource-intensive, it is not possible to internationalize as rapidly as in the manufacturing industry. As a result, markets are entered incrementally, in line with the Uppsala model (Johanson and Vahlne 1977, 1990).

Firms offering services to consumers face the highest barriers and need the most resources to grow internationally. Additionally, the home market is often big enough for their growth aspirations, and foreign expansion is not necessary. If they decide to grow internationally, they will need expensive marketing tools and may also need to adapt their services to different national cultures. Often it will be advisable to diversify into new products in the home market before the firm decides to go international.

However, there are resource-lean ways to grow internationally, such as franchising, and some quite successful concepts have been introduced internationally (such as McDonalds, Subway, etc.). Nevertheless, this strategy is hard to implement if you do not have a strong brand. As this study did not have any case examples of internationalization in this category, no conclusions are drawn here. This is also a category of firms where there are still regulations and differences among countries that hinder international expansion. These barriers are currently being intensively discussed in the European Union.

This study explores whether firms in different marketing contexts develop different international growth strategies, and whether some streams of internationalization literature are more applicable than others depending on the marketing contexts. This study does not imply that marketing contexts are the only factors influencing firms' international strategies; however, marketing contexts reveal varying barriers to internationalization that are important to deal with for firms intending to expand abroad. For managers, this study shows the importance of analyzing the characteristics of a firm's offer and market situation when decisions on international expansion are dealt with. These factors might influence the speed of internationalization, which markets are entered, and which market channels should be used. This study has also shown that different streams of literature and theory are appropriate to various marketing contexts.

LIMITATIONS AND FURTHER RESEARCH

This exploratory study carried out in Sweden cannot automatically be generalized to other countries. For example, developing countries may have too small a home market for some types of products, and firms in these countries may develop other types of internationalization patterns than shown in this study (cf. Andersson, Eriksson and Lundmark 2006). US firms with a large home market may, in contrast, have the opportunity to grow within their home market before international expansion. Firms in other small western European countries may show similar patterns as the firms treated in this study. Globalization changes the circumstances in different industries. In the fashion industry new Swedish firms (such Acne, Odd Molly, Filippa K, Hope, and Nudie Jeans) have been successful with an international growth strategy. Globally-minded entrepreneurs in the fashion industry have found opportunities worldwide; they have been able to attract venture capital and grow internationally by using resource-lean alternatives. That is, it seems that it is possible for entrepreneurs in different industries to overcome structural barriers and internationalize rapidly, which makes the research stream treating international entrepreneurship even more important. Further studies are needed to catch up and understand how globalization and other changes influence firms' international development. Additionally, studies that focus on firms' marketing contexts from different international settings are also recommended to enhance and deepen knowledge of different types of international growth strategies.

ACKNOWLEDGMENTS

Parts of this chapter were written when the author was a visiting scholar at the University of the Sunshine Coast, Australia and he wants to thank the Lars Erik Lundberg Foundation for Research and Education and the Swedish Foundation for International Cooperation in Research and Higher Education (STINT) for financial support. He appreciates also the constructive feedback given by Nicole Coviello, Joanne Freeman and Niina Nummela, which has helped him to develop the manuscript. This chapter builds on the author's earlier works, particularly Andersson 2006.

BIBLIOGRAPHY

Anderson, J.C., Håkansson, H. and Johanson, J. (1994) 'Dyadic business relationships within a business network context,' *Journal of Marketing*, 58 (4): 1–15.

Andersen, O. (1993) 'On the internationalization process of firms: a critical analysis,' *Journal of International Business Studies*, 24 (2): 210–231.

Andersson, S. (2000) 'Internationalization of the firm from an entrepreneurial perspective,' *International Studies of Management & Organization*, 30 (1): 65–94.

Andersson, S. (2002) 'Suppliers' international strategies,' *European Journal of Marketing*, 36 (1/2): 86–110.

Andersson, S. (2003) 'High-growth firms in the Swedish ERP industry,' *Journal of Small Business and Enterprise Development*, 10 (2): 180–193.

Andersson, S. (2006) 'International growth strategies in consumer and business-to-business markets in manufacturing and service sectors,' *Journal of Euromarketing*, 15 (4): 35–56.

Andersson, S., Eriksson, M. and Lundmark, L. (2006) 'Internationalization in Malaysian furniture firms—gradual internationalization or born globals?' *International Journal of Globalisation and Small Business*, 1 (3): 220–243.

Andersson, S., Gabrielsson. J. and Wictor, I. (2006) 'Born globals' market channel strategies,' *International Journal of Globalisation and Small Business*, 1 (4): 356–373.

Andersson, S. and Wictor, I. (2003) 'Innovative internationalisation in new firms—born globals the Swedish case,' *Journal of International Entrepreneurship*, 1 (3): 249–276.

Autio, E. (2005) 'Creative tension: the significance of Ben Oviatt's and Patricia McDougall's article 'Toward a theory of international new ventures',' *Journal of International Business Studies*, 36 (1): 9–19.

Axelsson, B. and Johanson, J. (1992) 'Foreign market entry—the textbook vs. the network view,' in B. Axelsson and G. Easton (eds.) *Industrial networks. A new view of reality*, 218–234, London: Routledge.

Bell, J. (1995) 'The internationalization of small computer software firms—a further challenge to 'stage theories',' *European Journal of Marketing*, 28 (8): 60–75.

Bilkey, W.J. and Tesar, G. (1977) 'The export behavior of smaller-sized Wisconsin manufacturing firms,' *Journal of International Business Studies*, 8 (1): 93–98.

Brown, S. (1995) *Postmodern marketing*, London: Routledge.

Carman, J.M. and Langeard, E. (1980) 'Growth strategies for service firms,' *Strategic Management Journal*, 1 (1): 7–22.

Cavusgil, S.T. (1980) 'On the internationalization process of firms,' *European Research*, 8 (6): 273–81.

Cowell, D. (1991) *The marketing of service*, Oxford: Butterworth Heinemann.

Coviello, N.E., Brodie, R.J. and Munro, H.J. (1997) 'Understanding contemporary marketing: development of a classification scheme,' *Journal of Marketing Management*, 13 (6): 501–22.

Coviello, N.E., Brodie, R.J., Danaher, P.J. and Johnston, W.J. (2002) 'How firms relate to their markets: an empirical examination of contemporary marketing practices,' *Journal of Marketing*, 66 (3): 27–46.

Coviello, N.E. and Martin, K. (1999) 'Internationalization of service SMEs: an integrated perspective from the engineering consulting sector,' *Journal of International Marketing*, 7 (4): 42–66.

Crick, D. and Jones M.V. (2000) 'Small high-technology firms and international high-technology markets,' *Journal of International Marketing*, 8 (2): 63–85.

Cyert R. and March, J.G. (1963) *A behavioral theory of the firm*, Englewood Cliffs, NJ: Prentice Hall.

Doole, I. and Lowe, R. (2008) *International Marketing Strategy*. London, Thomson Learning.

Eisenhardt, K.M. (1989) 'Building Theories from Case Study Research,' *Academy of Management Review*, 14 (4): 532–550.

Forsgren, M. and Johanson, J. (1992) 'Managing internationalization in business network,' In M. Forsgren and J. Johanson (eds.) *Managing networks in international business*, 1–16, Philadelphia: Gordon and Breach.

Gabrielsson, M., Kirpalani, V.H.M. and Luostarinen R. (2002) 'Multiple channel strategies in the European personal computer industry,' *Journal of International Marketing*, 10 (3): 73–95.

Grönroos, C. (1990) 'Internationalization strategies for services,' *Journal of Services Marketing*, 13 (4/5): 290–297.

Grönroos, C. (1994) 'Quo vadis marketing? Toward a relationship marketing paradigm,' *Journal of Marketing Management*, 10 (5): 347–360.

Gummesson, E. (1999) 'Total relationship marketing: experimenting with a synthesis of research frontiers,' *Australasian Marketing Journal*, 7 (1): 72–85.

Håkansson, H. (ed.) (1982) International marketing and purchasing of industrial goods, Chichester, UK: Wiley.

Håkansson, H. and Johanson, J. (1992) 'A model of industrial networks,' in B. Axelsson and G. Easton (eds.) *Industrial networks. A new view of reality*, 28–34, London: Routledge.

Hammarkvist, K.-O., Håkansson, H. and Mattson, L.-G. (1982) *Marknadsföring för konkurrenskraft*, Malmö: Liber.

Hofstede (2001) *Culture's consequences*, Thousand Oaks, CA: Sage.

Hollensen, S. (2007) *Global marketing*, Harlow, UK: Pearson Education.

Javalgi, R.G. and White, D.S. (2002) 'Strategic changes for the marketing of services internationally,' *International Marketing Review*, 19 (6): 563–581.

Johanson, J. and Vahlne, J.-E. (1977) 'The internationalization process of the firm—a model of knowledge development and increasing foreign market commitments,' *Journal of International Business Studies*, 8 (1): 23–32.

Johanson, J. and Vahlne, J.-E. (1990) 'The mechanism of internationalization,' *International Marketing Review*, 7 (4): 11–24.

Johanson, J. and Vahlne, J.-E. (2003) 'Business relationship learning and commitment in the internationalization process,' *Journal of International Entrepreneurship*, 1 (1): 83–101.

Johanson, J. and Wiedersheim-Paul, F. (1975) The internationalization of the firm—four Swedish cases, *Journal of Management Studies*, 12 (3): 305–322.

Knight, G.A. and Cavusgil, S.T., (1996) 'The born global firm: a challenge to traditional internationalization theory,' *Advances in International Marketing*, 8: 11–26.

Kotler, P. (2003) *Marketing management*, 11th ed., Englewood Cliffs, NJ: Prentice-Hall.

Madsen, T.K. and Servais, P. (1997) 'The internationalization of born globals: an evolutionary process?' *International Business Review*, 6 (6): 561–583.

Mason, J. (1996) *Qualitative researching*, London: Sage.

Melin, L. (1992) 'Internationalization as a Strategy Process,' *Strategic Management Journal*, 13: 99–118.

Mintzberg, H. and McHugh, A. (1985) 'Strategy formation in an adhocracy,' *Administrative Science Quarterly*, 30 (2): 160–197.

Oviatt, B.M. and McDougall, P.P. (1994) 'Toward a theory of international new ventures,' *Journal of International Business Studies*, 25 (1): 45–64.

Penrose, E.T. (1959) *The theory of the growth of the firm*. London: Basil Blackwell.

Petersen, B. and Welch, L.S. (2002) 'Foreign operation mode combinations and internationalization,' *Journal of Business Research*, 55 (2): 157–162.

Pettigrew, A. (1988) 'Longitudinal field research on change: Theory and practice,' paper presented at the National Science Foundation Conference on Longitudinal Research Methods on Organizations, Austin.

Reid, S.D. (1981) 'The decision maker and export entry and expansion,' *Journal of International Business Studies*, 12 (2): 101–112.

Rialp, A., Rialp, J. and Knight G.A. (2005) 'The phenomenon of early internationalizing firms: what do we know after a decade (1993–2003) of scientific inquiry?' *International Business Review*, 14 (2): 147–166.

Shostack, G.L. (1984) 'Breaking free from product marketing,' In C.H. Lovelock (ed.) *Services marketing—text, cases and readings*, 37–47, Englewood Cliffs, NJ: Prentice Hall.

Vargo, S.L. and Lusch, R.F. (2004) 'Evolving to a new dominant logic for marketing,' *Journal of Marketing*, 68 (1): 1–17.

Webster, F.E. and Wind, Y. (1972) *Organizational buying behavior*, Englewood Cliffs, NJ: Prentice Hall.

Welch C., Marschan-Piekkari, R., Penttinen, H. and Tahvanainen, M. (2002) 'Corporate elites as informants in qualitative international business research,' *International Business Review*, 11 (5): 611–628.

Welch, L.S. and Luostarinen R. (1988) 'Internationalization: evolution of a concept,' *Journal of General Management*, 14 (2): 34–55.

Yin, R.K. (1994) Case study research—design and methods, Newbury Park: Sage.

Zeithaml, V.A. (1984) 'How consumer evaluation processes differ between goods and services,' in C.H. Lovelock (ed.) *Services marketing—text, cases and readings*, 37–47, Englewood Cliffs, NJ: Prentice Hall.

Zeithaml, V.A., Parasuraman, A. and Berry, L.L. (2990) *Delivering Quality Service, Balancing Customer Perceptions and Expectations*, New York: The Free Press.

8 Analyzing the Moves of International Entrepreneurial Organizations
The Entry of SMEs to Complex Markets

Antonella Zucchella

INTRODUCTION

The realm of international entrepreneurship is very scattered and is even missing a generally agreed definition of the field. Definitions have been proposed in the literature, activities (Oviatt and McDougall 1995, 2000, Etemad 2004) and more recently a process-based view of international entrepreneurship (Jones and Coviello 2005, Zucchella and Scabini 2007). In this latter vein, there is a particular need for better understanding of how the entrepreneurial process addresses and confronts foreign markets.

This chapter aims at adopting a process-based view of international entrepreneurship (cf. Jones and Coviello 2005), following the idea that entrepreneurship is better represented as a process over time, rather than as an isolated act (such as the foundation of a company, for example). Additionally, it highlights antecedents and consequences of action, as well as the development of the capability of acting as entrepreneurial organizations (cf. Zucchella and Scabini 2007). In particular, this contribution focuses on the process related to the decision of entry to a complex market, this being an expression of the international entrepreneurial attitude of a small firm. The entry to a complex market is a demonstration of an international entrepreneurial organization, as it involves both orientation and capabilities to face the risks involved.

The definition of complex market is actually missing from the international business agenda. Traditionally foreign markets have been approached as:

- Being uniformly "different". For example, Schumpeter (1934) described internationalization as an act of entrepreneurship and innovation, without differentiating foreign markets. The mainstream literature on international business (IB) in explaining the reasons for internationalization focuses more on the difference between domestic and foreign markets (as well as between FDIs and exports) rather than among markets in general.
- Being progressively different. Interest in the characteristics of the single foreign markets (or clusters of foreign markets) is relatively more recent and finds its origins in the "behavioral turn" of IB studies. The

attention to the internationalization process (Johanson and Vahlne 1977) gave rise to studies on markets' psychic distance (Johanson and Wiedersheim-Paul 1975), paralleled by research on cultural distance in international organizations (Hofstede 1983). The concept of psychic distance is particularly relevant to this research because it underlines a subjective perspective of differences among countries, dependent on firm experience and vision.

- Becoming progressively more homogeneous. This perspective pertains to the seminal work of Levitt (1983) on the growing integration and interdependence of markets across the world, which has given rise to global strategies and global companies. The global strategy is also pointed out by other authors (Porter 1986), among other strategic orientations.
- Being organized in regional blocks, which shape international strategic behavior (Rugman 2007).

Of the above listed approaches, the second one is applied here, assuming that markets are

- subjectively different from the viewpoint of the internationalizing firm, depending on their knowledge base (cumulated experience);
- highly different with respect to institutional, sociocultural and economic dimensions; and
- perceived by firms as having different degrees of complexity in terms of risk/uncertainty, distance (geographic and psychic), and internal market structure, thus resulting in difficulties in managing market entry, penetration and stabilization of market presence.

The most complex markets represent a very relevant challenge, especially to smaller firms, which needs to be compensated by adequate opportunities. The quest for more opportunities, at the expense of taking higher risks, characterizes international entrepreneurial organizations (Zucchella and Scabini 2007). The analysis of when and how a firm takes this decision, how it is managed over time, and which learning and operation consequences it bears allows us to highlight a relatively neglected field both in IB and in IE studies. This chapter starts from a conceptualization of market complexity and related firm behavior, and then provides an exploratory analysis of two cases, concluding with suggestions for improved constructs and future research agenda.

THEORETICAL FRAMEWORK AND KEY CONCEPTS

This contribution rests on two conceptual pillars: (1) the firm, with its bundle of resources and capabilities, the ways it accumulates international knowledge through learning processes and how it approaches new markets, and (2) the construct of complex markets, which represents a relatively unexplored field of research.

Market Complexity

The concept of complexity has been adopted and studied across different disciplines and fields of research, but it has rarely been applied in the international business literature. An example of an exception to the rule is Duncan (1972), who states that "environmental complexity as perceived by foreign managers concerns the extent to which environmental factors in a host country are diverse and heterogeneous." Additionally, Luo (2002, 48) analyzed how MNEs exploit and develop their capabilities when entering a foreign complex market. In that study, "complex" referred to some emerging economies, and was defined as having a set of contextual hazards, such as "environmental complexity (the host country diversity), industrial structure uncertainty (its volatility), and business culture specificity (its culture uniqueness)."

Furthermore, it is proposed here that complexity may refer to both developed and developing countries. For example, the US market has been repeatedly reported as a complex one by many European firms, notably SMEs (Zucchella and Costa 2007). This is due to its institutional and consumer complexity, market structure, domestic competition, and quickly evolving managerial practices, among other factors. As an example, O'Grady and Lane (1996) reported that Canadian retailers expanding in the nearby US market experienced losses and even retreats due to underestimation of the two countries' differences. Although the authors concentrated exclusively on the firms' lack of knowledge and underestimation of the venture, and did not specifically explore the possibility that the high complexity of the US market might have been one of the reasons of these failures, these two issues may be strongly interrelated.

Psychic Distance—A Subjective Approach to Market Complexity

In the 1970s, as a part of the behavioral stream in IB studies, scholars explored the concept of psychic distance in relation to firms' behavior in foreign market entry. According to that view, the difficulty in entering a market is only partially dependent on the market characteristics (as expressed by their distance from the home country of the firm). In addition, the complexity of a foreign market is also dependent on the experiential knowledge possessed by the firm. This indicates that market complexity has also a subjective dimension, through the cognitive frame and knowledge base of the decision maker.

Psychic distance is a composite of the Greek word "psychikos," referring to an individual's mind and soul (Simpson and Weiner 1989), and "distance," which is based on perceived cultural differences between a "home" country and a "foreign" country, over and above the physical time and space factors that differ across diverse cultures (Usunier and Lee 2005). Consequently, the concept exists in the minds of individuals, and it is their subjective perceptions that uniquely determine the psychic distance in question (Sousa and Bradley 2005).

The origins of the concept "psychic distance" can be traced back to research conducted by Beckerman (1956) and Linnemann (1966). Later, Vahlne and Wiedersheim-Paul (1973) described it as "factors preventing or disturbing the flow of information between potential or actual suppliers and customers." These factors are associated with country-based dissimilarities and can be classified into four groups: (1) linguistic differences and translation difficulty, (2) cultural factors, (3) economic environment and (4) political and legal system.

Although the concept had already been described by the early 1970s, the study of Swedish multinationals by Johanson and Vahlne (1977) is generally accepted as the concept's real genesis (Sousa and Bradley 2005). Their study concluded that a firm's international expansion progresses into markets with successively greater psychic distance. In other words, firms enter new markets where they are able to identify opportunities with low market uncertainty, then enter markets at successively greater "psychic distance" (Johanson and Vahlne 1990). Since then, the concept has become very popular, and contemporary literature on the internationalization process cites "psychic distance" as a key variable and determinant for expansion into foreign markets.

However, there has been a recent surge in IE studies proposing models of international growth that are not necessarily influenced by gradualism and risk minimization. Research on born global firms (for a review, see Rialp et al. 2005) and international new ventures (Oviatt and McDougall 1994, 1997) highlight the fact that these firms approach foreign markets and entry modes differently. Johanson and Vahlne (1990) also recognized that firms may skip stages and enter quickly into distant markets, leveraging on other factors, such as networks. This implies that the learning processes about foreign markets are not necessarily dependent on experience, but may be complemented by other kinds of learning. Entrepreneurial organizations are driven by the need of exploring and exploiting opportunities quickly on a global sale, and need to develop learning processes that are not exclusively dependent on experiential learning.

Firm Orientation, Knowledge Base and Learning Processes

This chapter is built on the two pillars of market complexity and firm behavior toward market complexity. The two dimensions are interrelated, as market complexity may also be subjectively perceived in terms of psychic distance and firm experience.

The attitude of a firm toward complex markets is related to its entrepreneurial posture, as defined by Covin and Slevin (2002). Complex markets involve a wider set of opportunities, counterbalanced by a higher set of risks, related to the heterogeneity, variability or number of elements for the decision maker and to the uncertainty of performance. International entrepreneurial organizations possess the posture to face these challenges, as they are characterized by a strong international growth orientation (Zucchella and Scabini 2007).[1]

Together with its entrepreneurial posture and international growth orientation, a firm making decisions about entering complex markets needs resources and capabilities to enable it to exploit these opportunities. Financial and technological resources might be important, but human resources (especially at the top management level) and their knowledge base are particularly relevant. Therefore, the key question in this study is this: due to their high specificity, can complex markets be approached in the light of experiential learning and progressive extension of geographic scope, as the traditional Uppsala model suggests, or do they represent a discontinuity in firm's foreign operations, so that cumulated experiential knowledge is helpful only to a limited extent?

RESEARCH DESIGN

This study can be described as mainly exploratory and, to some extent, descriptive, as our aim is "to build a rich description of complex circumstances that are unexplored in the literature" (cf. Marshall and Rossman 1999, 33). Two main approaches or methods—quantitative and qualitative—are available to researchers. The qualitative approach implies an emphasis on processes and meanings that are not measured in terms of quantity, amount, intensity or frequency. This approach provides a deeper understanding of the phenomenon within its context. Moreover, qualitative researchers stress the socially constructed nature of reality, including the relationship between the researcher and the phenomenon under investigation. According to Sullivan (2001), when there is little theoretical support for a phenomenon, it may be impossible to develop precise hypotheses, research questions, or operational definitions. Thus, a qualitative approach was chosen here.

The empirical part of this study is based on two in-depth case studies. The subjects are two Italian companies, which provide rich longitudinal description of alternative internationalization processes, involving—at different stages of their life cycles and internationalization experience—an entry or entries to one or more complex markets. One of the firms operates in business-to-business markets, manufacturing espresso machines. The other one operates on business-to-consumer markets, in the food industry, producing rice and rice-based food products. The first one has been international since its inception, starting in the most complex market from their point of view, i.e., the US. The second one started selling abroad after many decades of growth in the domestic market, beginning in the nearest countries and only later entering the US market.

Data from the case companies were collected with face-to-face interviews, focusing on a predetermined set of discussion topics. However, in order to encourage free discussion, an interview guide was used, providing topics or subject areas within which the interviewer was free to explore, probe and ask questions that elucidated and illuminated the subject under investigation. It also enabled us to build a conversation within a particular subject area, to ask questions spontaneously, and to establish conversational style, but with the focus on a particular predetermined subject (cf. Marshall and Rossman 1999).

Between January and April 2009, four interviews were conducted in each company, with the CEO and the marketing/foreign operations manager of both firms, each interview lasting about two hours. The data and notes were carefully transcribed and read through in order to form a general understanding of the studied phenomenon. Information from the interviews was complemented with secondary sources, such as company documentation and press releases. Based on the case studies, a more refined conceptualization of complex markets will be provided, as well as a framework for successful management of this kind of entrepreneurial strategy.

CASE: RISO SCOTTI

Riso Scotti is the Italian industry leader in rice production and in the rice-related food products (such as rice flour pasta, biscuits, rice flakes and rice oil). The company was founded in 1860; since then it has grown and diversified its products and businesses, but still maintains a strong family business governance and management, being managed by Angelo Dario Scotti, the heir of the founding family. Today it employs about 150 employees and had a consolidated turnover in 2007 of 210 million Euros, with a forecast for 2008 of 240 million Euros.

The firm includes a number of companies, some specializing in cultivation, research and experimentation, others in manufacturing and processing rice and rice-based products. Today, the group features a strong international component as it sells its products in more than 50 countries (23 of which are non-European), and the proportion of exports in its annual turnover is approximately 22 percent. It was only in recent years—since the consolidation of the Italian market—that the company decided to internationalize, and it now aims at increasing market share and recognition as the best in its field in Europe.

Growth and Internationalization

The company started growing in the local, then in the domestic market. Only after reaching market leadership in Italy did they start searching for international growth (see Figure 8.1). Their growth pattern clearly resembles the "rings in the water" process proposed by Madsen and Servais (1997). In

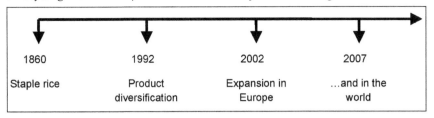

Figure 8.1   The growth process of Riso Scotti.

fact, in geographic terms the foreign expansion follows the Uppsala model: local-domestic-close countries-distant countries. It should also be noticed that continuous growth on domestic market first required product diversification and only later, when it had a good range of complementary rice-related products, could the company expand internationally.

Until 1992 the company had one product—packed rice–sold only on the Italian market. Although rice still remains the core product of the company, the stronger growth orientation of Dario Scotti resulted in developing, manufacturing and selling other rice-related products, such as bread sticks, rice flakes, rice milk, and rice-based pasta, biscuits and crackers. In 2002 the company started exporting through foreign distributors. However, internationalization was not only a question of straight exports; the first foreign investment of Riso Scotti was the Danube project, which focused on developing the production and marketing of rice in Romania. Since 2002 the company has also had an effective and planned international strategy, rather than the earlier unsolicited orders obtained from foreign customers contacted at trade fairs and exhibitions. Previously the company had also had no agreements with foreign distributors or distribution channels for foreign markets.

Their main geographic focus of internationalization is the European market, with special attention to Central and Western European countries. As for the countries of Eastern Europe, Riso Scotti plans to serve them in the next few years through its production in Romania, where land and climate conditions have been found appropriate for Italian rice cultivation. However, exports are not limited to Europe, but extend also to India, Canada, Africa, South America and North America. Since 2007, the company has been trying to enter directly into more complex markets; in the US and India, it has done so through the creation of a sales office and a joint venture respectively. Top management considers the North American market as their biggest challenge, but also probably their biggest opportunity.

Motives for internationalization are connected to the need of getting global visibility, at least in their niche (Italian rice and rice-related products).

> We have been striving hard in the domestic market to reach leadership through a differentiation strategy, based on overcoming the common perception of rice as a commodity and shifting competitive advantage from price to quality, innovation and brand. Lately we realized that our

competitive space was less and less the domestic one: with or without us, the competitive space was turning global.

Consequently, it is possible to distinguish three phases in the company's process of internationalization, as illustrated in Figure 8.2.

India is also an interesting market for the company from the point of view of both imports and exports. It offers the company a particular opportunity to learn more about the basmati rice, which is fairly different from the Italian variety and therefore cooked differently. The complexity of this market is related to its strong but different rice culture—a challenge where exports are concerned, but an advantage for imports from India and thus an opportunity to become a global player. However, exploiting this opportunity would require close collaboration with a strong local partner in the form of a joint venture.

In addition, Riso Scotti intends to expand its business on the North American market by establishing a sales office in the US. So far it has been exporting its products only occasionally, through local distributors and brokers, whose customers have been mainly Italian restaurants and shops. The top management considers the market to be a highly complex one and therefore a carefully planned strategy, clear commitment and investment of resources are needed.

Riso Scotti and the US Market

Entry to the US market can be considered as an entrepreneurial act. It requires risk-taking and considerable resource commitment—both financial

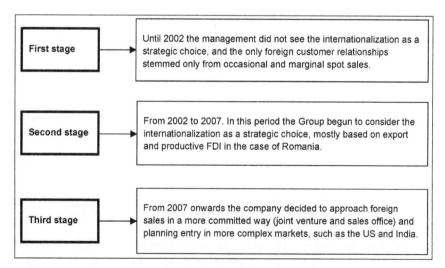

Figure 8.2 The internationalization process of Riso Scotti.

(the firm finances its operations mainly through its own cash flow) and human (the staff dedicated to foreign operations is small, consistent with the size of the company and its limited international business experience). On the other hand, the country-of-origin image of Italian food is very positive, and Italian rice might offer an interesting, novel and healthy alternative to the large and sophisticated customer base. All this probably facilitates the exploring and exploitation of the market opportunity, but offers the company the possibility to learn from the most advanced markets of the world.

However, the US market is not homogeneous. Although there is a growing trend toward eating healthy, organic and fat-free foods, the impact of this trend has been strongest in the western parts of the country, particularly in California. Therefore Riso Scotti has decided to enter the market through this state and set its sales office in San Francisco.

From the company point of view, the challenges of entering this complex market can be summarized as follows:

- the business risks/uncertainty and the different entry barriers;
- the dominant role of intermediaries, especially trade channels, in customer interface;
- the deep understanding of consumer preferences and their continuous evolution;
- the need of adapting the product to local conditions (regulations and consumers' orientations).

The three first challenges could also be labeled as barriers—the two first ones being both entry and permanence barriers—both typical for complex markets. These markets are not protected by very high traditional barriers of entry (such as duties, permissions, quotas) or natural barriers (such as physical access, cultural differences), but by less obvious ones. Whereas the traditional barriers of entry are easy to detect in advance, the US is perceived to be complex because as mentioned in the interviews: "It looks like an insidious ground, where barriers are mostly hidden and unexpected and come out when you are already investing money there."

These "invisible barriers" were also the reason why it took years for the company to actually enter the market and grow its business. Among the most significant barriers are the competitive and commercial ones. Local competition is quite strong and the competitors know the customers well. On the other hand, the distribution channels are dominated by large retailing chains, which have a very high bargaining power toward the manufacturers. From the viewpoint of Riso Scotti, however, the real gatekeepers are the buyers representing the specialty food shops and ethnic restaurants.

The interviews indicate that the entry to the US market is perceived as a point of discontinuity in the firm growth and internationalization process. The management considers that it has now reached for a different international scale, as well as a higher level of learning. The firm's knowledge base is still limited and has been built up mainly during the last few years. Even their recent entry to the UK market is not considered to facilitate preparation of the entry to the USA.

The complexity is further highlighted by the need to adapt the product to local conditions. It is not the rice in itself that needs adaptation; rather the company must select the most appropriate kind of products from their product range, the ones which will have the best chance to succeed in the US market, after which it then needs to obtain product certifications, and finally must adapt the packaging and other elements of the marketing mix. The case company decided to enter the American market with an organic and gluten-free product, and after analyzing the market carefully, California, and San Francisco in particular, was selected as the most suitable place to start. On the US market, certification of the products is crucial: the main approvals needed are from the USDA (organic: certification required for all companies wishing to export their products in the US), the NOP (National Organic Program; the products must be absolutely 100 percent organic), and OU Kosher certification (symbolized by a golden circled U).

The entry strategy of Riso Scotti in the US can be characterized as *committed* (in its careful pre-planning and considerable investment and definition of financial and human resources to employ), *selective* (in its choice of market area, small number of partnerships and limited range of products) and *learning-oriented*, rather than sales-oriented. Consequently, the process of internationalization in the US is incremental in terms of geographic areas involved and product offered, but committed in terms of entry modes, in order to maximize learning and business opportunities.

CASE: BRASILIA

Brasilia was founded in 1977 as a spin-off of Gino Rossi (now Rossi Corp), a family firm committed to the production of components for the espresso coffee machines since the 1950s. The entrepreneur, Giampiero Rossi, son of Gino, recognized a business opportunity when one of the leading Italian espresso machine manufacturers was suffering from a crisis. Instead of just providing the "engines" for the machine, they could supply the overall machinery to customers in the horeca (hotels, restaurants, cafeterias) sector.

The firm was international from its inception, mainly because the Italian market was already crowded by competitors (most of them its previous customers) and already had some good ties with foreign distributors and buyers in some countries. A decisive kick-off took place in 1983, when the company launched a line of compact machines. This was a start of an increasingly strong orientation toward exports and enabled their gain of a significant share of the world market. Currently, the company employs more than 200 people at its Italian headquarters, where the production and R&D are concentrated. Additionally, it has a number of foreign subsidiaries and partnerships in the main markets. In 2007 the products were available in more than 100 markets, the most important ones being Portugal, the US and France. It sells about 97 percent of its production abroad and is the second largest manufacturer of espresso machines in the world.

Growth and Internationalization

The company's growth has resulted from a couple of important early decisions. First, the company addressed those foreign markets where the coffee culture was less developed, but where, thanks to the presence of a significant community of Italians immigrants, it could take off quickly. This was the case in the North American market, where Brasilia began to sell its products in the early 1980s.

Second, by the 1980s the company had begun to explore the business opportunities of both coffee machines used at home and the so-called "office-coffee system." Particularly concerning the latter, the company chose not only to manufacture the machines but also to accompany them with complimentary offerings, such as equipment. In the manufacture of these machines the company collaborates with another company in the family group—Rossi Corp—in order to achieve some synergies in manufacturing.

Third, perhaps their most significant decision, they introduced the first, still unique, industrial espresso machine. In 1999 the company patented a machine for dairy industries, confectionery and beverages, with a production cycle capable of delivering 5 liters of pure espresso in the traditional 30 seconds, with chemical and organoleptic characteristics far exceeding those of a coffee obtained through the process of percolation.

Brasilia is still targeting high global growth, supported by consumers' increasing preference for Italian espresso. In order to achieve this global expansion, they must adequately develop the Italian coffee-making culture. For this reason they develop cooperative relationships with the customers (who are typically coffee-roasting companies and their baristas), through the offering of training courses, advisory services (such as coordination and project management for starting and conducting coffee shops, and the design and creation of innovative formats for the bar business), technical publications and dissemination.

Strategic factors for the international activity of Brasilia can be considered to be its knowledge about global competitors and local customers, and about the most effective ways to serve the latter through quality in product and service before and after sales, and the development of new products and new production technology. In a market where there is a strong presence of medium to large firms, Brasilia has implemented and still implements strategies to market entry based on export of machines produced in

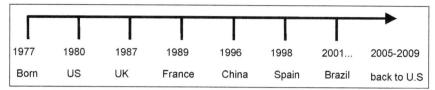

Figure 8.3 The growth process of Brasilia.

Italy. Exporting strategy is grounded on strong relationships with buyers/ importers and distributors, and on the presence of foreign sales offices, with the role of customer assistance. In recent years the firm has also turned to foreign production for some machines, through the acquisition of three production units in China, whose products are destined to be sold in the local market.

As Figure 8.3 indicates, Brasilia can be considered a born global company because it began operating abroad immediately after its foundation, starting from distant countries and expanding its foreign sales very quickly. The first market approached was the US one, thanks to the linkage with a US distributor. Relationships with foreign distributors are key factors for foreign market penetration for many businesses; this is particularly true when the product is primarily destined for a business-to-business market and requires technical understanding, user training and after-sales assistance. The nascent company was able to benefit from the previous experience of the entrepreneur in the production of

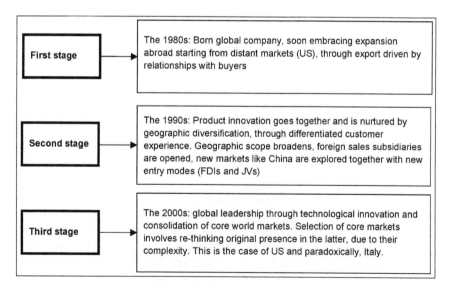

Figure 8.4 The internationalization process of Brasilia.

components for coffee-making machines and from his system of relationships abroad.

The company has already gained good experience in establishing subsidiaries abroad, a strategy which characterized its second stage of development, illustrated in Figure 8.4. All through the 1990s, geographic diversification was paralleled by the growth of foreign subsidiaries, especially in important markets (see Figure 8.4). In some cases the choice was to rely on strong relationships with local distributors; in other cases the firm established wholly-owned subsidiaries (Germany, Brazil) or joint ventures (UK, Spain) in order to get a stronger market presence.

The after-sales service is ensured through a network of centers coordinated either by subsidiaries in each country or by importers and dealers, who usually receive the necessary support in terms of technical documentation, a supply of spare parts and training courses from the headquarters.

Brasilia and the US Market

From the viewpoint of the case company, complexity is a function of market structure, in which local competition and access to the final customer (through knowledge and distribution channels) are fundamental factors. Also the size of the country matters, because it might oblige the company to organize its logistic activity and after-sales support in a complex, multi-located way. The marketing manager of the company named two markets as complex ones for them: the US and—quite surprisingly—the home market, i.e., Italy.

Although the company entered the US market at the time of inception—mainly because suitable distributors were available—the management still, after 30 years of experience, considers that they are unable to exploit the market potential fully. This is due to limited knowledge of local customers and the lack of brand awareness—the latter because the products are sold under the name of the US distributor who also takes care of the after-sales support. *"We found out that being there since 30 years did not turn into adequate experiential learning and local customer knowledge. The latter remained at the distributor level."* As a consequence, they realized that facing the challenges and capturing the opportunities of a complex market like the US one involves a stronger presence, branded products, a multi-located logistics strategy, and frequent visits by the Italian managers. Therefore, in 2005 a sales subsidiary and two logistic centers were established, but good relationships and commercial agreements with the former distributors were also maintained.

In the future, the company plans to serve new market segments and new areas (particularly the east coast) via its US branch. In addition to the existing distributor network, also new partnerships will be created with importers of different and complementary machines for cafeterias, bars and restaurants. The market has recently been divided into five areas:

inside each one they rely on a main distributor and on a consultant, who is responsible for the social network and is in charge of developing local relationships with final customers. The product range and characteristics have been simplified (only four products are actually offered in the US) and adapted to the market in order to provide the needed certifications, not only on the overall machine, but on all its components. In other words, a *multi-modal* and *multi-located* strategy with *a simplified offering* is considered more appropriate for the US market, particularly at a stage when the company considers it a core one, involving dedicated presence and localized learning.

What may seem surprising is that the definition of complex markets holds also for the domestic market, which seems to contradict any theory on gradual internationalization and psychic distance. According to the case company, "*The choice of being a born global firm led us to treat the home market with less attention from the beginning.*" As mentioned earlier, this was due mainly to the strong competition as well as the fact that some competitors had been their customers earlier. However, as the future strategy focuses on the leading markets in the world, Italy will certainly be among them and their presence there needs to be strengthened. Italy is a leading market, not just in terms of history or espresso consumption, but even more important, in terms of trendsetting, advanced technologies for coffee making and sophisticated customer tastes. This is why the case company has already challenged its main Italian competitors with its latest product: a machine especially addressed to espresso bars and serving a "perfect espresso," tasty and topped with a thick, long-lasting *crema*.

To sum up, for the case company, the definition of complex markets is based on the idea that these markets are dominated by distance: they do not mean inter-country distance, but the distance between the company and its final customer—this being dependent on the chosen entry mode and length of distribution channels. Therefore, complex markets need to be approached through strong commitment, close presence in the different areas (which may be approached gradually) and simplified product offerings, focusing on those products that are likely to fit the local needs best.

DISCUSSION

Early literature on foreign market entry concerned the choice between exporting and FDI. In this decision a crucial issue is the possession of firm-specific advantages that could compensate for the liability of foreignness. Firm-specific advantages connect to the literature on core competences as drivers of firm growth (Penrose 1959, Hamel and Prahalad, 1990). On the other hand, early literature (e.g., Knickerbocker 1973) also points out the perspective of market structure and its influence on entry strategy whereby oligopolistic reactions and exchange of threats are outlined.

According to a more dynamic perspective, markets are chosen according to "sequences" of firm behavior, and Vernon's (1966) life cycle, for example, highlights a sequence of internationalization decisions (concerning foreign markets and entry modes) based on the evolution of competitive conditions and the possession of a technological advantage to be exploited abroad. On the other hand, the Uppsala model (Johanson and Vahlne 1977) suggests that a gradual commitment is dependent on the firm's progressive acquisition of knowledge through experience, and that country/mode decisions follow an incremental, experience-driven path. Together with experiential learning, the construct of psychic distance between markets is fundamental to the model. Consequently, the characteristics of countries become more relevant, because they drive the entry sequence and influence the establishment (entry modes) chain. This literature highlights incremental changes among countries and thus supports a linear perspective of country selection as well as a linear perspective of entry modes selection.

Nevertheless, the two case studies reported contradict the linearity of the process, as some markets are characterized by complexity in terms of dynamism, heterogeneity, and uncertainty. These markets are not necessarily distant in cultural or geographic terms. For both companies the most complex market is the US one, even though both companies have international operations in many countries and in different continents. Moreover, as the first case indicates, the home market may also be considered complex.

Based on these cases, one may conclude that complexity refers to the following elements:

- Market knowledge, referring to the difficulty of knowing deeply a heterogeneous and sophisticated market and effectively serving customers. It is interesting to note that for both companies the US market is highly complex from this point of view, due to its high consumer behavior heterogeneity and change, to the level of advanced goods consumption, and to its trendsetting role in many markets, while the second market mentioned is for both companies the one where the consumption of the specific product is the more advanced one (India for rice, Italy for espresso coffee), even though India has a significant cultural distance for the Italian firm, while Italy is the home market for the other company. This creates *customer-related barriers* for entering these markets.
- Length and power of the distribution channels, referring to the challenge of using local distributors but retaining sufficient market knowledge and presence. Without shared knowledge with the partners, the company may meet considerable *distribution-related barriers* in these markets.
- Complex markets are also often mature markets with strong local competition. Because these competitors have an advantage in terms of their local market learning curve as well as in establishing their own distribution systems, companies may suffer from severe *competition-related* barriers.

These three elements of complexity create more barriers to market success than barriers to entry, because they are difficult to understand and analyze before the entry decision is taken. The case company Brasilia entered the US market at inception but did not achieve what they really wanted until they decided thirty years later to increase their market commitment and develop local learning and customer experience with their own branded products, sales offices and after-sales support. On the other hand, the other case company, Riso Scotti, adopted an exploratory strategy by selecting a geographic and market niche (health-food-oriented Californians) for learning purposes: based on that advance customer experience, the product could be better adapted to the market and distribution channels further developed.

Complex markets are also characterized by geographic complexity, which means not only distance but also size and topography of the country, leading to multi-located company presence and increased investments. Additionally, cultural distance may be involved, although the case companies did not emphasize this aspect. It is likely that cultural complexity better expresses what the management's perceptions of these markets, i.e., their heterogeneity and dynamism, their uncertainty and the level of commitment needed to handle it. For example, both case companies highlighted that the US is characterized by high institutional complexity, due to its federal organization and to the existence of a number of federal and national regulations.

Figure 8.5 summarizes the dimensions of complexity as perceived by the internationalizing firm. The upper three represent the barriers to market

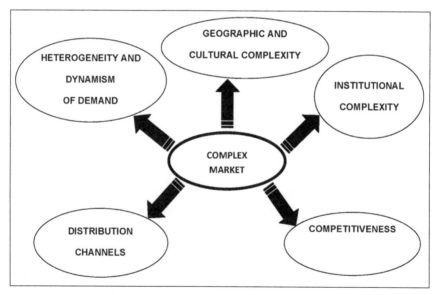

Figure 8.5   The dimensions of complexity.

knowledge and understanding, and the two below represent barriers to market/customer access. The decision to enter into these markets is driven by entrepreneurial posture and international growth orientation in particular. This decision involves a significant resource commitment.

Growth in complex markets needs to be supported by committed entry modes, which not only improve sales but also enhance learning, as a prerequisite of sales. In both case companies market complexity involved a significant marketing mix adaptation, starting from the product and implied also investments. Complex market were characterized as "resource-consuming" by both firms, meaning that they required not only financial investments for establishing local subsidiaries and for product adaptation, but also demanded significant input of valuable human resources, such as the time of members of the top management team.

On the other hand, the costs and risks (or better, uncertainties) of complex markets need to be balanced by relevant opportunities of doing business there and of developing learning that can enhance global competitive positioning, innovation and overall performance.

CONCLUSIONS

Foreign market expansion represents a critical incident for a firm, and influences its growth and performance over time. This contribution highlights the decision to enter into a complex market, which brings out novel challenges that have not been extensively discussed earlier. Bringing out the aspect of complexity does not mean rejecting the well accepted concepts of physical and psychic distance in the internationalization literature. However, it points out it is possible to complement this discussion with a perspective that more deeply considers the characteristics of some markets. To some extent, complexity is an expression of distance, and in particular of psychic distance, because it involves lack of specific market knowledge and experience. The construct of market complexity has thus both an objective dimension (market structure and evolution) and a subjective one (the firm's perception, orientation and knowledge).

The case companies share the idea that psychic distance is mainly—though not exclusively—a distance between the firm and the final customer, more than between the firm and the market in general. The former is mostly determined by the nature of local needs (heterogeneity and variability) and by the length and role of distribution channels, and determines the need of committed entry modes, adapted marketing mix and customer experience development.

Entering complex markets may represent a discontinuity in the international growth of a firm, which involves tolerating uncertainty and commitment of resources. Consequently, it includes a new, incremental process based on experiential learning. This apparently contradicts some recent streams in IB literature, which underline the relevance of learning through networks and foreign partners. The development of experiential learning involves committed entry modes from the beginning, thus highlighting that country and mode decision are neither linear processes (as a complex market entry represents a path discontinuity, and the establishment of a subsidiary before exporting constitutes a leapfrogging behavior) nor independent ones (the market complexity requires committed entry modes, whereas the establishment chain may prove ineffective and time consuming).

Finally, the subjective nature of market complexity also refers to strategic orientations of the firm and to its entrepreneurial posture: international growth orientation and willingness to trade higher risks (uncertainty) for higher opportunities. These seem to be required for succeeding in complex markets. However, as this study is exploratory in nature, the findings cannot be generalized to a larger population. Therefore, its main contribution is to shed some light on the international growth of SMEs, and in particular on the relationship between firms and foreign markets, introducing the concept of complexity and leveraging it to improve the understanding of non-linear international growth.

NOTES

1. International growth orientation is a construct meant to differentiate companies according to their motivation to seek growth in international markets, and thus for identifying the factors behind the chosen growth strategies (Nummela et al. 2005). It encompasses both external pressures and the internal factors that might drive the firm, such as the manager's attitude or global mindset (cf. Levy et al. 2007), and the assessment of the perceived risks in foreign operations (cf. Wiedersheim-Paul et al. 1978).

BIBLIOGRAPHY

Beckerman, W. (1956) 'Distance and the pattern of inter-European trade,' *The Review of Economics and Statistics*, 38 (1): 31–40.
Covin, J.G. and Slevin, D.P. (2002) 'The entrepreneurial imperatives of strategic leadership,' in M.A. Hitt, R.D. Ireland, S.M. Camp and D.L. Sexton (eds.) *Strategic entrepreneurship: creating a new mindset*, 309–327, Oxford, UK: Blackwell Publishers.
Duncan, R.B. (1972) 'Characteristics of organizational environments and perceived environmental uncertainty,' *Administrative Science Quarterly*, 17 (3): 313–327.
Etemad, H. (2004), 'International entrepreneurship as a dynamic adaptive system: towards a grounded theory,' *Journal of International Entrepreneurship*, 2 (1/2): 5–59.
Hamel, G. and Prahalad, C.K. (1990) 'The core competence of the corporation,' *Harvard Business Review*, 68 (3): 79–91.
Hofstede, G. (1983) 'National cultures in four dimensions: a research-based theory of cultural differences among nations,' *International Studies of Management and Organization*, 13 (2): 46–74.

Johanson, J. and Wiedersheim-Paul, F. (1975) 'The internationalization of the firm: four Swedish cases,' *Journal of Management Studies*, 12 (3): 305–322.

Johanson, J. and Vahlne, J-E. (1990) 'The mechanism of internationalization,' *International Marketing Review*, 7 (4), 11–24.

Johanson, J. and Vahlne, J.-E. (1977) 'The internationalization process of the firm: a model of knowledge development and increasing foreign market commitments,' *Journal of International Business Studies*, 8 (1): 23–32.

Jones, M. and Coviello, N.E. (2005) 'Internationalization: conceptualising an entrepreneurial process of behaviour in time,' *Journal of International Business Studies*, 36 (3): 284–303.

Knickerbocker, F.T. (1973) *Oligopolistic reaction and multinational enterprise*, Harvard University, Boston Division of Research, Graduate School of Business Administration.

Levitt, T. (1983) 'The globalization of markets,' *Harvard Business Review*, 61 (3): 92–102.

Levy, O., Beechler, S., Taylor, S. and Boyacigiller, N. (2007) 'What we talk about when we talk about "global mindset,"' *Journal of International Business Studies*, 38 (2): 231–258.

Linnemann, H. (1966) *An Econometric Study of International Trade Flows*, Amsterdam: North Holland Publishing Company.

Luo, Y. (2002) 'Capability exploitation and building in a foreign market: implications for multinational enterprises,' *Organization Science*, 13 (1): 48–63.

Madsen, T. and Servais, P. (1997) *The internationalization of born globals: an evolutionary process?* Odense University, Department of Marketing.

Marshall, C. and Rossman, G.B. (1999) *Designing qualitative research*, 3rd edition, London: Sage.

Nummela, N., Puumalainen, K. and Saarenketo, S. (2005) 'International growth orientation of knowledge-intensive SMEs,' *Journal of International Entrepreneurship*, 3 (1): 5–18.

O'Grady, S. and Lane, H.W. (1996) 'The psychic distance paradox,' *Journal of International Business Studies*, 27 (2): 309–333.

Oviatt, B.M. and McDougall, P.P. (1994), 'Toward a theory of international new ventures,' *Journal of International Business Studies*, 25 (1): 45–64.

Oviatt, B.M. and McDougall, P.P. (1995) 'Global start-ups: entrepreneurs on a worldwide stage,' *Academy of Management Executive*, 9 (2): 30–43.

Oviatt, B.M. and McDougall, P.P. (1997) 'Challenges for internationalisation process theory: the case of international new ventures,' *Management International Review*, 37 (2): 85–99.

Oviatt, B.M. and McDougall, P.P. (2000) 'International entrepreneurship: the intersection of two research paths,' *Academy of Management Journal*, 43 (5): 902–908.

Penrose, E. (1959) *The theory of the growth of the firm*, Wiley & Sons: New York.

Porter, M.E. (1986) *Competition in global industries*, Harvard Business School Press, Harvard.

Rialp, A., Rialp, J. and Knight, J.A. (2005), 'The phenomenon of early internationalizing firms: what do we know after a decade (1993–2003) of scientific inquiry?,' *International Business Review*, 14 (2): 147–166.

Rugman, A.M. (2007) *Regional aspects of multinationality and performance*, Oxford: Elsevier.

Schumpeter, J.A. (1934) '*The theory of economic development*,' Cambridge, MA: Harvard University Press.

Simpson, J.A. and Weiner, E.S.C. (1989) *Oxford English dictionary*, 2nd ed., London: Oxford University Press.

Sousa, C.M.P. and Bradley, F. (2005) 'Global markets: does psychic distance matter?' *Journal of Strategic Marketing*, 13 (1): 43–59.

Sullivan, T.J. (2001) '*Method of social research*,' Fort Worth, TX, and London: Harcourt College Publisher.

Usunier, J.C. and Lee, J.A. (2005) *Marketing across cultures*, 4th ed., Harlow, UK: Pearson Education.

Vahlne, J.-E. and Wiedersheim-Paul, F. (1973) 'Ekonomiskt avstånd—modell och empirisk undersökning' (Economic distance: model and empirical investigation), in E Hörnell, J.E. Vahlne and F. Wiedersheim-Paul (eds.), *Export och utlandsetableringar (Export and Foreign Establishments)*, 81–159, Stockholm: Almqvist & Wiksell.

Vernon, R. (1966) 'International investment and international trade in the product cycle,' *The Quarterly Journal of Economics*, 80 (2): 190–207.

Wiedersheim-Paul, F., Olson, H.C. and Welch, L.S. (1978) 'Pre-export activity: the first step in internationalization,' *Journal of International Business Studies*, 9 (1): 47–58.

Zucchella A. and Costa L. (2007) *Internazionalizzazione e innovazione nelle imprese*, Pavia, Italy: Federmanager.

Zucchella, A. and Scabini P. (2007) '*International entrepreneurship theoretical foundations and practices*, London: Palgrave Macmillan.

9 The Binary Choice Facing SME Internationalization

Colin Campbell-Hunt and Sylvie Chetty

INTRODUCTION

In this chapter we explore the internationalization paths of SME-scale competitors growing into the global economy, particularly those doing so from an isolated home market. We ask in particular whether the small size and isolation of these firms might lead to patterns of internationalization distinct from those theorized for much larger enterprises growing out from much larger and more globally integrated economies. Specifically, our study investigates what happens to a firm's marketing, product scope and manufacturing strategies as its geographic market scope expands. By comparing these trajectories to those predicted by current internationalization theory, we are led to conclude that SMEs face a binary choice between two radically different strategies for internationalization. While one of these has been recognized for some time in the born global model, the existence of its opposite has not previously been identified. Furthermore, the two pathways encourage SMEs to adopt strategies that are, in important respects, diametrically opposite to those predicted by the stages model of large-firm internationalization.

The context of our enquiry is a large-scale, long-term investigation into the evolution of competitive capability in a small number of New Zealand enterprises. A full account of the project, termed Competitive Advantage New Zealand—CANZ, is given in Campbell-Hunt et al. (2001).[1] These firms have achieved remarkable levels of internationalization, with offshore sales typically exceeding 90 percent of total, active participation in 50 to 60 countries globally, and leading market shares for their tightly focused product portfolio in major regional markets.

Like the country they spring from, these firms are distinctive for being small and having their home base as far removed as possible from the major markets of the world. These attributes separate these firms radically, we argue, from the bulk of contemporary internationalization theory. The fact that these firms have found ways to rise to these distinctive challenges has commanded our respect, and an acceptance that what they have learned might have greater validity for the context they experience than theorizations developed for other sizes and places of business. It is a context shared by many SMEs pursuing internationalization strategies from peripheral home markets such Finland (Autio et al. 2000) and Portugal (Fontes and Coombs 1997).

In the following sections, we first summarize the main tenets of contemporary internationalization theory. We then describe the internationalization strategies of the New Zealand companies in our study. Finally, we contrast our account of SME internationalization with that of contemporary theory, and attempt to identify the reasons for the sometimes radical differences that emerge between the two.

CONTEMPORARY INTERNATIONALIZATION THEORY

In this section we give a brief overview of two dominant models of firm internationalization as a basis for comparison to the findings of our study.

The Internationalization Process Model

The most widely-accepted view of the internationalization of firms is the "Uppsala Internationalization Process model" (IP model) by Johanson and Vahlne (1977). Despite critiques of its explanatory power (Millington and Bayliss 1990, Hedlund and Kverneland 1985), and of its continuing relevance in an age of radically-decreasing communication and transport costs (Oviatt and McDougall 1997), the IP model has been found to be consistent with the internationalization of firms in a broad range of countries and industries (Johanson and Vahlne 1990). The model's conceptualization of internationalization as a process of gradual learning, scale-expansion, and the internalization of value-adding functions in foreign markets, predicts that more globalized firms will display a greater preference for resource-intensive direct market representation and offshore manufacturing, while less globalized firms will use less resource-intensive strategies such as agents, distributors and licensing (Johanson and Wiedersheim-Paul 1975), and that markets will be developed in order of their cultural or psychic distance from the home market (Johanson and Vahlne 1977).

For the purposes of this chapter, it is helpful to recognize explicitly in the IP model an array of virtuous-cycle positive feedback loops, as shown in Figure 9.1. The inner loop describes the stages of successive value-adding internationalization in which exposure to (sales in) a market lead to learning about the potential of the market for the firm (both as an outlet for its products, and as a base for its own value-adding activities), then to increased resource commitment and a further cycle of increased exposure, learning and commitment. The addition of the inter-market stages model generates a further level of positive feedback processes. The firm's exposure to, and learning in, one market increases the firm's potential to learn about markets that are psychically close, setting off cycles of learning and commitment in those markets too. To the circular reinforcing dynamic of intra-market learning is added an expansive dynamic of inter-market

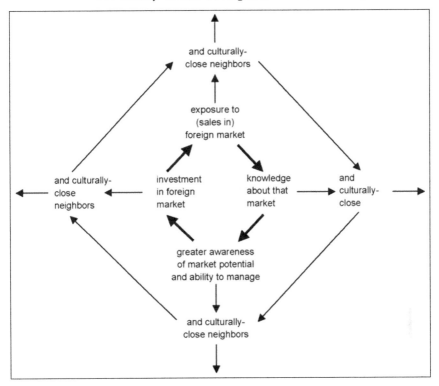

Figure 9.1 Learning cycles in stages theory.

learning. In systems terms, the entire array constitutes an attractor of considerable potential power to drive the firm's internationalization.

SME and New Venture Internationalization

Since the IP model was first developed, steady reductions in the economic, regulatory and informational barriers to trade have led to a burgeoning of internationalized businesses of SME scale (Oviatt and McDougall 1997). This in turn has attracted the interest of a growing number of researchers. In this section we summarize the emerging consensus on these internationalization trajectories.

First, it is suggested that smaller firms enter the internationalization experience with an notably smaller portfolio of resources than do larger firms and will, for that reason, realize better financial performance by extending their resource base through alliances with offshore partners (Agndal et al. 2008, Lu and Beamish 2001, Jones 1999). Although the IP model assumes that firms acquire knowledge and resources gradually as they mature, small and young firms can acquire these more quickly by forming strategic partnerships (Reuber and Fischer 1997). For example, the cost of direct modes of sales representation, such as developing a sales office in large markets, means that using a distributor will remain a more attractive option for SMEs (Burgel and Murray 2000).

Second, SMEs that are better equipped to progress through the learning-intensive experience of internationalization will be able to sustain faster international growth. For this reason it is argued that innovative SMEs such as knowledge-intensive new ventures will internationalize more rapidly, a result found to be consistent with the experience of Finnish new ventures in electronics (Autio et al. 2000). If such firms do not internationalize quickly enough they may lose their technological advantage (Burgel and Murray 2000). Consequently, they need to have the capability to accumulate knowledge and to learn quickly, as this will have an important impact on the rate and scope of internationalization (Autio et al. 2000, Jones 1999). An internationalizing SME has to develop the structures and routines that can support its internal resources and competencies, and help it acquire knowledge about its foreign markets (Eriksson et al. 1997).

The key differences that emerge between new venture internationalization and the stages model are thus:

- Knowledge-intensive SMEs will grow foreign sales at a faster rate than less knowledge-intensive SMEs, due to their superior ability to learn from the experience of internationalization.
- For any given degree of internationalization, SMEs will display greater use of indirect means of foreign market engagement, relative to larger firms.

METHODS

The methods used in this investigation are broadly those of theory development using multiple cases (Eisenhardt 1989, Yin 1989, Eisenhardt and Graebner 2007, Gibbert et al. 2008). We use multiple cases because they provide us with rich empirical evidence and the historical accounts of the phenomenon we wish to study (Eisenhardt and Graebner 2007). In addition, multiple cases allow replication logic to occur by comparing, contrasting, and extending each case to the emerging theory (Eisenhardt 1989, Yin 1989, Eisenhardt and Graebner 2007). We chose the case study method as it allows us to use multiple sources of data collection that includes interviews and secondary sources (Eisenhardt 1989, Yin 1989, Eisenhardt and Graebner 2007).

Sample Design

We selected a purposeful sample (Patton 2002) of companies that display the behaviors we wish to explain (Pettigrew 1990). Patton (2002, 40) describes purposeful sampling thus: *"Cases for study (e.g., people, organizations, communities, cultures, events, critical incidences) are selected because they are 'information rich' and illuminative, that is, they offer useful manifestations of the phenomenon of interest; sampling, then, is aimed at insight about the phenomenon, not empirical generalization from a sample to a population."*

Thus we used purposeful sampling to choose companies that have grown from New Zealand origins to display sustained competitive advantage in international markets. To identify these firms we were guided by an advisory panel of industry leaders, policy advisors, business support agencies and business journalists familiar with a wide range of New Zealand firms. The panel's task was feasible because of the limited size of the New Zealand economy, and the relatively small number of firms with exemplary histories of long survival and growth.

We chose to work closely with a small number of firms because resource-based sources of advantage are expected to be causally and socially complex and quite invisible to non-intrusive inspections (Rouse and Daellenbach 1999), and because a study of a firm's internationalization and the evolution of its advantage over time requires rich contextual material on the strategies and environmental conditions in which these processes are embedded (Pettigrew 1990).

Eight firms were studied over the first two years of the project, sufficient to allow the "constant comparisons" that are required for theory development (Eisenhardt 1989). Since then, other companies have been added in a process of theoretical sampling to explore the sensitivity of our conclusions to salient contingencies. The analysis presented here is based on the first eight firms studied.

Our focus on evolutionary processes, and the path dependencies expected in the internationalization of distinctive competitive assets (Dierickx and Cool 1989), argued for a historiographic approach (Goodman and Kruger 1988) as the only practical way to achieve the long perspectives required. Goodman and Kruger argue that historiographic methods are well suited to theory development because they produce contextually rich accounts of inter-temporal evolutions. In historiographic explorations, the theorization of causality is developed on the basis of inter-temporal relationships, rather than the more common correlational design of counterfactual control groups. For this reason, the sample design did not seek to match exemplar firms with lower-performing controls.

Data Acquisition

Over a two-year period, three waves of interviews were held with each organization. The first two involved the strategic apex of the organization, aimed at assembling a long historical overview of the firm's development, in a broad strategic context. The third involved more focused studies of aspects of each firm's development, including its internationalization; its manufacturing, human resource, and technology strategies; its decision-making processes; and the influence of leaders, owners, national culture and government regulatory change on the firm's evolution.

The limitations of data derived from participants' recollected accounts are discussed by Huber and Power (1985). We followed many of the procedures they recommend to minimize the motivational, perceptual and informational limitations they identify. We triangulated accounts of key events given to us by the several managers we talked to in each company, and complemented interview data with a comprehensive collection of all material on the company in the public record; company reports and documents; researchers' field notes; records of team discussions; and in several cases plant tours.

Interviews with CEOs were attended by a case writer[2] and at least two of the research team drawn from different disciplines. In this way, we acquired multiple-researcher, multidisciplinary perspectives on each interview (Eisenhardt 1989). We imposed very little structure on these interviews *ex ante* and allowed our informants to respond to broad areas of inquiry in their own terms and using their own constructs.

Data Analysis

As is common with these methods, we first constructed case histories for each of the eight companies from the various data sources we had assembled (Eisenhardt 1989).[3] These histories are of a type described by Pettigrew (1990) as chronologies: accounts constructed to assemble the story of a firm's evolution in rich contextual detail, and closely grounded in the sequencing of events. Data acquisition and case writing together took approximately six months, involving twelve case writers and all members of the core research team as reviewers.

Further analysis of these histories has involved a large research team, including specialists in human resource management, operations management, organization theory, decision theory, organization behavior, international marketing, and strategy. The design of the project has thus generated multiple perspectives on managers' accounts of events. All members of the research team read both case studies and transcripts, and perceptions were shared in meetings of the research team. In all cases, at least two of the research team had been present at the interview.

Triangulation of information was conducted by comparing information acquired from respondents with information from written documents and websites. We addressed issues of reliability and validity by checking for biases and accuracy of our interpretation of the data and for inter-coder agreement by moving between the transcripts and case studies. We regularly moved backward and forward between the tables, case studies and transcripts to confirm conclusions and interpretations. We discussed our findings with the rest of the research team to obtain multiple perspectives and to check for reliability and validity.

Feedback and Extension

Drafts of the histories were corrected and commented on by our sources. Interpretive work produced by the project has been fed back to participating executives in drafts, and to participating firms in management seminars at which the study's interpretation of events has been open to challenge. Interpretations have been altered where firms produced additional evidence to support a different view, or where errors made by the research team were pointed out.

Finally, a series of two dozen briefing seminars, involving approximately 400 people in total, have been held with practicing managers around the country, at which the conclusions of the study have been open to assessment and comment. These have allowed the project some ability to assess the validity of its interpretations beyond its immediate sample. Every seminar produced examples of firms not involved in the study that shared the experiences given salience in our interpretation of the competitive evolution and internationalization of sampled firms, and seminar assessments indicated high levels of approval for the relevance and accuracy of the interpretations offered.

In sum, we address validity (Andersen and Skaates 2004) and reliability issues raised by Gibbert et al. (2008) by using pattern making logic, data triangulation, review of transcripts by peers and key informants, feedback seminars to respondents, cross-case analysis, rationale for case study selection, and by developing a case study database that includes transcripts, case studies and secondary data for each case.

PATTERNS OF INTERNATIONALIZATION

The eight companies presented two distinct profiles of international scope. Four firms concentrated largely on the Australian and New Zealand markets, which represented about 80 percent of their total sales, and were active in fewer than ten countries beyond the region. They had a strong domestic market before they began to internationalize. These firms had established positions of leadership in both markets, and we have called this group *"regional leaders."*

The remaining four firms were active on a global scale, participating in 50 to 60 country-markets worldwide, with leading positions in major regional markets, and a significant or leading share in the global market as a whole, in some cases up to a third of the total. As can be seen in Table 9.1, they export up to 100 percent of their sales, with most of these sales going

Table 9.1 Strategic Configurations of the Case Firms

	Employees 2002	Sales NZ$ 2002	% sales international	Primary markets	Product scope	Primary int'l market	Manufacturing location
Regional Leaders							
BetaProducts	140	$50m	5% direct export plus sales in Australia	95% NZ and Australia	400 designs	Own sales staff offshore	Plants in NZ and Australia
GammaWorks	110	$40m	60%	NZ, Australia, US	Range of office furniture	Own sales staff offshore	Plants in NZ and Australia
DeltaCo	600	$200m	40%	NZ, Australia, UK	Range of products One beverage type	Own sales staff offshore	Plant in NZ
EpsilonCorp	336	$420m	65% est.	70% NZ and Australia	1000 distinct formulations	Own sales staff offshore	Plants in NZ and Australia
Global Leaders							
TabiSystems	158	$29m	100%	US	Industry-specific production equipment	Own sales staff offshore	Plant in NZ
RuaTech	250	$50m	80%	US, Europe	Single line Two niche markets	Distributors	Plant in NZ
ToruProducts	95	$30m	98%	US, UK	Single line Niche market	Distributors	Plant in NZ
WhaIndustries	750	$150m	90%	UK, Australia	Single line Niche market	Own sales staff offshore	Plant in NZ

Table 9.2   Configurations of Global and Regional Leadership

Market scope	Global leader	Regional leader
Innovation	World-leading Strong differentiator	Regional-leading or global-constrained
Product scope	Focus	Broad
Market representation	Most indirect	Direct
Manufacturing location	Consolidated in NZ	In NZ and Australia Strong differentiator

outside New Zealand and Australia. Global firms have a strong domestic market before they start to internationalize. We have called this group *"global leaders."*

We describe the internationalization paths of these two groups in turn, showing how the small size of these firms has had a profound influence on the internationalization strategies they have adopted. Table 9.2 gives a summary of the configurations of strategy emerging in each group.

Regional Leader Internationalization

Regional leaders have evolved a particular configuration of strategic responses to the challenges of internationalizing from a small isolated home market. The configuration represents a complex set of interdependent choices, each element of which is coherent to other choices in the set, and produces an array of mutually supportive strategies with its own internal logic. Our historiographic approach gives insight into how this configuration developed over time.

Fundamental to the regional leader configuration is a particular resolution to the challenge of building sufficient scale to meet the fixed costs of lumpy investments, such as manufacturing facilities and sales organizations, within markets that are too small to support product specialization. The *BetaProducts* (all company names are disguised) CEO portrays the choice faced by these small firms this way: "Narrow market, broader products; wider market, narrow [product] focus." *BetaProducts* has taken the first path: "We really looked for markets that we could get to amortize the cost of the machine over a larger range of products . . ." Regional leaders meet the challenge of scale by extending their product scope, and over time develop competitive advantage from this diversification. To take an extreme example of this phenomenon, *EpsilonCorp* has developed on the order of a thousand different products for a wide range of industrial uses. Like other regional leaders, *Epsilon* believes it gains competitive advantage over much larger, compartmentalized, global-scale competitors by being able to address clients' needs across a broader spectrum. To do so, however, direct relationships with customers and influencers are required, and all firms in the regional leader group have evolved a preference for direct representation. The following remarks from *Epsilon*'s CEO are typical of the logic behind the representation strategies of regional leaders: "We believe that we tailor our products for the customers' needs and nobody but ourselves can establish that relationship. We've tried agents but they really get in between you and the customer."

We summarize the essential features of product and marketing strategies in these firms as follows: (1) SMEs following the regional leader trajectory resolve the competitive limitations of small scale through developing a broad product scope. And (2), to develop competitive advantage from this diversity, regional leaders build close and direct relationships with customers to tailor solutions to customer needs. Regional leaders therefore have a preference for direct modes of market representation in both domestic and offshore markets.

The need to derive advantage from a diverse product portfolio, produced on a relatively small scale, has motivated in regional leaders the adoption of flexible manufacturing strategies suited to high-mix, low-volume operations. *BetaProducts*' CEO outlines his firm's manufacturing strategies as "shorter volume, just in time, being flexible, being able to produce many things [products] using high volume production techniques . . . It's set up for higher volumes but you are using your people to get the flexibility out of it." As the quotation shows, the pursuit of manufacturing flexibility at these small volumes requires a highly flexible production workforce: "If you have a skilled workforce, you can produce different things even in our processes. So we have set up cellular-based manufacturing, self-managed teams and activity-based costing systems down to those people." In these firms, flexible production capabilities have been developed to a point of competitive advantage, relative to the Australian economy where the challenges of small-scale production are less keen. This has been a necessary, but not sufficient, reason for these firms to locate manufacturing in both countries.

The further pressure motivating offshore manufacture has been the relatively low unit margins available to regional leaders. Regional leaders are active in industries with relatively low value-to-bulk ratios and, lacking the world-leading innovations that characterize global leaders, regional leaders do not demonstrate a capacity to defend high premiums for their products. The combination of low margins and competitive advantage in production capabilities has, in every case, motivated regional leaders to locate manufacturing facilities in the Australian as well as the domestic New Zealand market, wherever possible.[4] In sum, regional leaders locate manufacturing facilities in both domestic and offshore markets. The product diversity of these firms, combined with their small scale, has motivated the development of competitive advantages in flexible manufacturing that can be carried into the offshore plant. The absence of world-leading innovation in these firms has also produced relatively low unit margins, which discourage expensive transportation between countries.

The lack of world-leading innovation also appears to limit the geographic scope of these firms to a regional domain. Where global leaders are impelled to internationalize rapidly to realize the global potential for a product innovation, regional leaders have either never faced the opportunity, or, like *AlphaSystems*, have opted not to follow it. *Alpha* was the first company in the world to develop an electronically controlled dispensing system for its industry, but after assessing what would be involved in globalizing the innovation, the company decided instead to develop point-of-sale systems and security systems on a regional scale.

The experience of these cases leads us to characterize innovation as the portal that gives SME access to markets on a global scale; in the SME regional leader configuration, the lack of a world-leading innovation limits the geographic scope of firms to the proximate region.

Global Leader Internationalization

Global leaders have evolved a radically different configuration of strategies to deal with the same challenges of internationalizing from a small isolated home market. For them a world-leading innovation opened up the possibility of expanding the geographic scope of their business well beyond the home market. For *RuaTech*, new product technology offered greatly increased power and energy efficiency that increased global market size several fold; at *ToruProducts*, a revolutionary product design offered longer production lives and substantially lower operating costs; *WhaIndustries* was first to world markets with a product consistent with what became the global standard in their industry; *TahiSystems* was among the first in the world to apply full NC-control to the design of production lines in their industry. These innovations created the opportunity for these firms to enter a wide range of global markets.

We summarize the importance of innovation to the global leader trajectory as follows: in the SME global leader configuration, world-leading innovation is the strategy that makes possible a global scope of operations.

Of necessity, firms responded to this potential with strategies that accommodated their small size relative to the global markets opening before them. For these very small firms, the process of global expansion was characterized by a scale-up of very great magnitude and speed. For example, the first offshore order received by *TahiSystems* was for a system twenty times larger than anything it had done before. When starting from a very small base of operations, expansion on this scale dictates that the expansion will be experienced as rapid. Internationalization also places particular pressure on SMEs to develop offshore markets for their innovative products quickly before competitors can gain the lead. Thus *RuaTech* spent a hectic period of three to four years building a network of European dealers for their innovative systems before a local competitor with competitive technology could cover these markets. *RuaTech* won the race and today retains the dominant share of the European market. We have called these brief periods of rapid growth into multiple international markets "the gusher." Small firms also have very limited resources to fight off violations of their intellectual property, which adds to the urgency to capture markets quickly. These considerations suggest that in the SME global leader configuration, the rate of expansion into global markets must be rapid to capture the benefits of the firm's world-leading innovation.

In every case, these SME global leaders have had to respond to the pressures of very large-scale, very rapid expansion from a very limited resource base. Their small size has virtually required them to focus their entire operations on the rapidly-growing innovative product.

Another consequence of rapid internationalization is that global leaders have little choice but to develop foreign markets through indirect marketing channels such as dealers and distributors. Because they are still quite small firms and have to find a way to satisfy the diversity of multiple local markets, most global leaders retain a preference for indirect representation a decade or more after their period of rapid internationalization. Product and distribution strategies for global leaders are thus best summarized as follows:

- For SME global leaders, the competitive limitations of small scale are resolved by focusing product scope on the innovative product that opens up the possibility of global expansion.
- The rapid rate of expansion required to realize this potential leads to a preference for indirect modes of market representation in offshore markets, a preference sustained by the very much larger scale and diversity of offshore operations relative to the firm's home base.

Despite two decades of expansion to positions of global leadership in their tightly defined product markets, these firms remain of SME scale, typically employing no more than half of the 500 usually taken as the upper limit of the SME category (*WhaIndustries* is an exception, with a workforce of 750). As such, efficient scale of production has motivated all of these firms to concentrate their entire global manufacturing into one New Zealand–based site.

Several global leaders have built world-class, highly automated flexible manufacturing facilities to serve their diverse markets. With low labor costs, these plants are largely location-neutral and permit ongoing domestic manufacture. The manufacturing strategies of these firms are thus best summarized as follows: in the SME global leader configuration, the small scale of operations motivates firms to concentrate all manufacturing facilities in the domestic home base.

Table 9.3 Comparison of Theories on the Internationalization of the Firm

	Internationalization process of the firm	SME internationalization
Order of market entry	Gradual, in order of psychic distance	For global firms, rapid and universal exploitation
Direct market representation	Rises with degree of internationalization, but less in SMEs	Falls with degree of internationalization
Offshore location of manufacturing	Probability rises with degree of internationalization	Probability falls with degree of internationalization
Focused product portfolio		Required to achieve broad geographic scope; the result of innovation
Innovation	Permits faster international growth in SME	Required to achieve broad geographic scope Requires rapid internationalization

It is important to appreciate that regional and global strategic configurations represent radically different solutions to the challenges of SME internationalization from a small and isolated home market. There is no dynamic process inherent in the regional leadership strategy that allows an incremental mutation into global leadership of the kind described in the IP model. Rather this requires, in the experience of these cases, a product innovation of world-leading potential. Before its transformation into a global leader, *RuaTech* had developed a position of regional leadership in both Australia and New Zealand with less innovative products, but in the words of their CEO "We didn't really have a big strategic advantage. We never had an advantage until we joined the world economy." Conversely, when global leaders are presented with such an innovation, there is no motivation for them to begin its internationalization with a regional first step.

CONCLUSIONS ON SME INTERNATIONALIZATION THEORY

The conclusions developed in the previous section are grounded in the experience of SME internationalizing out of New Zealand's small and isolated economy. In this section we contrast these with contemporary internationalization theory, and to more recent attempts to adapt this theory to the SME domain (cf. Table 9.3).

The most striking point of contrast is that the core propositions of the IP model, in particular that more internationalized firms will prefer direct market representation and offshore manufacture, are reversed in the logic of SME internationalization (Table 9.3). As the discussion of the previous section has shown, this reversal is the result of a complex interplay of influences in which small size, product diversity, innovation and limited time interact to produce advantages to SMEs from strategies that are thought to be inferior in the general case. The salience that product diversity and innovation display in our view of SME internationalization has been absent from the IP model; but we argue that these strategies play a central role in SME internationalization, and are responsible for reversing the preferences of smaller firms for manufacturing and representation.

Placing innovation at the start of the complex process of SME internationalization opens up an evolutionary path with its own distinct strategic logic, undiscovered by larger firms. The first step down this novel path is to recognize the unique urgency of innovation-driven internationalization when experienced by a very small firm. Autio et al. (2000) have argued that a greater innovative capability in new ventures permits faster international growth. In our account this is appreciably strengthened to suggest that SMEs find themselves in a learning race to quickly and appreciably extend the geographical scope of their innovative product (Table 9.3).

The speed of this global exploitation of a world-leading product requires a very different form of learning from that envisaged by the stages model. In the stages model, learning involves the gradual accumulation of knowledge about successive local markets on what local agents (consumers, licensees and dealers) already know about the idiosyncrasies of each market. In our SME account, the internationalizing firm is racing into the unknown to discover what the global potential for its innovation may be–and in which markets it may be—before competitors capture the leading position for themselves (Table 9.3).

We have observed that the need to rapidly internationalize a world-leading innovation virtually forces SME following the global leader trajectory to focus all their limited resources on the internationalizing product. The consequences for the SME's product scope of the need for rapid internationalization have not previously been recognized to play an important role in the IP model of large-firm internationalization. In our model it plays a key role in linking the competitive appeal of innovation to the distinct marketing and manufacturing strategies adopted by regional and global leaders.

The result of this radical and sudden transformation or reconfiguration of the SME is a firm that is typically still small by world standards, but tightly focused on one world-leading product and engaging with a wide diversity of international markets. The distinctive challenges posed in this state to SMEs' manufacturing and representational strategies are best resolved, in our experience of these cases, with indirect local-market representation and consolidated manufacture. The slower evolution of much larger firms into multiple national markets, where the advantage stems from absorbing knowledge more than from creating it, has a quite different logic that leads the firm gradually to absorb functions into its own operations, as predicted by the IP model.

Conversely we argue that regional leader SMEs that have not experienced this innovation-led transformation, and whose broader product portfolios have no more than regional potential, seek advantage from their product diversity by establishing direct relationships with the much smaller range of clients that they serve. Use of direct representation among regionally focused SMEs has also been observed for Finnish SMEs (Holmlund and Kock 1998). We theorize that these results are the result of the mediating effect of the regional leader's broader product range.

Reflecting on the reasons for the sharp novelty of our representation, we observe that the great majority of work on internationalization has not concerned itself with the distinctive challenges of SMEs until very recent times. Well grounded as the IP model is for its own context, the roles of innovation and product diversity that are so salient in our account of SME internationalization have not emerged as being of any importance until recently.

More recent attempts to investigate SME and new venture internationalization have been primarily attracted to the phenomenon of small, innovative enterprises that internationalize extensively and very soon after founding: the born global model (Gabrielsson et al. 2008, Knight and Cavusgil 1996, 2004, McKinsey and Co. 1993). Contrasts between this model and the IP model have been sharply drawn on the pace and breadth of entry to foreign markets and the use of networks of business partners to substitute for the firm's own direct sales effort. The group of firms in our study we have termed global leaders share these attributes with the born global model. Our study has in addition uncovered consequential strategic choices on the location of manufacturing and product scope that have not previously been recognized as playing an important role in the born global model. Our case histories also support the claim by Bell et al. (2003) that the phenomenon of rapid and extensive internationalization of SMEs can also occur to firms later in life, consequent on a world-leading innovation: so-called born-again globals.

What is more novel in our model of SME internationalization is the existence of the third trajectory of the regional leader, distinct from both the large-firm IP model and the rapid internationalization of the born global firm. Where the IP model predicts steady and incremental growth in both the scope of international markets and the depth of engagement with those markets, the histories of firms in our study suggests that SME face a binary choice between on the one hand exploiting the global potential of an innovative product in many global markets but constrained by their small size to a limited depth of engagement in those markets, or on the other hand being constrained by a lack of innovative appeal to a limited geographic scope of proximate markets developed in depth with offshore marketing and manufacturing required to service a broad product line. The three trajectories are shown in Figure 9.2: the large-firm path moving up the diagonal in both geographic market scope and depth of engagement at the same time, the regional and global paths growing along one of these two axes, but not both. Figure 9.2 gives a graphical representation of the diametrically opposite predictions of our model of SME internationalization and the IP model on offshore marketing and manufacturing investment as a function of a firm's geographic scope. Where the IP model predicts that depth of engagement rises with geographic scope, our model predicts the reverse. The key role of innovation and product scope in producing and discriminating between the two trajectories of global and regional leader brings these strategies to the fore in SME internationalization theory.

We believe that the insights we have reached have also been greatly widened by our participation in a broad-based, multidisciplinary, multiple-researcher program of research. By this means we have been encouraged to see firms' internationalization experience as part of a wider process of evolving competitive capabilities. We have also been required to examine the evolving patterns of coherence between successive strategic choices across a broad domain of strategic action. We think that as a result we have been led to explore the distinctive interplay of size, innovation, product diversity and market scope that produces in SMEs a radically different set of preferences on manufacturing and representation strategies.

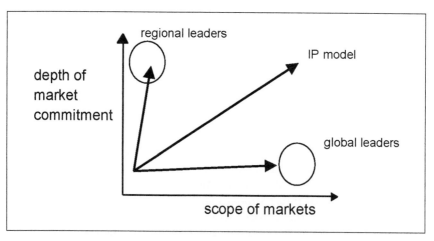

Figure 9.2   Internationalization trajectories of SME and large-firm models.

EXTENSIONS

We close by noting some features of the internationalization experience of our cases that deserve further investigation. Like other elements in our theorization, these are linked to the complex configurations of strategy that stem from the smallness and isolation of these firms. But we have yet to fully explore the extent of the differences between global and regional leaders on these features of SME internationalization.

The first concerns the search behaviors used by these firms to identify promising markets. We argue that SME global leaders must quickly identify promising markets for their world-leading innovations, yet consistent with Agndal et al. (2008) and Lu and Beamish (2001) they have a distinctively limited resource base with which to investigate this potential. We observe that many companies in this group adopt a strategy of broadcast exploration across a wide range of geographic markets, using low-cost strategies such as trade fairs, leaflets, and articles in trade and professional magazines. A salient example of this was the injunction by *RuaTech*'s CEO to his sales force that, since any country on earth was en-route between New Zealand and the company's emerging European markets, they should take a different route each time and take a day or two to scout the potential for the company's innovative product in each market. Only where promising leads are opened up are resources committed to further exploration and development. O'Farrell et al. (1998) have found a similar ad hoc approach to market selection in UK-based SME internationalization. We call the search strategy "sow and reap," and the consequent development of promising markets "focus and grow." These strategies combine broad and rapid exploration of global potential with a husbanding of limited resources for only those opportunities that show real market appeal. Both features are, we argue, dictated by the distinctive challenges of rapid SME internationalization.

These strategies are in contrast to the use of elaborate market-research studies that are the norm in large-firm internationalization practice. In our study, there is also some evidence that regional leaders adopt more considered search processes when investigating their much more focused market options in neighboring Australia; but our evidence on this is not extensive. We believe that similar issues are raised by the strategies used to protect intellectual property in these firms, but these too need further investigation.

The second issue concerns the distinctive risk faced by global leader SME in the "going global" transition. This conflates into one transforming experience three significant sources of risk, any one of which has the potential to destroy the firm. First, the "gusher" requires the firm to grow in scale very quickly, typically increasing ten-fold over a period of three to four years. In every case, our companies have struggled to maintain quality and delivery expectations that threatened the firm's emerging reputation in new markets. Second, the firm is expanding into several markets in a short space of time, many of them widely different (and distant) from the home market, which contradicts Johanson and Vahlne's (1977) model. Third, the entire expansion is driven by an innovative product whose global potential is unproven. This is consistent with the point made by Burgel and Murray (2000) that they might lose their technological advantage if they do not internationalize quickly.

Finally, the capacity of global leader SMEs to absorb learning at the pace and scale required raises important questions for investigation, relative to regional leader SMEs and large-firm transnationals. This contrasts with Johanson and Vahlne (1977) who do not make a distinction between size and strategic orientation of internationalizing firms. Given the preference of global leaders for indirect representation channels, it seems likely that their knowledge of individual markets is less complete than in other categories of internationalized firms. But we speculate that the wide scope of participation in global markets, and the extremely high levels of internationalization in these firms (typically on the order of 90 percent of total sales being foreign), requires in their executives a capacity to conduct strategy on a global scale that may match that of the most sophisticated large-firm transnational.

We share others' view that the phenomenon of SME internationalization is an important focus of study (Mathews and Zander 2007, McDougall and Oviatt 2000). We believe we have shown that the distinctive challenges of size and isolation faced by SMEs require an internationalization strategy that is radically different from that theorized for much larger firms. And we believe that there remains much more to learn about a remarkable group of very small, very internationalized enterprises that Simon (1996) has rightly called "hidden champions."

NOTES

1. See also the CANZ project website at www.vuw.ac.nz/fca/research/canz.
2. Case writers were all recent MBA graduates, familiar with the concepts of competitive advantage and the analysis of firm strategy.
3. Several of these are available on the CANZ website, www.vuw.ac.nz/fca/research/canz.
4. For DeltaCo, the nature of the product requires processing close to the domestic source of raw material.

BIBLIOGRAPHY

Agndal, H., Chetty, S. and Wilson, H. (2008) 'Social capital dynamics and foreign market entry,', *International Business Review*, 17 (6): 663–675.
Andersen, P.A. and Skaates, M.A. (2004) 'Ensuring validity in qualitative international business research,', in R. Marschan-Piekkari and C. Welch (eds.) *Hand-*

book of qualitative research methods for international business, 464–485, Cheltenham, UK: Edward Elgar.

Autio, E., Sapienza H.J. and Almeida, J.G. (2000) 'Effects of age at entry, knowledge intensity, and imitability on international growth,', *Academy of Management Journal*, 43 (5): 909–924.

Bell, J., McNaughton, R., Young, S. and Crick, D. (2003) 'Towards an integrative model of small firm internationalisation,', *Journal of International Entrepreneurship*, 1 (4): 339–362.

Burgel, O. and Murray, G.C. (2000) 'The international market entry choices of start-up companies in high-technology industries,', *Journal of International Marketing*, 8 (2): 33–62.

Chetty, S. and Campbell-Hunt, C. (2003) 'Paths to internationalisation amongst small to medium-sized firms: a global versus regional approach,', *European Journal of Marketing*, 37 (5/6): 796–820.

Dierickx, I. and Cool, K. (1989) 'Asset stock accumulation and sustainability of competitive advantage,', *Management Science*, 35 (12): 1504–1514.

Eisenhardt, K.M. (1989) 'Building theories from case study research,', *Academy of Management Review*, 14 (4): 532–550.

Eisenhardt K.M. and Graebner, M.E. (2007) 'Theory building from cases: opportunities and challenges,', *Academy of Management Journal*, 50 (1): 25–32.

Eriksson, K., Johanson, J., Majkgard, A. and Sharma, D. (1997) 'Experiential knowledge and cost in the internationalisation process,', *Journal of International Business Studies*, 28 (2): 337–360.

Fontes, M. and Coombs, R. (1997) 'The coincidence of technology and market objectives in the internationalisation of new technology-based firms,', *International Small Business Journal*, 15 (4): 14–34.

Gabrielsson, M., Kirpalani, V.H.M., Dimitratos, P., Solberg, C.A. and Zucchella, A. (2008) 'Born globals: propositions to help advance the theory,', *International Business Review*, 17 (4): 385–401.

Gibbert, M., Ruigrok, W. and Wicki, B. (2008) 'What passes as a rigorous case study?' *Strategic Management Journal*, 29 (13): 1465–1474.

Goodman, R.S. and Kruger, E.J. (1988) 'Data dredging or legitimate research method? Historiography and its potential for management research,', *Academy of Management Review*, 13 (2): 315–325.

Hedlund, G. and Kverneland, A. (1985) 'Are strategies for foreign markets changing? The case of Swedish investment in Japan,', *International Studies of Management and Organisation*, 15 (2): 41–59.

Holmlund, M. and Kock, S. (1998) 'Relationships and the internationalisation of Finnish small and medium-sized companies,', *International Small Business Journal*, 16 (4): 46–63.

Huber, G.R. and Power, D.J. (1985) 'Retrospective reports of strategy-level managers: guidelines for increasing their accuracy,' *Strategic Management Journal*, 6 (2): 171–180.

Johanson, J. and Vahlne, J.-E. (1990) 'The mechanism of internationalisation,' *International Marketing Review*, 87 (4): 11–24.

Johanson, J. and Vahlne, J.-E. (1977) 'The internationalisation process of the firm,' *Journal of International Business Studies*, 8 (1): 23–32.

Johanson, J. and Wiedersheim-Paul, F. (1975) 'The internationalisation of the firm—four Swedish cases,' *Journal of Management Studies*, 12 (3): 305–322.

Jones, M. (1999) 'The internationalisation of small high-tech firms,' *Journal of International Marketing*, 7 (4): 15–41.

Knight, G. and Cavusgil, T.S. (1996) 'The born global firm: a challenge to traditional internationalisation theory,' *Advances in International Marketing*, 8: 11–26.

Knight G.A. and Cavusgil, S.T. (2004) 'Innovation, organizational capabilities, and the born-global firm,' *Journal of International Business Studies*, 35 (2): 124–141.

Lu, J.W and Beamish, P.W. (2001) 'The internationalisation and performance of SMEs',' *Strategic Management Journal*, 22 (6/7): 565–586.

Mathews, J.A. and Zander, I. (2007) 'The international entrepreneurial dynamics of accelerated internationalisation,' *Journal of International Business Studies*, 38 (3): 387–403.

McDougall, P.P. and Oviatt, B.M. (2000) 'International entrepreneurship: the intersection of two research paths,' *Academy of Management Journal*, 43 (5): 902–906.

McKinsey and Co. (1993) *Emerging exporters. Australia's high value-added manufacturing exporters*, Melbourne: McKinsey and Company and the Australian Manufacturing Council.

Millington, A.I. and Bayliss, T. (1990) 'The process of internationalisation: UK companies in the EC,' *Management International Review*, 30 (2): 151–61.

Organisation for Economic Cooperation and Development (1990) '*Progress in Structural Reform*,' Paris: OECD.

O'Farrell P.N., Wood, P.A. and Zheng, J. (1998) 'Internationalisation by business service SMEs: an inter-industry analysis,' *International Small Business Journal*, 16 (2): 13–33.

Oviatt B.M. and McDougall, P.P. (1997) 'Challenges for internationalisation process theory: the case of international new ventures,' *Management International Review*, 37 (2): 85–99.

Patton, M.Q. (2002) *Qualitative research and evaluation methods*, Thousand Oaks, CA: Sage Publications.

Pettigrew, A.M. (1990) 'Longitudinal field research on change: theory and practice,' *Organisation Science*, 1 (3): 265–292.

Reuber, R.A. and Fischer, A. (1997) 'The influence of the management team's international experience on the internationalisation behaviours of SMEs,' *Journal of International Business Studies*, 28 (4): 807–26.

Rouse, M.J. and Daellenbach, U. (1999) 'Rethinking research methods for the resource-based perspective: isolating sources of sustainable competitive advantage,' *Strategic Management Journal*, 20 (5): 487–494.

Simon, H. (1996) *Hidden champions*, Boston: Harvard Business School Press.

Yin, R. (1989) *Case study research, design and methods*, Beverly Hills, CA: Sage.

10 Technology-based New Ventures and Critical Incidents in Growth

Jani Lindqvist, Olli Kuivalainen and Sami Saarenketo

INTRODUCTION

In this chapter we explore the critical incidents leading to new growth and internationalization of rapidly internationalized technology-based new ventures. The growth of technology-based new ventures plays a major role in wealth creation in most economies. However, despite the fact that there is a substantial number of frameworks describing the growth of the firms, there is still no comprehensive theory to explain which firms will grow and how they grow. Indeed, it is quite clear that not all the high-growth firms grow in the same way (Weinzimmer 2000, Delmar et al. 2003). This is partly due to the context specificity of growth; there are firm, industry and country-specific determinants which affect the growth patterns and pathways in pace, content and regularity.

Delmar et al. (2003) also note that there is a shortage of comprehensive studies in which not only are various growth measures used but also measures of potential causes and consequences of growth. In such studies life cycle models are useful tools in the conceptualization of the growth process, i.e., to analyze different types of phenomena which grow and mature over time. For example, they have been used to study dynamic relationships between the entrepreneurs or the management and the small business (e.g., Gibb and Davies 1990, Cope 2003) or the development of the product and market (e.g., Moore 2004).

The whole life cycle of the firm usually proceeds hand-in-hand with the life cycle of its products, services, customers and markets, and often also correspondingly with the internationalization life cycle. Much of the literature on internationalization of the firm concludes that the internationalization process involves a series of incremental stages. According to the so-called process or stage models, a firm incrementally builds up an involvement in international operations, starting with exporting in nearby countries (cf. Johanson and Vahlne 1990).

Although in the stage models the number of stages varies there has been a common underlying assumption that firms get well established in the domestic market prior to developing international operations. However, since the 1990s there has been a widespread emergence of studies reporting on companies that start operating internationally very early on—even from the first day of their existence. While these businesses—often referred to as *born globals*[1] (Rennie 1993, Knight and Cavusgil 1996), *international new ventures* (Oviatt and McDougall 1994) or *global start-ups* (Mamis 1989; Oviatt and McDougall 1995)—first emerged in countries with small domestic markets, they are now appearing in large numbers all over the globe. This indicates that it is an important phenomenon and there is a need to better understand the critical incidents that push or pull the firms forward in the process. Accelerated market entry can be seen as an important goal, as the shortening of the time span between foundation and foreign market entry can mean increasing the chances of fast and solid returns (Bloodgood et al. 1996, Oesterle 1997).

Despite the growing number of research on born global firms (see Rialp et al. 2005 for a review) and their differences with traditionally internationalizing companies (e.g., Knight and Cavusgil 1996, Moen and Servais 2002) accompanied by studies offering more holistic internationalization models (e.g., Bell et al. 2003, Crick and Spence 2005), the literature remains fragmented. There is still a lack of comprehensive theoretical explanations and a scarcity of studies focusing on the sequential growth and internationalization patterns of technology-based new ventures (the few exceptions include, e.g., Jones 1999). It seems that the question "what happens after initial rapid internationalization" remains partially unanswered.

Consequently, the aim of this chapter is to study the critical incidents leading to new growth and internationalization stages of technology-based new ventures following a born global pathway. These incidents are analyzed through the life cycle model of the firm. Accordingly, the chapter opens with a brief review of existing literature on life cycles and critical incidents in new venture growth and internationalization. Then, it proceeds to the research design of the study. Specifically, we have conducted four exploratory case studies of Finnish software companies, which we illustrate from the viewpoint of the critical incidents in their growth pathways. Software industry was chosen as the focus of our study, as the firms operating in this domain face numerous challenges in their internationalization. Finally, we conclude with a discussion of the findings and their scholarly and managerial implications.

LITERATURE REVIEW

Firm Life Cycle and Critical Incidents

Life cycle models are used in the analysis of different types of phenomena which grow and mature over time. In organizational theories the life cycle models are used to portray changes that take place in the set of activities and structures of an organization in the course of time. The *activities* along the life cycle refer to decision-making and operational procedures while the *structures* refer to relationships, distribution of power and different organizational forms (Lester and Parnell 2008).

The life cycle consists of stages that indicate the status and characteristics of the firm, with regard to, e.g., its size in terms of turnover or personnel, the rate by which it is growing, or the complexity of its organization structure. One of the most studied angles during life cycle is the perspective of the management. There seems to be a consensus that for long-term success, firm founders must be capable of 1) transforming themselves from entrepreneurs to managers, and 2) delegating responsibility in the organization, even to the extent of detaching completely from the firm (cf., e.g., Churchill and Lewis 1983).

In extant literature the number of stages varies between three and ten (cf. Hanks et al. 1993). However, most often the models consist of three to five stages, of which the five-stage model is the most common one (see Lester and Parnell 2008 for a review). The five stages in the firm life cycle include 1) *existence*, i.e., the initial phase of the firm with an accompanying high level of entrepreneurial spirit, 2) *survival*, or growth-seeking stage, 3) *success*, sometimes called professional phase or maturity, when delegation of responsibilities starts to take place, 4) *renewal*, or diversification and coordination and 5) *decline*, when grown bureaucracy may suffocate the company (cf., e.g., Hanks et al. 1993).

During its life cycle, the challenges a firm faces may snowball into crisis situations, in which the management is unable to cope with existing resources, methods or tools. Thus the management has to make greater changes or sacrifices to overcome the crisis (cf. Churchill and Lewis 1983, Quinn and Cameron 1983, Hanks et al. 1993, Oesterle 1997, Greiner 1972, Bell et al. 2001). Depending on how the organization faces each crisis situation defines whether it moves to a more mature life cycle stage or straight to decline. Thus, the company may enter the stage of decline anytime it cannot rise up to the crisis it is facing.

The often-cited crisis types that occur during growth include: 1) crisis of leadership, 2) crisis of autonomy, 3) crisis of control and 4) crisis of red tape (Greiner 1972). Further study on crises has been done by Dodge and Robbins (1992), who point out that the problems a firm faces may appear in an early stage, but accumulate as actual crises only later. Based on their empirical study of small firms, Dodge and Robbins (1992) argue that the problems in early life cycle stages are mostly related to external environment, e.g., in making contacts with the customers and in making accurate market assessments. In later stages, firms tend to have more difficulties with internal issues, such as financial and business planning as well as organization design and personnel.

For high-tech product firms in small open economies to grow, it has often been mentioned that internationalization is an inevitable undertaking. This makes internationalization an integrated part of the life cycle of a firm. Thus, to understand the development of high-tech firms originating from small markets, we need to add the determinants of international development to the life cycle.

Internationalization and Stimuli

Internationalization has been traditionally discussed in terms of "stage," or "incremental internationalization" models. The models are based on a typical risk-averse behavioral pattern of firms. Firms gradually increase their involvement (e.g., resource allocation) in international operations as they gain more knowledge of their target markets (cf. Johanson and Vahlne 1977). In a typical case, a firm first focuses on its domestic markets, and only after a while due to changes in internal or external environment, does it decide to enter the international marketplace as well. Moreover, frequently the target market is in a neighboring country and the form of internationalization is export via agents or answering to unsolicited orders (cf. Bell et al. 2001).

Although, for example, Oviatt and McDougall (1994) note that early internationalizers have existed for centuries, and that recent technological advances have increased possibilities for internationalization from the inception, these "born global" firms represent a special, rapid case of internationalization. They typically operate in a narrowly defined market niche and therefore, as mentioned above, cannot thrive in a single, small domestic market (Rialp et al. 2005). A high degree of specialization requires international expansion if the firm wants to achieve substantial sales growth. In addition, competition for typical high-technology born globals is very intense and their products may become obsolete in a short period of time. This leads to the above-mentioned situation in which a firm is forced to penetrate concurrently into all major markets, to be able to take the full advantage of the market potential before the so-called "window of opportunity" closes.

A firm's involvement in international markets can be measured by its "degree of internationalization" (DOI) (cf., e.g., Sullivan 1994). The indicators that are used in measuring the DOI include foreign sales compared to total sales, sales growth, operation mode and the number of countries where the company is present (Welch and Luostarinen 1988, Sullivan 1994). Thus DOI is a measure of the international structure of a firm together with its development speed and coverage in international marketplace.

Internationalization pathways are typical patterns or routes that a firm follows when it internationalizes, and they also depict typical forms of DOI development.[2] This means that in the same time span the DOI is different for firms following different pathways. For example, the DOI indicators for a born global firm after three years' time might look similar to those of a traditional firm after fifteen years. In Figure 10.1, a hypothetical example of such developments is presented.

After most researchers had moved their attention from incremental internationalization models to "born globals," Bell et al. (2001) in their study of

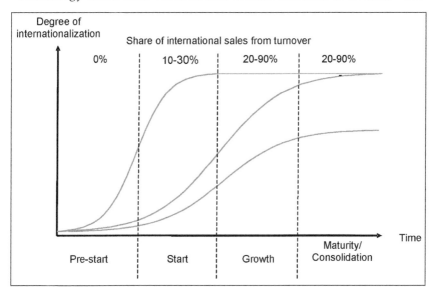

Figure 10.1 Indicators of internationalization in different stages.

so-called "born-again globals," raised the issue that the internationalization of the firm may comprise of "critical incidents," which launch "epochs" of internationalization. This means that a firm may quickly change its internationalization pathway due to changed circumstances. Bell et al. (2001) argue (in line with Dodge and Robbins 1992) that the critical incidents are brought forward by either internal or external *stimuli*. By internal stimuli they refer to new ideas, resources and skills or product development, etc. External stimuli, in turn, are stimuli that come from factors such as new customers, regulatory market changes or competitors.

In addition to the fact that small home market size pushes many firms to become international at an early age, researchers have been reporting many stimuli that initiate and accelerate internationalization process. Oesterle (1997) highlights the importance of "innovation set" of a new firm as a basis for the timing and speed of internationalization. This means that immediate internationalization is undertaken by firms that have radical innovations with little demand domestically, whereas sequential internationalization is promoted by positive domestic market situation for the innovation. Crick and Spence (2005) note that the rapid timing of initial internationalization decision is facilitated by the existing connections and networks of the owners/managers. Bell et al. (2001) found that a management change can get a firm to internationalize rapidly after many years of domestic operations. Moreover, Crick and Spence (2005) suggest "serendipitous encounters" as potential triggers for internationalization, or as a stimulus to such incidents as recruiting during growth and internationalization.

It is important to note that in many previous internationalization studies a combination of "critical incidents" and "forces" have been discussed in the sense that they are *initiating* the internationalization process (Oesterle 1997, Bell et al. 2001). Thus, we have a plethora of studies focusing on the antecedents and determinants of the born global phenomenon (cf. Rialp et al. 2005). However, to us it seems that there is a need to incorporate time in a more precise manner to born global studies (see also Coviello and Jones 2004) and that we could learn a lot from the life cycle literature, in which the view is more clearly on the development of the firm in the course of time.

As we explained, in organization life cycle research stream the focus is often set on "critical phases" (Steinmetz 1969), "growth hurdles" (Parks 1977) or developmental "problems/concerns" (Dodge et al. 1994). When company founders target internationalization from the beginning due to the external stimuli, the occurring "incidents" can be perceived as both prerequisites and accelerators for further growth of the firm. The involvement and maturity in international markets thus increase as accelerating incidents take place. In Table 10.1 we summarize the problems and stimuli that have been suggested in the literature on organizational life cycles and internationalization.

Having discussed the earlier literature on critical incidents in growth of technology-based new ventures and internationalization, let us now approach our research design.

Table 10.1   Stimuli and Problems Encountered in Different Internationalization Stages of Firms Following a "Born Global" Pathway (based on Churchill and Lewis 1983, Dodge and Robbins 1992, Hanks et al. 1993, Oesterle 1997, Bell et al. 2001, Crick and Spence 2005)

	Pre-start	*Start*	*Growth*	*Maturity*
Internal problems and stimuli	- Entrepreneurial spirit - Radical innovation - Matching of business and personal goals - Personal networks	- New ideas - Access to more resources - New skills - Product development - Change of ownership	- Cash flow - Delegation - Coordination - Business planning	- Maintaining flexibility (red tape) - Production and facilities - Organization design and personnel
External problems and stimuli	- No domestic demand - Lack of business knowledge - Cash availability - Market niche identification	- New customers - Regulatory market changes - Actions by competitors - Location	- Relocation - Keeping customer contact - Market assessment and identification	- Expansion - Planning of marketing operations

RESEARCH DESIGN

The case study is a research strategy which focuses on understanding of the dynamics either in a multiple or single settings and is especially feasible when studying new areas (Eisenhardt 1989). Although the extant literature has covered life cycle models in a detailed manner (e.g., Lester and Parnell 2008) the life cycles of rapidly internationalizing SMEs are studied in a lesser extent. The antecedents of born globals or international new ventures have been studied extensively (cf. Rialp et al. 2005) but the dynamics of the growth of these firms is less understood. Hence, we have chosen to utilize the case method in our study.

We adopted an exploratory multiple case study approach to analyze the critical incidents of four Finnish software companies. According to Pauwels and Matthyssens (2004, 128) [multiple case studies study design] "is built upon four pillars—theoretical sampling, triangulation, analytical pattern-matching logic and analytical generalization—and one roof—validation through juxtaposition and iteration."

Regarding sampling, the software industry was chosen as a case industry because most firms operating in this field face several challenges at the same time. These include, for example, constantly forming and growing new markets, short and rapidly changing product life cycles, existence of network externalities (the value of the product often depending on the number of other users of the product) and the need to harness emerging technologies and adapt to collapsing markets (cf. Äijö et al. 2005). Thus software industry was seen as a good example of an industry where rapid internationalization is almost imperative.

In the selection of the cases we followed the general criteria on sampling SMEs used by Bell et al. (2001):

- A firm should be a current exporter and fulfill the requirements of born global firms; it should have internationalized rapidly and operate in multiple countries (e.g., Knight and Cavusgil 1996).
- A firm should employ less than 250 staff and be independent and indigenous (not a subsidiary of a larger domestic or international company, to avoid potential resource and cultural influences on decision making). These criteria are in line with the EU criteria for defining SMEs, although in practice all the selected case firms had less than 50 employees.

The selection of the firms was made in spring 2004. All the chosen firms are, as noted above, born globals. However, they operate in different domains of software. Each of the firms is first analyzed independently regarding its internationalization life cycle and critical incidents, after which cross-case analysis is conducted. In constructing the critical incidents and growth paths of the case firms, we have utilized multiple, primarily secondary sources of information (on data triangulation, see, e.g., Tellis 1997). These sources include Finnish business magazines, business press databases such as Talentum, presentations, company websites, among others. In order to validate the drawn findings and interpretations of the group of four researchers the assembled texts were reviewed by the managers of the focal companies who confirmed their accuracy. In discussion section we aim for the analytical generalization by presenting a model which describe accelerated/born global pathway from the life cycle perspective.

CASES: FOUR FINNISH SOFTWARE COMPANIES

We now illustrate the growth and internationalization paths of the case companies and depict the stimuli and the subsequent critical incidents in their growth paths, which consist of four stages. Our intention is to analyze these companies to better understand their rapid international growth and reveal the critical incidents behind the growth processes. Concurrently, we will provide a framework for the following cross-case analysis.

Case Descriptions

Company A was founded in 1997, being the oldest of the four case companies. The company's main offering is a software product for data erasure. Its customers are companies who need to protect their business secrets, clients' privacy or otherwise sensitive information. Currently the company has a turnover of over €2.5 M, from which 90 percent comes from international markets. The company is operating in all the continents of the world, mostly through dealer network and partners. The company itself is still small; the number of employees is below thirty.

In terms of growth path, we can conclude that the company has reached "consolidation" phase nine years after it was established in 1997. During the first two years of operations, in a *pre-start phase*, the company focused on R&D-intensive projects and was supported by a local business incubator. The company developed two relatively unsuccessful innovations, but eventually the third innovation, a method for data overwriting, became a success. It was commercialized in 1999, and sold altogether 100,000 licenses within the first one and a half years.

The company actually *started* its operations in 2000, when it decided to concentrate its efforts on the development of the data erasure product and building its brand. The company started branding, and the product's brand name became the corporate brand. Soon afterward, the company became the market leader in Finland and was ready to aim for international markets. The company's approach to internationalization was to draw up country-specific strategies and create partnerships accordingly to support them. They entered several markets in Northern Europe, as well as Germany and Benelux countries.

High growth and internationalization strained the company's finances, and a venture capital investment was attained in early 2000. Due to the investment, the resources for further growth were assured. More experience of the markets in Northern Europe was added to the board by the venture capitalist (VC), and sales increased. After the increase in capital, the internationalization process continued with major leaps, when a global finance corporation became a client. This client led the company's markets to cover 23 countries, and its reference value was substantial for the company.

The company entered the major *growth* phase in 2002, when the half-million mark of sold licenses was reached, and the pace continued. Only a year after that, a total of a million licenses had been sold. It grew its international sales coverage through its own offices in order to improve the standard of service for its increasingly international or even global customer base. The growth was supported by the launch of a new product generation with more extensive features.

Since 2006 the company has entered a stable *consolidation* phase, where it focuses on managing its international operations actively and enters new partnerships when opportunities arise. It has increased its turnover and profitability by securing heavy users as customers while continuing to enter into partnerships. New markets are not proactively sought for, but the firm still intends to increase its share in current markets.

Company B was founded in 2000; its products are electronic patient diaries and wireless data collection solutions in all therapeutic areas. It targets a very narrow market segment with an innovative product. The customers are patients, clinical research professionals, site coordinators and data managers. The company has 13 out of 20 top pharmaceutical companies as clients, whose patients use their products in about 50 countries globally. The firm's main markets are the US and Europe, where the largest medical companies are located. The company's turnover has reached €8M, 50 percent of which comes from the US.

It seems that the company has gone through three distinct growth phases in its nine years of existence, and is currently in the "growth" phase. First, a short description of the *pre-start* phase: it was founded by people with experience from both the medical field and the telecom industry. Moreover, one of the founders has a famous relative in the telecom industry, and thus a highly recognizable name. Three months from establishment, the company introduced its first product. The commercialization of the product was successful and the company got three customers immediately. As the business idea appeared successful and the company targeted overseas, private investors also became interested in the company. The famous name among the founders brought even more credibility and lowered the threshold for investment. The first round of financing was used for speeding up R&D

process, sales and international expansion. A new, improved product was introduced after the first concept.

The company's activities started in 2001, and the actions taken toward international expansion were considered the right choice by the investors; a second round of financing followed soon after the first one. It decided to invest in customer service in its most important international markets. It had some 30 employees after establishing offices in the US, Sweden, and the Czech Republic. The internationalization efforts were supported by introducing internationally experienced board members and a third round of financing. By the end of 2002, the company already had 20 out of its 60 employees working in the US.

Since 2003, the company has been in the *growth* phase, starting from the funding it received from Tekes (Finnish Funding Agency for Technology and Innovation) and the other existing venture capitalists to develop a new product. The launch of the product was spurred by new international recruitment, including an American CEO. Increasing concentration on international markets also followed. Since then, the product and the company have received awards for innovativeness and the most recent evaluations suggest that the company's turnover will multiply in the following years.

Company C was founded in 1999 to develop mobile e-mail and office solutions. Its main product provides real-time access to different e-mail programs from mobile devices, and the customers are operators, device manufacturers, enterprises and individual consumers. The company is present in five major European markets through its own offices, and the product is available for corporate users in a number of European countries through partners, while individual users are able to obtain the product globally. In 2004, the company had a turnover of €200,000–400,000 and 40 employees; a year later was acquired by a US competitor in an all-stock trade.

In terms of growth, the company went through three distinct phases in its six years of existence. The acquisition in 2005 brought the company to its "consolidation" phase. When the company was in the *pre-start phase,* the mobile revolution was at hand in Finland and success in international markets was always the target. Consequently, English was the official company language from day one and foreign employees were deliberately hired soon. The company founders tried out several business and product ideas on industry experts, after which they adjusted them a few times before commercialization. Its original idea was to make the processes in field maintenance easier in several industries. The company introduced a business concept entailing a mobile middleware for enterprises.

Soon after foundation, the company's *start* had a major boost, when an experienced business angel joined the company as chairman. In addition to supporting decision making, and giving partner and customer leads, the business angel introduced the company to additional investors. The first round of financing from two venture capital companies was attained mostly due to the business angel's help. After that the venture capitalists, together with the business angel, contributed to fine-tuning the business plan. They decided to focus on developing mobile e-mail to telecom companies. The investments were used for speeding up the R&D process and building an international partnership network. The internationalization process was supported by recruitment: some 20 people were added to the company roster.

The *growth* spurt started when the company secured a second round of financing and attracted additional investments from Tekes. This led to new product introduction and establishment of a bridgehead in European markets with two lead customers in smaller markets. Soon after, it acquired a company in the UK, whose technology was wrapped with the company's existing application. More venture capital was attracted to support the new, larger company with a more extensive product. The larger company entity, the additional investments, and the increase in international presence were followed by a major recruitment effort. The company hired a foreign, internationally experienced CEO.

The internationalization development continued to be strong; partnerships and collaborative programs were used to increase recognition and market coverage. Additionally, their own network of offices was expanded in major markets. The consumer version of the product was made available globally, while its enterprise version had been licensed by partners and was available in major business centers in Europe and Asia. The year 2004 saw the turnover triple, but the company had not yet succeeded in making a profit.

In 2005, the company was acquired by a US competitor and reached the end of its independent growth phase. The acquirer revealed that the acquisition was based on the company's complementary market coverage and established partnerships with major players. The merged company now operates in all major markets and has many of the largest mobile operators as clients.

Company D was founded in 1999 to produce a wide range of digital entertainment. Currently it focuses on the development and publishing of downloadable games for mobile devices; the end customers are consumers, who are reached through a number of partners, including major telecom operators, media companies and entertainment portals. The company was acquired by a competitor in 2004 and remains as the European department of the acquiring company. Currently it has some 120 employees in Finland (out of a total of 400) and a turnover of €7.1 M from Finland.

The company went through three distinct growth phases in its five and a half years of independent existence, and the acquisition brought it to "consolidation" phase. The *pre-start phase* took place in 1999–2000, when the company was founded by two graphic designers, who initially employed a few software developers. There was little business or marketing knowledge in the firm. During the first one to two years, the company's business activities were very small-scale.

The activities started in 2000, when the business concept began maturing, as new people with experience from the wireless telecommunications and gaming field entered the management of the firm. The new CEO had experience in business analysis and his views led the company to focus on downloadable games for mobile devices. The number of employees rose to eight.

The *growth phase* started in the middle of 2002, when a hit game was released to take the company to a new level. The game suddenly sold a quarter of a million copies in 40 countries across the world, and gained approval both in the press and among the mobile game players. Awards and rewards followed. Next year the turnover reached €1.4 M and the number of employees increased to 15. In this rapid growth phase, the company needed to get new products to the market, and altogether 17 games were developed or bought from external game studios. A number of telecom operators and independent portals have been used for distributing the games since, which has guaranteed coverage in 50 countries worldwide.

During the observation period, the company was acquired by a US-based mobile application development company. It has a similar type of product offering, but with an emphasis on other types of entertainment than Company D. According to the acquirer, the value of company D was in its partnerships, geographical coverage, games and successful management team. The new company attracted €10 M of new venture capital right after the merger.

Cross-case Analysis

The previous section presented the internationalization of four Finnish technology-based new ventures. The growth paths and the critical incidents in them are gathered in Table 10.2.

It can be said as a summary that all the companies followed a "born global" path of internationalization according to the indicators presented in Figure 1. In the pre-start phase, companies A and D were founded on the basis of the individual skills of the founders. Company A tried to accomplish breakthrough technological innovations, while in company D the founders were using the dot-com boom as a means to capitalize their talent with the help of software programmers. They were seeking a radical innovation to lead them to more mature phases (cf. Churchill and Lewis 1983, Hanks et al.1993).

In contrast, companies B and C were founded on professional and business experience, which was to be capitalized through available connections and partnerships (also a factor promoting rapid initial internationalization, as suggested by Crick and Spence 2005). The commonly mentioned challenge that firms face early in their growth path, the lack of business knowledge (cf. Dodge and Robbins 1992), was not a problem for them. Companies A and D managed to solve their lack of business knowledge in

Table 10.2   Critical Incidents in the Case Companies

	Company A	Company B	Company C	Company D
Pre-Start	1997–1999 - Continuous search for innovation - 3rd product succeeds	2000–2001 - High profile management - Well-defined customer segment - 1st round financing	1999–2000 - Clear business profile from the beginning - Business angel: experience and contacts	1999–2000 - Propeller-heads producing digital entertainment - Lack of business and marketing approach
Start	2000–2001 - Image and corporate branding - VC - Unsolicited order from major global customer	2001–2002 - Commitment - Clear customer benefit - 2nd–3rd round financing	2000–2001 - First round financing: speeding up R&D process International partnership network development	2000–2002 - New CEO and other experienced recruits - Focus on mobile gaming
Growth	2002–2006 - Continuous growth through networks - Launch of new product generation	2003– - US markets started to take off - New product - New CEO and recruiting	2001–2005 - Product launch - Major contracts - Acquisition of a UK company - Additional financing - New CEO	2002–2004 - Hit product - Expansion of product line (17) - International distribution network development
Consolidation	2006– - Focus on most profitable customers - Global network of offices complemented by sales affiliates	*Potential future incidents:* *Exit of financiers: IPO, merger or acquisition*	2005– - Acquired by US competitor - Appreciated resources in acquisition: *markets* and *partnerships*	2004– - Acquired by US competitor - Appreciated resources in acquisition: *partnerships, markets, products, management team*

the start phase by getting experienced board members (A) or by recruiting a new CEO (D). The other external problems typically experienced in the pre-start phase (see Table 10.1) can also be identified in the case companies. Identification of a market niche and the resulting lack of sufficient domestic demand drove them all to internationalize rapidly. Moreover, availability of cash had to be guaranteed in the pre-start or start phase through venture capital in companies A, B and C. Only company D did not attain equity financing until the merger.

The start phase was characterized in all companies by product development and productization efforts, which were enabled by venture capital. There were no competition- or regulatory market change–driven external stimuli observed during the growth phase. Moreover, the difficulty of establishing new customer contacts has been mentioned both as one of the major problems in the early growth phases (cf. Dodge and Robbins 1992) and a stimulus for accelerated internationalization (Bell et al. 2001). Company A had a major stimulus to internationalize when it received an unsolicited order from a new customer. Companies C and D solved this problem by networking (company C already being in its start phase), whereas company B managed to get three large customers while still in its pre-start phase due to management contacts and well-planned segmentation.

In the growth phase, the case companies were determined to expand their market coverage and increase their involvement in their focal markets. In essence, this was a response to the challenge of location to reach customers better, but in a broad sense, it can also be interpreted as the delegation of responsibilities by the management (cf. Dodge and Robbins 1992, Hanks et al. 1993). The means used by case companies to increase their involvement in new markets were distribution contracts, partnerships, and their own offices. During the growth phase, companies B and C both recruited new CEOs in order to manage their further growth and international expansion. The problem of maintaining a cash flow (see Table 10.1) was not apparent in focal companies. This may be a result from the fact that venture capital was injected in all but company D.

Companies C and D have entered the consolidation phase in five to six years through mergers and ended their growth as independent companies. On the other hand, company A has slowed down its pace and entered a more stable state, while company B has not yet reached maturity even if it has some of the features that indicate such. It is still heavily financed by venture capitalists, which signals a major change coming in the near future.

DISCUSSION AND CONCLUSIONS

This chapter has sought to enhance understanding of how the life cycle theory of the firm and the "born global" model of internationalization intertwine. In order to do this, we have explored four case companies operating in the domain of software business and presented phases in their internationalization paths.

Transitions between the phases have been triggered by critical incidents, which have been solutions to either emerging or existing developmental challenges or "growth hurdles". The critical incidents leading to the decision to internationalize more rapidly, as presented by Bell et al. (2001) and Oesterle (1997) were supported by our findings. The case companies were established by people with high growth orientation. The external stimuli (e.g., the mobile revolution and the dot-com boom) during establishment promoted high growth and thus internationalization.

In companies B and C, the founders were determined to grow and internationalize their businesses. Nevertheless, an extra impetus to growth was given by the recruitment of new seasoned management (CEO). In general, it seems to be important for the advancement of many high-technology-based firms that the "father" of the original technological innovation is able to step back and accept the coming of professional management.

The development of an innovative product—often not the first one—acted as major internal stimulus for growth in the case companies. For example, in company A, the first two product concepts would probably not have offered such an opportunity for the firm outside its domestic markets, but the third one came with a clear customer benefit. Furthermore, this promoted external stimuli for growth in the form of new foreign customers.

The holistic approach to incidents triggering rapid initial internationalization of the firm (cf. Crick and Spence 2005) is supported to some extent by our study. Existing contacts and networks, together with earlier experience, have accelerated the first two phases of the internationalization process for companies B and C.

Indeed, firms following various internationalization pathways are expected to differ from each other regarding the prerequisites and accelerators of internationalization.[3] In this we follow the ideas of McHugh (1999), who, in his book focusing on the growth of the software business, notes that some characteristics of the firm are actually prerequisites for growth, whereas some characteristics accelerate the growth. These drivers include, e.g., international entrepreneurial orientation or global mindset (cf., e.g., Kuivalainen et al. 2004, Nummela et al. 2004). To summarize, as presented in the extant literature (cf. Oviatt and McDougall 1994, Knight and Cavusgil 1996, among others) and discussed above, a firm following the so-called born global pathway typically possesses the following characteristics:

- Growth-oriented, internationally experienced management team
- Credibility: ability to create "fast trust" and attract lead customers
- Innovation, core technology developed in-house
- Internationally experienced board, systematic international networking
- Packaged product/service and/or global niche market and strong product potential
- External financing (VC) and ability to attract it
- Growth is often gained through networking/use of partners or acquisitions enabled by external financing

These characteristics can be seen as prerequisites for a firm, as they enable it to follow the stereotypical born global internationalization pathway. In

Figure 10.2, the internationalization life cycle is divided into the previously defined four stages. Following the example of McHugh (1999) we have included so-called "steady state" into our model, as it is evident that many small firms are not willing or simply not able to grow after a certain stage.

In order to proceed to maturity, jump back to growth phase from the steady state, or be successful in the high growth phase which is characteristic of this born global pathway, the firm needs to be able to trigger fast international growth with several accelerators. Some of these critical incidents after the initial start of the internationalization seem to be a continuous stream of innovations, constantly improving product development, a sound business model and attractive value proposition for value-added resellers, distributors and customers, and the ability to attract further funding, thus securing the needed funds for accelerated growth, and finding suitable partners. In the case of our focal firms this is extremely important, as the average size of the Finnish venture capital investments is rather small. The question is not just about money either; the best possible option for a firm is to attract so-called smart money (which also incorporates business experience and contacts). However, the use of VC money may also determine the maturity/consolidation phase for a firm, as financiers typically aim for a relatively fast exit, either through an IPO or a trade sale of their portfolio companies.

Furthermore, growth management (i.e., the ability to leverage the firm's capabilities through effective knowledge management, recruiting and training) is needed. To sum up, a firm must succeed in numerous areas, rather than excelling just in just one area. This is naturally a challenge for managers in charge of rapid internationalization and public policymakers who wish to help them in this process. Providing tailor-made "right support at the right time" public support services for high-growth/high-risk firms is a challenge. Issues in such services or programs include assisting firms to access and leverage external sources of finance from venture capital

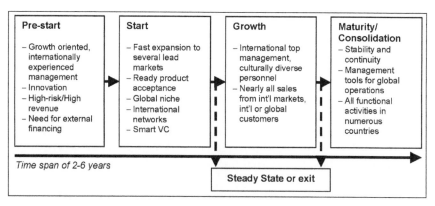

Figure 10.2 Accelerated growth/born global pathway.

providers, for example. They also involve helping improve firms' international market intelligence, in which online options need to be encouraged.

Overall, it is evident that more research into the longitudinal development of born global firms is needed. The literature to date has mostly neglected the fact that "born globals" experience gradually increasing commitment to foreign markets; only the length of the time span and the stages are shorter than in firms following the traditional "stages" pathway. Notable exceptions to this view have been presented by Hashai and Almor (2004) and Crick and Spence (2005), who noted gradual experience building even in rapid internationalization. Our chapter, with its four case studies, can hopefully add to this discussion.

Our opinion is that it is imperative to study the phases or stages even if the firm's life cycle is "condensed," in order to be able to understand how future firms may become born globals. Furthermore, we believe that analysis of critical incidents is an important means for gaining deeper understanding of the growth pathways in technology-based new ventures, and thus our results invite further empirical research into the topic.

ACKNOWLEDGMENTS

The authors wish to thank Toivo Äijö and Hanna Hanninen for their help in the process of developing the ideas behind this chapter and in the collection of the case materials.

NOTES

1. A common definition for a born global firm is that is has reached a share of foreign sales of at least 25 percent after having started export activities within three years of its foundation (e.g., Knight and Cavusgil, 2004).
2. Two main pathways for internationalization among new ventures seem to be the "traditional pathway," which closely resembles the incremental stage model of internationalization (cf. Johanson and Vahlne 1990), and the so-called "born global" pathway (e.g., Knight and Cavusgil 1996, Bell et al. 2003).
3. Naturally we have to accept the fact that there are also differences among firms following the same stereotypical pathway, just as there are individual differences in firms' internationalization paths (cf., e.g., Jones 1999). However, classifications are important tools for theory development (cf. Hunt 1991) and also have heuristic and analytical value. Managers can use them as exemplary cases in their strategic planning, for example.

BIBLIOGRAPHY

Äijö, T., Kuivalainen, O., Saarenketo, S., Lindqvist, J. and Hanninen, H. (2005) *Internationalization handbook for the software business*, Espoo, Finland: Centre of Expertise for Software Product Business.

Bell, J., McNaughton, R. and Young, S. (2001) '"Born-again global" firms—an extension to the "born global" phenomenon,' *Journal of International Management*, 7 (3): 173–189.

Bell, J., McNaughton, R. Young, S. and Crick, D. (2003) 'Towards an integrative model of small firm internationalization,' *Journal of International Entrepreneurship*, 1 (4): 339–362.

Bloodgood, J.M., Sapienza, H. and Almeida, J.G. (1996) 'The internationalisation of new high-potential U.S. ventures: antecedents and outcomes,' *Entrepreneurship: Theory and Practice*, 20 (4): 61–76.

Churchill, N. and Lewis, V. (1983) 'The five stages of business growth,' *Harvard Business Review*, 61 (3): 30–50.

Cope, J. (2003) 'Exploring the nature and impact of critical experiences within small business growth and entrepreneurial development,' *Lancaster University Management School Working Paper*, 2003/051.

Coviello, N.E. and Jones, M.V. (2004) 'Methodological issues in international entrepreneurship research,' *Journal of Business Venturing*, 19 (2): 485–508.

Crick, D. and Spence, M. (2005) 'The internationalisation of high performing UK high-tech SMEs: a study of planned and unplanned strategies,' *International Business Review*, 14 (2): 167–185.

Delmar, F., Davidsson, P. and Gartner, W.B. (2003) 'Arriving at the high-growth firm,' *Journal of Business Venturing*, 18 (2): 189–216.

Dodge, H. and Robbins, J. (1992) 'An empirical investigation of the organizational life cycle model for small business development and survival,' *Journal of Small Business Management*, 30 (1): 27–37.

Dodge, H., Fullerton, S. and Robbins, J.E. (1994) 'Stage of the organizational life cycle and competition as mediators of problem perception for small businesses,' *Strategic Management Journal*, 15 (2): 121–134.

Eisenhardt, K.M. (1989), 'Building theories from case study research,' *Academy of Management Review*, 14 (4): 532–550.

Gibb, A. and Davies, L. (1990) 'In pursuit of frameworks for the development of growth models of the small business,' *International Small Business Journal* 9 (1): 15–31.

Greiner, L.E. (1972) 'Evolution and revolution as organizations grow,' *Harvard Business Review*, 50(4): 37–46.

Hanks, S.H., Watson, C.J., Jansen, E. and Chandler, G.N. (1993) 'Tightening the life-cycle construct: a taxonomic study of growth stage configurations in high-technology organizations,' *Entrepreneurship Theory and Practice*, 18 (2): 5–29.

Hashai, N. and Almor, T. (2004) 'Gradually internationalizing "born global" firms: an oxymoron?' *International Business Review*, 13 (4): 465–483.

Hunt, S.D. (1991) *Modern marketing theory: critical issues in the philosophy of marketing science*, Cincinnati: South-Western Publishing Co.

Johanson, J. and Vahlne, J.-E. (1977) 'The internationalization process of the firm,' *Journal of International Business Studies*, 8 (1): 23–32.

Johanson, J. and Vahlne, J.-E. (1990) 'The mechanism of internationalization,' *International Marketing Review*, 7 (4): 11–24.

Jones, M.V. (1999) 'The internationalization of small high-technology firms,' *Journal of International Marketing*, 7 (4): 15–41.

Knight, G. and Cavusgil, S.T. (1996) 'The born global firm: a challenge to traditional internationalization theory,' *Advances in International Marketing*, 8: 11–26.

Kuivalainen, O., Sundqvist, S., Puumalainen, K. and Cadogan, J.W. (2004) 'The effect of environmental turbulence and leader characteristics on international performance: are knowledge-based firms different?' *Canadian Journal of Administrative Sciences*, 21 (1): 35–50.

Lester, D. and Parnell, J.A. (2008) 'Firm size and environmental scanning pursuits across organizational life cycle stages,' *Journal of Small Business and Enterprise Development*, 15 (3): 540–554.

Mamis, R.A. (1989) 'Global start-up,' *Inc.*, August: 38–47.

McHugh, P. (1999) *Making it big in software: a guide to success for software vendors with growth ambitions*, UK: Rubic Publishing.

Moen, O. and Servais, P. (2002) 'Born global or gradual global? Examining the export behavior of small and medium-sized enterprises,' *Journal of International Marketing*, 10 (3): 49–72.

Moore, G.A. (2004) 'Darwin and the demon: innovating within established enterprises,' *Harvard Business Review*, 82 (7/8): 86–92.

Nummela, N., Saarenketo, S. and Puumalainen, K. (2004) 'A global mindset—a prerequisite for successful internationalization?' *Canadian Journal of Administrative Sciences*, 21 (1): 51–64.

Oesterle, M.-J. (1997) 'Time span until internationalization: foreign market entry as a built-in mechanism of innovation,' *Management International Review*, 37 (2): 125–149.

Oviatt, B.M. and McDougall, P.P. (1994) 'Toward a theory of international new ventures,' *Journal of International Business Studies*, 25 (1): 45–64.

Oviatt, B.M. and McDougall, P.P. (1995) 'Global start-ups: entrepreneurs on a worldwide stage,' *Academy of Management Executive*, 9 (2): 30–43.

Parks, G.M. (1977) 'How to climb a growth curve: eleven hurdles for the entrepreneur-manager,' *Journal of Small Business Management*, 15 (1): 25–29.

Pauwels, P. and Matthyssens, P. (2004) 'The architecture of multiple case study research in international business,' in R. Marschan-Piekkari and C. Welch (eds.) *Handbook of qualitative research methods for international business*, 125–143, Cheltenham, UK: Edward Elgar.

Quinn, R.E. and Cameron, K. (1983) 'Organizational life cycles and shifting criteria of effectiveness: some preliminary evidence,' *Management Science*, 29 (1): 33–51.

Rennie, M.W. (1993) 'Global competitiveness: born global,' *The McKinsey Quarterly*, (4): 45–52.

Rialp, A., Rialp, J. and Knight, G.A. (2005) 'The phenomenon of early internationalizing firms: what do we know after a decade (1993–2003) of scientific inquiry?' *International Business Review*, 14 (2): 147–166.

Steinmetz, L.L. (1969) 'Critical stages of small business growth,' *Business Horizons*, 12 (1): 29–36.

Sullivan, D. (1994) 'Measuring the degree of internationalization of a firm,' *Journal of International Business Studies*, 25 (2): 325–342.

Tellis, W. (1997) 'Application of a case study methodology,' *The Qualitative Report*, 3 (3), http://www.nova.edu/ssss/QR/QR3–3/tellis2.html (accessed 15 December 2005).

Weinzimmer, L.G. (2000) 'A replication and extension of organizational growth determinants,' *Journal of Business Research*, 48 (1): 35–41.

Welch, L.S. and Luostarinen, R. (1988) 'Internationalization: evolution of a concept,' *Journal of General Management*, 14 (2): 36–64.

Part III

How Should We Study International Growth?

11 Toward a Typology of Rapidly Internationalizing SMEs

Jim Bell, Sharon Loane,
Rod B. McNaughton and Per Servais

INTRODUCTION

A longstanding criticism of export research is that a "mosaic of autonomous endeavors" (Aaby and Slater 1989) has contributed to conflicting findings that have only served to obfuscate our understanding of the issues. Contradictory results have often been explained by differences in contexts, definitions and methodological approaches (Leonidou 1995) and the failure to build on existing research has not been helpful. Regrettably, a similar situation is occurring in the allied field of SME internationalization (Coviello and Jones 2004) where the actors have been variously referred to as "committed internationalists" (Bonaccorsi 1992, Jolly et al. 1992) "born global" firms (Rennie 1993, Knight and Cavusgil 1996), "international new ventures" (McDougall et al. 1994, Oviatt and McDougall 1995, Shrader et al. 2000), or even "micromultinationals" (Dimitratos et al. 2003).

There is no doubt that the impact of new technologies and an increasingly interconnected global business environment influenced the growing incidence of SMEs that have rapidly entered international markets (Knight and Cavusgil 1996). Given widespread recognition of their growing importance (Bell et al. 2003, Rialp et al. 2005, Zahra 2005, Weerawardena et al. 2007, Zucchella et al. 2007), an attempt to clarify some mistaken assumptions and definitional ambiguities surrounding such firms is both apposite and overdue.

The objectives of this contribution are fourfold. First, we attempt to understand exactly what differences, if any, exist between alternative conceptualizations of rapidly internationalizing firms. Second, we discuss and critique a number of widely held assumptions regarding such firms. We illustrate the argument with examples from recent research conducted by the authors in different locations, within and across a variety of industry sectors. Third, we examine some of the existing definitions to clarify what constitutes "rapid" and "dedicated" internationalization. Finally, we propose a typology of rapidly internationalizing SMEs that attempts to integrate diverse, yet complementary, views, in order to offer a more holistic perspective for researchers and public policymakers alike. We conclude that this framework has important implications for policy, theory and future research.

THE GENESIS OF "BORN GLOBAL" AND RELATED TERMS

Although preceded by Bonaccorsi's (1992) Italian study on firm size and export intensity that identified "committed internationalists," it was really Rennie's (1993) seminal research among Australian firms that first drew widespread public policy and research attention to the phenomenon of rapid SME internationalization. Conducted under the auspices of McKinsey & Company, it coined the catchy "born global" sobriquet that rapidly entered the academic and business lexicon. While the study of this phenomenon quickly became a legitimate area of inquiry, (Madsen and Servais 1997, Coviello and McAuley 1999, Jones 1999, Harveston and Davis 2000, Knight and Cavusgil 2004, Rialp et al. 2005) we challenge the notion of "born global" firms (notwithstanding that the term is widely used as shorthand for rapid internationalizers), and a number of the assumptions that surround them in the following section.

Our challenge is consistent with the fact that, despite the emergence of the "BRIC" nations (Brazil, Russia, India and China) as important trading nations, a significant proportion of world trade is still concentrated between and within Ohmae's (1985) "triad" region of Europe, Japan and North America (UNCTAD 2008). It also reflects the findings of Rugman and Verbeke (2004) that only nine Fortune 500 companies were truly global, with the remaining MNEs engaging in regional business (cf. also Ohmae 1995, Rugman 2003, 2005).

Around the same time, McDougall et al. (1994) identified a similar phenomenon, where firms pursued "rapid and dedicated internationalization from inception . . . or shortly thereafter." These firms were considered "international new ventures" (INVs) if they generated more than 25 percent of sales from exports, served multiple markets (typically more than five) and internationalized within two years of formation. The significant contribution of these authors is evidenced in a series of key articles (Oviatt and McDougall 1995, 2005, McDougall and Oviatt 1997, 2000, Shrader et al. 2000). In their later articles, the definition of INVs was extended to include firms that had internationalized in less than six years.

More recently, Dimitratos et al. (2003) have provided evidence from a Scottish study of emergent international business players they term "micro-multinationals" (mMNEs). These firms operate in both high and low technology sectors, but tend to employ foreign investment modes, as well as contractual approaches, to enable them to internationalize more rapidly. In common with the notion of "born global" firms, there are some aspects of the INV and mMNE definitions that merit further scrutiny.

ASSUMPTIONS IN THE LITERATURE ON BORN GLOBAL FIRMS

We begin by exploring some typical assumptions regarding "born global" firms; first, that all *"born global" firms are truly born global*, when, in fact, few really are. At best, some may be "born international," operating in multiple markets; others may have a presence in regional markets ("born regional"), or target specific "lead" markets for their offerings (Madsen et al. 2000, Moen and Servais 2002, Chetty and Campbell-Hunt 2004). This behavior is quite common among software firms from many countries, where the US is often regarded as a key target market, as it consumes around 80 percent of all such products (Bell 1995). Similarly, many Finnish software firms also target Japan, the second largest market for software after the US, which is highly dependent on imported software products (Ojala and Tyrväinen 2007, 2008, Ojala 2009).

Furthermore, there is evidence that firms will target "lead" markets irrespective of location. Loane (2006) found that the US was a lead market for a large number of Australian, Canadian, Irish and New Zealand knowledge-based firms. As a major user/producer of new technology, with high per-capita income, demanding and innovative consumers and flexible innovation-friendly framework conditions for suppliers and users alike, it was often the first market targeted. However, regional influences were also evident. For example, all the Australian firms were also active in Asian countries such as China, Korea, Malaysia, the Philippines, Singapore and Thailand, with 30 percent of them active in Japan and New Zealand. Similarly, New Zealand firms were exporting to Australia and ASEAN countries. Conversely, while over 90 percent of Canadian firms exported to the US, as expected, many also targeted EU markets. Irish firms were particularly active in the EU, as well as the US. Industry and/ or sectoral considerations may also lead firms to target specific "lead" markets.

Cases A and B illustrate these exceptions to the notion of "born global." They show the importance of "lead" markets, and that firms may be quite content to focus on key international and/or regional markets. In pursuing key market concentration strategies, rather than market spreading (Piercy 1981), many demonstrate no real ambition to achieve a "global presence" by extending into other markets that present fewer opportunities and/or greater challenges.

Case A: "Lead/Key market player"

A New Zealand producer of sports motion analysis software made their first sale to the UK. Thereafter the firm entered Australia and India. This pattern reflected the cricket-playing nations of the world, as the motion analysis software was an invaluable training tool for coaches. Cricket boards in these countries represent "lead" markets for the software.

Case B: "International seller/Key markets"

This New Zealand designer and producer of an innovative, versatile container loading system, believed to be the first of its kind to operate on both sides of the host vehicle, made their first international sale to the US. The CEO commented, "The US military market is huge; if you want to sell to any military market that's the one to go for." Subsequent sales were made in the UK, Australia, Dubai and the United Arab Emirates.

Case C illustrates how a domestic market focus and strategy may result in international expansion into regional markets, where internationalization is not a primary objective but is clearly a secondary outcome. Again, in such cases the notion of establishing a "global presence" is notably absent.

Case C: "Born regional"
Not long after start-up, this small Finnish ICT consulting firm acquired the rights to distribute a financial software application from a US developer. It had originally intended to serve only the home market, but the US firm also included the rights for Norway and Sweden. Consequently, the Finnish firm rapidly entered these markets. It subsequently expanded its consulting services to other regional markets such as the Baltic States and Russia.

A second assumption is that *"born global" firms are new*. Although there is clear evidence that more firms are internationalizing rapidly and the recent "drivers" of this phenomenon are clearly identified in the literature (e.g., Knight and Cavusgil 1996), "born global" firms have existed for at least 100 years and probably more. For example, the rapid internationalization of the New Zealand dairy and meat industry came about with the development of refrigerated shipping in the 1880s. Similarly, new process technologies and materials influenced the rapid internationalization of an Irish firm, Belleek Pottery, following their participation at the Great Exhibition at the Crystal Palace in London in the 1850s. Thus, it may be argued that innovations in communication, transport or process technologies accelerate internationalization in any era, increasing the volume of activity and attracting new actors (Knight et al. 2001).

A third assumption is that *"born global" firms are exclusive to knowledge-based sectors* (such as IT, software or biotech). Analyses of the internationalization patterns of such firms dominate the current research on early and rapid internationalization, and some firms do owe their existence to emergent technologies and tend to internationalize rapidly because they possess unique knowledge and are at the leading edge of developments. However, many rapidly internationalizing firms operate in more traditional industries (see, e.g., Knight et al. 2001). These industries are becoming more knowledge-intensive with advances in process technologies or new materials (for example, in clothing and textiles or food and drink sectors). An Irish manufacturer of beverage dispensing systems for beer and soft drinks that developed a more efficient production process, enabling it to be internationally competitive from inception, provides an illustration of this point (Bell et al. 2003).

Fourth, a frequent assumption is that *"born global" firms are only located in advanced Western economies*. While past inquiry has tended to focus on such locations, there is evidence of rapid internationalization of firms located in the new EU member states, Latin America, the Middle East and the BRIC nations. In part, this reflects economic transformation and greater economic integration, but technological "drivers" are also a major factor (e.g., case D).

Case D: Rapid internationalization from emerging market

This Indian engineering services company was founded in late 2005, and is focused on enabling the capital equipment industries to better leverage higher capability at lower cost from India. Within 14 months, the company had 65 employees and international Fortune 1000 clients in the semiconductor equipment, instrumentation and renewable energy industries. In 2006, it received US$4 million funding from Intel Capital, JAFCO Asia and the KT Venture Group. The company now has offices in North America and a European office in the Netherlands.

Finally, both the *"born global" and INV literatures focus almost exclusively on "outward" internationalization*, which is often measured by level of export sales. However, as Welch and Luostarinen (1988) assert internationalization is both an inward and outward process (see also Korhonen et al. 1996). What has been largely ignored to date are the "inward" activities of firms that source internationally and therefore have an international orientation, but do not have any significant export activities. Moreover, in other cases "inward" activities, such as the acquisition of new technologies or networks, may influence future "outward" movements. Cases E and F provide an illustration of the latter.

Case E: "Born international sourcer"

This small Australian firm was originally set up in the early 1980s to distribute imported foreign-language films to a large immigrant population. Subsequently it began to subtitle and dub films into English. In 1992, as the Australian film industry gained worldwide notoriety (e.g., through the *Neighbours* soap), it was approached by an Australian filmmaker to dub films into foreign languages for international distribution. Several years later, on the recommendation of a local client, it was asked by an overseas production company to dub foreign films into English for international distribution. The firm formed a strategic alliance with this contact and now has export sales of more than US$2 million.

Case F: "Born international sourcer"

Established in the early 1980s, this Irish firm produced anodized aluminum profiles used in kitchens and showers. It also made picture frame profiles. Even before starting production, it had to source equipment and machinery from Germany and the US. Once it entered production, profiles were purchased from Norway, chemicals from the UK and other components from Italy. Initial sales were to the Irish and UK markets, but within a few years it was also selling to Belgium, Holland, Germany, Switzerland and even Iran. Within three years only 10 percent of sales were obtained in the Irish market.

In both these cases, inward technology transfers improved the firms' capabilities and influenced subsequent internationalization.

DIFFICULTIES IDENTIFYING BORN GLOBAL FIRMS

We now turn our attention to several difficulties in identifying, classifying and measuring both "born global" firms and INVs (for an extensive discussion of these issues, see Hurmerinta-Peltomaki 2004). These relate to the scope and pace of internationalization and to the time span from inception. As defined in the INV literature (McDougall et al. 1994, Shrader et al. 2000), achieving an export ratio of 25 percent in multiple markets within two (or six) years of inception constitutes "rapid" and "dedicated" internationalization.

Such performance may be regarded as impressive in firms operating in a large domestic market such as the US, but is not especially noteworthy for those located in small open economies. High-technology firms located in small countries may have no domestic sales whatever, or have export ratios in excess of 70–80 percent (Loane 2006). Moreover, active internationalizers in "traditional" sectors in are also likely to have higher export ratios because of a smaller domestic market.

Several issues merit further discussion: First, *not all firms that meet the INV criteria may actually be INVs*, nor can they really be regarded as "born global." For example, a Canadian firm that exports 25 percent of its output to the US within 2–6 years and has a further 1 percent of total sales in four or five other countries may be an "international seller," but cannot really be regarded as an INV or a "born global" firm. Similarly, an Irish or Danish firm that sells more than 25 percent of its output to other EU countries may be "born regional," but cannot truly be regarded as "born global". Indeed, in the context of EU integration, it is debatable if these sales even qualify as "export" activity. Furthermore, employing export ratios as a key internationalization performance measure is not wholly satisfactory, particularly if, as suggested by Dimitratos et al. (2003), some SMEs use investment modes in order to enter foreign markets.

Second, *not all rapid internationalizers are INVs or "born globals."* There is clear evidence from the literature that some firms internationalize very rapidly after concentrating exclusively on the home market for a long period. Bell et al. (2001) call these firms "born-again globals" as a change in market focus follows a critical incident or a combination of events, such as new ownership or management, an acquisition, involvement of venture capitalists or relationships with new clients with extensive international operations (Barkema and Vermeulen 1998). Cases G through K illustrate a variety of circumstances in which older firms suddenly began to internationalize rapidly.

Case G: Late rapid internationalizer (via new client)
    Established in 1983, this Irish bakery internationalized very rapidly in the mid-1990s. Subway had just established its Irish operations and was seeking a local supplier of chilled part-baked bread. So successful was this relationship that in less than two years it was also supplying Subway franchisees in Egypt, Portugal, the UK and a number of other European countries. These contracts provided the impetus for the firm to develop other markets on its own behalf in Sweden and Holland, by supplying produce direct to large retail chains. Currently, almost half its production is destined for export markets.

Case H: Late rapid internationalizer (via acquisition)
    Formed in 1986, this UK firm manufactures remote-operated underwater vehicles used in the offshore oil exploration industry. Originally the main target market was the UK, but orders were also obtained from Norwegian operators in the North Sea in 1990. Conscious that these oil reserves were finite, the firm acquired a foreign company in the early 1990s to enable it to develop alternative products and new markets. It currently employs 30 staff and exports 55 percent of its US$5 million turnover; new markets resulting from the acquisition include Singapore and Brazil.

Case I: Born-again global (under new management)
    Founded in 1848 to print railway tickets, this New Zealand firm now supplies printed security products (e.g., postage stamps). It first exported on a sporadic basis, but a turning point came in late 1991 when it won a contract to print 79 million definitive stamps for New Zealand Post. As a result, Crown Agents in London gave it accreditation to produce stamps for up to 40 Commonwealth countries that do not have their own production facilities, although export volumes remained small. It went into receivership in 1999, and was bought by existing management. They invested in new technology and the company has become a niche supplier of "special" stamps in the southern hemisphere. It is now an aggressive exporter, with an export ratio of 60 percent, serves over 30 markets, and has 80 employees and a sales turnover of $NZ 9 million.

Case J: Born-again international (taken over)
    A "specialist" engineering firm in New Zealand established in the early 1970s, until 1988, it had primarily focused on the domestic market, with sporadic contracts in Australia, and had a turnover of less than US$1 million. In 1988, it was acquired by a US company and expanded rapidly into

a number of export markets where the new parent had business (including Argentina, Chile and Ireland). It also obtained significant new business in the US via the parent company. It remains a small operation with less than 30 permanent staff. Exports currently account for most of its US$5 million turnover; these involve individually negotiated turnkey projects

Whether or not "late" rapid internationalizers like these firms are more successful than their INV counterparts is the subject of much current speculation and requires further inquiry. However, what is certain is that internationalization is unlikely to have taken place in the absence of one or more critical incidents that influenced the firms' subsequent strategies.

In terms of speed of entry to international markets, vital pre-export activities in the domestic market may need to precede international activities. For example, firms seeking to internationalize via a franchising mode may first have to spend time to develop the business concept and format successfully at home. Similarly, biotechnology firms may have new offerings at a research and development (R&D) stage for five years, or even longer, before they can be commercialized. Thus, there may be an extensive "prenatal" phase required to establish proof of concept, meet legal requirements, etc., sometimes even before the firm has incorporated, and certainly before they can be classified as "born global." However, once necessary approvals have been obtained, they may internationalize very rapidly. Case K is an example of a firm whose internationalization fits this pattern.

Case K: Late technology-based "born global"

This Hungarian company was founded in 2001 with the goal of becoming a product, service and solution provider in the field of molecular diagnostics and pharmaceutical R&D. Its aim was to provide high-throughput screening of drug candidates for the pharmaceutical and agrochemical industries. The company refined the processes involved and was ready to commercialize by 2005. It then obtained patents and the necessary permissions, which took 18 months and went to the US market, and later to the rest of Europe. In all, it took more than six years before it was fully able to operate internationally.

Another example is in computer software where firms often provide consultancy services to local clients in order to obtain the revenue stream needed to develop and commercialize applications internationally. In such cases, the time span from inception to internationalization may be longer than envisaged in the born global and INV literature. This raises the issue of whether inception should be regarded as the date the firm was formed, or if it should it be judged from when the firm first has its offer ready for commercialization.

In many cases, the management of such firms will have a global vision from inception, even if they are unable to implement an internationalization strategy straight away. Conversely, some firms may have been established with the intention of serving clients in the domestic market, but have subsequently internationalized because of referrals from clients based in the domestic market, as illustrated by Case L (see also Cases E and G).

Case L: Initial domestic focus/late rapid internationalization

This Northern Ireland firm developed a range of card-operated electronic management systems used to monitor usage of multiple-user copiers. Founded in 1983, it obtained orders from UK subsidiaries of large MNC office equipment suppliers such as Xerox and Fuji. Following an MBO in 1987, it began to pursue more aggressive international strategies and several of its UK MNC clients recommended its offerings to corporate headquarters or subsidiaries in other countries. Before being acquired by a US company in 2005, it employed more than 50 staff and exported over 70 percent of its products to more than 40 markets including Australia, the Netherlands and the US.

In these cases, the activities of a domestic client, either a local firm or an MNE subsidiary, led to rapid internationalization because of existing relationships with affiliated subsidiaries in other countries or other client/supplier networks.

DISCUSSION AND CONCLUSION

We hope the points raised in the previous sections are a catalyst for debate around rapid internationalization and not the somewhat narrower INV perspective, or the increasingly nebulous "born global" view. Researchers need to recognize that rapid internationalization may occur at various points during a firm's development and not just at inception. Moreover, inward internationalization may occur in advance of any outward activities and the latter may be initiated through contacts established in the domestic market.

Similarly, public policy in support of internationalization should reflect cognizance that different rapid internationalization trajectories will necessitate diverse forms of intervention, assistance and support (see Bell et al. 2003, Wright et al. 2007). In order to advance this argument, we present a typology of rapid internationalizing firms that seeks to encapsulate and integrate the extant perspectives in a more holistic manner (see Figure 11.1).

The typology of rapidly internationalizing SMEs shown in the figure suggests that International New Ventures may take the form of firms that operate in global markets, adopt a regional focus, target a limited number of key countries or operate in multiple markets, but are not truly global in terms of reach. Additionally, such firms may source internationally, whether or not they have any export activity. Those engaged in outward internationalization may employ investment modes as well as contractual approaches.

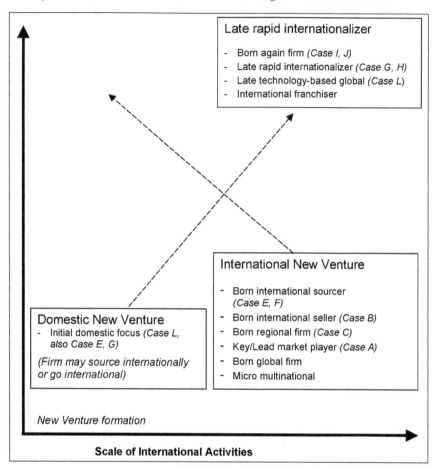

Figure 11.1   Typology of rapidly internationalizing SMEs.

Late rapid internationalizers may be "born-again" firms that become active internationally due to a critical incident or a combination of events that has forced them to look outside the domestic market. Alternatively, they may be firms that always intended to internationalize as soon as they had the requisite capabilities, conditions and resources.

Domestic new ventures are, as the name implies, firms that focus their initial sales efforts on the domestic market. Such firms may or may not source internationally. They may also subsequently go international via referrals from clients located in the domestic market or because they identify other exporting opportunities.

Born-again local ventures may be ones that have restructured, for whatever reason (such as an MBO, an acquisition, or being acquired), but might also include those that significantly changed their business model, entered new market segments/sectors, or acquired new processes or technologies. Again, these firms may or may not source internationally, but if they do, they may be very active in terms of the wider definition of internationalization.

From an academic perspective, the proposed typology allows researchers to move on from merely classifying firms as "born global" or "INVs" to focusing on much more critical issues, such as if and how rapidly internationalizing firms can achieve sustained international competitiveness. To date there is a dearth of longitudinal inquiry into "born globals" and INVs. Are they able to continue to internationalize rapidly and if so, how? In the long run, are late rapid internationalizers more successful than those that start the process early, or vice versa? And if so, how and why?

From a public policy perspective, recognition of a wide range of internationalization patterns raises many questions. Are the support needs of early and rapid internationalizers the same as those of born-again global firms? Do they have the same information needs? Do they require different forms of financial support or other assistance? Are current policy measures best configured to assist firms that have different international trajectories, or is it still a one size fits all approach? For example, biotechnology firms are likely to have much higher up-front R&D costs, necessitating greater financial support compared to other knowledge-intensive sectors.

Should policymakers recognize that firm internationalization is much broader than exporting, and consider how to enable firms to benefit from "inward" activities such as acquiring new technologies, or sourcing lower-cost raw materials or components from abroad? Should they be more active in supporting other forms of outward internationalization and not just exporting? Finally, to what extent could they influence the development of domestic market networks that might influence future international activities?

We believe that the answers to these and other important questions lie, at least in part, in persuading academic researchers to focus much more clearly on the issues that surround rapid internationalization, regardless of whether it occurs at inception or at a subsequent point in time. To do so requires us to reach a better consensus on definitional and theoretical issues. Our intention is that the typology presented herein, together with the holistic perspective it seeks to provide, may prove useful in this process.

BIBLIOGRAPHY

Aaby, N.E. and Slater, S.F. (1989) 'Management influences on export performance: a review of the empirical literature 1978–88,' *International Marketing Review*, 6 (4): 7–26.

Barkema, H.G. and Vermeulen, G.A.M. (1998) 'International expansion through start-up or through acquisition; an organizational learning perspective,' *Academy of Management Journal*, 41 (1): 7–27.

Bell, J. (1995) 'The internationalisation of small computer software firms—a further challenge to 'stage' theories,' *European Journal of Marketing*, 29 (8): 60–75.

Bell, J., McNaughton, R. and Young, S. (2001) '"Born-again global" firms—an extension to the "born global" phenomenon,' *Journal of International Management*, 7 (3): 173–189.

Bell, J., McNaughton, R., Young, S. and Crick, D. (2003) 'Towards an integrative model of small firm internationalization,' *Journal of International Entrepreneurship*, 1 (4): 339–362.

Bonaccorsi, A. (1992) 'On the relationship between firm size and export intensity,' *Journal of International Business Studies*, 23 (4): 605–635.

Coviello, N.E. and Jones, M.V. (2004) 'Methodological issues in international entrepreneurship research,' *Journal of Business Venturing*, 19 (4): 485–508.

Coviello, N.E. and McAuley, A. (1999) 'Internationalisation and the smaller firm: a review of contemporary empirical research,' *Management International Review*, 39 (3): 223–256.

Chetty, S. and Campbell-Hunt, C. (2004) 'A strategic approach to internationalisation: a traditional versus "born global" approach,' *Journal of International Marketing*, 12 (1): 57–81.

Dimitratos, P., Johnson, J., Slow, J. and Young, S. (2003) 'Micromultinationals: new types of firms for the global competitive landscape,' *European Management Journal*, 21 (2): 164–174.

Harveston, P.D. and Davis, P.S. (2001) 'Entrepreneurship and the born global phenomenon: theoretical foundations and a research agenda,' in J. Butler (ed.) *E-commerce and entrepreneurship: research in entrepreneurship and management*, 1–30, Charlotte, NC: Information Age Publishing.

Hurmerinta-Peltomaki, L. (2004) 'Conceptual and methodological underpinnings in the study of rapid internationalizer,' in M.V. Jones and P. Dimitratos (eds.) *Emerging paradigms in international entrepreneurship*, 64–88, Cheltenham, UK: Edward Elgar.

Jolly, V.K., Alahuhta, M. and Jeannet, J.P. (1992) 'Challenging the incumbents: how high technology start-ups compete globally,' *Journal of Strategic Change*, 1 (2): 71–82.

Jones, M.V. (1999) 'The internationalization of small high-technology firms,' *Journal of International Marketing*, 7 (4): 15–41.

Knight, G. and Cavusgil, S.T. (1996) 'The born global firm: a challenge to traditional internationalization theory,' *Advances in International Marketing*, 8: 11–26.

Knight, G. and Cavusgil, S.T. (2004) 'Innovation, organizational capabilities, and the born-global firm,' *Journal of International Business Studies*, 35 (2): 124–141.

Knight, J., Bell, J. and McNaughton, R. (2001) '"Born globals": old wine in new bottles?' Paper presented at the Australian and New Zealand Marketing Academy Conference, http://smib.vuw.ac.nz:8081/WWW/ANZMAC2001/anzmac/AUTHORS/pdfs/Knight.pdf (accessed 20 May 2010).

Korhonen, H., Luostarinen R. and Welch, L.S. (1996) 'Internationalization of SMEs: inward–outward patterns and government policy,' *Management International Review*, 36 (4): 315–329.

Leonidou, L.C. (1995) 'Empirical research on export barriers: review assessment and synthesis,' *Journal of International Marketing*, 3 (1): 29–43.

Loane, S.P. (2006) 'The role of the internet in the internationalisation of small and medium sized companies,' *Journal of International Entrepreneurship*, 3 (4): 263–277.

Madsen, T.K., Rasmussen, E. and Servais, P. (2000) 'Differences and similarities between born globals and other types of exporters,' *Advances in International Marketing*, 10: 247–265.

Madsen, T.K. and Servais, P. (1997) 'The internationalisation of born globals: an evolutionary process?' *International Business Review*, 6 (6): 561–583.

McDougall, P.P., Shane, S. and Oviatt, B.M. (1994) 'Explaining the formation of international new ventures: the limits of theories from international business research,' *Journal of Business Venturing*, 9 (6): 469–487.

McDougall, P.P. and Oviatt, B.M. (1997) 'International entrepreneurship literature in the 1990s and directions for future research,' in D.L. Sexton and R.W. Smilor (eds.) *Entrepreneurship 2000*, 291–320, Chicago: Upstart Publishing.

McDougall, P.P. and Oviatt, B.M. (2000) 'International entrepreneurship; the intersection of two research paths,' *Academy of Management Journal*, 43 (5): 902–906.

Moen, O. and Servais, P. (2002) 'Born global or gradual global? Examining the export behavior of small and medium-sized enterprises,' *Journal of International Marketing*, 10 (3): 49–72.

Ohmae, K. (1985) *Triad power: the coming shape of global competition*, New York: Free Press.

Ohmae, K. (1995) *The end of the nation state: the rise of regional economies*, New York: Free Press.

Ojala, A. (2009) 'Internationalization of knowledge-intensive SMEs: the role of network relationships in the entry to a psychically distant market,' *International Business Review*, 18 (1): 50–59.

Ojala, A. and Tyrväinen, P. (2007) 'Entry barriers of small and medium-sized software firms in the Japanese market,' *Thunderbird International Business Review*, 49 (6): 689–705.

Ojala, A. and Tyrväinen, P. (2008) Best practices in the Japanese software market,' *Global Business and Organizational Excellence*, 27 (2): 52–64.

Oviatt, B.M. and McDougall, P.P. (1995) 'Global start-ups: Entrepreneurs on a worldwide stage,' *Academy of Management Executive*, 9 (2): 30–43.

Oviatt, B.M. and McDougall, P.P. (2005) 'Defining international entrepreneurship and modeling the speed of internationalization,' *Entrepreneurship Theory and Practice*, 29 (5): 537–554.

Piercy, N. (1981) 'British export market selection and pricing,' *Industrial Marketing Management*, 10 (4): 287–297.

Rennie, M.W. (1993) 'Global competitiveness: born global,' *McKinsey Quarterly*, (4): 45–52.

Rialp, A., Rialp, J. and Knight, G.A. (2005) 'The phenomenon of early internationalizing firms: what do we know after a decade (1993–2003) of scientific inquiry?' *International Business Review*, 14 (2): 147–166.

Rugman, A.M. (2003) 'The regional solution: triad strategies for multinationals,' *Business Horizons*, 46 (6): 3–5.

Rugman A.M. (2005) *The regional multinationals: MNEs and 'global' strategic management*, Cambridge: Cambridge University Press.

Rugman, A.M. and Verbeke, A. (2004) 'A perspective on regional and global strategies of multinational enterprises,' *Journal of International Business Studies*, 35 (1): 3–18.

Shrader, R.C., Oviatt, B.M. and McDougall, P.P. (2000) 'How new ventures exploit trade-offs among international risk factors: lessons for the accelerated internationalization of the 21st century,' *Academy of Management Journal*, 43 (6): 1227–1247.

UNCTAD World Investment Report (2008) http://www.unctad.org/en/docs/wir2008_en.pdf (accessed 15 March 2009).

Weerawardena, J., Mort, G.S., Liesch, P.W. and Knight, G. (2007) 'Conceptualizing accelerated internationalization in the born global firm: a dynamic capabilities perspective,' *Journal of World Business*, 42 (3): 294–308.

Welch, L.S. and Luostarinen, R. (1988) 'Internationalization: evolution of a concept,' *Journal of General Management*, 14 (2): 36–64.
Wright, M., Westhead, P. and Ucbasaran, D. (2007) 'Internationalization of small and medium-sized enterprises (SMEs) and international entrepreneurship: a critique and policy implications,' *Regional Studies*, 41 (7): 1013–1030.
Zahra, S. (2005) 'A theory of international new ventures: a decade of research,' *Journal of International Business Studies*, 36 (1): 20–28.
Zucchella, A., Palamara, G. and Denicolai, S. (2007) 'The drivers of early internationalization of the firm,' *Journal of World Business*, 42 (3): 268–280.

12 Sampling Frames for Cross-national Survey Research in International Entrepreneurship

Scott Paul Johnston, Marian V. Jones, Anna Morgan-Thomas and George I. Vlachos[1]

INTRODUCTION

Internationalization research concerns the increasing exposure and involvement of firms in international business activities, whereas international entrepreneurship (IE), is currently defined as the "discovery, enactment, evaluation, and exploitation of opportunities—across national borders—to create future goods and services," (Oviatt and McDougall 2005, 540), processes which ipso facto include internationalization, i.e., the transfer of goods services and business activities across borders. Research in this field (using the wider concept of IE) entails study of entrepreneurial behavior, at the level of the individual and the firm, and comparison across countries. In this chapter we focus on IE as a process of behavior manifest at the level of the firm rather than the individual.

The collection of data in multiple country settings is essential to increasing our understanding of international entrepreneurship and cross-country comparisons facilitate the search for universality and highlight the nature of differences in business processes and behaviors at individual and firm level. The identification of suitable sampling frames presents a key challenge in that context. The sampling frame in the first instance is a list representing the population under study. If it is considered that the population of interest is the population of firms that are involved in international business activity, including those that are small and young as well as established and large, those at various stages of international development, and those that are international new ventures, born globals, multinationals and so on, the sampling frames used must accommodate those types of firms and enable their selection in the sampling process.

In cross-national research of IE, the sampling frames must not only capture the range of international activity with which firms are involved, they also need to enable sampling equivalence across the countries of interest and provide some degree of homogeneity across national samples. This is a challenge in IE research, given that identification of firms at the early stages of internationalization in single countries from existing databases has consistently proved to be problematic (OECD 1997).

The selection of sampling frames for cross-national surveys has received much attention in the broader social science literature. Indeed, one study of 703 journal articles on organizations found that the majority of researchers do not pay sufficient attention to population and sampling issues (Drabek et al. 1982). In the international entrepreneurship (IE) context limited discussion has addressed the methodological issues and effects associated with population identification and the adequacy of sampling frames (Coviello and Jones 2004). Moreover, Coviello and Jones (2004) call for more attention to be paid to the discussion of sampling frames in IE research. The purpose of this chapter is to make a preliminary selection and evaluation as a basis and stimulus for further investigation and debate. The purpose of this chapter is to raise questions and discussion concerning the identification and use of sampling frames for survey research in internationalization and IE. To that end we explore the literature on sampling frames for criteria guiding the selection and usefulness of databases available for survey research. For reasons of parsimony, we assume that the planned survey for which a database is being sought will be a cross-national survey of small and medium-sized enterprises (SMEs) in the European Union (EU). After identifying suitable selection and evaluation criteria, we choose and evaluate four databases that have potential for use as sampling frames to identify internationalizing SMEs, and support survey-based primary research studies. In this chapter we do not investigate the potential of any databases for secondary data analysis.

SAMPLING FRAMES IN CROSS-NATIONAL RESEARCH

A sampling frame is understood as a complete list of all cases in the population from which the sample is drawn, and represents a vital component of every survey (Lohr 2008). From a pragmatic perspective, the sampling frame often represents a starting point for the survey, providing the definition for the surveyed population and information needed for stratifying, sampling and contacting businesses (Colledge 1995). Provision of a sampling frame and correcting frame errors can account for a significant proportion, sometimes exceeding 20 percent, of the research budget (Colledge 1995). The costs concern the outlay for the frame as well as the cost of correcting and adjusting the frame to suit the research objectives. In the context of international entrepreneurship research, for example, identification of smaller and younger enterprises represents a common problem (Jones 1999).

The choice of sampling frame has important consequences for the generalizability and the impact of research findings (Kohn 1987). The classical statistical theory and the inferential paradigm provide legitimacy to the IE research practice of building general theories from research on samples. The theory allows drawing general conclusions because it assumes that the probability distribution limits the possible biases and errors in data and that the findings from samples can be extended to populations (Handwerker and Wozniak 1997). This assumption only stands if probability sampling is used, i.e., when any element of the population has a known and equal probability of being included in the sample (Groves and Peytcheva 2008). Finding a suitable sampling frame represents a key precondition for probability sampling ensuring that any element of the population has an equal probability of being selected (Levy and Lemeshow 1999).

The sampling frame also affects the generalizability of findings: by providing the definition of the surveyed population, the sampling frame delineates the group of research units to which the researcher wishes to generalize (Miller and Salkind 2002). Importantly, the findings apply only to the surveyed population and one cannot generalize beyond the sampling frame (Cowan 1991, Levy and Lemeshow 1999). For example, from a purist perspective, the findings derived from a sample of Danish born global firms can only be extended to the population of born globals in Denmark.

The search for high-impact, generally applicable theory is but one reason for extending the research beyond national borders (Harkness 2008, Kohn 1987). Cross-national research studies either compare countries or regions on different dimensions, or aggregate estimates from different countries (Lynn 2003). The aggregation of data permits the extension of findings to a larger population, thus affecting the generality and the validity of interpretations derived from single-nation studies (Kohn 1987). In the context of IE research, these studies are fundamental to the search for universality and the nature of differences between SMEs (Coviello and Jones 2004).

Compared with surveys carried out within a single nation, cross-national surveys involve an extra layer of complexity in terms of both organization and design (Lynn et al. 2007). In comparative research, data must not only be valid and reliable for a given national context but also comparable across contexts (Harkness 2008). The search for comparability of results, referred to as equivalence (Usunier 1998) represents the most important methodological aspect of cross-national research. Within that context, the choice of sampling frame has important implication for sampling equivalence— the extent to which samples are comparable (Coviello and Jones 2004). Sampling equivalence assures the validity of results and valid results mean that any differences detected in cross-national surveys can be attributed to dissimilar characteristics of the countries and not caused by differences in research samples (Sin et al. 1999). For example, Busenitz et al. (2000) and Mueller and Thomas (2001) administered their questionnaires to business students rather than entrepreneurs, across six and nine countries respectively, in order to ensure homogeneity across respondents and avoid the need for controls for differences in demographic variables.

Comparable sampling frames and the resulting equivalent cross-national samples reduces the likelihood of two types of error: sampling frame error and coverage error. Sampling frame error is the degree to which the sampling frame fails to account for the whole population (Lohr 2008). An incomplete or inaccurate list means that some cases will have been excluded, so it will be impossible for every case in the population to have a chance of selection. In extreme cases, a potential sampling frame may be "empty" if the frame contains no elements of the target population (Kish 1965). If a frame includes lists of liquidated companies, efforts to contact defunct sampling units and distinguish them as non-respondents can significantly increase survey costs and bias (Colledge 1995).

For accurate coverage a sample must include all units in the population of interest and coverage might be defined as a percentage of population of interest that is included in the sampling frame (Lohr 2008). The main concern about undercoverage is that it can lead to misleading or a biased estimate of population quantities particularly if a segment is missed that differs on key measurements from the surveyed population (Lohr 2008). For example, it is relatively easy to identify older and larger, particularly if they are limited companies or registered for VAT (value added tax, applicable across EU countries at varying levels). By comparison, it is difficult to find sampling frames accounting for very young or very small firms (Cowan 1991, Jones 1999). Sampling frames for business surveys concerned with the study of small companies are harder to find, as smaller enterprises tend to be more specialized and localized than larger firms (Coviello and Jones 2004, Cowan 1991). The overrepresentation of a particular segment of the population or overcoverage can also be problematic. For example, the sample might include a disproportionately large number of firms from certain industries: in the IE context, typically, high-tech enterprises.

In summary, identifying suitable sampling frames for cross-national research in the context of SME internationalization represents a key stumbling block in moving the field forward. Sampling frames affect what we know about small firm internationalization by influencing the generalizability of results and research errors. Sampling frames play a significant role in integration of survey data, and their presence ensures that the data can be meaningfully related for a synergic gain, where the combined data sets contains more information that the sum of separate parts (Colledge 1995). The lack of adequate sampling frames precludes the identification and delineation of and access to comparable research samples.

ASSESSMENT CRITERIA FOR CROSS-NATIONAL SAMPLING FRAMES

Given the complex nature of cross-national research, the assessment of sampling frames must take into account the validity and reliability of national samples, as well as their appropriateness of the sample for cross-national design (Harkness 2008). In terms of general assessment criteria for sampling frames, Kalleberg et al. (1990) examined five common databases using three criteria including the *publisher details*, inclusion criteria, search criteria, and electronic availability; *timeliness*, how often the database is updated; *auxiliary information*, what auxiliary information is available for each company, such as company name and address; and *units of analysis*, whether or not the directory includes information to head office detail or branch detail, which may lead to issues regarding duplicate entries. According to Aldrich et al. (1989), two additional useful measures for assessing potential sampling frames are *practicality*, the ease of identifying units of analysis, and *costs*, in monetary terms (costs stated in this article were correct at the time of research).

Furthermore, Kish (1965) posits a five-dimensional model for assessing bias: *missing elements*, whether or not the sampling frame excludes units intended to be represented in the study population; *clusters of elements*, whether or not a sampling unit represents a cluster of units (for example, a household rather than an individual); *foreign elements*, whether or not the possibility of including units outside of the target population exists; *duplicate listings*, whether or not a sampling unit is listed more than once; and *factual and temporal inaccuracies*, such as the inclusion of liquidated businesses or provision of incorrect addresses. Unless a database is electronic and updated frequently, however, this dimension is likely to render most paper-based databases obsolete immediately after publication, due to the frequency of firms' going out of business. It should be noted that although the aforementioned headings provided suitable criteria for the purposes of this paper, formal use of this framework would require further methodological evaluation and verification.

Finally, Saunders et al. (2007) consider five criteria: *relevance* (whether cases listed in the sampling frame are relevant to the topic), *timeliness* (how up-to-date the data is), *comprehensiveness*, *precision* and *control* (whether the researcher can establish and control how the sample is selected).

In addition to the general criteria, in the context of cross-national research the problem of sampling equivalence should be considered. Two aspects of equivalence merit particular attention for a study concerned with IE. First, there is the issue of sample equivalence and the notion of comparability of samples obtained from different national settings (Coviello and Jones 2004). This issue pertains to the notion of population coverage within a country. A separate question concerns international coverage of the sampling frame and the issue of whether populations from different countries are represented adequately. We assume that a suitable sampling frame for cross-national research would be accurate in terms of representing the population of enterprises within each country and have sufficient breadth to provide data concerning several different countries.

Based on the above discussion and considering the context and purpose of the IE research, this study evaluates the relevant databases based on and extending Saunders' (2007) criteria. Thus, the criteria we use are: 1) practicality, 2) coverage, 3) precision, 4) equivalence and 5) cost. *Practicality* refers to the ease of use including researchers' ability to identify the units within the database and to control them through relevant search criteria. *Coverage* is defined as the extent to which the listing includes the all relevant units of analysis. This dimension encompasses *comprehensiveness* (whether all units are listed), *relevance* (whether cases are listed in the sampling frame relevant to the topic), and *timeliness* (how up to date the listings are). *Precision* refers to the ease of identification of the relevant units of analysis made possible through auxiliary information, and its freedom from bias. Finally, *equivalence* denotes the extent to which the frame generates samples that can be compared cross-nationally, and *cost* relates to the price of data elements and the overall costliness of the sampling process (Aldrich et al. 1989, Kish 1965, Saunders et al. 2007).

EVALUATION PROCEDURE

The evaluation procedure we adopted was as follows. First, based on our knowledge of internationalization and international entrepreneurship we established a set of criteria for the selection of databases. Next, we accordingly selected four databases as examples and examined them with regard to inclusion of the elements identified in the previous section as being relevant to the process of sampling and the subject discipline. We then prepared a descriptive overview of each database before proceeding to an evaluation based on our five criteria.

We were concerned with the identification and evaluation of suitable sampling frames for IE research. To be considered suitable, the potential sampling frame had to meet four criteria. The first is that the database should include firms of all sizes. While IE research is not confined to SME studies their importance is such that a potential sampling frame ideally should include listing of SMEs. There is no single, uniformly acceptable definition of a small firm (Storey 1994) and the definition adopted here follows that of the European Commission (2003), which describes SMEs as firms employing fewer than 250 employees.

The second is that the database should have international coverage in order to be suitable for cross-national research. Although global coverage would have been desired, in this study we considered European coverage as a minimum inclusion criterion. We defined European as involving the EU countries: that is, Austria, Belgium, Bulgaria, Cyprus, the Czech Republic, Denmark, Estonia, Finland, France, Germany, Greece, Hungary, Ireland, Italy, Latvia, Lithuania, Luxembourg, Malta, the Netherlands, Poland, Portugal, Romania, Slovakia, Slovenia, Spain, Sweden, and the UK.

The third is that the database should be reasonably universally accessible. One aspect we considered concerned the availability of listings to the researcher. Some countries such as Norway and Sweden maintain lists of all businesses, containing very comprehensive information, and make these available to researchers under certain conditions (Kalleberg et al. 1990). Although the UK Office of National Statistics collects comprehensive information on 99 percent of UK businesses, including details such as industry classification, employee numbers, and turnover, such data is not universally available to researchers by legislation. Consequently, this chapter will discuss a selection of databases generally available to all researchers in all locations that might be used for the purposes of cross-national as well as nationally focused studies. The availability of such sampling frames was a noted as a problem faced by 61 percent of countries in a 1997 OECD study. Coviello and Jones (2004), commenting on this problem, suggest that list brokering tends to prevent access by researchers with tight budgets. Another aspect of accessibility concerns the ease of use. Although there are several business directories and listings available to the authors, limited language capability made it difficult for the authors to access and use foreign equivalents of, for example, the UK Companies House listings. Furthermore, local technical barriers prevented access to telnet-based databases.

The fourth, and perhaps most important, criterion is that the database should potentially include firms at all stages of internationalization, including those that have not yet commenced international activity, as well as those that may have abandoned it. Export directories, commonly used in studies of exporting, international marketing, and international trade, do not necessarily include firms that are involved in other modes of international business activity. Therefore they are not fully representative of the population of internationalizing firms.

Export directories are not the most appropriate sampling frames if the purpose of the study is to identify internationalizing firms from a holistic perspective in which inward, outward and cooperation modes of activity as well as, or instead of, "export" sales are relevant. Finely grained studies seeing to examine, for example, the instances of born global firms, the development of cross-national relationships, networks or firms' transfer of knowledge need to use databases that cover a wider population of firms than that provided by export directories. Notwithstanding their obvious suitability for export studies, we excluded export directories from this evaluation for the reasons discussed.

We selected four databases for evaluation that met the above selection criteria: Yellow Pages, Kompass, Amadeus, and MarketEurope. Following selection, we scrutinized each database for key elements for comparison and on which to base our evaluation (Bureau van Dijk 2009, Dun & Bradstreet 2009, Kompass 2009, Yellow Pages 2009). The elements, listed as headings in Table 12.1, are: *Units of Analysis, Search Criteria, Auxiliary*

Table 12.1   A Summary of the Databases Examined

	Units of analysis	Search criteria*	Auxiliary information returned†	Timeliness	Potential sources of bias	European coverage	Estimation of country equivalence
Electronic Yellow Pages	Head offices and branches for various organizations	Company name; business type; location	Telephone number; facsimile number; e-mail address; and Internet address	Real-time updates	- No formal industry codes used - Registration (paid) required - No distinction made between branches and headquarters - Individual directories are non-equivalent - Liquidated firms likely to be in database	Can be considered as fully comprehensive as equivalents exist in all EU countries	Medium—Various companies in different countries collect Yellow Pages data
Kompass	Head offices of manufacturers	Company name; sales bands; number of employees; trade names; registered number; year incorporated; legal form; product (using a unique classification system); executive name; executive job title; country; town/city; postcode; region; state; export indicator; import indicator; export countries; know-how; trademarks; e-mail indicator; web address indicator; telephone indicator; fax indicator; telephone STD code; fax STD code	Financial information; trade association memberships; branch addresses; agents; and quality assessments	CD/DVD ROM editions updated bi-annually Internet edition updated weekly	- Focuses on manufacturers - Duplication issues arising from the fact companies can pay to have additional listings - Only represents a selection of the population despite its larger size	Subscriptions to other databases necessary for fully comprehensive coverage of the EU	High—Collected by one source

AMADEUS	Head offices of private and public organizations	Company name; identification numbers; geographic location; activity/industry; brand names; no. of employees; financial data and ratios; credit score or rating); ownership status; holding companies; shareholders; subsidiaries; group of companies; M&A deals; stock data; publicly listed status; directors/contacts; advisors/auditors; auditors; legal form; accounts type; miscellaneous	As search criteria	CD/DVD ROM edition updated monthly; Internet edition updated weekly	Only represents a selection of the population despite its larger size	Fully comprehensive	High—Collected by one source
MarketEurope	Head offices and branches for various organizations	D-U-N-S number; business number; company name; address details; executive name; executive gender; executive function; US 1987 SIC codes (line of business); no. of employees; sales in Euros; sales in US dollars; legal status; year started; import/export indicator; company status (headquarters/branch/single location)	Profit and loss information; turnover information; and the name of the company secretary	Weekly updates	- Only represents a selection of the population despite its larger size	Subscriptions to other databases necessary for fully comprehensive coverage of the EU	High—Collected by one source

*AMADEUS contains more than 150 different types of search criteria. Consequently, only the broad criteria headings have been included.
†In addition to search criteria.

Information Returned, Timeliness, Potential Sources of Bias, European Coverage and Estimation of Country Equivalence. Drawing on these tabulated details and experience gained through online exploration of the database websites, we prepared a descriptive overview of each before making a more in-depth evaluation following the set of five evaluative criteria drawn from the literature as discussed.

OVERVIEW OF THE SELECTED DATABASES

Electronic Yellow Pages Directories

The Yellow Pages is an easily accessible directory of business names, addresses and telephone numbers classified under occupationally-related headings. In terms of the search criteria available, the researcher is restricted to searching by company name, business type or location in each respective version of the Yellow Pages. Companies, defined as "advertisers," are included on payment of an annual fee. Provided by the Yell Group, the UK edition was first launched in 1966, and contains over 448,000 unique companies listed within its database. In addition to its paper-based database, its online equivalent, Yell.com provides a free-to-search database of over 1.7 million UK businesses. Although the Yell Group produces directories only for the UK and USA, all other EU countries have their own equivalent of the Yellow Pages, both in paper format and online. They include the Portuguese *Páginas Amarelas*, containing more than 400,000 businesses, the French *Les Pages Jaunes*, containing more than 556,000 businesses, and the Dutch *Gouden Gids*, containing more than 650,000 businesses. As some directories are displayed in the local language, a comprehensive critique of all EU country listings is not feasible in the scope of this chapter; instead we have focused on the Internet editions, which are more widely accessible.

Kompass Database of Industrial and Commercial Companies

The Kompass database of industrial and commercial companies is a commercial database for business-to-business commerce that, in total, encompasses over 1.7 million companies. Kompass Group products are franchised to major international publishers such as Reed Elsevier and Bonnier. The researcher is given the option of accessing the databases in print format, on CD-ROM, or via the Internet. The Western European edition of the Kompass databases contains over 700,000 companies, who can register a base level of data with Kompass for free, and may elect to include additional information for a fee payment. The largest group of users, 40 percent, access Kompass for some form of research, including academic investigation. A wide range of search criteria are available to the researcher (examples are listed in Table 12.1), including company name, number of employees, trade names, product, and year incorporated. Kompass uses its own unique product classification system instead of generic codes such as the US Standard Industrial Classification (SIC) Codes. English is the primary language of all products, although the databases have been indexed in 40 other languages to allow foreign users to explore the database in their own languages. There appears to be no in-depth examination of Kompass databases in a peer-reviewed literature search.

Amadeus

Amadeus is a pan-European database containing information on 6.5 million public and private companies. Within this figure 1.5 million companies are located in the UK. Published by Bureau van Dijk, Amadeus data derive from around thirty varied sources designed for both commercial and academic researchers. Indeed, Fame, a localized version of Amadeus covering the UK and Ireland, was accessible at local university and city libraries. The database is available on the Internet, as an intranet feed or on CD/DVD-ROM. The authors were able to secure free-trial access to the Internet Version of Amadeus. Company listings are compiled on the basis of the content of about thirty different databases, including data from local chambers of commerce. It is not possible for companies to register directly with Amadeus, and drawing as it does on so many other sources, Bureau van Dijk suggests that Amadeus is the most representative databases for European companies. The researcher is offered a very large number of search criteria (examples listed in Table 12.1), including company name, number of employees, trade names, industry, and year incorporated. It should be noted that Amadeus uses multiple industry classifications in addition to the US SIC. The software also enables the user to include any exclusion criteria in searches, such as EU members-only options, for example, to eliminate countries such as Switzerland, before presenting final results. As with Kompass, there appears to be no in-depth examination of Amadeus in a peer-reviewed literature search.

Dun & Bradstreet MarketEurope Database

Dun & Bradstreet (D&B) Corporation was formed in 1841 as the Mercantile Agency to provide company information for US merchants. D&B offers a variety of commercially available databases to suit various organizational functions; the database of interest in this discussion is designed for sales departments to identify new prospects within Europe. Referred to as MarketEurope, this Internet-only database contains information on around 9.5 million active European businesses. It is compiled from a variety of sources, including official government sources. Furthermore, companies are able to register on MarketEurope free of charge. The researcher is offered a very large number of search criteria (see examples in Table 12.1), including company name, number of employees, trade names, industry, and year incorporated. In addition to the US SIC codes, D&B databases, like Kompass, have a unique classification system, known as D-U-N-S numbers, to identify businesses for data-processing purposes.

In the academic literature relating to business and management, D&B databases are evaluated on the basis of their usefulness for building sampling frames. The general points from this literature suggests that D&B databases tend to give varied coverage of individual industries (Murphy 2002); concerns regarding its representativeness (Aldrich et al. 1989; Kalleberg et al. 1990), and timeliness (Buss et al. 1991) are reported. Nevertheless, it should be cautioned that three of these papers were written prior to the popular adoption of the Internet, and more up-to-date reports from researchers using them are called for. Furthermore, D&B claim to have increased the size of their database eightfold to reduce the bias towards particular industries, as well as making the basic level of registration free for new companies.

COMPARATIVE EVALUATION OF THE SELECTED DATABASES

The suitability of each database for cross-national research in the IE context is assessed using five general criteria suggested in the literature on sampling frames: *practicality, coverage, precision, equivalence* and *cost* (Kalleberg et al. 1990, Aldrich et al. 1989, Kish 1965, Saunders et al. 2007). Each criterion draws on several of the elements listed in Table 12.1.

Practicality

Practicality refers to the ease of use, including researchers' ability to identify the units within the database and control them (Saunders et al. 2007). In terms of *practicality*, access to Yellow Pages is readily available via the Internet. However, a researcher may be restricted in using international versions of the Yellow Pages, as language barriers may prevent accurate searching. In addition, the Yellow Pages offer no facility to export records into database or spreadsheet software, resulting in the researcher having to enter each record manually before conducting a mail survey. Furthermore, a researcher wishing to access the paper edition may be restricted to listings from their own country, as their own municipal or academic libraries may only stock their national editions. By contrast, Kompass, Amadeus and MarketEurope allow higher levels of control, enabling the researcher to search for companies using various criteria that can be exported into any spreadsheet or database software. Amadeus and MarketEurope also provide custom-designed record management software.

Coverage

Coverage is defined as the extent to which the listing includes all relevant units of analysis. This dimension encompasses comprehensiveness (whether all units are listed), relevance (whether cases are listed in the sampling frame relevant to the topic), and timeliness (how up to date the listings are). Considering the problem of self-selection (firms have to pay to register), Yellow Pages is likely to have *missing elements*, thus questioning its comprehensiveness. The Yellow Pages may also exclude companies without a telephone number, though these are likely to be few in number: a problem which may increase as the range of alternative communication technologies (e.g., mobile telephones) increases. As regards *clusters of elements*, the Yellow Pages includes company branches as well as head office addresses, therefore suggesting there is a risk of incorrectly selecting units outside the target population. This also increases the risk of *duplicate listings*, as does the fact that businesses may pay to have more than one listing within a directory under different categories. Other *foreign elements* include the fact that large-scale enterprises (with 250 or more employees) and public sector organizations are listed alongside SMEs. No defining criteria or search terms, other than broad categories, are provided by the Yellow Pages to allow manual removal of such elements. The database is updated weekly, although no mention is given concerning what is done to remove businesses that have been liquidated.

A different set of limitations affects the coverage of the Kompass database. Kompass is mainly restricted to companies who manufacture components or end products; service providers, for example, are likely to be a *missing element*. Not all manufacturers have registered with Kompass, subjecting the database to a degree of bias. As regards *clusters of elements*, Kompass lists branches under a main head office heading, which reduces the risk of *duplicate listings*. However, companies may be listed more than once if they pay for additional listings. Although large-scale enterprises are listed alongside SMEs, the search criteria provided allow *foreign elements* to be filtered with ease. Indeed, the majority of the database contains SMEs. For example, 157,000 out of 180,000 companies in the United Kingdom Gold database had 249 or fewer employees. Finally, as regards *factual and temporal inaccuracies*, CD-ROM editions are issued biannually and Internet editions are updated in real time. Kompass markets their product as being continuously updated by extensive research involving company visits and follow-up telephone calls to ensure accurate data. The database lists only active businesses.

Amadeus does not cover all 20 million SMEs within the EU, and could not therefore be considered comprehensive. Furthermore, inclusion is based on minimum financial performance criteria that are sufficiently high to exclude very small, very new firms, or those operating at low revenues. Nevertheless, the database is not based on registration by individual businesses, broadening the general scope of the database. As regards *clusters of elements*, Amadeus lists branches under a main head office heading, reducing the risk of *duplicate listings*. The two-level search facility also enables *foreign elements*, such as large-scale enterprises or non-EU members, to be filtered with ease. Finally, as regards *factual and temporal inaccuracies*, updated CD/DVD-ROM editions are issued monthly and are available for an additional fee. Internet editions are updated in real time, and Bureau van Dijk will, purportedly, e-mail the researcher any changes to the data of the selected companies. Such facilities cannot be verified using the trial edition.

MarketEurope includes companies with eleven or more employees (note that other Dun and Bradstreet databases, such as Global Reference Solution, include firms as small as one employee). As our working definition of SMEs includes companies of between one and ten employees, this would bias the final sampling frame as the population would not be fully represented. As the database is partially dependent on registration, not all companies will have registered with the database. As regards *clusters of elements*, MarketEurope lists branches and company headquarters separately. However, branch listings are easily identifiable as a "branch entry" as opposed to an "HQ entry" and removable, reducing the risks of *duplicate listings*. As regards *foreign elements*, some criteria, such as large-scale enterprises, can be filtered with ease using the search criteria, though others, such as non-EU members, need to be removed manually. Finally, as regards *factual and temporal inaccuracies*, updated CD/DVD-ROM editions are issued quarterly and are available for an additional fee. Internet editions are updated in real time. Each edition, according to D&B, is updated using 2,000 separate auditing procedures. Although D&B are ready to admit that their information changes rapidly, they offer no facility to keep the researcher informed of the changes.

Precision

Precision refers to the ease of identification of the relevant units of analysis made possible through auxiliary information. For example, for IE studies that focus on smaller, younger enterprises, the auxiliary information providing information regarding the foundation of the firm would enable one to select a representative sample of firms based on age. In the Yellow Pages the *auxiliary information* provided to the researcher is restricted to basic details such as company name, address telephone number, facsimile number, e-mail address, and Internet address. By contrast, Amadeus provides a wealth of auxiliary information including geographic location, industry, brand names, financial data, etc. The search facility allows a high level of precision, for example, the researcher would be able to search for the desired target population between types of foundation year, types of product manufactured, and countries, superficially supporting the creation of a statistically representative sampling frame.

Kompass and MarketEurope records provide additional information such as financial information, return, profit and loss information, turnover information, and the name of the company secretary, in addition to the search criteria in Table 12.1. *Units of analysis* for both databases are provided on the basis of branch and head office listings, with branch addresses listed as separate records. If the sampling frame is intended to represent the population of small, young and new firms, the researcher would be able to search for the desired sample using the type of firm, the foundation year, or the industry (using US SIC codes), which would support the creation of a statistically representative sampling frame before carrying out a main survey.

Cost

As regards *costs*, all Internet editions of the Yellow Pages are free to search, but lack of facilities to manage and effectively search for the relevant listings means that substantial costs would be incurred in selecting and sorting the relevant entries. These expenses have to be considered when comparing the Yellow Pages with the paid listings such as Kompass, Amadeus or MarketEurope. In contrast to the Yellow Pages, all the other databases charge per unit. The unit price is based on the amount of information being retrieved: each additional detail about the unit incurs additional cost. To provide some indication of the cost, MarketEurope, for example, charges £0.14–0.15 for each company name accompanied by telephone number. Additional information, such as the address, company size, or its age are priced separately and added to the unit price. The researcher using these databases faces a trade-off between either paying a high initial price for each entry in order to assure precision and limit the number of questionnaire questions, or paying a lower initial price for each unit with a risk of lower accuracy and lower response rate.

Estimated Equivalence

As the data is collected by a single source, MarketEurope can be considered to have high estimation of sampling equivalence. However, subscriptions to additional Dun & Bradstreet databases would be necessary to achieve a fully comprehensive sample from all EU countries.

Similarly, Kompass data is collected by a single source and can be considered to have high estimation of sampling equivalence. However, as with Dun & Bradstreet, subscriptions to additional Kompass databases would be necessary to achieve a fully comprehensive sample from all EU countries. As the data is collected by a single source, Amadeus can be considered to have high estimation of sampling equivalence, and is also fully comprehensive of all European countries. The Yellow Pages can be considered to be fully comprehensive as equivalents exist throughout the EU; however, due to the other limitations discussed above, researchers are advised to cross-check data with other lists and be prepared to spend time cleaning the sample of duplicate listings.

A detailed literature search has indicated that, in terms of sampling frames, the Yellow Pages is a database well used and discussed in academic literature across disciplines. Indeed, various studies have described the UK Yellow Pages as a useful sampling frame for business research (Burton and Wilson 1999, Emerson and MacFarlane 1995, Errington 2008). However, using Chi-Squared statistical procedures, Emerson and MacFarlane (1995) found Yellow Pages to be only 62.9 percent representative of a population census. To counter this, Kalleberg et al. (1990) suggests that the Yellow Pages should be used in conjunction with a standard telephone directory, referred to as the White Pages. The White Pages generally suffer from the same problems regarding bias as the Yellow Pages. Businesses do not pay for a White Pages listing, which increases coverage; however the White Pages are updated less frequently (annually in the UK), will exclude companies that have chosen to be unlisted, and only certain telecommunications companies provide directories listing their own customers, with few cable companies producing any form of directory. These problems are compounded when cross-country comparative research is planned and sampling equivalence using these listings seems unlikely to achieve without considerable cross-checking and referencing on the part of the research team.

DISCUSSION AND CONCLUSIONS

In conclusion, this chapter has defined sampling frames as master lists of a population from which a non-biased sample can be drawn. Sampling frames, typically constructed using various types of databases, are subject to various forms of sampling error that can affect the quality and reliability of finished research. By conducting a systematic review of databases, the researcher should be able to determine the best possible database for the least possible cost. Despite this, studies and discussions concerned with sampling frames in business and management research are limited in general and yet are of particular importance in IE research in which the units of analysis may be difficult to find. To this end, we proposed a multi-stage process of selection and evaluation and by way of demonstration applied it to four commercially available databases for potential use in a cross-national survey of SMEs in the EU.

Cross-national surveys differ from national surveys in a number of ways. Their main use is to compare countries and regions on different dimensions or to aggregate estimates from a number of countries in order to provide an estimate relating to supra-national regions (Lynn et al. 2007). A two-step procedure is typically involved in designing the cross-national survey; first, to decide which countries to include and second, how to select units within the countries (Lynn et al. 2007). We suggest that for IE research a prior step is needed: to determine whether the population of interest is the population of internationalizing firms, or the population of (for example) SMEs, of which those with international activities are a subgroup, and select a database representative of that population. To date, for example, the extensiveness of the born global phenomenon is undetermined, but research addressing that question is overdue.

Our evaluation of four example databases is preliminary and invites more detailed analysis in future research. As Table 12.1 indicates, databases vary considerably in the breadth and depth of information that they contain. Further research in this area could statistically compare the representativeness and coverage of these databases regarding their inclusion of internationalizing firms and data relevant to the study of international entrepreneurship across countries.

Outside the IE field, studies in the UK and US have been carried out at the state or county level to this effect, commenting on the exact representativeness of the database concerned, and any industrial or sectoral biases within that database (Aldrich et al. 1989, Burton and Wilson 1999, Buss et al. 1991, Emerson and McFarlane 1995, Errington 1985, Kalleberg et al. 1990, Murphy 2002). These authors also suggest that, where possible, more than one database should be used in the construction of a sampling frame.

Future research may wish to include formal tests to give statistical provenance to any subjective criteria. Our preliminary database evaluation procedure was derived from a review of literature on sampling frames and with insight from our work in the IE field. Future research may involve developing formal sub-criteria to make the review procedure more methodologically robust, such as following a content analysis approach (Titscher et al. 2000). More immediately, full and critical evaluation by researchers of the usefulness and limitations of the databases, directories and lists used to identify populations and samples for IE research will help in defining the parameters of the field, the extensiveness of IE activity among firms and across countries, and contribute to the development of robust empirical enquiry. Most important, cross-national collaboration and sharing of datasets among IE researchers will enhance and strengthen the field.

NOTES

1. Authors' names are listed alphabetically.

BIBLIOGRAPHY

Aldrich, H., Kalleberg, A., Marsden, P. and Cassell, J. (1989) 'In pursuit of evidence: sampling procedures for locating new businesses,' *Journal of Business Venturing*, 4 (6): 367–386.

Bureau van Dijk (2009) Company website, available at http://www.bvdep.com (accessed 9 June 2009).

Burton, R.J.F. and Wilson, G.A. (1999) 'The Yellow Pages as a sampling frame for farm surveys: assessing potential bias in agri-environmental research,' *Journal of Rural Studies*, 15 (1): 91–102.

Buss, T.F., Lin, X. and Popovich, M.G. (1991) 'Locating new firms in local economies: a comparison of sampling procedures in rural Iowa,' *Journal of Economic and Social Measurement*, 15 (1): 45–55.

Busenitz, L.W., Gómez, C. and Spencer, J. (2000) 'Country institutional profiles: unlocking entrepreneurial phenomena,' *Academy of Management Journal*, 43 (5): 994–1003.

Colledge, M.J. (1995) 'Frames and business registers: an overview,' in B.G. Cox, D.A. Binder, B.N. Chinnappa, A. Christianson, M.J. Colledge and P.S. Kott (eds.) *Business survey methods*, 21–47, New York: John Wiley and Sons Inc.

Coviello, N.E. and Jones, M.V. (2004) 'Methodological issues in international entrepreneurship research,' *Journal of Business Venturing*, 19 (4): 485–508.

Cowan, C.D. (1991) 'Coverage issues in sample surveys: a component of measurement error,' *Marketing Research*, 3 (2): 65–68.

Drabek, T.E., Braito, R., Cook, C.C., Powell, J.R. and Rogers, D. (1982) 'Selecting samples of organizations: central issues and emergent trends,' *Pacific Sociological Review*, 25 (3): 377–400.

Dun & Bradstreet (2009) Company website, available at http://www.dnb.com (accessed 9 June 2009).

Emerson, H. and MacFarlane, R. (1995) 'Comparative bias between sampling frames for farm surveys,' *Journal of Agricultural Economics*, 46 (2): 241–251.

Errington, A. (1985) 'Sampling frames for farm surveys in the UK: some alternatives,' *Journal of Agricultural Economics*, 36 (2): 251–258.

European Commission (2003) 'Commission Recommendation of 6 May 2003 concerning the definition of micro, small and medium sized enterprises 2003/362/EC,' *Official Journal of the European Union*, 46 (124): 36–41.

Groves, R.M. and Peytcheva, E. (2008) 'The impact of nonresponse rates on nonresponse bias,' *Public Opinion Quarterly*, 72 (2): 167–189.

Handwerker, W.P. and Wozniak, D.F. (1997) 'Sampling strategies for the collection of cultural data: an extension of Boas's answer to Galton's problem,' *Current Anthropology*, 38 (5): 869–875.

Harkness, J. (2008) 'Comparative survey research: goals and challenges,' in J.J. Leeuw and D.A. Dillman (eds.) *International handbook of survey methods*, 456–477, New York, London: Lawrence Erlbaum Associates.

Jones, M.V. (1999) 'The internationalization of small high technology firms,' *Journal of International Marketing*, 7(4): 15–41.

Kalleberg, A.L., Marsden, P.V., Aldrich, H.E. and Cassell, J.W. (1990) 'Comparing organizational sampling frames,' *Administrative Science Quarterly*, 35 (4): 658–688.

Kish, L. (1965) *Survey sampling*, New York: John Wiley and Sons Inc.

Kohn, M.L. (1987) 'Cross-national research as an analytic strategy,' *American Sociological Review*, 52 (6): 713–731.

Kompass (2009) Company website, available at http://www.kompass.com (accessed 9 June 2009).

Levy, P.S. and Lemeshow, S. (1999) *Sampling of populations: methods and applications*, 3rd ed., New York: John Wiley and Sons Inc.

Lohr, A. (2008) 'Coverage and sampling,' in J.J. Leeuw and D.A. Dillman (eds.) *International handbook of survey methods*, 97–112, New York, London: Lawrence Erlbaum Associates.

Lynn, P. (2003) 'Developing quality standards for cross-national survey research: five approaches,' *International journal of Social Research Methodology*, 6 (4): 323–336.

Lynn, P., Hader, S., Gabler, S. and Laaksonen, S. (2007) 'Methods for achieving equivalence of samples in cross-national surveys: the European Social Survey experience,' *Journal of Official Statistics*, 23 (1): 107–124.

Miller, D.C. and Salkind, N.J. (2002) *Handbook of research design & social measurement*, London: Sage Publications.

Mueller, S.L. and Thomas, A.S. (2001) 'Culture and entrepreneurial potential: a nine country study of locus of control and innovativeness,' *Journal of Business Venturing*, 16 (1): 51–75.

Murphy, G.B. (2002) 'The effects of organisational sampling frame selection,' *Journal of Business Venturing*, 17 (5): 237–252.

OECD (1997) Globalisation and Small and Medium Enterprises, Vol. 1, Synthesis Report, Publications of the Organisation for Economic Co-operation and Development, Paris.

Oviatt, B.M. and McDougall, P.P. (2005) 'Defining international entrepreneurship and modelling the speed of internationalization,' *Entrepreneurship Theory and Practice*, 29 (5): 537–553.

Saunders, M., Lewis, P. and Thornhill, A. (2007) *Research methods for business students*, London: Prentice Hall.

Sin, L.Y.M., Cheung, G.W.H, and Lee, R. (1999) 'Methodology in cross-cultural consumer research: a review and critical assessment,' *Journal of Business Ethics*, 9 (6): 457–471.

Storey, D.J. (1994) *Understanding the small business sector*, London: Thomson Learning.

Titscher, S., Meyer, M., Wodak, R. and Vetter, E. (2000) *Methods of text and discourse analysis* (B. Jenner, Trans.), London: Sage Publications.

Usunier, J.-C. (1998) *International and cross-cultural management research*, London: Sage Publications.

Yellow Pages (2009) Company website, available at http://www.yell.com (accessed 9 June 2009).

13 Export Behavior, Growth and Performance of SMEs

Does Ownership Matter?

Jorma Larimo

INTRODUCTION

The intensification of competition on a global scale has led to an increasing number of firms seeking opportunities in international markets to achieve their objectives, as well as to safeguard their market positions and survival. The most common mode of foreign operation in small and medium-sized companies (SMEs) has been export. Research into firms' export behavior, strategies and performance can be considered to date back to the early 1960s, the study of Tookey (1964) being the first one trying to analyze the factors associated with successful exporting. Since then the amount of research focusing on exports and other forms of foreign operations has increased significantly, especially since the 1980s. At the same time, the earlier focus on large companies has expanded to cover the exports and internationalization of SMEs as well.

According to statistics from IFERA (International Family Enterprises Research Academy) the role of family-owned firms is very important in various European countries. Their share of all firms ranges from 60 to 93 percent, of all employees from 40 to 60 percent and of GNP from 40 to 60 percent (IFERA 2003). The share of family-owned companies is especially high (approximately 80 percent or more) in European countries like Finland, Greece, Italy, and Sweden. Their role among the exporting SMEs is also important and increasing all the time. Therefore, it is really surprising that there are only a few studies focusing on the internationalization of family-owned companies. According to the review by Zahra and Sharma (2004)—which covers 190 international journal articles focusing on family-owned companies—only 3 percent of them focused on exports/internationalization. In a more recent review by Casillas et al. (2007), the authors found only twelve international journal articles focusing on internationalization of family firms published in 1991–2005 in five key entrepreneurship journals. Thus there is definitely a need for more research.

The aim of this chapter is to analyze the export behavior and export performance of SMEs, and especially to analyze the similarities and differences in the behavior and performance depending on the ownership background of the companies. In addition, the study takes into account the impact of the timing of the establishment of the firms, the field of industry, and the speed of their internationalization. The study contributes to the hitherto limited knowledge on the impact of ownership on export behavior and company performance. To our knowledge, this study is the first large-scale study of the topic in Finland, and apparently in all Nordic countries.

LITERATURE REVIEW

Based on the results of an extensive STRATOS (Strategic Operations of Small and Medium-sized Enterprises) project (including SMEs from several European countries: Austria, Belgium, Germany, Finland, France, the Netherlands, Switzerland, and the UK), Donckels and Fröhlich (1991, 158–159) found the following characteristics typical for family-owned SMEs (see also Kets de Vries 1993):

1. They are rather inwardly directed or closed family-related systems: they are considered as family businesses, the management is in the hands of the family, family traditions are maintained, and building up a business for the family is a major objective.
2. Their managers are less often pioneers, more often all-rounders and organizers, and are rather risk-averse.
3. They need fewer socioeconomic networks, and less cooperation with other firms, including subcontracting and production.
4. They are more inclined to pay wages above the level set by wage agreements and to care significantly more about the satisfaction of their employees. However, they pay less attention, e.g., to the participation of the employees in decision making or the education of employees.
5. Their attitude towards strategy was rather conservative, linked especially to the all-rounder and organizer types of entrepreneurs, who often are less prepared for exports and other types of internationalization. Furthermore, their businesses are more stable, because their managers have weaker profit- and growth-orientation than managers in non-family firms.

Additionally, some other studies on family firms indicate that they are on the average older than non-family firms, but based on the number of employees and sales they are smaller (Binder Hamlyn 1994, Graves and Thomas 2003).

Exports and Family Firms

Donckels and Fröhlich (1991) state that the share of exports was lower in family than in non-family firms, though they do not give exact figures of exports in family firms. Later studies in the same project (e.g., Donckels and Aerts 1998) also indicate similar results. Findings from other studies in various countries are contradictory: for example, Westhead and Cowling (1997) did not find statistically significant differences in the exports of UK-based family and non-family firms, whereas the study of Binder Hamlyn (1994) indicated a clear difference in the probability of their exporting.

Furthermore, based on an Australian sample Kotev (2005) did not find any statistically significant difference either in the probability of exporting or in the share of exports among small firms (less than 20 employees), but among bigger companies (20–199 employees) the probability of exporting and the share of exports compared to total sales was higher in non-family than in family firms. And yet another Australian study, Graves and Thomas (2003), found that though the probability of exporting was clearly lower in family than in non-family firms, after starting exports no statistically significant difference was found in the share of exports.

In contrast to this, a study among US-based firms (Zahra 2001) indicated that the family firm background had a positive impact on the probability of exporting but a negative impact on the number of target countries for exports. In a later study in the US, Zahra (2003) made this relationship even more explicit: family firms had a significantly lower share of foreign sales and number of target countries for exports than non-family firms.

A study among Spanish firms (Fernández and Nieto 2002) also supported that the share of exporting companies and average share of exports was lower in family than in non-family-owned firms. In another Spanish study, Nieto Sanchez (2003) found that the international sales of the reviewed firms had clearly increased in 1991–1999, and that the share of exports was still lower in family than in non-family firms. Also based on a Spanish sample, Gallo and Garcia Pont (1996) found that family firms started their internationalization more slowly than non-family firms.

Internationalization of Family Firms

The motives for international expansion in SMEs can also be very diverse. Usually the motives are classified as proactive and reactive, or internal and external (see, e.g., Leonidou et al. 2007). In the case of proactive motives the company takes the initiative, e.g., based on the international experience of its management, whereas in the case of reactive motives the company reacts to an unsolicited inquiry or to the moves of their competitors. According to the results in several studies, an outside triggering factor—such as an unsolicited inquiry—has very often initiated the exports of SMEs (see, e.g., Albaum et al. 2005). For example, Okoroafo (1999) found that the exports of family firms had very often started after an unexpected foreign inquiry (89.5 percent). The situation seems to have been very similar in Finnish SMEs (cf. Larimo and Arola 1998).

It is also possible that family firms differ in terms of their internationalization process. Harris et al. (1994) have argued that because of their conservatism and risk aversion family firms tend to adopt a gradual (step-by-step) approach to exporting. In other words, they would increase their commitment to internationalization incrementally, first developing the home market and then gradually expanding the operation to more distant countries (Johanson & Wiedersheim-Paul 1975, Luostarinen 1979).

Luostarinen and Hellman (1995) have reviewed in more detail the internationalization of Finnish firms, taking into account the outward, inward and cooperative activities. From our point of view, their most interesting results were that the time lag from establishment to the first export delivery was clearly longer in family firms than in non-family firms, and that the role of psychic distance to markets was clearly more important for family firms entering their first export markets than for non-family firms in a similar situation.

Internationalization is generally expected to be linked to company performance. Findings concerning the performance of family firms compared to others are quite mixed. According to some studies, family firms have performed better and grown more rapidly than non-family firms, whereas results in some studies have indicated just the opposite or have found non-significant differences between the two groups (see, e.g., London Economics 2002). And so far, no study particularly addressing the export performance of family firms exists—although some studies do show a lower share of exports in family firms, thus also indicating lower export performance.

Synthesis

Earlier literature—although limited—indicates that family firms do differ from other firms in terms of growth-orientation, risk taking and need for networking, for instance. All these characteristics are bound to have an influence on their internationalization, too. Based on the literature review, the following hypotheses are drawn, to be tested in the empirical part of the study:

H1: Proactive motives are more important triggers for internationalization in family firms than in non-family firms.

H2: Family firms start their internationalization later than non-family firms.

H3: The internationalization of family firms proceeds more slowly than the internationalization of non-family firms.

H4: In family firms, the first export countries are more often culturally and geographically close countries than in non-family firms.

H5: The share of international sales is lower in family than in non-family firms.

H6: The market strategy of family firms is more concentrated than in non-family firms.

H7: The performance in exports has been lower in family than in non-family firms.

METHODOLOGY

The data for the study was collected as a part of a larger survey analyzing the export behavior, strategies and performance of Finnish SMEs in spring 2002. The target population consisted of industrial and service (firms in software, engineering and advertising) having 10 to 500 employees and with export experience. Altogether 2,856 companies meeting the criteria were found from the Yritys-Suomi 2000 database, as well as from earlier surveys made by the author. However, a closer look revealed that 202 of these did not actually belong to the target population, as they were in bankruptcy, were too big etc. As a result, the final target population was 2,654 firms.

In total 489 answers were received, of which 343 were usable for this study,[1] resulting in a response rate of 12.9 percent. Based on the number of employees, annual turnover and field of industry, there seemed not to be any great differences between responding and non-responding companies.

Table 13.1   Sample Description

	Total sample		Family firms		Non-family firms	
	N/Mean	%	n	%	n	%
Establishment	343	100	182	100	161	100
mean	1976		1972[d]		1980	
before 1990	241	70.3	137	75.3	104	64.6
1990–	102	29.7	45	24.7	57	35.4
Number of employees						
mean	66.0		51.5		82.4[c]	
below 50	248	72.5	142	78.0[a]	106	66.25
50–250 missing info=1	94	27.5	40	22.0	54	33.75
Total sales (M€)						
mean	10.1		9.0		11.1[c]	
below 7 M€	235	68.5	136	74.7[c]	99	61.5
7 M€ or more missing info=1	108	31.5	46	25.3	62	38.5
Fields of industry						
Industrial goods	229	66.8	125	68.7	104	64.6
Consumer goods	66	19.2	36	19.8	30	18.6
Service	48	14.0	21	11.5	27	16.8

Statistical significance levels: a–0.1, b=0.05; c=0.01; d=0.001

Furthermore, no noticeable differences were found between early- and late-responding companies.

Approximately 70 percent of the responding firms were established before 1990 and the rest after 1990 (see Table 13.1). Similarly, over 70 percent of the firms had fewer than 50 employees and some 30 percent between 50 and 249 employees. Furthermore, two-thirds of the firms were industrial firms, some 20 percent consumer goods firms, and some 14 percent service companies. About half of the companies were family-owned,[2] (53 percent) and the other half (47 percent) were non-family firms. Family firms were somewhat older and smaller and concentrated more on production goods industries than non-family firms.

FINDINGS

Motives for Exports

For all the respondents—independent of company ownership—the main motive for internationalization had been the management's interest in international sales (see Table 13.2). This motive can be classified as a proactive one, and thus in the case of family firms goes against expectations. Other significant motives included unsolicited inquiry and limited home market. These two motives can be classified as reactive ones, which is quite in line with earlier studies (see, e.g., Okoroafo 1999). Although the rank order of the motives was different in the two subgroups, against expectations the difference was not statistically significant.

In the ranking of importance, the next motives were related to marketing outside Finland, the international experience of the management and strong competition on the home market. The first two can be classified as proactive internal motives, whereas the third is a reactive external motive. The proactive motives were more important for non-family than family firms, whereas the reactive motive was more important for the family firms.

Other motives were clearly of less importance; in most cases no significant difference between family and non-family firms existed. The only exception was the measures taken by the competitors and the positive impact of internationalization on the competitors—both proactive external motives—which had influenced the internationalization of non-family firms to a statistically significant extent.

Management's interest in internationalization was the main motive for both older and younger firms, and for both industrial and service firms, but for firms in the consumer sector unexpected inquiries were of more importance. Also, in terms of the internationalization process, some differences could be identified. Whereas for incrementally internationalized firms management's interest was decisive, for companies who internationalized

Table 13.2   Importance of Various Motives for Starting Exports

	Total sample N=316	Family firms n=163	Non-family firms n=153
Management's interest in internalization P/I	3.99	4.03	3.94
Foreign inquiry about the company's products/services R/E	3.78	3.82	3.73
Inadequate demand in the home market R/E	3.69	3.62	3.76
The company has never considered its home market as the only market P/I	3.18	2.97	3.40[b]
Management's international experience P/I	2.84	2.59	3.10[d]
Increasing competition in home market R/E	2.78	2.86	2.69
Internationalization of customer P+R/E	2.48	2.43	2.53
Internationalization of competitors R/E	2.33	2.13	2.54[c]
Success of competitors in international markets P/E	2.31	2.17	2.46[b]
Competitive foreign subcontractors P/E	2.09	2.07	2.11
Export subsidies/subsidies for international operations P/E	2.08	2.09	2.06
Lack of subcontractors in home market R/E	1.65	1.69	1.60
Contact from the chamber of commerce/other support organization R/E	1.59	1.63	1.55

P=proactive & R=reactive motive, E=external & I=internal motive; scale 1 . . . 5; 1=not at all important, 5=very important
Statistical significance levels: a=0.1; b=0.05; c=0.01; d=0.001

more rapidly, the markets outside Finland were the most important motive for starting exports. However, in terms of motives, family and non-family firms seem to resemble each other considerably, and thus our *hypothesis 1 does not receive support.*

Speed of Internationalization

Target firms started exporting on the average 9.6 years after their establishment (see Table 13.3). However, there was great variation, because some of the firms had started exports in the year of establishment, whereas in some almost 100 years had passed before starting exports. The mean year of

Table 13.3 Start and Expansion of Exports

	Total sample N=316/283				Family firms n=164				Non-family firms n=152			
	1	2	3	4*	1	2	3	4*	1	2	3	4*
Total sample	9.6	2.8	2.2	4.5	13.5ᵈ	2.9	2.2	5.0	7.2	2.1	2.0	4.0
Establishment												
before 1990 (n=241)	14.3	3.0	2.6	5.6	17.4ᵈ/ᵈ	3.8ᵈ	2.7ᵃ	6.0ᵈ	10.2ᵈ	2.9ᵇ	2.8ᶜ	5.3ᶜ
1990—(n=102)	1.8	1.4	0.9	2.1	1.5	1.4	1.5	2.0	1.7	1.4	0.8	2.2
Fields of industry												
Industrial goods (n=229)	11.5	2.2	1.8	3.8	13.8ᵇ	2.9ᵃ	2.4ᵃ	4.8ᵇ	8.7	2.0	1.4	3.0
Consumer goods (n=66)	10.8	2.9	3.2	6.1	15.7ᶜ	4.0	2.8	6.5	4.9	2.1	3.9	6.0
Service (n=48)	5.6	3.8	2.3	5.7	7.7ᵃ	3.6	1.9	4.6	3.9	4.0	2.5	6.6
Speed of internationalization												
Traditional (n=274)	12.8ᵈ	3.2ᵈ	2.3	5.2ᶜ	14.8ᵈ/ᵈ	3.1	2.4	5.5ᵇ	8.4ᵈ	2.5	1.9	4.2
Born internationals (n=77)	1.6	1.4	1.9	2.9	1.5	1.9	0.9	2.0	0.9	1.1	2.3	3.4

(1) From the establishment to the start of exports; (2) expansion from first to second target country (years); (3) expansion from second to third country (years); (4) expansion first to third country (years)

Statistical significance levels: a=0.1; b=0.05; c=0.01; d=0.001

*Not all companies had expanded as far as their third target countries. Means in column 4 include only cases of expansion to three or more countries.

starting exports in the sample was 1986. The time lag from the establishment to the starting of exports had clearly shortened: in companies established before 1990, it was over 14 years, whereas in companies established in 1990 or more recently the time lag was only about 2 years, which is in line with earlier research both in Finland (e.g., Hurmerinta-Peltomäki 1995 and 2001) and elsewhere (see, e.g., Rialp et al. 2005). The time lag has clearly been shorter in service than in the other sectors, which can partly be explained by the fact that the service firms in this study had been established mostly in the 1990s.

In earlier studies several criteria have been used to classify firms in terms of speed of internationalization (see, e.g., Rialp et al. 2005), and two criteria were used in this study. First, according to the looser criterion (starting to export within the first three years of the firm's establishment) 45 percent of the respondents were traditional companies and 55 percent born international companies. Using the tighter criterion (starting to export within three years and also having an export share of 25 percent or more within three years) resulted in the classification of 78 percent of respondents as traditional and 22 percent as born international companies.

A clear difference could be found in the time lag from the establishment to the starting of exports between family vs. non-family firms. In the latter group the average time lag was 7.2 years, whereas in the former the time lag was 13.2 years (difference statistically significant at the 0.001 level). So *the hypothesis 2 assuming a slower start of exports in family firms received support.* The exports of family firms had started on the average in the year 1985, which is two years later than the non-family firms. The more detailed results indicated that the starting of exports had clearly been slower in those family-owned SMEs that were established before 1990 (difference significant at the 0.001 level), whereas in the more recent period no statistically significant difference between family-owned and non-family-owned companies could be found. The greatest difference was found in SMEs operating in consumer goods industries, but among traditionally internationalized companies a clear difference was also found between family vs. non-family firms, whereas among born international companies the difference in speed was clearly smaller, as might be expected.

In terms of speed of internationalization family firms also differed. According to the looser criterion, 54 percent from the family firms were traditional and 46 percent born internationals, whereas in non-family firms the respective figures were 35 percent and 65 percent (difference statistically significant at the 0.01 level). Taking into account the 25 percent export share requirement showed that from the family firms 84 percent were traditional and only 16 percent born internationals, whereas in non-family-owned the respective shares were 71 percent and 29 percent (difference statistically significant at the 0.001 level). Thus, even based on the stricter criteria, almost one-third of the non-family-owned companies were born internationals.

No statistically significant difference could be found in the average expansion time between family vs. non-family firms after starting exports except in the industrial goods sector. Additionally noteworthy is that those born international family firms that had expanded to three or more countries had expanded more quickly than the non-family born internationals.

The First Target Countries in Exports

The most common first export market had been Sweden—a country geographically and culturally close to Finland. Over 45 percent of the respondents had started their export operations in Sweden. The other typical first export countries were Germany and Russia. Over two-thirds of the respondents had started their exports from one of those three countries. Besides these, first export countries included other economically and culturally close countries, such as Norway and Estonia, but also the UK—a somewhat more distant country—and the US—a clearly more distant country. The same countries—except the US—were also commonly the second and third target countries of exports. In the list of most common third target country appeared another Nordic country, Denmark.

The US was more common as the first target country for companies which were established (and therefore also started their exports) in 1990 or more recently. Results related to the first export markets in this study were relatively similar to those in earlier studies focusing on exports by Finnish firms (cf. Luostarinen 1979, Larimo and Sutinen 1995).

Sweden, Germany and Russia were the three most common first export countries both for family and non-family firms. Sweden, however, was clearly more often the first market for the former (103 vs. 53). Thus, geographical and cultural closeness seems to have influenced family firms slightly more than non-family firms. This becomes even clearer when the fourth most common first export countries are reviewed: among family firms it was Estonia and among non-family firms the UK. Among the second and third export countries family firms had clearly preferred Norway and Denmark more often than non-family firms. Among the latter, the role of Denmark was lower, and that of the US higher.

Because all three Scandinavian countries are clearly geographically and culturally closer to Finland than are the US and UK, the results support the view that family firms prefer economically and culturally close countries as first target countries of exports more often than non-family firms (concerning the first target countries, the difference was significant at the 0.001 level, and concerning the three first target countries, the difference was significant at the 0.1 level). Hence, *the results give support for hypothesis 4.*

Sweden had been the most common first target country in all reviewed subgroups both among family and non-family firms. The role of Sweden as the first target country was, however, clearly higher in the older, industrial and consumer goods sector, and in traditionally internationalized family than in non-family firms, whereas among born internationals hardly any difference was found between family vs. non-family firms.

Share of Exports

The average share of exports among the respondents was 41 percent, which is more than twice as high as in US-based family firms (see Zahra 2003; mean 14.8 percent). The year of establishment (before or after 1990) did not have any significant impact on the share of exports. The average share was some 5 percent higher in consumer and industrial products companies than in the service companies. In companies having started their international-ization slowly—the traditional companies—the average share of exports was about one-third from total sales, whereas in rapidly internationalized companies—born internationals—the share was over two-thirds. Thus these results give additional support to earlier studies' findings of the great significance of foreign sales in born international firms.

The ownership background of the firms also significantly influenced the average share of exports. In family firms the average share was about 38 per-cent, whereas in non-family firms almost 44 percent (difference significant at the 0.1 level). Thus, *hypothesis 5 is supported*. The difference was clearly higher in companies established before 1990—some 6 percentage points—than in the more recently established companies where the difference was about 3 percentage points. The average share of exports was somewhat lower in family and in non-family firms in all three reviewed fields of industries. Furthermore, the share of exports, both among family and non-family firms, was almost twice as high among the born internationals as in traditional firms. Noteworthy also is that the born international subgroup was the only reviewed subgroup where the average share of exports exceeded (by some 1.5 percent) the respective figure in non-family firms.

Market Strategies

The most companies studied had on the average ten target markets for exports, which is four times more than the respective number of US-based family firms (Zahra 2003; mean 2.3 countries). Many of the companies had only one to three target countries, but some had as many as twenty or more. The older companies had had naturally more target countries than the young ones, and the companies operating in business-to-business markets had more target countries than firms operating in business-to-consumer markets. Furthermore, as might be expected, traditional exporters had on the average fewer target countries for exports than born internationals.

Family firms had on average 8.4 target countries for exports, whereas non-family firms had 11.2 (difference statistically significant at the 0.05 level). Thus, *the results support hypothesis 6*. Young family and non-family firms had a smaller number of target countries than older ones. Among firms established before 1990, there was also a statistically significant difference in the average number of export countries between family and non-family firms. Furthermore, both family and non-family industrial companies had on the average more export countries than the others. However, among family firms, producers of consumer goods had on average more target countries than firms operating in the service sector, whereas among non-family firms the situation was the opposite. Nevertheless, this notion is valid only concerning the average number of target countries for family vs. non-family firms in the industrial product sector. Traditionally internationalized companies had, on average, a smaller number of target countries than born internationals, both among family and non-family firms. A statistically significant difference was found between family and non-family traditional exporters, but not between the born international subgroups. Finally, a statistically significant difference was also found in family-owned firms between traditional and born international firms.

Although the respondents had on average almost ten target countries for exports, their exports were often very concentrated, as on average the share of the three main target countries of exports was more than 75 percent. The share of exports was highest among the consumer goods producers—85 percent. As discussed earlier, the average amount of target countries in the total sample was also lowest in the consumer goods industry. Although the number of target countries was higher among born internationals than among traditional exporters, the concentration ratio of exports was also very high among born internationals—about 70 percent from total exports to the three main target countries. The most important target country's share of exports was on the average 43 percent.

The results indicated that the share of the three most important target countries of exports was higher (79.2 percent) in non-family than in family firms (72.2 percent) (the difference being statistically significant at the 0.1 level). Thus *these results also support hypothesis 6*. The concentration ratio of exports was higher in family firms, both in companies established before and after 1990, but a statistically significant difference between family and non-family firms was found only in the older subgroup. The concentration ratio was lower both in family and non-family firms in the industrial products sector than in the other sectors. In total, the lowest concentration ratios were found among the born international subgroups, both among family and non-family firms. However, in these subgroups the concentration ratio of sales to the three most important countries was still around 70 percent.

Export Performance

Three measures of export performance were selected: the management's view of the performance in relation to the goals set for exports, the total performance in foreign markets, and the total performance of the main product in export markets.

Based on the management's views, the means of all three measures were very close to each others (means between 3.29 and 3.41—see Table 13.4).

Table 13.4   Performance in Exports Compared to the Goals Set during the Last Three Years

	Total sample N=340			Family firms n=179			Non-family firms n=161		
	1	2	3	1	2	3	1	2	3
Total sample									
mean	3.30	3.29	3.41	3.28	3.20	3.30	3.30	3.39[b]	3.53[b]
Establishment									
before 1990 (*n*=240)	3.45	3.30	3.46	3.31	3.23	3.36	3.34	3.44[a]	3.61[b]
1990–(*n*=100)	3.23	3.28	3.30	3.19	3.09	3.14	3.23	3.30	3.39
Field of industry									
Industrial goods (*n*=229)	3.36	3.31	3.45	3.41[b]	3.25	3.35	3.25	3.37	3.58[b]
Consumer goods (*n*=66)	3.28	3.20	3.30	2.91	3.00	3.14	3.17	3.43[a]	3.40
Service (*n*=48)	3.23	3.23	3.30	3.10	3.19	3.29	3.63[b]	3.44	3.48
Speed of internationalization									
Traditional (*n*=265)	3.27	3.25	3.37	3.23	3.40	3.22	3.31	3.27	3.56
Born internationals (*n*=74)	3.36	3.45[b]	3.57[b]	3.52[a]	3.38	3.72[d]	3.27	3.36	3.47

(1) Performance compared to the goals set during last three years; (2) Total performance; (3) Performance of the main product in main markets (scale: 1=Very unsatisfied . . . 5=Very satisfied)
a=0.1, b=0.05, c=0.01, d=0.001

Thus, the companies were on the average relatively satisfied with their export performance, independent of the measure used. The results show that older firms performed somewhat better than younger firms, industrial firms better than consumer goods producers or service companies, and born internationals performed somewhat better than traditionally internationalized firms.

Family firms performed relatively similarly on all three measures, whereas the performance of non-family firms was more dependent on the measure used. When the performance was evaluated based on the goals set for exports, the results did not indicate any significant difference between family and non-family firms. When the other two measures were used, the results indicated that non-family firms had clearly performed better than non-family firms (differences statistically significant at the 0.05 level) thus giving *support to hypothesis 8.*

The performance in both ownership groups was better among older than among younger companies. On two performance measures older non-family firms clearly performed better than older family-owned firms, whereas in the case of younger firms the values of performance means were more similar. Non-family firms performed better than family-owned firms on all three measures, although the difference was statistically significant only for one measure of the three (a different measure in each case for each of the three industries).

Among family firms, those operating in the industrial products sector performed better than firms in the other fields, and those in the consumer goods sector more poorly than the others. The results were clearly different among non-family firms, where service companies clearly performed better on the first performance measure than firms in other industries, and also slightly better than the other firms on the second measure, whereas industrial producers had performed best on the third measure. The most surprising results were found to be related to the speed of internationalization.

The findings indicated that born internationals had performed better than traditionals according to all three measures (the difference being statistically significant on the second and third measures). Among family-owned firms, the performance was better in born internationals on the first and third measure, and about equal based on the second measure, whereas among the non-family firms the differences were much smaller, with traditional firms performing slightly better than born internationals on the first and third measure. Furthermore, it is noteworthy that among traditional firms the non-family firms had performed better than the family firms on two measures, whereas on one measure the situation was the opposite, though no statistically significant differences were found. The born international family-owned firms performed better on all three measures than non-family firms.

Thus, these last more detailed results *do not support hypothesis 8.* As noted earlier, the share of foreign sales was also higher among the family-owned born internationals than among non-family-owned born internationals. Thus family-owned born internationals seem to have succeeded very well in export markets.

Because the export performance and performance-related factors between family and non-family firms have not previously been thoroughly analyzed, some additional tests were made. Based on a correlation analysis, the firm size correlated positively and significantly with export performance both in the whole sample as well as in the non-family firm sub-sample (although in the case of the performance of the main product, the results were only marginally better in non-family firms). Also, among family firms, bigger firms performed better, but no statistically significant difference was found. Concerning the share of exports, sampled firms having 33 percent or lower share of exports clearly had poorer performance than companies having a higher export share (difference statistically significant at the 0.001 level). The non-family firms having a higher export share had clearly performed better than family firms, especially based on management evaluation of total performance and the performance of the main product in foreign markets, whereas in the latter subgroups no statistically significant differences were found between family and non-family firms. Thus, as a whole, the results support better export performance by non-family firms, especially on two of the measures of performance.

SUMMARY AND CONCLUSIONS

The internationalization of SMEs has received increased attention during the last twenty years. However, the impact of the type of ownership on firms' export behavior and performance has so far received surprisingly limited attention. Therefore, this study has tried to analyze the possible differences both in the starting phase and later phases of exports between family and non-family-owned firms from diverse points of view. Based on the literature review, eight hypotheses were developed for the empirical part of the study. The empirical part was based on a survey made among Finnish exporting SMEs. The sample included 182 family-owned and 161 non-family-owned firms.

In sum, the international sales of family-owned firms seem to start more slowly, and the first target countries are clearly more often other Nordic countries than is the case with non-family firms. Furthermore, family-owned firms choose fewer target countries for their foreign sales, and their sales are more concentrated on their three main markets than in the case of non-family firms. Their export performance is also lower, independent of the measure used for evaluating export performance. However, in terms of their motives for beginning to export or their speed of internationalization, no statistically significant differences were found between family and non-family firms. These findings concerning the time lag from the establishment to the start of export, the role of exports, and the number of target countries are very similar to the results in earlier studies (see, e.g., Donckels and Aerts 1998, Fernandez and Nieto 2005, 2006).

A more detailed analysis of the findings indicated that differences between family and non-family firms can be identified among older companies, companies operating in the industrial sector, and among the firms who have internationalized at a slower pace. Among younger companies, those operating in the consumer goods and service sectors, the ones who had internationalized rapidly, fewer statistically significant differences were found. These slightly contradictory findings indicate that it is not enough to take into account the ownership background; other factors also need to be considered.

In terms of target countries (number and scope), the findings give support to the view that when family members are involved in management they may approach internationalization with caution. In line with Zahra (2003), the results indicate that family firms may seek to maximize revenues from foreign markets rather than aggressively try to pursue intensive internationalization (that is, a really high share of exports, expansion to distant markets and targeting a high number of countries).

The study had several limitations. First, the distribution of sample companies into family vs. non-family-owned companies was based on the management's view without any more specific conditions. Thus, for example, the role of the family in decision making and management, was not analyzed in terms of whether the company was a first, second or third generation family firm. For instance, Menéndez-Requejo (2005) found that the internationalization of the family-owned companies proceeded faster when the company was not a first-generation family firm, whereas Zahra (2003) did not find any significant difference in the share of foreign sales or number of target countries depending on the family generation in management. However, this aspect could be analyzed in further studies.

Additional avenues for further research might include more detailed analysis of the background and attitudes of the management toward internationalization, and the impact of the strategies used on the export performance. A third alternative would be to do a follow-up study of the development of export strategies and export performance. Finally, it would be interesting to compare the internationalization and export performance of Finnish family and non-family firms with that of firms from other Nordic countries and from other European countries.

NOTES

1. Export performance studies made in 1996–2001 had an average sample size of 146 cases (Manolova and Manev 2004). Thus the sample size of this study can be considered appropriate, as it was clearly above the average.

2. The ownership of the company was classified based on the respondent's answer to the question "Is your company family-owned?"

BIBLIOGRAPHY

Albaum, G., Duerr, E. and Strandskov J. (2005) *International marketing and export management*, Harlow, UK: FT, Prentice Hall.

Binder Hamlyn (1994) *The quest for growth: a survey of UK private companies*, London: Binder Hamlyn.

Casillas, J., Acedo, F. and Moreno, A. (2007) *International entrepreneurship in family businesses*, Cheltenham, UK: Edward Elgar.

Donckels, R. and Aerts, R. (1998) 'Internationalization and ownership: family versus non-family enterprises,' in A. Haahti, G. Hall and R. Donckels (eds.) *The internationalization of SMEs. The interstratos project*, 153–163, London: Routledge.

Donckels, R. and Fröhlich, E. (1991) 'Are family businesses really different? European experiences from STRATOS,' *Family Business Review*, 4 (2): 149–160.

Fernandez, Z. and Nieto, M.J. (2002) 'International involvement of SMEs: the impact of ownership,' Business Economics Series Working Paper No. 02–58 (21), Universidad Carlos III de Madrid.

Fernández, Z. and Nieto, M.J. (2005) 'Internationalization strategy of small and medium-sized family businesses: some influential factors,' *Family Business Review*, 18 (1): 77–88.

Fernández, Z. and Nieto, M.J. (2006) 'Impact of ownership on the international involvement of SMEs,' *Journal of International Business Studies*, 37 (3): 340–351.

Gallo, M.A. and Garcia Pont, C. (1996) 'Important factors in family business internationalization,' *Family Business Review*, 9 (1): 45–59.

Graves, C. and Thomas, J. (2003) 'Venturing beyond the backyard: internationalisation of the family business,' paper presented at the 16th Annual Conference of Small Enterprise Association of Australia and New Zealand, 28.9.–1.10.2003, Ballarat, Australia.

Harris, D., Martinez, J.I. and Ward, J.L. (1994) 'Is strategy different for the family-owned businesses?,' *Family Business Review*, 7 (2): 159–174.

Hurmerinta-Peltomäki, L. (2001) 'Time and internationalisation: the shortened adoption lag in small business internationalisation,' Publications of the Turku School of Economics and Business Administration, Series A-7:2001.

Hurmerinta-Peltomäki, L. (1995) 'Shortened adoption lag in small businesses' internationalization—fact or fiction?' Publications of the Turku School of Economics and Business Administration, Series D-6.

IFERA (2003) 'Family businesses dominate,' *Family Business Review*, 16 (4): 235–239.

Johanson, J. and Wiedersheim-Paul, F. (1975) 'The internationalization of the firm—four Swedish cases,' *The Journal of Management Studies*, 12 (3): 305–322.

Kets de Vries, M. (1993) 'The dynamics of family controlled firms: the good and bad news,' *Organizational Dynamics*, 21 (3): 59–71.

Kotev, B. (2005) 'Goals, management practices, and performance of family SMEs,' *International Journal of Entrepreneurial Behaviour & Research*, 11 (1): 3–24.

Larimo, J. and Arola, M. (1998) 'Pk-yritysten vienti ja kansainvälistyminen. Kirjallisuusyhteenveto aihealueen tutkimuksista vuosilta 1976–1998,' Publications of the University of Vaasa, Reports 37.

Larimo, J. and Sutinen, K. (1996) 'Vaasan läänin yritysten kansainvälistyminen. 1990-luvun kehitys ja tulevaisuudennäkymät,' Publications of the University of Vaasa, Reports 17.

Leonidou, L.C., Katsikeas, C.S., Palihawadana, D. and Spyropoulou, S. (2007) 'An analytical review of the factors stimulating smaller firms to export: implications for policy-makers,' *International Marketing Review*, 24 (6): 735–770.

London Economics (2002) Family businesses: do they perform better? Literature review by London Economics. European Foundation for the Improvement of Living and Working Conditions, http://www.eurofound.eu.int.

Luostarinen, R. (1979) 'Internationalization of the firm: an empirical study of the internationalization of firms with small and open domestic markets with special emphasis on lateral rigidity as a behavioural characteristics in strategic decision-making,' Acta Academiae Oeconomicae Helsingiensis, Series A:30.

Luostarinen, R. and Hellman, H. (1995) 'The internationalization processes and strategies of Finnish family firms,' Helsinki School of Economics and Business Administration Centre for International Business Research, CIBR Research Papers Y-1.

Manolova, T. and Manev, L. (2004) 'Internationalization and the performance of the small firm: a review of the empirical literature between 1996 and 2001'. In M. Jones and P. Dimitratos (eds.) *Emerging Paradigms in International Entrepreneurship*, 37–63, Cheltenham, UK: Edward Elgard.

Menéndez-Requejo, S. (2005) 'Growth and internationalisation of family businesses,' *International Journal of Globalisation and Small Business*, 1 (2): 122–133.

Nieto Sanchez, M.J. (2003). Las pyme familiares en Espana: Que nos dicen los datos? *Investigaciones Europeas de Dirección y Economía de la Empresa*, 9 (2): 115–128.

Okoroafo, S.C. (1999) 'Internationalization of family businesses: evidence from Northwest Ohio, U.S.A,' *Family Business Review*, 12 (2): 147–158.

Rialp, A., Rialp, J. and Knight, G. (2005) 'The phenomenon of international new ventures, global start-ups, and born-globals: what do we know after a decade (1993–2002) of exhaustive scientific inquiry?' *International Business Review*, 14 (2): 147–166.

Tookey, D.A. (1964) 'Factors associated with success in exporting,' *Journal of Management Studies*, 1 (1): 48–66.

Westhead, P. and Cowling, M. (1997) 'Performance contrasts between family and non-family unquoted companies in the UK,' *International Journal of Entrepreneurial Behavior and Research*, 3 (1): 30–52.

Zahra, S. (2001) Ownership and involvement and international expansion: an empirical test of the stewardship theory among family firms: theories of the family enterprise: establishing a paradigm for the field, Canada: University of Alberta School of Business.

Zahra, S. (2003) 'International expansion of U.S. manufacturing family businesses: the effect of ownership and involvement,' *Journal of Business Venturing*, 18 (4): 495–512.

Zahra, S. and Sharma, P. (2004) 'Family business research: a strategic reflection,' *Family Business Review*, 17 (4): 331–346.

Part IV
The Role of Networks in the International Growth of SMEs

14 New Venture Internationalization and Technological Learning

A Social Capital Perspective

Shameen Prashantham

INTRODUCTION

The manifestation of entrepreneurial behavior in international new ventures (INVs) has attracted substantial research attention (Jones and Coviello 2005, Keupp and Gassmann 2009, McDougall and Oviatt 2000). Although the prospect of growth is often an incentive to pursue entrepreneurial internationalization (Lu and Beamish 2001, Oviatt and McDougall 2005b), the literature indicates other potential consequences as well, notably *learning* outcomes, i.e., the generation of new knowledge (Sapienza, De Clercq and Sandberg 2005, Zahra 2005). Indeed, learning is a central theme in the international entrepreneurship literature (Johanson and Vahlne 2006, Prashantham 2008, Sapienza et al. 2006).

However, "important gaps remain concerning learning" (Sapienza et al. 2006, 926), probably because the literature emphasizes learning as an antecedent, rather than consequence, of internationalization (Autio 2005). Yet within limits of cognition and resource, the extent of internationalization is positively associated with learning attained (Zahra et al. 2005). As Forsgren (2002) notes, internationalization scholars have not adequately examined various aspects of learning. An important—but seldom articulated—outcome of entrepreneurial internationalization is the potential for technological learning. Technological learning refers to "the ways firms build and supplement their knowledge bases about technologies, products and processes, and develop and improve the use of the broad skills of their workforces" (Dodgson 1991, 142). Put simply, it is the acquisition of technological knowledge. While entrepreneurial internationalization may yield new market knowledge and new technological knowledge (Autio 2005), the literature emphasizes the former. Technological learning is an underresearched (and perhaps non-obvious) outcome of entrepreneurial internationalization by comparison to market learning—and yet of potentially great value to the firm (Hitt et al. 2000). Yli-Renko et al. (2002, 283) note that "improved technological learning translates into greater knowledge intensity."

Two broad objectives are addressed: first, to explain how entrepreneurial internationalization could lead to technological learning and second, to shed light on how this outcome could be amplified i.e., to identify moderating factors that strengthen the relationship between internationalization and technological learning in INVs. While internationalization is multidimensional, this discussion is confined to one facet of internationalization that appears overlooked in international entrepreneurship research, viz., choice of entry mode (Shrader 2001). Building upon Zahra et al.'s (2000) study of INVs, the focus is the role of entry mode commitment in fostering technological learning.

In the paragraphs that follow, in relation to the first objective, a theoretical explanation of the relationship between entry mode commitment and technological learning is proffered by viewing technological learning in terms of the interplay between knowledge and social capital. The central argument is that presence within (as distinct from exporting to) international markets, arising from the use of high-commitment modes, leads to technological learning as interorganizational social capital is built, which, in turn, facilitates the acquisition and creation of technological knowledge. Then, in relation to the second objective, relevant literatures are synthesized to identify conditions relating to international markets under which the relationship between the use of high-control modes and technological learning may be amplified. The resultant ideas—pertaining to regional clusters, national culture and industry knowledge intensity—have potentially useful theoretical and normative implications, which are subsequently discussed.

TECHNOLOGICAL LEARNING IN INTERNATIONALIZATION

Knowledge—both market and technological—is a key driver of entrepreneurial behavior in general (Wiklund and Shepherd 2003) and INV activity in particular (Yli-Renko et al. 2002). Traditional views have focused on the role of market knowledge (Johanson and Vahlne 1977), which regulates the level of resources committed to international expansion activities (Eriksson et al. 1997). However this approach provides only a partial perspective of learning in an internationalization context (Forsgren 2002). More recently, the role of technological knowledge has been emphasized, particularly to explain accelerated internationalization (Oviatt and McDougall 1994), as it allows knowledge-intensive firms to create globally mobile offerings (Autio et al. 2000, Bloodgood et al. 1996, Sapienza et al. 2006). Internationalization typically involves *both* capability-leveraging and capability-building, i.e., learning (Forsgren 2002, Kuemmerle 2002, Sapienza et al. 2005). Thus, INVs can be expected to be able to enhance their market knowledge as well as their technological knowledge as a *consequence* of internationalization (Zahra et al. 2000). Yet technological learning appears to be an overlooked outcome in the international entrepreneurship literature.

Technological learning can aid further success in internationalization (Autio et al. 2000), potentially resulting in a virtuous cycle. A primary distinction between technological learning and market learning pertains to the *nature of knowledge* that is acquired through each of these outcomes: technological knowledge and market knowledge, respectively (Wiklund and Shepherd 2003). Specifically, technological knowledge may be more dynamic in that it ages rapidly, entailing "a dynamic interplay between a firm's technological knowledge and strategy" (Hitt et al. 2000, 237). Hence, in the case of technological learning, there may be a greater need for continuous refreshment of knowledge through social interactions and for a relatively longer tenure in relationship in order for knowledge to accrue. This of course is not to belittle either the relevance of, or challenge involved in, market learning; indeed, a key ingredient for INVs' success is the integration of market and technological learning (Dougherty et al. 2000).

One of the few studies that does deal with technological learning outcomes in the context of entrepreneurial internationalization, and arguably the definitive study on the subject, is by Zahra et al. (2000). They studied 321 American new ventures from 12 knowledge-intensive industries (including biotechnology, software and telecommunications) to test the effect of two aspects of international expansion—entry modes used and foreign markets entered—upon technological learning. Using an essentially capability-based perspective, they hypothesized that the use of high-control modes and international diversity (e.g., number of foreign markets entered) would be positively associated with the extent (breadth, depth and speed) of technological learning. Empirical support for these assertions was found. The authors also correctly predicted that these relationships would be positively moderated by the firm's ability to integrate knowledge; this is important because "technological learning is a multifaceted, and sometimes chaotic, process yielding knowledge that is often fragmented and unfocused" (Zahra et al. 2000, 925). Finally, they found that firm performance was enhanced by international expansion and the resultant technological learning, which could aid better adaptation of offerings to local conditions, rapid new product development and identification of emerging technological changes.

INVs' use of high-commitment modes appears overlooked in the literature (Shrader 2001); moreover, there are limits to international diversity's effects on learning owing to information overload (Zahra et al. 2000). The identification by Zahra et al. (2000) of the relationship between the use of high-commitment modes and technological learning is thus a valuable insight. However there is scope (and need), it may be argued, for a clearer articulation of a theoretical explanation for this relationship in order to help identify ways in which this relationship can be strengthened. According to Zahra et al. (2000), close interaction with other actors is the primary means by which the use of high-control mode translates into technological learning outcomes. However, while Zahra et al. (2000, 929) argue that high-control modes permit "interactions with markets, suppliers and customers," "close observation of other companies" and "closeness to customers," they stop short of articulating a theoretical causal mechanism for how these interactions translate into the acquisition of knowledge. There is potential for further theoretical development. Zahra et al. (2000, 927) note that INVs' "access to '"soft' resources (such as interorganizational relationships) also promotes learning and innovation." Their observations, it is argued below, could be fruitfully reframed in terms of a social capital theory of knowledge creation, formulated by Nahapiet and Ghoshal (1998).

EXPLAINING THE ENTRY MODE COMMITMENT-TECHNOLOGICAL LEARNING RELATIONSHIP

Nahapiet and Ghoshal's (1998) ideas build upon the view that firms are repositories of knowledge (Kogut and Zander 1992) and the Schumpeterian notion that knowledge is created through generic processes of combination and exchange. The likelihood of these processes occurring can be greatly increased under certain conditions, of which Moran and Ghoshal (1999) identified three: the opportunity for these processes to take place, motivation to engage in them and an expectation or perception that they are viable. Recognizing that knowledge is fundamentally socially embedded, Nahapiet and Ghoshal (1998) formulated a model of knowledge creation—i.e., of how such conditions are created or intensified—that is rooted in social relationships, by invoking social capital theory.

Social capital is "the sum of the actual and potential resources embedded within, available through, and derived from the network of relationships possessed by an individual or a social unit" (Nahapiet and Ghoshal 1998, 243). The central tenet of social capital theory is that resources accrue from network relationships (Adler and Kwon 2002). Nahapiet and Ghoshal (1998) argue that social capital improves the conditions under which knowledge-creating exchange and transfer take place in two ways: first, through the efficient transfer of information by reducing opportunistic behavior, and second, by enhancing cooperative behavior and greater creativity. Thus, the intensive interactions with customers and other firms in a foreign market on the part of INVs using high-commitment modes can be seen as a socially embedded process that generates interorganizational social capital, which in turn facilitates the acquisition and creation of knowledge (i.e., learning). In other words, the key to learning is firms' *presence* in a foreign market, made possible by the use of high-commitment modes. Conversely, exclusive usage of a low-commitment mode such as exporting deprives firms of such presence.

Indeed, a strong and explicit connection has been made between intensive interaction resulting in technological learning and Nahapiet and Ghoshal's (1998) work. For instance, in a study on technological learning from *key customers* by new knowledge-intensive firms (albeit within the domestic market), Yli-Renko, Autio and Sapienza (2001) emphasize the importance of "repeated, intense action" and, drawing upon Nahapiet and Ghoshal (1998), demonstrate that the ensuing social capital leads to technological learning outcomes. They argue that technological learning is facilitated by social capital through improved efficiency in communication, evaluation of new technical information and problem-solving heuristics. In a similar vein, Inkpen and Tsang (2005, 146) note that "knowledge transfer is facilitated by intensive social interactions of organizational actors." Thus Zahra et al.'s (2000) important finding can be fruitfully explained, in terms of a causal mechanism, through the lens of a social capital theory of knowledge.

Nahapiet and Ghoshal's (1998) social capital perspective is conceptually consistent with the mechanism of high-commitment modes encapsulated in Kogut and Zander's (1993) work on mode choice. Kogut and Zander's (1993, 625) main argument is that "the choice of transfer mode is determined by the efficiency of the multinational corporation in transferring knowledge relative to other firms." Of particular relevance is the transfer of tacit technological knowledge. Put differently, tacit technological knowledge flows more easily through high-commitment modes. This is due to the greater social interaction that high-commitment modes permit among individuals working for—or *with*—the firm, because INVs are more likely to possess an *inter*organizational, rather than intraorganizational, network of affiliates (Dimitratos et al. 2003). Here, this logic is applied in reverse. That is, insofar as mode commitment is a function of efficiency of knowledge transfer in the direction of the host market, it *also* provides a conduit for technological knowledge flow in the *reverse* direction, i.e., to the home market. The emphasis here is not on "technology exploitation" (Kogut and Zander 1995, 422) but on technology *exploration* via high-commitment modes. Indeed, Kogut and Zander (1995, 424) allude to this possibility when they observe, "Technology cost need not be static, but may represent the forward-looking quality of experimentation and exploration in new markets."

Thus, the argument made here is that high-commitment entry modes facilitate technological learning by creating greater opportunities for INVs to build social capital in international markets. The above theoretical explanation can help identify means through which the relationship between entry mode commitment and technological learning can be amplified. Consistent with other theory-building efforts (e.g., Inkpen and Tsang 2005, Simsek, Lubatkin and Floyd 2003), this quest is guided by three inter-related dimensions—structural, relational and cognitive—of social capital (Nahapiet and Ghoshal 1998). These dimensions are used as stimuli to explore a variety of literatures to arrive at moderating factors. The moderators pertain to market characteristics, each of which relates in some way to the structural, relational and cognitive dimensions of social capital, respectively. These arguments represent a preliminary model, depicted in the figure below.

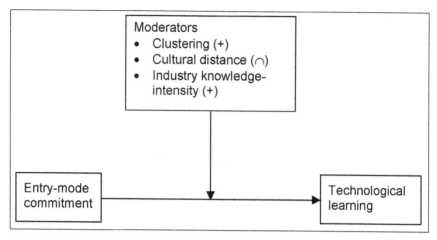

Figure 14.1   Entrepreneurial internationalization and technological learning.

AMPLIFYING THE ENTRY MODE COMMITMENT-TECHNOLOGICAL LEARNING RELATIONSHIP

Regional Clusters

The structural dimension of social capital pertains to the "network of relationships as a whole" (Nahapiet and Ghoshal 1998, 244). Social capital theorists emphasize *spatial proximity* in relation to social capital structure (McEvily and Zaheer 1999). In this context, the regional cluster, defined as "a geographically proximate group of interconnected companies and associated institutions in a particular field, linked by commonalities and complementarities" (Porter 1998, 78), has been emphasized as a network where social capital is developed and leveraged to generate knowledge (Inkpen and Tsang 2005). The proximity that clusters afford affects learning largely because of its network *structure* characteristics, of which Inkpen and Tsang (2005) highlight three: network ties, configuration and stability. They argue that in a cluster, network ties are based on social ties, the formation of which is facilitated by proximity. Network configuration, which relates to patterns of linkages within a network, is non-hierarchical and dense in a cluster, allowing greater connectivity among members; such connectivity is "usually established through informal interpersonal relations" (Inkpen and Tsang 2005, 53). Finally, in terms of network stability, clusters are dynamic, which would seem to be particularly well suited to the transfer of technological knowledge, which itself is dynamic, with new members being potential harbingers of new ideas and technologies.

Porter (1998) talks of a global-local paradox: even though globalization drivers appear to be on the rise, sources of competitive advantage are increasingly embedded locally. For this reason, Leamer and Storper (2001) have argued that the rise of technologies like the Internet heightens, not diminishes, the importance of spatial proximity to firm behavior and performance. The notion that geographic proximity facilitates knowledge flows and exchange among firms has long been recognized (Marshall 1920). Clusters are characterized by high levels of inter-firm interaction as a consequence of labor force mobility, supplier-customer interaction and the spinning-off of ventures (Keeble and Wilkinson 1999). Such interactions often result in the generation of social capital (Westlund and Bolton 2003), which in turn facilitates the acquisition and creation of knowledge (Inkpen and Tsang 2005). The contemporary perception of clusters appears to be as communities of knowledge (Tallman et al.2004).

In response to calls from scholars (Zahra and George 2002), the literature has recently begun to consider the role of location within a cluster, albeit in the context of the firm's *home* market. Fernhaber, Gilbert and McDougall (2008) found that ventures located within industry clusters were more likely to engage in entrepreneurial internationalization compared to ventures that were not cluster-based. Also, Brown and McNaughton (2003) have illustrated the potential for joint promotion activities to be readily undertaken by firms headquartered in clusters. Here, a different point is made: that presence (through the use of high-commitment modes) within a cluster in a *foreign* market is likely to increase the odds that technological learning will occur as a consequence of heightened intensity of interaction with often demanding customers, exposure to high quality innovation and competitive pressure. This, too, is consistent with Zahra's (2005) suggestion that economic geography influences internationalization. The main logic is that greater proximity to actors in a network—as afforded by a cluster—increases the opportunities for interaction and of forming ties (Inkpen and Tsang 2005). Some evidence for this can be found in the context of large MNCs. Birkinshaw and Hood (2000) found that multinational subsidiaries embedded within dynamic clusters contribute more significantly to the parent's performance and innovation output than do subsidiaries based outside clusters. They also make the point, however, that clusters are heterogeneous in terms of, for instance, the level of (local) political salience and foreign investment, and clearly INVs will have to take this into account. Also, location within a cluster is no passive activity—certainly not if technological learning outcomes are sought. This is because in a network such as a cluster, there is likely to be greater demand on and competition for actors' time and attention (Sapienza et al. 2005). In sum, it is proposed:

P1: For an INV, the relationship between entry mode commitment and technological learning is stronger when it locates within a cluster than when it locates elsewhere in an international market.

National Culture

The relational dimension of social capital pertains to "the kind of personal relationships people have developed with each other through a history of interactions" (Nahapiet and Ghoshal 1998, 244). Relevant characteristics of relationships include respect and friendship, which facilitate identification; i.e., individual actors perceive themselves to belong to a group (Adler and Kwon 2002). A recurring theme in the literature on network relationships is the importance of *trust*. Inkpen and Tsang (2005, 154) note that "trust plays a key role in the willingness of network actors to share knowledge." This is facilitated by a low fear of opportunistic behavior on the part of other network actors. Conversely, a lack of trust can be detrimental to the creation and acquisition of knowledge and can result in competitive confusion (Powell et al. 1996). A major barrier to the development of trust is differences in national *culture* (Currall and Inkpen 2002). Cross-cultural social relationships involving customers and suppliers often break down unintentionally due to miscommunication, thereby constraining the development, or even diminishing the stock, of social capital (Fink and Holden 2005). Moreover, trust is conceived differently across cultures and could result in differential attitudes to trust, i.e., trust asymmetries, that could adversely affect knowledge transfer (Zaheer and Zaheer 2006).

In the internationalization literature, the impact of national culture is implicit in the concept of psychic distance which relates to the sociocultural disparity between markets (Johanson and Wiedersheim-Paul 1975). Internationalizing firms are expected to initially enter psychically proximate firms owing to factors such as similarity of market needs, commonalities in ways of doing business and lower political resistance. The basic logic is that learning in culturally different settings is difficult, owing to barriers to trust and therefore the free flow of information. In Nahapiet and Ghoshal's (1998) terms this can also be seen as cultural differences impeding the formation of social capital. However, it cannot be argued that technological learning will only arise in markets at low cultural distance. Indeed, some research indicates the danger of over-embeddedness within networks (Simsek et al. 2003, Yli-Renko et al. 2001) and of complacence when cultural distance is very low (O'Grady and Lane 1996), resulting in underperformance. Technological learning may be somewhat less dependent on cultural factors relative to market learning and could benefit from a certain amount of "diversity of a venture's international business environment" which allows "interactions with local knowledge bases and exposure to different systems of innovation" and therefore "exposure to new and diverse ideas from multiple market and cultural perspectives" (Zahra et al. 2000, 927).

Furthermore, firms must deal with the empirical reality that knowledge-intensive markets are primarily situated in the Triad: the advanced economies of Asia Pacific, Europe and North America. Given the considerable differences between Western and Asian cultures it may not be a realistic option for firms to locate exclusively in culturally proximate markets (Forsgren 2002). These differences often have implications for the manner in which social capital is developed and leveraged. Indeed, social capital may acquire added significance in Asian markets whose importance in the context of global knowledge-intensive industries is growing. It has been asserted that Asian cultures have a propensity for developing and relying upon network relationships. As Hitt et al. (2002, 354) note,

> "In the West (i.e., North America, Western Europe), business dealings have been largely based on the concept of transactions. However, in most Asian societies, they are based on relationships. For example, when an executive is regarded as successful in Western societies, s/he is often described as wealthy. However, an executive of similar success in China is referred to as well connected."

Therefore, Western INVs seeking a presence in Asia will do well to adopt a social capital orientation, albeit in a manner that is culturally appropriate, and to mitigate cultural distance through collaborating with local partners. When cultural barriers can be overcome, interaction with multiple cultures can result in greater technological learning in the long run (Zahra et al. 2000). In sum, it is proposed:

P2: For an INV, the relationship between entry mode commitment and technological learning is stronger at moderate levels of cultural distance between the home country and the international market than at very high or very low levels of cultural distance.

Industry Knowledge Intensity

The cognitive dimension of social capital pertains to "resources providing shared representations, interpretations and systems of meaning among parties" (Nahapiet and Ghoshal 1998, 244). An example would be the concept of the dominant logic of the firm (Prahalad and Bettis 1986), i.e., a mindset embodied in the cognitive map of the dominant coalition in organizations, which influences their worldview of, for instance, worthy goals and appropriate decision-making tools. When firms interact, the extent of a shared understanding on their part is vital to the development of social capital, and thereby knowledge. Tsai and Ghoshal (1998) indicate that shared goals and values lead to *shared vision*, which is an important virtue of the cognitive dimension of social capital, which in turn "can be viewed as a bonding mechanism" (Inkpen and Tsang 2005, 157) that facilitates knowledge creation and acquisition. For INVs, the entrepreneur's vision is especially influential (Johanson and Vahlne 2006, Zahra et al. 2005).

It is particularly beneficial for an INV to have a shared vision with its *key customer(s)* in a given market (Lane and Lubatkin 1998, Yli-Renko et al. 2001). An important source of shared vision between an INV and its potential key customer(s), it is argued, is the degree of industry knowledge intensity of the market segment that it primarily targets. The main target industry in a given international market is vital, because an INV is likely to focus its new business development activities at this segment, and consequently to build its key customer relationship(s) in this industry. Although Porter (1998, 80) argues that "all industries can employ advanced technology; all industries can be knowledge-intensive", it is clear from his own and other work that knowledge intensity varies across industries (e.g., the biotechnology industry is more knowledge-intensive than the cement industry) and for the same industry across markets (e.g., the American bio-technology industry is more knowledge-intensive than the Korean biotech-nology industry). Knowledge-intensive industries are major consumers of technological products and services, suggesting that firms in such indus-tries will welcome any technological learning on the part of their suppliers, including INVs of which they are clients. To that extent, the client(s) and INV have the potential to develop mutual expectations (Yli-Renko et al. 2001) and collective goals (Inkpen and Tsang 2005).

A shared vision between firms and their customers increases the likeli-hood of a high quality of reciprocal exchanges in terms of a match in the level of dependence, equivalence and immediacy. In other words, mutual sharing of knowledge is greater when the firms feel that their exchange is interdependent, of broadly equal value to each other and immediately deployable (Simsek et al. 2003). Not surprisingly, therefore, it has been noted that—especially in knowledge-intensive industries where customer-supplier relationships are often of a collaborative nature—an INV's key customer within a market plays a crucial role in this learning process, both in the context of innovation (Yli-Renko et al. 2001) and interna-tionalization (Yli-Renko et al. 2002). This is particularly true when there is a certain amount of longevity in inter-firm relationships that allows trust to be built and enhances the prospect of new opportunities emerg-ing (Johanson and Vahlne 2006). Learning outcomes for the supplier are often beneficial for the customer and therefore there is reason to expect exchanges of knowledge (Simsek et al. 2003), facilitated by social capital. Thus, it is proposed:

P3: For an INV, the relationship between entry mode commitment and technological learning is stronger at higher levels of industry knowledge intensity of the primary target market segment(s) in the international mar-ket than at lower levels of industry knowledge intensity.

DISCUSSION AND IMPLICATIONS

An important but little articulated outcome of new ventures' entrepreneurial internationalization is technological learning. Building upon prior interna-tional entrepreneurship research, an explanation is provided in this concep-tual paper of how high-commitment entry modes can yield technological learning. The central argument is that presence within (as distinct from exporting to) international markets, arising from the use of high-commit-ment modes, leads to technological learning by allowing the development of social capital which in turn facilitates the acquisition and creation of knowledge (Nahapiet and Ghoshal 1998). This insight is used to identify conditions under which the relationship between the use of high-control modes and technological learning may be enhanced. The resultant ideas— pertaining to regional clusters, national culture and industry knowledge intensity—have potentially useful theoretical and normative implications.

This paper has sought to explain better how technological learning outcomes may potentially occur through the use of high-commitment modes. Relative to other internationalization behaviors such as speed, entry mode has attracted relatively little attention in the international entrepreneurship literature. The entry mode literature has little to say in relation to small and new ventures, which are largely viewed as exporters (Brouthers and Hennart 2007). Yet the Zahra et al. (2000) study—which this paper builds on—does indicate that some INVs do use high-commitment modes that place increasingly more complex demands on the firm in terms of required resources, the need for coordination, and the necessity of interacting with customers and other key stakeholders in foreign markets.

An important implication of the conceptualization in this paper is that, consistent with scholars at the strategy/entrepreneurship interface, internationalization is simultaneously entrepreneurial *and* strategic (Hitt et al. 2001). Research on INVs has understandably emphasized the entrepreneurial aspects of their accelerated internationalization. And, of course, the very act of going beyond exporting in terms of entry mode is entrepreneurial for INVs (Zahra 2005). It calls for inertia to be proactively overcome, is fraught with risk and calls for the innovative use of limited resources (Jones and Coviello 2005, Lu and Beamish 2001). Although traditional perspectives of internationalization would not predict that high-commitment entry modes would be manifested early in a firm's internationalization trajectory (Johanson and Vahlne 1977), opportunity recognition and entrepreneurial learning could result in such behaviors (Forsgren 2002, Oviatt and McDougall 2005a).

However, the model presented in this paper suggests that internationalization is strategic as well, and decision makers in INVs could make choices that are more or less conducive to technological learning outcomes. In particular, the choice of sub-national target markets—in terms of their clustering, cultural and knowledge-intensive characteristics—represents an important strategic decision for INVs. A vital routine associated with making sound location decisions is international market screening (Young et al. 1989). Furthermore, once a high-commitment mode is established, the social capital logic posited in this paper implies that managerial networking (Luo 2003), forming new alliances (Eisenhardt and Martin 2000, Kale et al. 2001) and collaborative learning (Powell 1998) are key strategic capabilities. Thus, this paper provides a more complete perspective of internationalization that encompasses strategic aspects along with entrepreneurial facets. These ideas are synthesized in the table below.

Table 14.1 High-commitment Entry Modes and Technological Learning in INVs

Facilitating factor	Network benefit	Relevance to INVs vis-à-vis large MNCs	Impact on technological learning vis-à-vis market learning	Implications for market screening	Associated practices
P1 (Structural): Regional cluster	Opportunity for tie formation	Potentially more crucial given lesser likelihood of multiplicity of locations within a country-market	Relevant to both types of learning, in terms of providing cutting-edge information.	Relatively unorthodox and may lead to a cluster-by-cluster, rather than a country-by-country, perspective	Networking—proactively interacting and engaging with other actors (Luo, 2003)
P2 (Relational): National culture	Trust	Potentially more crucial given fewer HR resources or lack of a network of subsidiaries	Relatively less sensitive to cultural distance compared to market learning	Helps to short-list culturally compatible clusters	Alliancing—forming formal or informal partnerships with local actors (Eisenhardt and Martin, 2000; Kale et al., 2001)
P3 (Cognitive): Industry knowledge-intensity	Shared goals/vision	Potentially more crucial as expertise across a range of industry settings is less likely	More dependent on knowledge intensity owing to corresponding technology usage	Helps to identify suitably knowledge-intensive markets; trade-offs may need to be made	Collaborative learning—acquiring new knowledge through mutually beneficial ties (Powell, 1998)

This paper also provides a rationale for why some INVs may choose to be what Dimitratos et al. (2003) call a "micromultinational." The micromultinational notion distinguishes between smaller firms (including INVs) that are predominantly exporting (low commitment mode) from those that use higher-commitment modes (e.g., alliances and subsidiaries). They note that such firms "were believed not to proceed beyond exporting in their internationalization routes . . . [but] may service their foreign markets through subsidiaries, and particularly, interorganizational networks and alliances" (Dimitratos et al. 2003, 164). This paper suggests that this is a conceptualization that warrants further research attention, as noted below.

The ideas in this paper open up fresh lines of inquiry that can advance understanding of entrepreneurial internationalization. First, more research is required to consider the antecedents, processes and consequences pertaining to INVs' use of entry modes other than exporting; one promising avenue may be to explore Dimitratos et al.'s (2003) notion of micromultinationals and to compare their financial and non-financial (e.g., learning) performance with that of pure exporters. Second, the moderating effect of the three contingent factors identified in the paper should be studied empirically to further refine and test the propositions, through in-depth case studies and large-scale surveys, respectively. Longitudinal research that explores changes (if any) in the extent of these moderating variables' influence would also be useful. Additionally, attempts could be made to uncover other moderating variables that have not been touched upon here. Third, a useful research avenue would be to distinguish among high-commitment modes (e.g., alliance- vs. ownership-based entry modes) and explore their differential role in technological learning (e.g., acquisitive vs. experimental learning). In other words, it would be of interest to specify the variations in terms of technological learning outcomes, for different high-commitment entry modes employed by INVs.

There are some limitations that should be noted. First, the moderating factors that have been identified do not by any means constitute an exhaustive list. Rather, they are a set of important market characteristics that affect the relationship between entry mode commitment and technological learning. But considering them is useful because, as noted, when taken together they inform a related practice of INVs, viz., international market screening. Second, the use of the dimensions of social capital—structural, relational and cognitive–has been primarily as "steers" to identify relevant literature. Consequently, the factors highlighted (e.g., clusters) may not be classical network characteristics per se (e.g., tie density or centrality) but are highly relevant, given recent emphases on broader network-related concepts, including clusters, in the social capital literature (e.g., Inkpen and Tsang 2005) and the importance of economic geography to international entrepreneurship (Zahra 2005). Third, the theorizing primarily deals with acquisitive learning which "takes place as the firm acquires and internalizes knowledge external to its boundaries" Hitt et al. (2000, 236). Excluded from the scope of the theorizing is internal experimental learning.

Despite its limitations the paper has not only useful theoretical implications (as noted earlier) but also provides useful guidance for managerial practice. First, INVs must be cognizant of valuable benefits, such as technological learning, when they use high-commitment entry modes. Admittedly, the transition to entry modes beyond exporting should be undertaken with care, given the risks involved. However, the recognition of the potential for technological learning, along with other benefits such as firm growth, should be factored into the risk assessment that firms make of the option of high-commitment modes. Second, the decision of what entry mode to employ is made in conjunction with another important decision: which market(s) to enter. The theorizing in this paper offers useful insight into the process of market screening—including the suggestion that INVs pay at least as much attention to the sub-national level as to the national level. They should also take into account cultural distance (while recognizing that some cultural distance may be beneficial) and industry knowledge intensity of their target segments, with a view to enhancing technological learning outcomes. Managerial attention should be most focused on markets where technological learning is likely to be the greatest. Third, INVs must develop competence in networking and collaborative learning in order to better develop, and gain knowledge through, social capital in international markets.

BIBLIOGRAPHY

Adler, P.S. and Kwon, S.-W. (2002) 'Social capital: prospects for a new concept', *Academy of Management Journal*, 27 (1): 17–40.

Autio, E. (2005) 'Creative tension: the significance of Ben Oviatt's and Patricia McDougall's article "Toward a theory of international new ventures",' *Journal of International Business Studies*, 36 (1): 9–19.

Autio, E., Sapienza, H.J. and Almeida, J.G. (2000) 'Effects of age at entry, knowledge intensity, and imitability on international growth,' *Academy of Management Journal*, 43 (5): 909–924.

Birkinshaw, J. and Hood, N. (2000) 'Characteristics of foreign subsidiaries in industry clusters,' *Journal of International Business Studies*, 31 (1): 141–154.

Bloodgood, J., Sapienza, H.J. and Almeida, J.G. (1996) 'The internationalization of new high-potential US ventures: antecedents and consequences,' *Entrepreneurship Theory and Practice*, 20 (4): 61–77.

Brouthers K. and Hennart J.M.A. (2007) 'Boundaries of the firm: insights from international entry mode research,' *Journal of Management*, 33 (3): 395–425.

Brown, P. and McNaughton, R. (2003) 'Cluster development programmes: panacea or placebo for promoting SME growth and internationalisation?' in H. Etemad and R.W. Wright (eds.) *Globalization and Entrepreneurship: policy and strategy perspective*, 106–124, Cheltenham: Edward Elgar.

Currall, S.C. and Inkpen, A.C. (2002) 'A multilevel approach to trust in joint ventures,' *Journal of International Business Studies*, 33 (3): 479–495.

Dimitratos, P., Johnson, J.E., Slow, J. and Young, S. (2003) 'Micromultinationals: new types of firms for the global competitive landscape,' *European Management Journal*, 21 (2): 164–174.

Dodgson, M. (1991) The management of technological learning: lessons from a biotechnology company, Berlin: de Bruyter.

Dougherty, D., Borrelli, L., Munir, K. and O'Sullivan, A. (2000) 'Systems of organizational sensemaking for sustained product innovation,' *Journal of Engineering and Technology Management*, 17 (3–4): 321–355.

Eisenhardt, K.M. and Martin, J.A. (2000) 'Dynamic capabilities: what are they? *Strategic Management Journal*, 21 (10–11): 1105–1121.

Eriksson, K., Johanson, J., Majkgård, A. and Sharma, D. (1997) 'Experiential knowledge and cost in the internationalization process,' *Journal of International Business Studies*, 28 (2): 337–360.

Fernhaber, S.A., Gilbert, B.A. and McDougall, P.P. (2008) 'International entrepreneurship and geographic location: an empirical examination of new venture internationalization,' *Journal of International Business Studies*, 39 (2): 267–290.

Fink, G. and Holden, N. (2005) 'The global transfer of management knowledge,' *Academy of Management Executive*, 19 (2): 5–8.

Forsgren, M. (2002) 'The concept of learning in the Uppsala internationalization process model: a critical review,' *International Business Review*, 11 (3): 257–277.

Hitt, M.A., Ireland, R.S. and Lee, H.-U. (2000) 'Technological learning, knowledge management, firm growth and performance: an introductory essay,' *Journal of Engineering and Technology Management*, 17 (3–4): 231–246.

Hitt, M.A., Ireland, R.D., Camp, S.M. and Sexton, D.L. (2001) 'Strategic entrepreneurship: entrepreneurial strategies for wealth creation,' *Strategic Management Journal*, 22 (6–7): 479–491.

Hitt, M.A., Lee, H.-U. and Yucel, E. (2002) 'The importance of social capital to the management of multinational enterprises: relational networks among Asian and Western firms,' *Asia Pacific Journal of Management*, 19 (2–3): 353–372.

Inkpen, A.C. and Tsang, E.W.K. (2005) 'Social capital, networks, and knowledge transfer,' *Academy of Management Review*, 30 (1): 146–165.

Johanson, J. and Vahlne, J.-E. (1977) 'The internationalization process of the firm—a model of knowledge development and increasing foreign market commitment,' *Journal of International Business Studies*, 8 (1): 23–32.

Johanson, J. and Vahlne, J.-E. (2006) 'Commitment and opportunity development in the internationalization process: a note on the Uppsala internationalization process model,' *Management International Review*, 46 (2): 165–178.

Johanson, J. and Wiedersheim-Paul, F. (1975) 'The internationalization of the firm—four Swedish cases,' *Journal of Management Studies*, 12 (3): 305–322.

Jones, M.V. and Coviello, N.E. (2005) 'Internationalisation: conceptualising an entrepreneurial process of behaviour in time,' *Journal of International Business Studies*, 36 (3): 284–303.

Kale, P., Dyer, J. and Singh, H. (2001) 'Value creation and success in strategic alliances: alliancing skills and the role of alliance structure and systems,' *European Management Journal*, 19 (5): 463–471.

Keeble, D. and Wilkinson, F. (1999) 'Collective learning processes, networking and "institutional thickness" in the Cambridge region,' *Regional Studies*, 33 (4): 319–332.

Keupp, M.M. and Gassmann, O. (2009), 'The past and the future of international entrepreneurship: a review and suggestions for developing the field,' *Journal of Management*, 35 (3): 600–633.

Kogut, B. and Zander, U. (1992) 'Knowledge of the firm, combinative capabilities, and the replication of technology,' *Organization Science*, 3 (3): 383–397.

Kogut, B. and Zander, U. (1993) 'Knowledge of the firm and the evolutionary theory of the multinational corporation,' *Journal of International Business Studies*, 24 (4): 625–645.

Kogut, B. and Zander, U. (1995) 'Knowledge, market failure and the multinational enterprise: a reply,' *Journal of International Business Studies*, 26 (2): 417–426.

Kuemmerle, W. (2002) 'Home base and knowledge management in international ventures,' *Journal of Business Venturing*, 17 (2): 99–122.

Lane, P.J. and Lubatkin, M. (1998) 'Relative absorptive capacity and interorganizational learning,' *Strategic Management Journal*, 19 (5): 461–477.

Leamer, E.E. and Storper, M. (2001) 'The economic geography of the Internet age,' *Journal of International Business Studies*, 32 (4): 641–665.

Lu, J.W. and Beamish, P.W. (2001) 'The internationalization and performance of SMEs,' *Strategic Management Journal*, 22 (6–7): 565–586.

Luo, Y. (2003) 'Industrial dynamics and managerial networking in an emerging market: the case of China,' *Strategic Management Journal*, 24 (13): 1315–1327.

Marshall, A. (1920) *Principles of economics*, London: Macmillan.

McDougall, P.P. and Oviatt, B.M. (2000) 'International entrepreneurship: the intersection of two research paths,' *Academy of Management Journal*, 43 (5): 902–906.

McEvily, B. and Zaheer, A. (1999) 'Bridging ties: a source of firm heterogeneity in competitive capabilities,' *Strategic Management Journal*, 20 (12): 1133–1156.

Moran, P. and Ghoshal, S. (1999) 'Markets, firms and the process of economic development,' *Academy of Management Review*, 24 (3): 390–412.

Nahapiet, J. and Ghoshal, S. (1998) 'Social capital, intellectual capital, and the organizational advantage,' *Academy of Management Review*, 23 (2): 242–266.

O'Grady, S. and Lane, H. (1996) 'The psychic distance paradox,' *Journal of International Business Studies*, 27 (2): 309–333.

Oviatt, B.M. and McDougall, P.P. (1994) 'Toward a theory of new international ventures,' *Journal of International Business Studies*, 25 (1): 45–64.

Oviatt, B.M. and McDougall, P.P. (2005a) 'The internationalization of entrepreneurship,' *Journal of International Business Studies*, 36 (1): 2–8.

Oviatt, B.M. and McDougall, P.P. (2005b) 'Defining international entrepreneurship and modeling the speed of internationalization,' *Entrepreneurship Theory and Practice*, 29 (5): 537–554.

Porter, M.E. (1998) 'Clusters and the new economics of competition,' *Harvard Business Review*, 76 (6): 77–90.

Powell, W.W. (1998) 'Learning from collaboration: knowledge and networks in the biotechnology and pharmaceutical industries,' *California Management Review*, 40 (3): 228–240.

Powell, W.W., Koput, K.W. and Smith-Doerr, L. (1996) 'Interorganizational collaboration and the locus of innovation: networks of learning in biotechnology,' *Administrative Science Quarterly*, 41 (1): 116–145.

Prahalad, C.K. and Bettis, R. (1986) 'The dominant logic: a new linkage between diversity and performance,' *Strategic Management Journal*, 7 (6): 485–501.

Prashantham, S. (2008) *The internationalization of small firms: a strategic entrepreneurship perspective*, London: Routledge.

Sapienza, H.J., Autio, E., George, G. and Zahra, S.A. (2006) 'A capabilities perspective on the effects of early internationalization on firm survival and growth,' *Academy of Management Review*, 31 (4): 914–933.

Sapienza, H.J., De Clercq, D. and Sandberg, W.R. (2005) 'Antecedents of international and domestic learning efforts,' *Academy of Management Review*, 20 (4): 437–457.

Shrader, R.C. (2001) 'Collaboration and performance in foreign markets: the case of young high-technology manufacturing firms,' *Academy of Management Journal*, 44 (1): 45–60.

Simsek, Z., Lubatkin, M.H. and Floyd, S.W. (2003) 'Inter-firm networks and entrepreneurial behavior: a structural embeddedness perspective,' *Journal of Management*, 29 (3): 427–442.

Tallman, S., Jenkins, M., Henry, N. and Pinch, S. (2004) 'Knowledge, clusters, and competitive advantage,' *Academy of Management Review*, 29 (2): 258–271.

Tsai, W. and Ghoshal, S. (1998) 'Social capital and value creation: the role of intra-firm networks,' *Academy of Management Journal*, 41 (4): 464–476.

Westlund, H. and Bolton, R. (2003) 'Local social capital and entrepreneurship,' *Small Business Economics*, 21 (2): 77–113.

Wiklund, J. and Shepherd, D. (2003) 'Knowledge-based resources, entrepreneurial orientation, and the performance of small and medium-sized businesses,' *Strategic Management Journal*, 24 (13): 1307–1314.

Yli-Renko, H., Autio, E. and Sapienza, H.J. (2001) 'Social capital, knowledge acquisition, and knowledge exploitation in young technology-based firms,' *Strategic Management Journal*, 22 (6–7): 587–613.

Yli-Renko, H., Autio, E. and Tontti, V. (2002) 'Social capital, knowledge and the international growth of technology-based new firms,' *International Business Review*, 11 (3): 279–304.

Young, S., Hamill, J., Wheeler, C. and Davies, D. (1989) *International market entry and development: strategies and management*, London: Harvester Wheatsheaf.

Zaheer, S. and Zaheer, A. (2006) 'Trust across borders,' *Journal of International Business Studies*, 37 (1): 21–29.

Zahra, S.A. (2005) 'A theory of international new ventures: a decade of research,' *Journal of International Business Studies*, 36 (1): 20–28.

Zahra, S.A. and George, G. (2002) 'International entrepreneurship: the current status of the field and future research agenda,' in M.A. Hitt, R.D. Ireland, S.M. Camp and D.L. Sexton (eds.) *Strategic entrepreneurship: creating a new mindset*, 255–288, Oxford: Blackwell.

Zahra, S.A., Ireland, R.D. and Hitt, M.A. (2000) 'International expansion by new venture firms: International diversity, mode of market entry, technological learning, and performance,' *Academy of Management Journal*, 43 (5): 925–950

Zahra, S.A., Korri, J.S. and Yu, J. (2005) 'Cognition and international entrepreneurship: implications for research on international opportunity recognition and exploitation,' *International Business Review*, 14 (2): 129–146.

15 Change in SME Internationalization

A Network Perspective

Niina Nummela

INTRODUCTION

Surprisingly, the concept of change in literature related to the internationalization of the firm has not been of much interest (Nummela et al. 2006, Schuh 2001). However, implicitly, as most researchers consider internationalization as a process evolving in time, change must be a central element in this phenomenon. Changes due to internationalization can be internal to the company (see Kalinic and Forza 2009, Nummela et al. 2006, Nummela 2004), but changes that happen in the company network are also of importance. This aspect is highlighted in the context of small and medium-sized enterprises (SMEs), as for them the role of network is decisive. A number of researchers have suggested that access to external resources through a network facilitates and accelerates the internationalization process of a small firm (e.g., Chetty and Wilson 2003, Jones 1999, Holmlund and Kock 1998, Coviello and Munro 1995, 1997, Bell, 1995, Bonaccorsi, 1992, Welch 1992). But how this happens and what actually changes in company network due to internationalization, remains unclear.

The objective of this study is to shed some light on this topical issue by describing and analyzing change in the networks of internationalizing SMEs. The study combines the analysis of change both at the company level and at the network level, but the emphasis is on the latter.

LITERATURE REVIEW

Networks and SME Internationalization

Until the early 2000s, research on networks and internationalization was quite modest (Sadler and Chetty 2000, Coviello and Munro 1995), and was concentrated on a few specific areas. A much cited piece of research in this area is the study of two Swedish researchers, Johanson and Mattsson (1988). They argued that internationalization was inherently a network-embedded phenomenon: when entering new markets, a company also enters a new network, and has to create new relationships. Additionally, they emphasized that the network in which a company operates also affects its internationalization.

Discussion of networks and internationalization has often been brought to the level of individual relationships that need to be managed during the process (Ruzzier et al. 2006). Continuing from the seminal work of Johanson and Mattsson (1988), researchers have argued that the internationalization process is about establishing more and more relationships abroad, allowing the firm to advance in the internationalization process (Jansson and Sandberg 2008). In the development of relationships, mutual learning and the acquisition of experiential knowledge are decisive (Johanson and Vahlne 2003).

Consequently, prior research offers a substantial knowledge base on which to build, but gaps also exist. For example, the earlier discussion focuses mainly on direct business relationships between companies. And yet we know that non-exchange relationships (Ojala 2009) and social networks may also be significant in the internationalization of SMEs (Komulainen et al. 2006, Holmlund and Kock 1998).[1] Additionally, the number of empirical studies describing the role of networks in SME internationalization is limited. The body of this work suggests that SME internationalization partly depends on a company's set of network relationships (for a review of these studies, see Coviello and McAuley 1999). In general, empirical studies support Johanson and Mattsson's (1988) argument that the network has a significant effect on SME internationalization. What kind of impact remains unclear, and especially how firms should utilize these relationships (Ojala 2009).

The significance of the different actors in the network seems to vary during the process of internationalization (Ruokonen et al. 2006, Coviello and Munro 1995). In the pre-export stage—when the firm is still searching for information and considering the possibility of entering international markets—the problems are mainly related to the lack of different resources, and small companies may turn to public and semi-public actors for assistance (cf. Ojala 2009) or to their social networks to learn about markets and international business (Bonaccorsi 1992).

On the other hand, when a small company is already involved in international operations, it faces competition and environmental turbulence in the market. It is also probable that, at this stage, the network of the company requires more proactive management than earlier (cf. Ruokonen et al. 2006, Hite and Hesterly 2001). These new circumstances create novel needs, and the company's interests also turn to different network actors. Other firms, such as customers and suppliers, are the normal partners in this stage, when new strategy alternatives, and also business partners with market knowledge and long-term relationships, are sought. The emerging alliances may be collaborative or competitive, or even both (on "co-opetition" between small companies, see e.g., Bengtsson and Kock 1999, Chetty and Wilson 2003).

To sum up, it is assumed here that existing networks can offer small and medium-sized enterprises assistance in their internationalization, particularly in a case when the internationalization process proceeds rapidly (e.g., Belso-Martinez 2006, Freeman et al. 2006, Madsen and Servais 1997, McDougall et al. 1994). Unfortunately not all SMEs are aware of all the potential partners in their networks and, even if they are, they do not know how to exploit them (Nummela et al. 2004, Bell et al. 1992, Rothwell and Dodgson 1991). Such ignorance probably means that very few small companies exploit their networks effectively.

Change on the Network Level

This study focuses on changes in the network that are due to internationalization. In general, literature on small-firm internationalization describes an evolutionary process of slow-moving change, mostly at the company level (Nummela et al. 2006). Therefore, here too the dynamics of networks are investigated by taking the so-called IMP Group's network approach, because in that approach the change in networks is considered to be continuous, although this evolutionary, incremental change may be interrupted by radical changes (e.g., Halinen et al. 1999, Easton and Lundgren 1992, Gadde and Håkansson 1992, Lundgren 1992). The change in a network is due to the fact that it is never complete or in equilibrium (Håkansson 1992). The most important change agents in the network are the companies themselves, as the origin of the change is related to the interface between the actor and the environment (Gadde and Håkansson 1992).

Changes in a network may concern the actors, the activities or the resources that exist between companies (Halinen et al. 1999). Therefore, in this study the changes due to internationalization in the network are analyzed with the help of the A-R-A model (see Håkansson and Johanson 1992), which has been commonly used in studies of business-to-business marketing. The key elements in the model are the actors, the resources and the activities in the network. The actors perform and control the activities with the help of the resources, and through exchange processes they develop and maintain relationships with each other.

Again, this study is concerned less with the process of network evolution, and more with the changes in the actors, resources and activities in SME networks. Such changes are analyzed over the course of time. First, the relevant actors in the network are identified, then their activities are examined, and finally, the resources acquired through these contacts are analyzed. As Gadde and Håkansson (1992) suggest, both major and minor changes in the network are considered as important study objects, as the minor changes may lead to major ones in the future.

Changes are also evaluated in actor bonds, resource ties and activity links[2] (cf. Håkansson and Snehota 1995). In other words, here too the interest is in the connection between the activities, resource elements and different actors in the company's network. We are also interested in the strengths of these connections (cf. discussion of strong and weak ties, originating from Granovetter 1973), and whether their development has been proactive or reactive (cf. Chetty and Blankenburg-Holm 2000, Ojala 2009).

The network of a small firm is a complex combination of the several embedded networks to which it belongs (cf. Halinen and Törnroos 1998, Easton 1992). It is recognized that both business and social relationships may have a role in SME internationalization (Holmlund and Kock 1998), although it is sometimes difficult to separate business and social relationships from each other—not least because a relationship may change from one to the other in course of time (Agndal and Chetty 2007). In this study, business relationships are institutionalized connections between organizations, whereas social relationships are based on interaction between individuals. The latter would not exist without the involvement of these particular individuals (Agndal and Chetty 2007).

The activities between the actors may be business-based, dealing with economic transactions between the organizations, but this is not always the case. Sometimes collaboration is based on other types of exchange of resources, such as knowledge or finance. Business relationships may also extend beyond normal business transactions; they may lead to obtaining market knowledge or access (Holmlund and Kock 1998), opportunity recognition and exploitation (Agndal and Chetty 2007, Lin and Chaney 2007, Johanson and Vahlne 2006) improvement in strategic positions or a gain in legitimacy and visibility (Belso-Martinez 2006, Freeman et al. 2006).

In line with Van de Ven and Poole (1995), change is defined here as the difference in form, quality or state over a selected time period. The focus is mainly on changes due to internationalization, but sometimes they are so intertwined with other changes that they are very difficult to separate (cf. Nummela et al. 2006).

RESEARCH DESIGN

This study describes and analyzes changes in the networks of internationalizing SMEs. For this exploratory study, a multiple-case approach was considered to be an appropriate research strategy. Case study allows inductive investigation of the research topic, analysis of the phenomenon in its contextual setting, and more holistic coverage of the companies selected (Ghauri 2004). In order to minimize the effects of environmental and situational factors, we limited the number of cases to three Finnish industrial companies. However, in order to preserve the anonymity of the informants, the case companies were disguised (they are given fictional names in the case descriptions, for example.)

The selection of cases is a crucial decision in the research process and should therefore be made after careful consideration and a critical evaluation of the alternatives. Random selection is neither necessary nor desirable, and theoretical sampling is recommended (Eisenhardt and Graebner 2007). This involves choosing cases that are likely to replicate or extend the emergent theory (Eisenhardt 1989). The theoretical qualifications of the case must also be kept in mind; in other words, how well they fit the conceptual categories and the extent of their explanatory power (Eisenhardt 1989, Smith 1991).

Because of the significance of the context in studying change, the timing of internationalization was particularly important. Additionally, in this kind of exploratory study, a broad overview and variety in results is preferable; therefore companies with diverse internationalization histories were included in the study.[3] The study comprises three companies that all started exporting in the 1990s, but were in different stages of internationalization at the time of the data collection. Fork Ltd could be labeled as a "born-again global" and Specs Ltd and Spiral Ltd as "traditional" companies. This variety was considered to increase the richness of the data and the diversity of the cross-case analysis.

This study takes a retrospective perspective, although the research design is not necessarily longitudinal, as the data was collected at only one point of time. In line with the recommendations of Huber and Power (1985), we gathered the data for the research in face-to-face interviews with the most knowledgeable informants available, in other words the entrepreneurs in the case companies. Our investigation is based on the perception of the owner-manager, who is at the core of the change process, as networks in small firms are highly personalized to the entrepreneur or the top management team (see e.g. Loane et al. 2004, Manolova et al. 2002, Holmlund and Kock 1998). In the interviews, the owner-managers were asked to look back and describe the changes during the company's internationalization.

Secondary data was also collected to complement the personal interviews. All gathered data was further analyzed in several phases (Yin 1994). First, the interview recordings were transcribed and a within-case analysis of each company was conducted (Eisenhardt 1989). Consequently, the information from the interviews was reorganized to form descriptive narratives. Finally, we included a cross-case comparison in order to reveal the similarities and differences between the companies.

CHANGES IN THE CASE COMPANIES

Fork Ltd

Fork Ltd is a family-owned company, which specializes in the design, manufacture and marketing of forest harvesting heads. The harvester heads are used in forest machines for wood harvesting all over the world. At the time of the interviews, the turnover of the company was about €3 million and it employed approximately 20 persons.

The company was founded in the mid-1980s as an engineering office focusing solely on designing harvester heads. The managing director has a strong background in the business since the early 1980s, first in his father's company and thereafter as an independent entrepreneur. Design of an own product for the company started in 1993, and the product was launched on the market in 1995.

The product was originally planned for global markets: it was tested in Australia and the first delivery was made in 1995 to Canada. The first export order was obtained through the entrepreneur's social network; he had a personal contact to a potential customer who was interested in their new product. Since then the company has proceeded to the main European markets and now operates worldwide. During the last few years the share of exports has been almost 100 percent of the annual turnover. At the moment the main market area is North America, which covers approximately 25 percent of exports. In the future, besides North America and Europe the importance of more distant markets, such as Southeast Asia and Japan as well as South America, will continue to increase.

The company has a worldwide dealer and importer network. The local dealers have their own customer network, consisting mainly of small and medium-sized forest contractors who own less than ten machines. Customers sometimes also include forest companies, firms that install additional products, and sellers of secondhand machines. The dealer network is under constant development process, and at the moment Fork Ltd is trying to withdraw from cooperation with the weakest dealers and create strong partnerships with the most effective ones.

In the forest machine industry, cooperation between companies is quite rare. In the case of Fork Ltd, however, cooperation has been one of the key characteristics of the company's business idea. Since 1993 and the development of its own product, the company has invested strongly in the development of a subcontractor network. At the moment it has a few key subcontractors who take care of selected processes (e.g., automation, welding, painting) in production, and also a few key component suppliers with whom a long-term partnership is the objective. The subcontractors are small local companies, whereas most of the suppliers are large foreign companies. Approximately half of production has been outsourced, but key activities (testing, assembly, etc.) are still done in-house.

In addition to its cooperation with other companies, Fork Ltd has also cooperated with public and semi-public organizations as well as universities. For example, it has financed its growth partly through support from a governmental organization and trained its personnel in courses organized by semi-public and public organizations. It has also used the services of Finnish commercial counselors abroad as well as students from the local polytechnic. The company has participated in two export circles, one aimed at the Russian markets, and the other at the Brazilian. These export circles are cooperative ventures comprising four small companies that jointly attempt to enter the markets in question, and for this purpose jointly hire an export manager. The circles are initiated by a governmental organization, which covers half of the resultant expenses for a period of three years.

Specs Ltd

Specs Ltd manufactures and markets products for contact-lens care as well as contact lenses, spectacle frames and other related products. The turnover of the company exceeds €4 million and it employs almost 50 persons. Contact lenses cover approximately one-third of the turnover, and the other two-thirds come from lenses and spectacle frames. The company is family-owned and in addition to this business, the managing director and his family also own a small optician's business and a photographer's studio.

The company was established in the late 1970s when the managing director, who is an optician by education, and his friend, who has a degree in chemistry, noticed the invasion of imported liquids for contact-lens care. They deduced that there would be a niche for a corresponding Finnish product at a more reasonable price. After three years of extensive product development, they introduced their own product to the Finnish market. They initially developed three different products for contact-lens care, which then led to the manufacture and marketing of a range of contact lens care products.

In Finland, the products are sold directly to opticians through the company's sales representatives in the field. The brand is quite well known in Finland, not least because the company prominently sponsored a local team in the national basketball league in the late 1990s. Domestic markets are stable, although the demand has decreased slightly. The company has, however, been able to cover this loss with an increase in exports.

The internationalization of the company started in the mid-1980s when it began importing stock lenses and spectacle frames, but exports started later, in 1994. Because of strict legislation, entry to the main European markets was quite difficult; therefore Poland was selected as the first target market. From these markets, the company soon expanded into Estonia and Sweden. Finland's entry to the European Union in 1995 offered access to EU markets, and at present the company is operating in most European countries. Now the company exports to 30 countries, and the proportion of exports exceeds 60 percent in the main export product group (contact lens care solutions). Customers on international markets are mainly local distributors and wholesalers who specialize in optical products. Exported products are sold both under the company brand name and as private-label products.

The company has created a network based on long-lasting relationships in some activities. For example, in product development the company cooperates closely with the University of Turku. They use the laboratory facilities of the Institute of Microbiology for the testing needed for product development and other related purposes. The managing director finds this arrangement very effective as it allows the company to use the facilities only when they are needed, and thus to incur costs only during this time.

On the other hand, the company has cooperated with several governmental organizations in order to seek additional financial resources for investments needed. Cooperation with public organizations has also been necessary when organizing tailor-made training for its workforce, as the public education system does not offer any training in this field. The personnel have also occasionally participated in seminars and courses related to exports that have been organized by governmental organizations. The managing director himself is an active member in several entrepreneurial associations, but, according to him, the role of these activities in internationalization has been very limited.

Most of the raw materials used for production are purchased from foreign suppliers, as potential suppliers do not exist on the domestic market. Long-lasting relationships with key suppliers have been established and, in order to stay competitive, the company has invested a considerable amount of time in searching for the best possible supplier for each component. This has led to a relatively tight supplier network, as new entrants, usually internationally well known and respected suppliers, have always replaced the older ones in the network. As competitiveness is of particular importance on international markets, it seems that these changes have been—at least partly—due to internationalization. In addition to the supplier network, the company has also created an international dealer network, which is based on long-lasting relationships with the local dealers.

Spiral Ltd

Spiral Ltd is a small company operating in the metal and engineering industry, its main products being screw conveyors and pumps. The company employs 20 persons and its annual turnover exceeds €4 million. The company was established in the late 1970s as a joint company of the managing director and his father-in-law. Business operations started when the managing director and his father-in-law bought machinery and some preliminary sketches from a company that had gone bankrupt. The company has remained in the family, although the older generation has already withdrawn from it.

During the company's history, the main products have been conveyors, which are used in various industries in order to move raw materials from one place to another. These are also the products that the company exports. Customers include the pulp and paper industry, mechanical woodworking, mining and the metallurgical industry, as well as sewage treatment and power plants. The conveyors have an important role in process industries, where undisturbed production and dust-free material transfer are crucial issues.

Both in Finland and abroad, the products are sometimes sold to end users, i.e., manufacturing companies in various process industries. However, the majority of products are sold to large, often globally operating systems suppliers as a part of a larger system consisting of complementary products. The number of potential customers in each country is limited; for example, in Austria the company has only one customer, a globally operating systems supplier. In other export markets too, the number of customers is very small.

The company started exporting in 1990 with a delivery to Sweden, although there had occasionally been direct deliveries to Norway and indirect deliveries to Russia before that. The export share has varied considerably; at most direct exports exceeded 25 percent of turnover. The relative importance of the different markets has clearly varied. At the time of the interviews, Austria was its main export country, accounting for 80 percent of exports. In the early 1990s the main focus of export operations was on Sweden, and one person was employed almost full-time for two to three years to try to gain access to this market (the production manager, who had Swedish as his mother tongue). The first deliveries were made to Austria in 1993, and exports there have been regular ever since. At the moment, the share of exports is approximately 10 percent of annual turnover. The proportion of indirect exports has also remained high, and at present is approximately 70 percent of turnover.

The core competence of Spiral Ltd lies in the manufacture of conveyors for demanding industrial applications. Most of the production is done in-house, although less important activities are outsourced to small subcontractors (e.g., in automation) that operate on the company's premises. All components are bought from suppliers with whom the company has long-term relationships.

The role of public and semi-public actors has been quite limited in Spiral Ltd's internationalization. The managing director has occasionally participated in seminars and courses related to exports and internationalization, but otherwise the company has been rather self-sufficient when it comes to internationalization. In addition to this, the company has also participated in two export circles initiated by a semi-public organization. The export circles focused on the Swedish and Norwegian markets, but did not bring in any notable business.

Cross-case Analysis

The three case companies have clear similarities and differences. First, their internationalization process has occurred mostly at the same time, in the 1980s and 1990s. Second, they all operate in rather traditional industries. However, from the perspective of change due to internationalization, they also differ significantly from each other. The networks of the case

Table 15.1 A Summary of the Case Companies' Networks in Internationalization

	Actor bonds with	Nature of resources	Activity links
Fork Ltd	1 public and semi-public support organizations 2 domestic SMEs 3 domestic suppliers 4 international dealers	1 knowledge, finance 2 risk sharing, market knowledge 3 material 4 knowledge, customer contacts	1 administrative 2 other 3 commercial 4 commercial
Specs Ltd	1 university 2 international suppliers 3 international dealers	1 knowledge 2 material 3 knowledge, customer contacts	1 technological 2 commercial 3 commercial
Spiral Ltd	1 professional service providers 2 domestic SMEs 3 domestic suppliers 4 international system suppliers and end customers	1 knowledge, expertise 2 risk sharing, market knowledge 3 material 4 business transactions	1 administrative 2 other 3 commercial 4 commercial

companies are analyzed in the table below, in relation to actors, resources and activities in internationalization.

During its internationalization, the network of Specs Ltd changed noticeably. The process, which began with ad hoc contacts through the entrepreneur's social network, has developed into an international business network with strong, long-lasting relationships with suppliers and dealers. The supplier side in particular seems to be proactively managed. Contrary to our expectations, the various semi-public and public organizations do not seem to have played a major role in the company's internationalization, although it has used their services in its business in general. The changes in networks were mostly a result of proactive development resulting in long-lasting relationships between the parties. However, the proactive development often arose from the entrepreneur's social network; in other words social networks were developed into business relationships (cf. Agndal and Chetty 2007).

On the other hand, the networks of Fork Ltd were much more diverse than those of the other companies. Within a relatively short space of time, the company had entered into short-term transactions with various public and semi-public organizations, participated in two short-term collaborative ventures with other Finnish SMEs and had created an international dealer network. The collaboration with semi-public and public actors and other non-exchange relationships was created for temporary purposes only, and the relationships remained weak. These relationships can be considered to have been valid only for a short time, and after a while became "saturated," once learning and the exchange of resources reached the desired level.

The third of the case companies, Spiral Ltd, made the most limited use of its network in its internationalization, and the social network of the entrepreneur was not utilized at all. Although the company entered into some transactions with public and semi-public organizations and engaged in some collaboration with other Finnish SMEs, none of these activities seemed to have much impact on the company's internationalization. The only strong, long-lasting relationships were created with system suppliers; otherwise the company's network was developed on a more ad hoc basis.

DISCUSSION AND CONCLUSIONS

The dynamics of networks in SME internationalization seems to be an under-investigated area. In contrast to many earlier studies, this study attempted to look at change in company networks throughout the internationalization process, not only at initiation, as often seems to be the case. Networks were also analyzed from multiple perspectives, but the main focus was on two dimensions: (1) the change in the network and (2) the value added by the network.

The networks of all case companies had *changed* due to internationalization, but the degree and nature of change varied. The cases partly verify earlier knowledge on networks; e.g., in the early phases of internationalization, social relationships act as triggers for change, and these relationships may later be developed into business ones (cf. Agndal and Chetty 2007). However, this is not always the case, and, contrary to Jack et al. (2008), our cases indicate that networks may develop based on business transactions only. The findings also point out the importance of looking at the dynamics of networks in more detail—maybe in later research—particularly taking into account exits, withdrawals and re-entries. This aspect has been rather neglected so far, but if it could be combined with discussion on de-internationalization, the results could be very interesting.

The findings also indicate that various changes in a company network are not necessarily connected, although they might somehow be related to internationalization of the company. It can be assumed that the "connectedness" depends on the company's commitment to internationalization, and particularly on the company's strategic decisions. In a company where internationalization is strongly based on a deliberate strategy, the changes probably follow a more predefined pattern, and thus are also more closely connected to each other. Consequently, in future studies on change and internationalization, the aspect of strategy should also be taken into consideration.

The strategy viewpoint and our case company, Fork Ltd, also highlight the need carefully to consider the definition of change. Fork and other "born-again globals" pose extra challenges for studying change and internationalization. Namely, if the situation at the time of founding is compared with today, noticeable changes can be identified, as the engineering office at that time operated in a totally different network. However, internationalization actually began much later, in 1993, at a time when radical change in the company and its business idea was taking place, when it turned its attentions from being just an engineering office to being a manufacturer. Its activities were reorganized according to a new business idea, so this point in time would seem a more suitable time for comparison. If the time of this "rebirth" is used as a comparison point, the changes that occurred are less notable, although not insignificant. After making the strategic decision to change its business idea, the company has quite proactively followed its chosen path; since this one radical change the other changes have been minor in nature. The changes in the network were the results of the proactive development of business relationships, with social networks playing only a minor role in the internationalization of the company.

In terms of *value added by the network*, these exploratory cases indicate that the internationalization of SMEs is unique, especially when evaluated from the viewpoint of networks. A small company can internationalize with rather limited support from its network, as Spiral Ltd has done, and also with relatively few changes to the network, as in the case of Fork Ltd. Social and business networks can also be used in a variety of ways in the internationalization process. It is also noticeable that, for a company operating worldwide, some parts of its value network may remain quite domestic (cf. Fork Ltd).

From a managerial perspective, it is interesting to observe the case companies' different strategies used in network management. Our cases seemed to support the argument of Jack et al. (2008) that, in the growth phases of SMEs, network management becomes more calculated and intentional. In particular, the two companies whose internationalization had progressed successfully had been developing their networks in quite a proactive manner. However, some changes to the networks of both companies can still be expected—not all changes in the network are "voluntary," and sometimes because of time and resource constraints, a small company may have to decrease the number of partners in its network or make some of its connections more latent (cf. Jack et al. 2008). This might be particularly relevant for Fork Ltd, whose number of dealers exceeds its number of employees.

Despite the interesting results, this study also has some limitations. First, the findings are based on only three cases and thus the results can only be considered tentative. Nevertheless, they open new avenues for further research and point out topics that need more elaboration. It would be worthwhile, for example, to study sources of radical change in detail. When do they actually occur and why? Additionally, the study could be extended to companies whose internationalization has proceeded from exporting to more demanding modes of operations. McDougall and Oviatt (1996) have argued that modes of operation that require more resource commitment also call for more strategic changes, and it would no doubt be rewarding to examine if this is really so.

This study was retrospective in nature, focusing on the change from the viewpoint of a single company. It would be quite attractive to broaden the perspective from the micro level to the industry or country level and examine whether SMEs in general have changed the way they internationalize their operations. Recent studies on born globals suggest that this is the case. It has been argued that these companies should have been created to fit the international business environment from inception (McDougall et al. 1994). In other words, it could be assumed that these companies should exhibit fewer changes as a result of internationalization. A broader empirical study would be required to justify of this argument.

NOTES

1. For a thorough review of the business and social network traditions in entrepreneurship research, see Slotte-Kock and Coviello 2010.
2. *Activity links* regard technical, administrative, commercial and other activities of a company that can be connected in different ways to those of another company as a relationship develops. *Resource ties* connect various resource elements (technological, material, knowledge resources and other intangibles) of two companies. *Actor bonds* connect actors and influence how the two actors perceive each other and form their identities in relation to each other (Håkansson and Snehota 1995, 26–27).
3. Bell et al. (2001) have classified internationally operating firms into three categories: born globals, born-again globals and traditional firms. Traditional firms follow the incremental internationalization process, born globals are international from inception and born-again globals are well-established firms that focus on domestic markets at start-up, but later start a rapid internationalization process (Bell et al. 2001, 174).

BIBLIOGRAPHY

Agndal, H. and Chetty, S. (2007) 'The impact of relationships on changes in internationalisation strategies of SMEs,' *European Journal of Marketing*, 41 (11/12): 1449–1474.

Bell, J. (1995) 'The internationalization of small computer software firms: a further challenge to stage theory,' *European Journal of Marketing*, 29 (8): 60–75.

Bell, J., McNaughton, R. and Young, S. (2001) 'Born-again global' firms. An extension to the 'born global' phenomenon,' *Journal of International Management*, 7 (3): 173–189.

Bell, J., Murray, M. and Madden, K. (1992) 'Developing expertise: An Irish perspective,' *International Small Business Journal*, 10 (2): 37–53.

Belso-Martinez, J.A. (2006) 'Why are some Spanish manufacturing firms internationalizing rapidly? The role of business and institutional international networks,' *Entrepreneurship & Regional Development*, 18 (3): 207–226.

Bengtsson, M. and Kock, S. (1999) 'Cooperation and competition in relationships between competitors in business networks,' *The Journal of Business and Industrial Marketing*, 14 (3): 178–193.

Bonaccorsi, A. (1992) 'On the relationship between firm size and export intensity,' *Journal of International Business Studies*, 23 (4): 605–635.

Chetty, S. and Blankenburg-Holm, D. (2000) 'Internationalisation of small to medium-sized manufacturing firms: a network approach,' *International Business Review*, 9 (1): 77–93.

Chetty, S.K. and Wilson, H.I.M. (2003) 'Collaborating with competitors to acquire resources,' *International Business Review*, 12 (1): 61–81.

Coviello, N. and McAuley, A. (1999) 'Internationalisation and the smaller firm: a review of contemporary empirical research,' *Management International Review*, 39 (3): 223–256.

Coviello, N. and Munro, H. (1997) 'Network relationships and the internationalisation process of smaller software firms,' *International Business Review*, 6 (4): 361–384.

Coviello, N.E. and Munro, H.J. (1995) 'Growing the entrepreneurial firm. Networking for international market development,' *European Journal of Marketing*, 29 (7): 49–61.

Easton, G. (1992) 'Industrial networks: a review,' in B. Axelsson and G. Easton (eds.) *Industrial Networks. A New View of Reality*, 1–27, London: Routledge.

Easton, G. and Lundgren, A. (1992) 'Changes in industrial networks as flow through nodes,' in B. Axelsson and G. Easton (eds.) *Industrial Networks. A New View of Reality*, 89–104, London: Routledge.

Eisenhardt, K.M. (1989) 'Building theories from case study research,' *Academy of Management Review*, 14 (4): 532–550.

Eisenhardt, K.M. and Graebner, M.E. (2007) 'Theory building from cases: opportunities and challenges,' *Academy of Management Journal*, 50 (1): 25–32.

Freeman, S., Edwards, R. and Schroder, B. (2006) 'How smaller born-global firms use networks and alliances to overcome constraints to rapid internationalization,' *Journal of International Marketing*, 14 (3): 33–63.

Gadde, L-E. and Håkansson, H. (1992) 'Analysing change and stability in distribution channels—a network approach,' in B. Axelsson and G. Easton (eds.) *Industrial Networks. A New View of Reality*, 166–179, London: Routledge.

Ghauri, P. (2004) 'Designing and conducting case studies in international business,' in R. Marschan-Piekkari and C. Welch (eds.) *Handbook of qualitative research methods for international business*, 109–124, Cheltenham, UK: Edward Elgar.

Granovetter, M.S. (1973) 'The strength of weak ties,' *American Journal of Sociology*, 78 (6): 1360–1380.

Halinen, A., Salmi, A. and Havila, V. (1999) 'From dyadic change to changing business networks: An analytical framework,' *Journal of Management Studies*, 36 (6): 779–794.

Halinen, A. and Törnroos, J.-Å. (1998) 'The Role of Embeddedness in the Evolution of Business Networks,' *Scandinavian Journal of Management*, 14 (3): 187–205.

Hite, J.M. and Hesterly, W.S. (2001) 'The evolution of firm networks: from emergence to early growth of the firm,' *Strategic Management Journal*, 22 (3): 275–286.

Holmlund, M. and Kock, S. (1998) 'Relationships and the internationalisation of Finnish small and medium-sized companies,' *International Small Business Journal*, 16 (4): 46–63.

Huber, G.P. and Power, D.J. (1985) 'Retrospective reports of strategic-level managers: Guidelines for increasing their accuracy,' *Strategic Management Journal*, 6 (2): 171–180.

Håkansson, H. and Johanson, J. (1992) 'A model of industrial networks,' in B. Axelsson and G. Easton (eds.) *Industrial Networks. A New View of Reality*, 28–34, London: Routledge.

Håkansson, H. and Snehota, I. (1995) *Developing relationships in business networks*, London: Routledge.

Jack, S., Drakopoulou Dodd, S. and Anderson, A.R. (2008) 'Change and the development of entrepreneurial networks over time: a processual perspective,' *Entrepreneurship & Regional Development*, 20 (2): 125–159.

Jansson, H. and Sandberg, S. (2008) 'Internationalization of small and medium sized enterprises in the Baltic Sea Region,' *Journal of International Management*, 14 (1): 65–77.

Johanson, J. and Mattsson, L.-G. (1988) 'Internationalisation in Industrial Systems—A Network Approach,' in N. Hood and J.-E. Vahlne (eds.) *Strategies in Global Competition*, 287–314, London: Routledge.

Johanson, J. and Vahlne, J.-E. (2006) 'Commitment and opportunity development in the internationalization process: A note on the Uppsala internationalization process model,' *Management International Review*, 46 (2): 165–178.

Johanson, J. and Vahlne, J.-E. (2003) 'Business Relationship Learning and Commitment in the Internationalization Process,' *Journal of International Entrepreneurship*, 1 (1): 83–101.

Jones, M.V. (1999) 'The Internationalization of Small High-Technology Firms,' *Journal of International Marketing*, Vol.7 No.4, 15–41.

Kalinic, I. and Forza, C. (2009) 'Internationalisation of SMEs and changes in organisational elements,' Proceedings of the 36th Annual Conference of the Academy of International Business (UK and Ireland Chapter), April 2–4, Glasgow.

Komulainen, H., Mainela, T. and Tähtinen, J. (2006) 'Social networks in the initiation of high-tech firm's internationalisation,' *International Journal of Entrepreneurship and Innovation Management*, 6 (6): 526–541.

Lin, K-H. and Chaney, I. (2007) 'The influence of domestic interfirm networks on the internationalization process of Taiwanese SMEs,' *Asia Pacific Business Review*, 13 (4): 565–583.

Loane, S., McNaughton, R.B and Bell, J. (2004) 'The internationalization of Internet-enabled entrepreneurial firms: Evidence from Europe and North America,' *Canadian Journal of Administrative Sciences*, 21 (1): 79–96.

Lundgren, A. (1992) 'Coordination and mobilisation processes in industrial networks,' in B. Axelsson and G. Easton (eds.) *Industrial Networks. A New View of Reality*, 144–165, London: Routledge.

Madsen, T.K. and Servais, P. (1997) 'The internationalization of born globals: an evolutionary process?' *International Business Review*, 6 (6): 561–583.

Manolova, T.S., Brush, C.G., Edelman, L.F. and Greene, P.G. (2002) 'Internationalization of Small Firms. Personal Factors Revisited,' *International Small Business Journal*, 20 (1), 9–31.

McDougall, P.P. and Oviatt, B.M. (1996) 'New venture internationalization, strategic change, and performance: A follow-up study,' *Journal of Business Venturing*, 11 (1), 23–40.

McDougall, P.P., Shane, S. and Oviatt, B.M. (1994) 'Explaining the formation of international new ventures: The limits of theories from international business research,' *Journal of Business Venturing*, 9 (6): 469–487.

Nummela, N. (2004) 'Change in SME internationalisation. Three case studies from Finland,' in L.P. Dana (ed.) *Handbook of Research on International Entrepreneurship*, 404–430, Cheltenham, UK: Edward Elgar.

Nummela, N., Loane, S. and Bell, J. (2006) 'Change in SME internationalisation: an Irish perspective,' *Journal of Small Business and Enterprise Development*, 13 (4): 562–583.

Nummela, N., Saarenketo, S. and Puumalainen, K. (2004) 'Rapidly with a rifle or more slowly with a shotgun? Stretching the company boundaries of internationalising ICT firms,' *Journal of International Entrepreneurship*, 2 (4): 275–288.

Ojala, A. (2009) 'Internationalization of knowledge-intensive SMEs: The role of network relationships in the entry to physically distant market,' *International Business Review*, 18 (1): 50–59.

Rothwell, R. and Dodgson, M. (1991) 'External linkages and innovation in small and medium-sized enterprises,' *R & D Management*, 21 (2): 125–137.

Ruokonen, M., Nummela, N., Puumalainen, K. and Saarenketo, S. (2006) 'Network management—the key to successful rapid internationalisation of a small software firm?' *International Journal of Entrepreneurship and Innovation Management*, 6 (6): 554–572.

Ruzzier, M., Hisrich, R.D. and Antoncic, B. (2006) 'SME internationalization research: past, present and future,' *Journal of Small Business and Enterprise Development*, 13 (4): 476–497.

Sadler, A. and Chetty, S. (2000) 'The Impact of Networks on New Zealand Firms,' *Journal of Euromarketing*, 9 (2): 37–58.

Schuh, A. (2001) 'Strategic change during the internationalisation of the firm,' Proceedings of the 27th EIBA Conference, 13.–15.12.2001, Paris.

Slotte-Kock, S. and Coviello, N. (2010) 'Entrepreneurship research on network processes: A review and ways forward,' *Entrepreneurship: Theory and Practice*, 34 (1): 31–57.

Smith, N.C. (1991) 'The case-study: a vital yet misunderstood research method for management,' in N.C. Smith and P. Dainty (eds.) *The management research handbook*, 145–158, London: Routledge.

Van de Ven, A.H. and Poole, M.S. (1995) 'Explaining development and change in organizations,' *Academy of Management Review*, 20 (3): 510–540.

Welch, L.S. (1992) 'The Use of Alliances by Small Firms in Achieving Internationalization,' *Scandinavian International Business Review*, 1 (2): 21–37.

Welch, L.S. and Luostarinen, R. (1988) 'Internationalization: Evolution of a concept,' *Journal of General Management*, 14 (2): 34–55.

Yin, R.K. (1994) *Case study research: design and methods*. 2nd ed., Thousand Oaks, CA: Sage Publications.

Part V
Illustrative Cases

16 A Different Story on Rapid International Growth
CV Online

Tiia Vissak

THE BIRTH OF CV ONLINE

Young Estonian entrepreneurs Jürgen Tamm, Jüri Kaljundi and Randel Min established a predecessor of CV Online—Amendion—in November 1996. It began as a traditional recruitment company, mainly helping the founders' co-students from Tallinn Technical University to find jobs. The firm hired two recent graduates in psychology to interview and test job-seekers. In the beginning, the enterprise was not very successful although its services were cheaper than their competitors': Jürgen Tamm even had to sell his brother's car (he later got some shares in return) to stay in business. Online services were developed in autumn, 1997, when the company was renamed CV Online.

The first system cost 511 Euros; at first, the firm just created a homepage with a database in which job-seekers could enter their resumes, but this database had no searching opportunities. In 1998, the new services were developed further (photos, test results and interview clips were added later in addition to CVs) and the firm started offering them more intensively as the founders understood that the uniqueness of their services would bring more profit than standard services with low prices. Still, their operations remained relatively modest: in 1998, the firm's turnover was only €0.01 Million.

RAPID EXPANSION TO INTERNATIONAL MARKETS

In 1999, the company started paying even more attention to online services, but also continued with traditional offline services. Until August 1999, CV Online operated locally. Then it decided to expand to several Eastern and Central European countries because the owners saw how successful recruitment and IT firms were in the US and Western Europe, and understood that the population and the number of Internet users were too small in the Baltic region to provide for world-scale competitiveness and covering the development costs of its online services. Thus it decided not only to enter Latvia and Lithuania as many other Estonian firms had done, but also several other countries. In December 1999, the company went to its first foreign market, Latvia. In that year, its database included 10,500 CVs and 750 job offers, its sales were €0.16 million, net profit €0.01 million, and assets €0.08 million, and it had 12 employees. It needed external financing to expand further. Moreover, the founders expected the investors to raise the company's efficiency and goodwill and participate in forming its strategy.

In January 2000 CV Online expanded its capital base by including New Economy Ventures (then belonging to an Estonian firm, LHV Ventures; its current name is GILD Bankers) and Esther Dyson (US). The former was selected for their entrepreneurial experience and the latter for contacts in Europe and knowledge of the Internet's future perspectives. They invested approximately €0.62 million in total and obtained a 35 percent ownership. In addition, the firm took loans in the sum of €1.40 million. The inflow of capital quickened its expansion. The office in the Czech Republic was opened in March, the Lithuanian branch in April, the Hungarian subsidiary in May and the one in Poland in June, 2000. Two months later, the firm also opened a homepage in Russia but did not create a subsidiary there. In the Czech Republic, the firm bought an online recruitment service provider Profese.cz, in Hungary, it bought 75 percent of the shares of a local site Munkaforum.hu (paying €0.5 million), while the other offices were started from scratch, so the firm also had to find local employees and managers. In addition, it hired representatives in Bulgaria and Romania and established a holding company, CVO Holdings, in Amsterdam, Holland.

In foreign markets, the firm offered both online and offline recruitment services, including evaluations, interviews and background studies. In 2000, CV Online Estonia's turnover was €0.39 million, its net loss was €1.03 million and assets €1.32 million. In total, the firm invested €0.64 million to its subsidiaries that year and gave them loans in the sum of €0.78 million. The group's total turnover (both from Estonia and abroad) was €0.45 million. The firm had 100 employees in 7 countries (32 in Estonia) and expected to double their number every year (this plan was not realized) although the company's equity capital had become negative. Thus, it needed additional investments.

CHALLENGES OF RAPID INTERNATIONAL GROWTH LEADING TO REORGANIZATION OF BUSINESS

In January 2001, the following expansion in the firm's capital base took place: this time, LHV Ventures, Esther Dyson and 3TS Venture Partners (a Central European investment fund) participated. The total investment was about three million Euros. Through the deal, the investors gained a majority stake in the firm's holding company, Dutch-registered CVO Holdings.

In 2001, the firm's managers realized that it had grown too fast and become too large for managing efficiently. Moreover, some offices were not able to sell enough in their markets, as the firm lacked time to customize its services to every country's needs. The economic slowdown in some countries was also a problem, as it reduced the need for traditional offline recruitment services.

Consequently, CV Online decided to lay off a third of its Estonian employees and temporarily suspended its operations in Russia, Romania and Bulgaria (in the latter two countries, the firm's offices had not yet actively started their operations, so it was relatively easy to pull back, while the Russian office was spending a lot—at least €50,000 a month—but earning almost nothing). The company considered entering Slovakia instead, but did not yet establish a subsidiary there (this was done in 2005). The firm's headquarters were moved to Budapest and some founders drew back from active management of the firm. Norrie Sinclair (who was originally from Scotland, but had lived for several years in Budapest and who had experience as a top manager of a large international recruitment company) became the new CEO of the company (renamed CVO Group).

The new CEO agreed that the firm should remain focused on Central and Eastern Europe as this market was not as developed as Western Europe, so the competition was lower. He also considered Asia as a potential future market, but the firm has not yet entered there. Moreover, he decided to increase prices and pay more attention to increasing the value added by the firm's services, as it had to differentiate from its competitors on these markets (though in Estonia and Latvia the company had the first-mover advantage, while in Poland and Hungary, it had more than 100 competitors). In 2001, the group's turnover was €1.30 million and net loss €2.41 million, while CV Online Estonia's turnover was €0.49 million, net loss €0.80 million (all foreign subsidiaries also had losses) and total assets €1.45 million.

Although in 2002 the firm had planned to reopen its operations in Russia and Romania through a joint venture and possibly enter Croatia, these plans were not fully realized because of lack of capital (in 2001, the firm had to write off a hopeless loan and thus that year ended with a loss; moreover, only its Latvian subsidiary managed to earn profit in 2002, while all others had losses) and the global economic slowdown after the September 11th events. A Romanian homepage was later reopened, but closed again in 2008, while entry into Croatia was canceled.

Still, product development continued: the company launched a new personnel recruitment service Professional People (by in the first half of 2002, this division had already reached almost 30 percent of the group's total revenues) and started developing a recruitment software program called CVO Selector. It also decided to try entering other market niches: business consulting, technology development and labor renting. CVO Group's turnover from the services of CV Online was about €1.82 million and net loss €0.79 million, while CV Online Estonia's turnover was €0.68 million, net loss €0.09 million and total assets €1.40 million. In October 2002, the enterprise had over 330,000 registered users as job-seekers in the CEE region. In that year, it had about 100 employees, 25 of them in Estonia.

INTERNATIONAL GROWTH THROUGH DIVERSIFICATION AND SUBSIDIARIES

In 2003, the company's Estonian branch changed its name to CVO Group OÜ. It hoped to increase the sales of its service Professional People, but this did not happen. It had 26 employees in Estonia (the group's total number of employees was still about 100). The firm's turnover was €0.73 million (the group's total turnover from the services of CV Online was €1.96 million and net loss €0.67 million), net profit €0.01 million and total assets €1.44 million. In addition to the Latvian subsidiary, the Lithuanian subsidiary also managed to earn profit. In the three Baltic countries, the company was a market leader, while elsewhere it did not have such a strong position. It received a loan of €0.19 million for developing its recruitment software CVO Selector (at that time unique in the Central and Eastern European market) helping employers to manage and track the entire recruitment process from behind their own desks.

In 2004, the firm restructured the service Professional People and employed more people for developing and offering it. As a result, the sales of this service increased by 31 percent. It also paid more attention to its labor renting service under the trademark Contract People, as several local and foreign enterprises were interested in it. Estonia's and the firm's other subsidiaries' home countries' accession to the European Union increased the demand for its services. It had 31 employees in Estonia. The firm's turnover in Estonia was €1.04 million (the group's total turnover from the services of CV Online was €3.3 million), net profit €0.29 million and total assets €1.61 million. The Lithuanian subsidiary and the head office in Hungary ended that year with a loss, while the others earned profit.

The firm also established a subsidiary in Russia and an office (CVO International) in London for entering Western European markets (later, this function was moved to Budapest, Hungary: currently, CVO International offers its services in Austria, Germany, Switzerland, the United Kingdom, Finland, Sweden, Denmark, Netherlands and Belgium, but also countries outside Europe: Egypt, Ethiopia, Kenya, Mauritius, Morocco, Namibia, Rwanda, South Africa, Sudan, Tanzania, Tunisia and Uganda) as it did not want to be perceived as only an Eastern European company. The company also considered opening subsidiaries in Holland, Germany, Austria and some other countries, but decided not to do it at this time.

In 2005, the firm's growth continued as the business climate was favorable (the expansion of the European Union in May 2004 had increased the need for Central and Eastern European workforce in Western Europe) and the efficiency of its subsidiaries increased. The firm's turnover in Estonia was €1.88 million (the group's total turnover was €13.6 million, €5.15 million of that from the services of CV Online), net profit €0.25 and total assets €2.21 million. It opened a new subsidiary in Estonia, JobCenter, for offering labor-renting services, and an international site, EMEAjobs, in cooperation with Monster, Posao, CyprusJobs, Bestjobs, Jobtiger and others, offering jobs in 40 countries in Europe, the Middle East and Africa. In Estonia, the number of employees was increased to 150. The group's Latvian and Hungarian subsidiaries earned profit, though the others had losses. The firm also opened a subsidiary in Slovakia.

THE END OF A MICROMULTINATIONAL?

In 2006, the company continued offering online recruitment under the trademark CV Online, classical offline recruitment (under the new trademarks CVO Technology Recruitment, CVO Finance Recruitment and CVO Sales & Marketing Recruitment) and labor renting under the trademark Simplika. The group's total turnover was €18 million (€7.4 million came from the services of CV Online). Due to the creation of a new unit, JobCenter, and moving most of labor renting services there, the Estonian firm's overall turnover decreased to €1.57 million, but net profit increased to €0.70 million. JobCenter's turnover in Estonia was €1.0 million; it also created subsidiaries in Latvia and Lithuania and offered its labor renting and recruitment services in Russia. In the end of 2006, the Estonian firm had 36 employees. Many of its former employees went to JobCenter. The firm's assets increased to €2.63 million. Only its Latvian and Lithuanian subsidiaries managed to earn profit.

In 2007, the firm continued with online and offline recruitment services. JobCenter took a new name, OÜ Simplika, and continued with labor renting, but also took over some consulting services from the mother company. Its turnover increased to €1.04 million (it continued with its two subsidiaries in Latvia and Lithuania, but also offered its services in Russia, Poland and the Czech Republic), while its Estonian mother company's turnover decreased to €1.47 million, net profits increased to €1.90 million and total assets to €3.98 million (the firm sold one of its trademarks for €0.80 million, which increased its profit). In Estonia, it had 234,000 registered users and published more than 26,000 job ads in its online portal. The Estonian firm's average number of employees decreased to 31, but the group itself had 240 employees and its turnover was €22 million, about five million coming from the services of CV Online in different countries. In total, it had 1.1 million users and 1.1 million CVs. As the Russian subsidiary did not manage to start earning profit, the firm decided to close it down in 2007. Of the other subsidiaries, only the Latvian one earned a profit, but the activities of others were also continued: it was decided to close down only the London office in 2008.

In February 2008, the firm's Estonian branch active in online services (including pre-screening) took the name CV Online Estonia OÜ, while a new branch, CVO Recruitment Estonia OÜ, specialized in offering recruitment services, mostly for specialists in finance, technology, sales and marketing. OÜ Simplika continued with labor renting and consulting services. In February 2008, the owners decided to sell CV Online, but not CVO Recruitment (including CVO Finance Recruitment, CVO Technology Recruitment and CVO Sales and Marketing Recruitment) or Simplika. The firm's estimated market value was at that time €19.2 million. In April the company informed the public that several firms were interested in buying it. In August 2008, it was announced that Alma Media—a large media company from Finland with net sales of €341.2 million in 2008 (also a part-owner of a recruitment company, Monster Finland, with 75 percent)—had started negotiations for buying the enterprise, but by spring 2009, the acquisition had still not taken place, as the economic slowdown and a relatively high price reduced its appeal.

DISCUSSION

From the above, it can be concluded that CV Online was local for three years and one month and then entered eight CEE countries—Latvia, Lithuania, Poland, the Czech Republic, Hungary, Russia, Bulgaria and Romania—in a very short time period: from December 1999 to August 2000. Such a beginning of the internationalization process does not fit the one described in the Uppsala model (Johanson and Vahlne 1977, 1990, Johanson and Wiedersheim-Paul 1975) because the entry to several foreign markets was very fast, so the firm did not have much time for acquiring foreign market knowledge from one country to the next; moreover, the company did not enter all the psychically closest countries (as it skipped neighboring countries Finland and Sweden, which are also very popular for Estonian internationalizers) and started its internationalization from the establishment of foreign subsidiaries.

On the other hand, this company was not a classic born-global, either, even though it "leapfrogged" into internationalization instead of making incremental steps (Oviatt and McDougall 1994), because it did not start exporting within three years after its foundation (this aspect has been emphasized in Knight et al. 2004) and it still has not established any subsidiaries outside its home region, Europe (according to Gabrielsson et al. 2004, such firms should also enter countries outside their own continent). Moreover, it did not intend to internationalize from inception (cf. Oviatt and McDougall 1994), the managers started considering this in 1999, more than two years after the company's establishment. The company was also not a born-again global (Bell et al. 2001) as it did not have international activities before the domestic-market-oriented period right after its establishment.

The relatively early and fast internationalization of this firm was triggered by several factors mentioned in the literature as *"critical incidents"* (Bell et al. 2001). They received foreign direct investments (Dunning 1994) from owners who helped with knowledge and useful network relationships (Johanson and Vahlne 2003), but also offered ideas and assistance in formulating the group's management team. They also raised the firm's efficiency and goodwill, helped in developing new offices abroad and finding new customers in the CEE. Expansion to the European Union was also a favorable "critical incident" for this company. In addition, the firm's internationalization was also fast because of favorable entrepreneurial and managerial attitude toward international expansion (Kutschker et al.1997; Madsen and Servais 1997), relatively unique resources, capabilities and services (Zahra and George 2002) and low entry costs (Roberts and Tybout 1997).

Although in the first year of its international activities, the firm expanded very fast, such an expansion in the number of foreign countries did not continue: on the contrary, in 2001, the company decided to freeze its operations in Russia, Romania and Bulgaria. This partial de-internationalization (cf. Benito and Welch 1997) happened because of the firm's newness, inexperience and limited resources and networks (cf. Wickramasekera and Bamberry 2003). It was also easy because of low exit costs (cf. Roberts and Tybout 1997); in Romania and Bulgaria, the company's operations were relatively minor and the Russian unit had not managed to create much revenue, either. Despite such a slowdown in the firm's development, it did not wish to stop its international expansion. By 2002, it was already planning to re-enter Russia and Romania (this means, to re-internationalize partially, cf. Pauwels and Matthyssens 1999)—which was easy due to low re-entry costs (cf. Roberts and Tybout 1997) and the firm's previous experience in these markets (cf. Johanson and Vahlne 2003)—and enter Croatia, but it did not succeed. It re-established its Russian subsidiary in 2004, but closed it down again in 2007; the Romanian operations were also restarted and closed down again in 2008, while the Croatian subsidiary was never created. The corporation also established an office in London in 2004 but closed it down in 2008 (its operations were moved to Budapest). Thus as Axinn and Matthyssens (2002) state, during their internationalization, firms often use combinations of entry and exit strategies.

Still, it cannot be concluded that the firm's international development was unsuccessful in the first decade of the 21st century. It entered Slovakia in 2005 and has cooperated with several firms to develop new services and enter additional markets. It has access to other recruitment sites through the online recruitment network EMEAjobs, but has also cooperated with CEO Europe, UCMS Group EMEA and StepStone ASA, and thus it can also find employees for its customers' enterprises, not only in Western and Eastern Europe, but also in some Middle Eastern, American and Asian countries. The turnover of the firm has increased from €0.01 million in

1998 to €0.45 million in 2000 and €22.0 million in 2007, of which 93.3 percent came from outside Estonia. It is no longer an Estonian firm, as its headquarters have been moved to Budapest and its holding firm to Amsterdam, and the initial founders have retained only a minority stake—it has become truly international and its development continues. To sum up the total internationalization experience of this firm, it can be agreed with Bell et al. (2001) and Oesterle (1997) that there are many situations in between instantly internationalizing companies, slow internationalizers and the ones that never enter any foreign countries: this company is one of such examples and its internationalization path cannot be explained by a single research stream in IB.

ACKNOWLEDGMENTS

The research was financed by the Estonian Science Foundation's Grant No. 7405 and target financing from the Estonian Ministry of Education and Research No. 0180037s08.

BIBLIOGRAPHY

Axinn, C.N. and Matthyssens, P. (2002) 'Limits of internationalization theories in an unlimited world,' *International Marketing Review*, 19 (5): 436–449.

Bell, J., McNaughton, R. and Young, S. (2001) '"Born-again global" firms: an extension to the 'born global' phenomenon,' *Journal of International Management*, 7 (3): 173–189.

Benito, G.R.G. and Welch, L.S. (1997) 'De-internationalization,' *Management International Review*, 37 (Special Issue 2): 7–25.

Dunning, J.H. (1994) 'Re-evaluating the benefits of foreign direct investment,' *Transnational Corporations*, 3 (1): 23–51.

Gabrielsson, M., Sasi, V. and Darling, J. (2004) 'Finance strategies of rapidly-growing Finnish SMEs: born internationals and born globals,' *European Business Review*, 16 (6): 590–604.

Johanson, J. and Wiedersheim-Paul, F. (1975) 'The internationalization of the firm: four Swedish cases,' *Journal of Management Studies*, 12 (3): 305–322.

Johanson, J. and Vahlne, J.-E. (1977) 'The internationalization process of the firm: a model of knowledge development and increasing foreign market commitments,' *Journal of International Business Studies*, 8 (1): 23–32.

Johanson, J. and Vahlne, J.-E. (1990) 'The mechanism of internationalisation,' *International Marketing Review*, 7 (4): 11–24.

Johanson, J. and Vahlne, J.-E. (2003) 'Business relationship learning and commitment in the internationalization process,' *Journal of International Entrepreneurship*, 1 (1): 83–101.

Knight, G., Madsen, T.K. and Servais, P. (2004) 'An inquiry into born-global firms in Europe and the USA,' *International Marketing Review*, 21 (6): 645–665.

Kutschker, M., Bäurle, I. and Schmid, S. (1997) 'International evolution, international episodes, and international epochs—implications for managing internationalization,' *Management International Review*, 37 (Special Issue 2): 101–124.

Madsen, T.K. and Servais, P. (1997) 'The internationalization of born globals: an evolutionary process?' *International Business Review*, 6 (6): 561–583.

Oesterle, M.-J. (1997) 'Time span until internationalization: foreign market entry as built-in mechanism of innovation,' *Management International Review*, 37 (2): 125–149.

Oviatt, B.M. and McDougall, P.P. (1994) 'Toward a theory of international new ventures,' *Journal of International Business Studies*, 25 (1): 45–64.

Pauwels, P. and Matthyssens, P. (1999) 'A strategy process perspective on export withdrawal,' *Journal of International Marketing*, 7 (3): 10–34.

Roberts, M.J. and Tybout, J.R. (1997) 'The decision to export in Columbia: an empirical model of entry with sunk costs,' *The American Economic Review*, 87 (4): 545–564.

Wickramasekera, R. and Bamberry, G. (2003) 'Exploration of born globals/international new ventures: some evidence from the Australian wine industry,' *Australasian Journal of Regional Studies*, 9 (2): 205–217.

Zahra, S.A. and George, G. (2002) 'International entrepreneurship: the current status of the field and future research agenda,' in M.A. Hitt, R.D. Ireland, S.M. Camp and D.L. Sexton (eds.) *Strategic entrepreneurship: creating a new mindset*, 255–288, London: Blackwell Publishers.

17 A Path of International Growth
Case PurFilec Ltd

Leila Hurmerinta

THE BIRTH OF PURFILEC

PurFilec (a pseudonym) was established at the end of 1987 by two partners, each having equal ownership of the shares. The company produces
equipment for water purification, i.e., apparatus for desalination and fil-
tering, and operates in business-to-business markets. About 80 percent of
PurFilec's clients are end users, and the remaining products are subcon-
tracted for other firms. The products are tailor-made for each project. The
owner-manager had 15 years' working experience before establishing the
company: first he spent a couple of years in marketing in the pharmaceutical industry, and after that worked as a water chemist in another company,
responsible for the water purification processes. His partner, coming from
the same company, had worked as a planning engineer for 20 years. The
previous employer of both partners is now one of their competitors, and a
few clients also followed the partners.

In the beginning the company produced components for Finnish clients only, but even then the products were indirectly exported to Russia
as a part of clients' end products. The owner-manager was also involved
in the *negotiations with the foreign end customers*, so in that respect he
had some experience of conducting international business. His previous
work had included similar tasks and he had a *good knowledge of languages*
(four languages), as well as *of business practices* in general. Furthermore,
his attitude toward internationalization was very positive, as the following quote indicates: "Actually, exporting has never been strange to me; I
worked abroad during my student days. It just seems so natural." In sum, it
can be concluded that the prerequisites for international growth existed in
the company from the very beginning.

THE FIRST STEPS TOWARD INTERNATIONALIZATION—
THE PERIOD OF PASSIVE GROWTH

Decision making in the company is quite democratic: the decisions are discussed between the partners, and sometimes also with the employees. The

board of directors also has a central role in the decision making. However, when asked about the decision to go international, it seems that an explicit decision was never made. Exporting was based more on identified needs in the market, and was also influenced by the economic recession. Since the attitudes toward internationalization were positive from the beginning and the importance of language skills has been emphasized (even the assemblers knew three languages), starting exports was very natural.

The first export delivery was made in 1987, as a part of a larger project. At that time, exporting was based on the contacts of the Finnish clients—mostly inherited from the previous employer. With these customers business continued as earlier, but in terms of volume the business was still rather modest, only some 50 thousand Euros a year. Gradually, the project business developed, and before the year 1991 the company participated in several larger export projects as an active subcontractor, having direct contacts to foreign markets and negotiating with the final users. This active role was required because the complex processes of water purification demanded expertise in the field.

Exporting had been an essential part of the company's activities since the earliest stage of its life cycle. However, at the beginning the company's role was very passive: *they made none of their own initiatives to develop the business.* The product/market decisions were accepted as given, i.e., they were made by others. New customers contacted the company, not the other way around. Knowledge about the company's products was spread by existing customers and through business negotiations abroad. Nevertheless, participation in trade fairs abroad took the company a bit closer to the potential clients. It also had a stand at a Finnish trade fair that was visited by many Russians.

LIKE RIPPLES IN A POND—FROM PASSIVE TO ACTIVE

Given the company's passiveness in creating its early export relations, the year 1991 could be considered as a turning point. Business in this field is based on a process of long negotiations, taking from one to three years. Negotiations with the first new foreign client started in 1990, leading to the first direct export order in 1991. At the same time the company also gained some large Finnish clients, who had exports to the Baltic countries and Russia. Information about PurFilec was spread abroad through these clients, thus creating more and more export contacts. As a result, exporting to Poland started in 1992.

The spread of the economic recession in the domestic markets created a temporary setback for its business. Cooperation with Finnish building companies gradually ended in 1992–1994, which motivated the company to search for new foreign contacts. Although the export projects did help the company to survive through its worst times, the situation was still very difficult. At the time of the deepest recession, in 1993, the company was contacted by an agent of a Danish company, who was interested in buying the business. The partners did not see any other way out, so the shares were gradually sold to the Danish company between 1994 and 1998. At the time when the decision was made, PurFilec employed six persons directly and another six as subcontractors and its turnover had increased to €1.3 million.

The management took the change of ownership as an opportunity and a potential source for competitive advantage. Information about new projects and market opportunities was obviously needed. The company turned to the east, where market information was obtained by visiting foreign engineering offices in Moscow. The need to make direct contact with foreign clients without domestic intermediaries challenged the company in terms of doing business abroad. This new challenge forced the company to utilize private expert services, particularly concerning the legal aspects: "You have to think differently when you make the contract. And financial questions are difficult; how to finance the project and then how to get the money from the clients. The banks have been cooperative."

The company gradually succeeded in creating new cooperative relationships in Russia. This time the partner in the Russian market was a consulting and engineering company—either Finnish or foreign—but not a Finnish constructing company, as earlier. In practice, business in the Russian market may be initiated elsewhere, in Turkey or the US, for example. This adds another dimension to the international growth of the company, but also sets new requirements for its own competence. It uses the knowledge of its partners—the consulting and engineering offices abroad—but the benefits of public service providers have remained limited. For example, it has participated twice in an "export circle," i.e., a collaborative venture of SMEs aiming at exports, which receives financial support from the Ministry of Trade and Industry. In both cases the concrete output was considered inadequate, except in the form of shared costs on marketing expenses.

SIX YEARS AFTER THE FIRST EXPORT DELIVERY— FROM SPORADIC TO CONTINUOUS GROWTH

By 1993, exports were a primary part of the business: the first export clients were still regular customers and exports had continued without any major setbacks. However, the owner-manager was still responsible for all international operations; no export personnel was employed. This is due to the fact that his technological expertise was needed throughout the negotiations and delivery. Additionally, because of the nature of the project business and lack of time, careful planning of international growth was considered quite difficult.

The volume of exports grew gradually, as the number of international clients increased. Until 1992, the proportion of exports was about 30 percent of turnover, but this rose to 80 percent in 1993 with the large, successful international projects. In its international operations the company focused on the east, the main export countries being Russia, Belarus, Kazakhstan, Ukraine (Russia and CIS countries together comprised 92 percent of exports), the Baltic countries (5 percent) and Poland (3 percent). However, the future already seemed to lie further east—in China.

The business continued to grow, for several reasons. First, the demand for water-filter apparatus continued to increase in the 1990s as a result of the development of a new coating technique, and at the end of the 1990s it already accounted for 70–80 percent of the company's turnover. R&D got a further boost from its collaboration with the Helsinki University of Technology in the late 1990s, which resulted in novel know-how and new clients.

Second, growth was supported by the change of ownership—the shares of the company were sold to Danish ownership by 1998, and the company became a member of a water technology group which was the biggest water-treatment organization in the Nordic countries. This resulted in significant decreases in purchasing prices, as the procurement was centralized to headquarters, which again helped the company in the tough competition. Additionally, the new ownership also gave the company credibility in the eyes of clients. As a result, in 1998 the company employed eight persons directly, and its turnover had increased to €2.3 million.

In spite of its continuous growth, at the end of 1990s the company still did not have any specific objectives for exports, or growth in general. However, its international operations had become less sporadic: if in the beginning it took every project which was offered, by this time it had the possibility of being more selective. Also long-term projects, ranging from planning to delivery and after sales activities (including supply of spare parts etc.), facilitate planning in the company. Planning is done at all levels of organization: groups, management team and the board of directors.

ELEVEN YEARS AFTER THE FIRST EXPORT DELIVERY—GROWTH ON LIMITED MARKETS

International growth comes with experience. During the first decade in international markets, the company had learned that having more than one market decreases the potential market risk; this is why it invested in both domestic and international markets. Additionally, the Danish owners expect the company to take care of its home market for the group. The balance is still in favor of exports—in 1998 its share was 70 percent of the turnover.

Membership of the water technology group means that *the markets are divided* within the group. PurFilec had two main export areas: Russia and the Baltic countries, of which Russia was the more important, accounting for 95 percent of the exports. In Russia the company concentrated particularly on Moscow and its surroundings. Another eastern market was China, where the company started to export in 1994/1995, and in summer 1998 it established a sales subsidiary there. Additional sporadic deliveries had also been made to other countries, such as Tanzania, Guatemala, Poland, Cyprus and Israel. Relationships with these clients will continue too, because of the need for spare parts. Earlier contacts in Belarus, Kazakhstan and Ukraine had gradually faded.

The company continued to grow. In 1999, an engineering company that produces equipment and plans processes for water purification plants was merged into PurFilec. Through the merger the expertise in water purification increased. In 2003, the Danish parent company joined a leading European water technology group having more than 70 subsidiaries all around the world. This European group operates globally and joining it limited potential markets of PurFilec even further, as it cannot operate in the same markets where the group already has local activities. By the end of 2005 the turnover had increased to €3.7 million, and the number of employees had grown to 18, the latter mostly due to the merger with the engineering company.

EIGHTEEN YEARS AFTER THE FIRST EXPORT
DELIVERY—THE END OF INTERNATIONAL GROWTH

In 2005, the managing director and founder of PurFilec retired, and a new managing director replaced him. At the same time, a person responsible for exports was employed. Although the company's turnover had increased, the share of direct exports had decreased to 5 percent and indirect project exports to 16 percent. Decisions on markets are no longer made within PurFilec but determined at the group headquarters. Although the focus on the home market has been made very explicit, the company still continues to export to Russia and Estonia, which have remained the most important export countries throughout the company's history. Russia still accounts for 95 percent of the exports, which consist mostly of extensive and customized water treatment systems to the power industry. In Estonia the products are individual components and equipment for households and small-business needs.

Being a part of the European water technology group requires more detailed planning, budgeting and reporting from the company. The development strategies have also been made more explicit. The strategies focus on the home market and selected export markets—such as Russia and Estonia. Since the beginning of the 2000s, exports to other countries have been sporadic and geographically dispersed, including deliveries to Sweden, Kazakhstan, the US, Colombia, Yemen and Egypt, for example. Many markets that were significant earlier are now the responsibility of other units of the group, and the sales subsidiary in China has been closed down.

DISCUSSION

PurFilec could be characterized as *an entrepreneurial spin-off* (see Ahlström Söderling 1999). Its exports already had roots prior to the establishment of the company, as the customer relationships were inherited from the previous employer. The owner-manager just continued with the same business (products, employees, customers) he had previously been involved with. This is in line with earlier research, as small-business owners often establish businesses in sectors in which they have prior experience or product knowledge in order to utilize their own skills and knowledge (Hogarth-Scott et al. 1996).

The internationalization process proceeded rather quickly and without setbacks. It could be characterized as circular, combining the previous knowledge of the entrepreneur with a broad international outlook. While knowledge is the key resource for international growth (Yli-Renko, Autio and Tontti 2002), the experiential knowledge is the most critical determinant in it (Johanson and Vahlne 1977, Majkgård 1998).

The year 1991 was important for the company. That was the year when the home market collapsed and the importance of exports increased. It was also the time of the company's first direct export delivery, and the *customer base* for project exports expanded. In this totally new situation for the entrepreneur and the company, the company decided to use external consultants. This indicates that the experiential knowledge of the entrepreneur, especially in terms of business practice, was not sufficient. At the stage when a company experiences newness and uncertainty, the process of internationalization seems to slow down until the gap in knowledge is successfully filled. Again, this is in line with earlier research—for example, Reuber and Fischer (1999) found that there may be diminishing returns on experience, rather than the usually assumed linear relationship between experience and its consequences.

The company has succeeded in deepening its export involvement by expanding its business operations. Throughout the company history the entrepreneur's previous knowledge of export practice was the main source of information. Cooperation with Finnish construction companies gradually ended in the late 1990s, which forced the company to increase its direct contacts abroad, thereby enhancing the role of the entrepreneur as an active initiator of negotiations. The company was also compelled to establish new contacts directly with foreign consulting and engineering offices, i.e., to create a new business network. *Business networks often provide the market knowledge and contacts* needed for export. Furthermore, the company strengthened its product knowledge in collaboration—again supporting the fact that an experienced owner-manager understands what he or she does not know and could learn from others (McGee et al. 1995). Prior experience may also encourage the search for and use of information (Hart et al. 1994) when needed. The new parent company and the European group of firms did not directly affect the process of internationalization, but rather implicitly influenced it by strengthening the company's credibility and resources.

The company subsequently successfully deepened its internationalization through the end of the 1990s, when it was compelled to focus on the home market and follow the division of markets within the group. As the company was only one member of a larger group, it was not surprising that the relevance of individual prior experience decreased when the power structure and management of the company were changing (see Forsgren 2002).

Thus, this case highlights the value of pre-entrepreneurial experience of a small firm's owner-manager. It can be divided into business and market-related experience, but the international outlook of the manager is also of importance. Prior export-market experience supports rapid initiation of exports and also deep involvement in international operations (see Bilkey 1978, Dichtl et al. 1990). The value of pre-entrepreneurial export experience for the company seems to be twofold; it has its own value until the export confirmation stage, after that it appears especially in ability in building business networks and utilization of them. The more experienced owner-managers are better able to contact, create and use external sources of knowledge (e.g., Blomstermo et al. 2004) that may further the international growth of the firm.

BIBLIOGRAPHY

Ahlström Söderling, R. (1999) 'Entrepreneurial spin-offs: do we understand them?' 44th ICSB World Conference, 20–23 June, Naples, Italy. ICSB152–1/152–19.

Bilkey, W.J. (1978) 'An attempted integration of the literature on the export behavior of firms,' *Journal of International Business Studies*, 9 (1): 33–46.

Blomstermo, A., Eriksson, K, Lindstrand, A. and Sharma, D.D. (2004) 'The perceived usefulness of network experiential knowledge in the internationalising firm,' *Journal of International Management*, 10 (3): 355–373.

Dichtl, E., Köglmayr, H.-G. and Müller, S. (1990) 'International orientation as a precondition for export success,' *Journal of International Business Studies*, 21 (1): 23–40.

Forsgren, M. (2002) 'The concept of learning in the Uppsala internationalisation process model: a critical review,' *International Business Review*, 11 (3): 257–277.

Hart, S.J., and Webb, J.R. and Jones, M.V. (1994) 'Export marketing research and the effect of export experience in industrial SMEs,' *International Marketing Review*, 11 (6): 4–22.

Hogarth-Scott, S., Watson, K. and Wilson, N. (1996) 'Do small businesses have to practise marketing to survive and grow?' *Marketing Intelligence & Planning*, 14 (1): 6–18.

Johanson, J. and Vahlne, J.-E. (1977) 'The internationalization process of the firm—a model of knowledge development and increasing foreign market commitments,' *Journal of International Business Studies*, 8 (1): 23–32.

Majkgård, Anders (1998) 'Experiential knowledge in the internationalization process of service firms,' Doctoral thesis no. 70. Department of Business Studies. Uppsala University. Uppsala.

McGee, J.E., Dowling, M.J. and Megginson, W.L. (1995) 'Cooperative strategy and new venture performance: the role of business strategy and management experience,' *Strategic Management Journal*, 16 (7): 565–580.

Reuber, A.R. and Fischer, E. (1999) 'Understanding the consequences of founders' experience,' *Journal of Small Business Management*, 37 (2): 30–45.

Yli-Renko, H., Autio, E. and Tontti, V. (2002) 'Social capital, knowledge, and the international growth of technology-based new firms,' *International Business Review*, 11 (3): 279–304.

18 The International Growth of a Privately-owned Enterprise from China

Peter Zettinig and Churu Lin

BACKGROUND

In 1978 Deng Xiaoping became the head of the People's Republic of China. Under his leadership China committed to economic reforms which stimulated uninterrupted economic growth and the Open Door Policy. This policy introduced reciprocal trading rights among countries enabling firms to take up international business activities. The regulatory bodies could use vast international connections, especially to overseas Chinese and their "bamboo networks." Initially starting from the provinces geographically neighboring Hong Kong, Macau and Taiwan, these activities soon expanded to more distant provinces. The economic reforms in effect made it possible to modernize China and gave rise to new economic actors entering the organizational landscape.

Prior to the reforms Deng initiated, economic activity was exclusively run by large centrally controlled state-owned enterprises (SOEs), which had a considerable role in producing inefficiencies resulting in the people of the republic suffering from poverty and technological backwardness. With economic reforms the locus of decision making became gradually decentralized and shifted from state-controlled organizations to lower hierarchical levels, permitting collective-owned enterprises (COEs), which spurred considerable entrepreneurial imagination and activity under local authorities' supervision (Liao and Sohmen 2001). This type of company soon successfully reformed agriculture and diversified into many different industries. Another type of company, made possible subsequent to the 1978 reforms, allowed private individuals to use their own capital in pursuit of economic wealth. These private and individually-owned firms soon became a real powerhouse of the Chinese economy, due to the legendary Chinese entrepreneurial spirit (Dana 2007) and the culturally rooted desire to be the master of one's faith. A Chinese proverb saying "It is better to be a chicken's head than a phoenix's tail" is a good illustration of this inherent desire. The fourth type of company established through reforms can be summarized as firms targeting joint ownership types, most prominently allowing international joint ventures, which were rather important in developing China's human capability pool and in organizing operations more efficiently (Lin et al. 2008).

For China as a whole these reforms have led to breathtaking economic change, and have put China on the path to once again become the world's largest, and maybe one day wealthiest, economy. The last thirty years have witnessed China's GDP increase from USD 50 billion in 1978 to over USD 3,000 billion in 2007, representing an average annual growth rate of over 10 percent. Exports have been growing on average by around 11 percent per annum since 1980, reaching an overall contribution of 40 percent to China's GDP by 2006. An inward foreign direct investment (FDI) flow of USD 80,000 in 1978 compares to more than USD 72 billion in 2005. The outward FDI flow of 440 million in 1982 has to be compared to outward flows of USD 11.3 billion in 2005 and USD 21.2 billion in 2006. By 2005, FDI stock in China had reached a level of USD 318 billion, and China's invested capital stock abroad amounted to USD 46.3 billion in the same year (Lin 2009). China's sustained economic growth rate over this 30-year timeframe was largely driven by its newly open status and rapid economic integration with the world trading and production systems. During this process and promoted by a 1985 directive by the Ministry of Foreign Economic Relations and Trade the number of internationally active Chinese subsidiaries grew considerably from 185 firms investing USD 0.154 billion abroad in 1985 to a stunning 7,470 subsidiaries making international investments of USD 33.2 billion by 2003 (Lin 2009).

SMES IN CHINA

The internationalization process of the case company Alpha (a pseudonym) must be understood against the background of the economic development of China. In today's China small and medium-sized enterprises (SMEs) play a role comparable to that in OECD (Organisation of Economic Co-operation and Development) countries. This is especially valid when measured in terms of new company formations, employment growth and innovative output (OECD 2002). Even though SMEs are usually understood as a rather homogeneous group, there is no internationally consistent classification for such firms. What constitutes a SME is largely relative to national standards defined by the size and the type of organization. The OECD loosely defines SMEs "as non-subsidiary, independent firms which employ less than a given number of employees" (OECD 2005, 17).

From the Chinese point of view, the definition of a SME is complex and varies by industry category due to regulatory purposes. Generally, three criteria in addition to industry category are applied. According to the law, an industrial SME (such as Alpha) is defined to have less than 3,000 employees, receives revenues of less than RBM 300 million and possesses assets of less than RBM 400 million. These dimensions are in clear contrast to European or US standards, especially in relation to the employment size of the firm (less than 250 for the EU, or 500 in the case of the US).

SMEs in China face a number of business obstacles to which larger firms are less exposed. In comparison to larger corporations, a Chinese SME often has very limited access to financial resources and investment facilities. These firms further struggle to attract sufficient capabilities and know-how for their businesses, they employ personnel with less formal business and technical education, and they suffer from lower economies of scale and scope compared to their larger peers (Lin 2009). On the other hand, SMEs in China have a number of advantages in relation to their larger competitors. Less formal structures and a lower level of hierarchical complexity allow entrepreneurs to make decisions quickly and to exercise full control over their operations, business focus, technologies and target markets. These are strategically important traits, especially in very quickly changing environments such as the consumer electronics industry where the case company is active. Based on these characteristics it can be assumed that the lack of resources is often made up for by resourcefulness, which allows SMEs in China to outperform their larger counterparts. The lack of resources paired with the will to succeed and inherent structural agility pushes these types of firms to utilize partnerships and networks that provide continuous learning, spur innovativeness to flexibly combine resources, and result in the generation of economies on a cooperative inter-firm level.

LOCATION FACTORS AND INDUSTRY MEMBERSHIP

Alpha was founded as a privately owned enterprise in 1981 in Guangdong province, with an initial focus on the young electronics industry and the purpose of producing videocassette recorders for the domestic market. The circumstances, the home base in Guangdong and the firm being part of China's early electronics industry, need a more specific assessment in order to understand the company's subsequent development.

First, the Chinese electronics industry changed dramatically with the 1978 reforms. Prior to that time, the industry had a strict military focus, with very limited consumer product output and with modest technology compared to Western standards at the time. For instance, in 1965 only 4,400 television sets and 810,000 radios were made. The number increased to a modest 517,000 TV and 11.6 million radio sets by 1978 (Tilley and Williams 1997). Especially the fact that the industry was considered sensitive from the viewpoint of national defense created barriers for acquisition of foreign technology, although some was created in collaboration with the USSR. Until the period of economic reforms this definitely limited, if not excluded, any foreign investments in the industry.

Soon after the reforms this changed rapidly, and the government addressed the needs of the industry by obtaining technology for state companies overseas, and by actively encouraging investments in the Chinese electronics industry. International business activity started in the industry, with the first joint venture investments by Japanese companies, firms like Toshiba and Hitachi being at the forefront. They established production lines for consumer electronics—such as color television sets—to be sold mainly for domestic consumption in China. The inward-investment flow by foreign electronics companies increased steadily and European and US firms began to invest into Chinese joint venture operations by the early and mid 1980s (Tilley and Williams 1997).

Second, Alpha is based in Guangdong, whose main city is Shenzhen—the first Special Economic Zone (SEZ). Shenzhen, which was formally established in May 1980, was originally a small fishing village, located right across the border from Hong Kong, which at that time was a prosperous British territory. The strategic location, with its geographic proximity to the highly industrialized Hong Kong and its many cultural and family links, had been chosen to experiment with Chinese-style capitalism within a socialist system. Since then, the province of Guangdong has become the most industrialized region in the world, and the city of Shenzhen one of the world's fastest growing cities, giving home and work to more than 8.5 million people. After 1980 Guangdong quickly opened up and developed intensive business ties with Hong Kong businesses, which took the lead in investing in manufacturing (Tilley and Williams 1997).

While Hong Kong business had a central role in brokering many international joint ventures between international companies and Guangdong firms, they themselves preferred *processing agreements* to enter mainland China. This practice provided the foreign investors with cheap production sites without giving up control or capital gains to equity partners. As a result, the electronics industry in the region shifted much of its production from the Hong Kong side of the border to Guangdong (Tilley and Williams 1997). Subsequently, many Western companies followed this practice, either establishing international joint ventures with Guangdong businesses, or using processing agreements with local partners. In effect these practices have developed the electronics industry through the stage of foreign direct investments to serve the local Chinese markets in becoming a production base that now exports nearly 100 percent of its outputs.

THE STORY OF ALPHA

For most of the 1980s Alpha focused on production of videocassette players for the domestic markets. During the early years most of the technology was licensed, and operations ran on a rather modest scale. In the early 1990s the demand for this technology slowed down, forcing the management of the company to take action in order to survive. The management developed two strategies for survival. The first one was to diversify its business areas. This resulted in a reorganization of the firm, which developed diversified business divisions with extensive product ranges in perceived high-growth areas. These divisions focused on product areas such as mobile communication, consumer audio and video systems, portable entertainment products, an information technology department and the production of electronic accessories and equipment. The second strategy was to aggressively pursue internationalization, due to soaring domestic competition among firms that were trying to build their competitive advantages on very similar factor conditions. The firm subsequently targeted countries and sub-markets that were less developed, where they perceived competitive opportunities due to lower competition levels, as for instance in the main western or Asian markets. This led them initially to serve markets like Eastern Europe and Africa, using agents and pursuing exports as a means to enter markets. Both strategic changes were reactive, the first influenced by product innovations and obsolete technologies, and the second due to increasing domestic competition, in which the firm had to face their limited ability to develop distinct competitive advantages compared to their domestic rivals.

During that time the company developed their international network of agents abroad, and for their telecommunication products they pursued a strategy of building partnerships with local telecommunication operators in many countries, serving as distributors for their handhelds. Though especially at first the internationalization of the mobile phone business served as an addition to their domestic revenues in that market category, a decision by the Chinese government would change this strategy. The firm early on decided to follow the latest technological developments in the mobile-handheld business, even though their products did not reach the level of sophistication demonstrated by globally leading companies in the industry. Part of that behavior led the company to develop third-generation mobile technology (3G).

At that time, the roll out of 3G in China was very limited, with the Chinese government delaying 3G licensing to mobile phone operators. The Chinese government followed the strategy of favoring the development of its own national mobile phone standard instead. The rationale for that was to put Chinese firms, which could gain a temporal technological advantage, in the position to build a strong industry based on a proprietary standard in order to utilize the fast growing national market for mobile communication. Alpha's investments into 3G forced them to consider more strongly the prospect of internationalization of the mobile phone division, which again led them first to foreign direct investments and to focus on key markets through two wholly-owned subsidiaries in the US and Singapore. This development strongly influenced the firm's further pattern of market selection, because markets which launched 3G were seen as strategically important to facilitate their growth aspirations in one of the most promising business areas at the turn of the millennium.

The manager responsible for international operations stated that now, after so many years of international activity and expansion, the firm has accumulated much international knowledge and has a good network of business partners. He also mentioned that internationalization is deemed to be successful for this firm due to a high share of sales abroad accounting for more than 30 percent of their overall revenues (in 2005) and continuous strong international growth rates. Internationalization for this firm is seen as an important opportunity to compete with international industry leaders and to learn from these interactions for future business development. Internationalization is also seen to be essential for another aspiration, to build their own brands, achieving a high level of awareness abroad and on the domestic market.

In order to fully capture learning from international business operations the firm is changing its management processes to allow more systematic technology transfer. At the same time, the firm tries to increase the level of product standardization considerably. This can be seen as a further move in following a global strategy, in line with the global leaders of the electronics industry. While internationalization is considered as vital to the firm's further development and survival, the domestic market is seen as equally important. That is due to the fast growing demand for consumer electronics in China and the fact that competitive advantage is very much born out of local factor conditions, their combinations and their efficient and effective use in production. By the end of 2006 the company had 2,250 employees, with 50 permanent offices overseas, and employing more than 200 expatriates in its foreign market operations. Turnover by that time had reached RMB 213 million, close to a third of which was from international operations, and the firm possessed total assets of RMB 305 million.

TRYING TO UNDERSTAND THE STORY OF ALPHA

Why has a relatively small company, in an industry dominated by globally acting players, decided to grow internationally, even though their home market is rapidly growing to become the world's largest market for consumer electronics?

Alpha's motivation to seek international exposure tended to be of a reactive nature. The downturn in the VCR market forced the firm to seek new business focuses in order to survive. Besides product diversification the firm chose to geographically diversify their sales efforts. Through internationalization the company has been able to expand its market space, increase its asset base and acquire sophisticated technologies, both in terms of product development and in terms of management and marketing knowhow. During that time the Chinese business and institutional environment played an important role in the development of this firm's strategies. On the one hand, domestic competition in the consumer-electronics field grew exponentially, with the Guangdong region being one of the world's densest industrial areas for this type of production.

On the other hand, the institutional environment and the central government's aspirations to develop a national mobile phone standard pushed the firm abroad in order to utilize its developments in 3G technology and to exploit investments that had already been made in that business area. International growth started in markets that required lower-priced products and that had less competition from global players at the time. For instance, markets in Africa and Eastern Europe soon developed their market offerings in line with leap-frog developments in these markets. Later, especially in regard to their mobile phone division, they started to enter more developed markets, and started to build up 3G networks early.

Simultaneously, the market entry modes changed. In the early days of internationalization the firm put most emphasis on exports via agents, while later on, especially in regard to mobile phones, the firm pushed harder to build partnerships with local operators of mobile networks and other local gatekeepers in different markets. This developed further, often through learning to work in local market environments overseas and by acquiring modern management techniques, and resulted in the establishment of two wholly-owned subsidiaries (WOS). While the US subsidiary serves mainly to keep in touch with the latest consumer developments and trends in one of the major foreign markets, the Singapore unit is mostly concerned with production of more sophisticated mobile phones, liquid crystal display television sets and notebook computers. Still, the major resource base the firm is drawing from is located in China, where the company runs its three R&D centers and where most products and technologies are produced to be exported. In terms of control, the firm has a great desire to keep to itself, either by engaging in agent-based exporting under close supervision, or by internalizing operations through its WOS.

In regard to the firm's international market selection and expansion sequence the firm is not following what would be predicted by the psychic distance theory. Currently the company focuses on higher-end markets in the US, Eastern Europe, Africa and also recently the Middle East, which are somewhat institutionally distant countries, with very diverse socioeconomic realities and not close to the home country. This can be seen to be mostly due to the choice of the firm to follow the latest technological advances, rather than introducing older technology to less-developed markets.

DISCUSSION

The case of Alpha is an interesting one, because it shows the limited explanatory value of domestic market size for internationalization. Rather than approaching the limits of growth on the domestic market, this firm is an example of how the external environment can push a firm's international growth. On the one hand, there is an increasingly favorable institutional environment, which over the last thirty years has been revising its regulatory policy from an absolute restrictive to a positive (i.e., the *go-out policy*, Wu 2005) and finally to a supportive (i.e., *go-global*, Child and Rodrigues 2005) policy in regard to international business expansion. At the same time this regulatory environment has put up restrictions forcing the company to take its 3G technology to international markets. This government decision led the firm to enter markets which were ready for this technology early on. Entering these markets in turn helped the firm to meet the most sophisticated demand, and with it globally acting competitors. From interactions with them the case company quickly became a comparatively small but viable international player in very diverse markets.

Reflecting on this case of the international expansion of a Chinese SME invites us to evaluate briefly some of the main theories of internationalization. Overall, we conclude that this firm has similar motives and behaviors to those we would find in many western firms. And yet, this overall assessment is in agreement with other analyses concluding that western management theories suffice for understanding Chinese firms' management approaches (e.g., Floyd 1999; Pheng and Leong 2001).

However, it is interesting also to note that this case displays characteristics of two major internationalization theories (Autio 2005), which often have been portrayed as competing concepts. On the one hand, the firm has internationalized incrementally, from agent-based export to wholly-owned subsidiary, as the Uppsala School model prescribes (e.g. Johanson and Vahlne 1977). On the other hand, it shows that a quite established firm, once the internationalization decision had been taken, could aggressively expand into multiple markets and globally integrate important functions being carried out in different, non-psychically close markets. This complies with some, although not all, of the aspects documented in the literature on "international new ventures" (e.g., Oviatt and McDougall 1994), while at the same time building strongly on the domestic resource base for some of its most crucial operations.

BIBLIOGRAPHY

Autio, E. (2005) 'Creative tension: the significance of Ben Oviatt's and Patricia McDougall's article "toward a theory of international new ventures,"' *Journal of International Business Studies*, 36 (1): 9–19.

Child, J. and Rodrigues, S.B. (2005) 'The internationalization of Chinese firms: a case for theoretical extension?' *Management and Organization Review*, 1 (3): 381–410.

Dana, L.-P. (2007) Asian models of entrepreneurship—from the Indian Union and the Kingdom of Nepal to the Japanese archipelago: context, policy and practice, Singapore: World Scientific.

Floyd, D. (1999) 'Eastern and Western management practices: myth or reality?,' *Management Decision,* 37 (8): 628–632.

Johanson, J. and Vahlne, J.-E. (1977) 'The internationalisation process of the firm: a model of knowledge development and increasing foreign market commitments,' *Journal of International Business Studies,* 8 (1): 23–32.

Liao, D. and Sohmen, P. (2001) 'The development of modern entrepreneurship in China,' *Stanford Journal of East Asian Affairs.* 1: 27–33.

Lin, C., Zettinig, P. and Rose, B. (2008) Internationalisation patterns of Chinese entrepreneurial firms. Proceedings of the 34th EIBA Annual Conference 2008. Tallinn, Estonia.

Lin, C. (2009) 'Exploring Chinese privately-owned enterprises internationalisation,' Master's thesis. Victoria University of Wellington, New Zealand.

OECD (2002) *The OECD SME Outlook 2002,* Paris: OECD Publications.

OECD (2005) OECD SME and Entrepreneurship Outlook: 2005, Paris: OECD Publications.

Oviatt, B.M., and McDougall, P.P. (1994) 'Toward a theory of international new ventures,' *Journal of International Business Studies,* 25 (1): 45–64.

Pheng, L.S., and Leong, C.H.Y. (2001) 'Asian management style versus Western management theories: a Singapore case study in construction project management,' *Journal of Managerial Psychology,* 16 (2): 127–141.

Tilley, K.J. and Williams, D.J. (1997) 'The Greater China electronics industry—an external view,' *Annual Journal of IIE (HK),* 1996–1997: 24–30.

Wu, F. (2005) *Corporate China goes global,* Singapore, Nanyang Technological University.

Epilogue
Where to Head from Here?

Niina Nummela

This book provides its readers with a comprehensive overview of international growth of small and medium-sized enterprises from diverse points of view. It verifies that SMEs in all parts of the globe share similar characteristics, but also differ significantly. Additionally, it suggests concrete measures how to support the international growth of these companies. For example, although early internationalizing firms are still in the minority in Latin America, with well-targeted education and development of human capital through extended networks, their number could be increased (cf. Federico et al., this volume).

Theoretically, the book contributes to our body of knowledge on international growth by revealing that SMEs worldwide seem to experience the *cyclical nature of international growth*. The critical incidents and turning points of the life cycle may differ, and be determined by, for example, earlier decisions of the company (cf. Zettinig and Lin, Lindqvist et al., this volume), but they may also originate outside the firm, from its network (cf. Nummela, this volume) or its significant stakeholders (cf. Hurmerinta, this volume). As a result, internationally growing SMEs are by no means a homogenous group, *their life cycle and growth process may differ considerably*, as the studies in the book show. Therefore, classifications of the companies, such as the one suggested by Bell et al., or suggestions how this should be taken into account when conducting empirical studies (cf. Johnston et al., this volume), are very valuable for research purposes. And yet, anomalies which will not fit the rules will always exist, as the illustrative case of CV Online demonstrates (see Vissak, this volume).

We have to also keep in mind that not all SMEs are interested in international growth (cf. Federico et al. and Kuuluvainen and Paavilainen-Mäntymäki, this volume), and internationalization and growth are not necessarily linked (cf. Nlemvo et al., this volume). *New explanations for explaining* this and other differences between SMEs emerge, such as ownership (cf. Larimo, this volume), steering of the company (cf. Nisuls et al., this volume), or the negative consequences of international growth (cf. Heinonen and Hytti, this volume). The changing external environment of SMEs also pushes them to create innovative solutions in order to survive and succeed, such as the configuration of value chain activities and hybrid organizational forms (cf. Nummela and Saarenketo, this volume).

All this means that although seminal concepts of internationalization research—such as learning and market—still remain powerful in explaining the international growth of SMEs, their proper use requires *new interpretations* (cf. Andersson, Prasantham, Zucchella, this volume). The studies reviewed also indicate that *the definition of international growth*—the key concept in this book—may be in need of revision. Instead of treating international growth as an extension of operations across borders, a definition taking into account the multidimensionality and complexity would be preferred. The definition suggested by Paavilainen-Mäntymäki (2009, 262) could offer a starting point for this discussion:

> International growth is a multidimensional change process, enabled and accelerated by entrepreneurial orientation and opportunity seeking behavior, in which small and medium-sized enterprises increase the magnitude, scale and/or breadth of their operations and develop their organization while expanding their international operating scope within the pressures of external environment.

The definition itself and its key concepts—entrepreneurial orientation and opportunity-seeking behavior—offer interesting avenues for further research in the field of international entrepreneurship. The story is continued—by us and many, many others.

BIBLIOGRAPHY

Paavilainen-Mäntymäki, Eriikka (2009) *Unique paths: the process of international growth among selected Finnish SMEs*, Series A-17:2009, Turku School of Economics, Turku, Finland.

Contributors

Svante Andersson is professor of business administration at Halmstad University, Sweden. His research interests lie in internationalization, growth, entrepreneurship and marketing. He has published in several journals, including Journal of Business Venturing, Journal of Small Business and Enterprise Development, Journal of International Entrepreneurship, Canadian Journal of Administrative Sciences, and European Journal of Marketing.

Arild Aspelund is associate professor of marketing at the Norwegian University of Science and Technology. His main research interest is the internationalization of new firms and new industries, but he also does research within innovation and entrepreneurship, economic development and change management in multinational corporations.

Jim Bell was professor of international business entrepreneurship at the University of Ulster, Northern Ireland. He lectured in international marketing and had research interests in the internationalization of knowledge-based SMEs, and international marketing and business education. He had published widely in this area.

Mathieu Cabrol is an assistant professor at the Montpellier Business School, France. His research interests include internationalization and entrepreneurship, particularly from the viewpoint of the internationalization process and strategies, as well as networks.

Colin Campbell-Hunt is professor of strategic management at the University of Otago, New Zealand. His research focuses on competitive strategy and competitive advantage, with a particular interest in SME-scale enterprises of global scope. His work is published in a range of journals including Human Relations, Journal of International Marketing, Journal of Operations Management, R&D Management, and Strategic Management Journal.

Sylvie Chetty is professor of marketing at Massey University, Auckland, New Zealand, and an associated researcher at Uppsala University, Sweden. Her research interests are in internationalization, export performance and the business network approach. She has published widely in these areas, including in such journals as Journal of International Business Studies, Regional Studies, International Business Review, European Journal of Marketing and International Small Business Journal.

Juan Federico has worked as research assistant in the Institute of Industry at the Universidad Nacional de General Sarmiento, Argentina. Currently he is doing his PhD courses at the Department of Business Economics of the Universitat Autònoma de Barcelona (Spain). His main research interests are new venture growth, strategy, entrepreneurial policies and international entrepreneurship.

Jarna Heinonen is professor of entrepreneurship and director of TSE Entre— a research group at the Turku School of Economics at the University of Turku, Finland. Her research interests include business growth, family businesses, enterprise education and corporate entrepreneurship as well as entrepreneurship and innovation policies. She has published in a number of international journals.

Leila Hurmerinta is professor of marketing at the Turku School of Economics at the University of Turku, Finland. Her research interests include international entrepreneurship, time and experience in internationalization, entrepreneurial marketing and methodological issues. She has published in Academy of Entrepreneurship Journal, International Small Business Journal, Journal of International Entrepreneurship, Journal of Small Business and Enterprise Development, and Management International Review, among others.

Ulla Hytti is adjunct professor and research director of the TSE Entre research group at the Turku School of Economics at the University of Turku, Finland. She has contributed to the new theoretical and methodological approaches in entrepreneurship research. She has published in a number of international journals.

Scott Paul Johnston is a graduate of the University of Glasgow, and currently working as a statistician with HM Revenue and Customs, UK. His interests are diverse, including organizational behavior, corporate strategy, project management, quality assurance, marketing research, macroeconomics, foreign policy, statistics and banking. He has published in Active Learning in Higher Education, European Journal of Engineering Education, and the International Journal of Management Education.

Marian V. Jones is professor of internationalization and entrepreneurship and co-director of the Centre for Internationalization and Enterprise Research (CIER) at the University of Glasgow, Scotland, UK. Her research on the internationalization of high-technology small firms has been widely published in internationally recognized journals such as the Journal of International Business Studies, Journal of Business Venturing and Journal of International Marketing.

Hugo Kantis is professor in the Institute of Industry and the director of the Master's Program in Industrial Economics and Development at the Universidad Nacional de General Sarmiento, Argentina. His research interests are entrepreneurship, new venture growth, entrepreneurial policies, SMEs and strategy. He is a member of the editorial board of Venture Capital and the International Small Business Journal.

Sören Kock is professor of management at the Hanken School of Economics in Vaasa, Finland. His research interests include business networks, international business, cooperation, "co-opetition," purchasing and market orientation. He has published in a number of international journals, including Industrial Marketing Management, International Marketing Review, International Business Review, European Journal of Marketing, International Small Business Journal, and Journal of Business & Industrial Marketing.

Olli Kuivalainen is professor of international marketing at the Lappeenranta University of Technology, Finland. His research interests are in the areas of strategic management, marketing and internationalization of firms and international entrepreneurship, the focus being in knowledge-intensive firms. He has published articles in the Journal of World Business, International Journal of Production Economics, Technovation and Journal of International Entrepreneurship, among others.

Arto Kuuluvainen is a doctoral student at the Turku School of Economics at the University of Turku, Finland. His research interests are in growth entrepreneurship, serial entrepreneurship, entrepreneurial behavior, dynamic capabilities, sports management and marketing, and international business.

Jorma Larimo is professor of international marketing at the University of Vaasa, Finland. His research interests include internationalization of SMEs, export performance, foreign direct investment strategies, and investment performance. His studies have been published in several international journals such as Journal of International Business Studies, Management International Review, Journal of International Marketing, and Journal of Business Research.

Churu Lin graduated from Victoria University of Wellington, New Zealand with a master's in commerce and administration and is currently an entrepreneur in Shenzhen, Guangdong, People's Republic of China.

Jani Lindqvist is a doctoral student at the Lappeenranta University of Technology, Finland and a management consultant at Compass Management Partners. His research interests are in the areas of strategic management and internationalization of firms, the focus being especially on knowledge-intensive firms and information and communication technologies.

Sharon Loane is a lecturer in the School of International Business at the University of Ulster, Northern Ireland. Her research interests are in the area of small firm internationalization, Internet-enabled start-ups, bio and life sciences and digital content. Her publications have appeared in Journal of World Business, Canadian Journal of Administrative Sciences, International Marketing Review and the Irish Journal of Management.

Rod B. McNaughton is Eyton Chair in Entrepreneurship at the University of Waterloo, Canada. His specialty is international marketing strategy, with a focus on the internationalization of small, knowledge-intensive firms. He has published widely on international channels of distribution, exporting and export policy, market orientation and value creation, strategic alliances, foreign direct investment and the venture capital industry.

Anna Morgan-Thomas is a lecturer at the University of Glasgow, Scotland. Her research focuses on global impacts of e-commerce, with particular reference to internationalization and export performance of smaller firms. Her articles on e-commerce, internationalization and global entrepreneurship have been published in International Marketing Review, International Small Business Journal and European Journal of International Management.

Johanna Nisuls is a doctoral student at the Hanken School of Economics, Vaasa, Finland. Her current research interests lie within the field of boards of directors and the internationalization process in SMEs.

Frederic Nlemvo is a professor at the Reims Management School, France. He has published in European Journal of Management, International Journal of Entrepreneurship and Innovation, Small Business Economics and Technovation, among others.

Niina Nummela is professor of international business at the Turku School of Economics at the University of Turku, Finland. She has published in the area of international entrepreneurship, small business management, interfirm cooperation, and research methods. She has contributed to Journal of World Business, Management International Review, European Journal of Marketing, International Small Business Journal, and Journal of Engineering and Technology Management, among others.

Eriikka Paavilainen-Mäntymäki is a post-doc researcher at the Turku School of Economics at the University of Turku, Finland. Her research interests are in research methods and methodology, company internationalization, growth, international growth, life cycle and process models, entrepreneurial behavior and orientation, and small and medium-sized enterprises.

Shameen Prashantham is a senior lecturer in international business and strategy at the Centre for Internationalization and Enterprise Research (CIER), University of Glasgow Business School, Glasgow, Scotland. His research concerns social capital and the internationalization of small and new firms, particularly in the Bangalore software industry. His work is published or forthcoming in California Management Review, Entrepreneurship Theory & Practice and International Business Review.

Erik Rasmussen is associate professor of marketing at the University of Southern Denmark. His research interests include born global firms and other international new ventures as well as international entrepreneurship as a phenomenon. An emerging research area is also the use of languages in international operations. He has published in, e.g., Corporate Communications, Asia Pacific Journal of Marketing and Logistics, and Advances in International Marketing.

Alex Rialp is associate professor of business organization at the Universitat Autònoma de Barcelona, Spain. He has contributed to books, book chapters and articles published in journals such as International Business Review, International Marketing Review, Advances in International Marketing, Journal of International Entrepreneurship, and Journal of Euromarketing. He also serves as an editorial board member of Journal of International Marketing.

Josep Rialp is associate professor of marketing and market research at the Universitat Autònoma de Barcelona, Spain. He has published books, book chapters and articles in both national and international scientific journals, such as Journal of World Business, International Business Review, Management Decision, Regional Studies, Advances in International Marketing, Journal of International Entrepreneurship, and Journal of Euromarketing.

Sami Saarenketo is professor of international marketing at the Lappeenranta University of Technology, Finland. His research interests are international marketing and entrepreneurship in technology-based small firms. He has published on these issues in Journal of World Business, European Journal of Marketing, Canadian Journal of Administrative Sciences, International Journal of Production Economics and Journal of International Entrepreneurship, among others.

Per Servais is associate professor of marketing at the University of Southern Denmark. His research interests are international entrepreneurship, international purchasing and sourcing and e-business, among others. He has published widely, including books and articles in Industrial Marketing Management, International Marketing Review, Journal of International Marketing, Advances in International Marketing and International Business Review.

Anette Söderqvist is a doctoral student at the Hanken School of Economics, Vaasa, Finland. Her current research interests lie within the field of entrepreneurship, international business and boards of directors.

Tiia Vissak is a senior researcher at the University of Tartu, Estonia. Her research interests include international entrepreneurship, internationalization, business networks, strategic alliances, foreign direct investments and transition economies.

George I. Vlachos is a doctoral student at the Centre for Internationalization and Enterprise Research (CIER) at the University of Glasgow, Scotland, UK. His research currently focuses on small firm internationalization and opportunity recognition theory, and he intends to extend his research towards the broader area of entrepreneurial cognition and decision making.

Peter Zettinig is assistant professor of international business at the Turku School of Economics at the University of Turku, Finland. His research interests concern the intersection of international business, strategy and entrepreneurship, in addition to interests in human and organizational cognition and their evolutionary outcomes.

Antonella Zucchella is professor of innovation management and international entrepreneurship at the University of Pavia, Italy and vice dean of the Faculty of Economics. She has also been a visiting professor of international marketing at the University of Strasbourg since 2003.

Index

Note: Page numbers followed by 'f' refer to figures and page numbers followed by 't' refer to tables.

*For Product Safety Concerns and Information please contact
our EU representative GPSR@taylorandfrancis.com Taylor & Francis
Verlag GmbH, Kaufingerstraße 24, 80331 München, Germany*

T - #0060 - 230425 - C0 - 229/152/18 - PB - 9780415648691 - Gloss Lamination